MUSIC

IN

AMERICAN

LIFE

A list of books

in the series

appears at the

end of this book

SI

'Twas

Only

an

Irishman's

Dream

The Image of Ireland

and the Irish in

American Popular Song Lyrics,

1800–1920

William H. A. Williams

University of Illinois Press

Urbana & Chicago

'Twas Only an Irishman's Dream

*Publication of this book was
supported by a grant from the
Milwaukee Irish Fest Foundation, Inc.*

1   2   3   4   5   C   P   5   4   3   2   1

This book is printed on acid-free paper.

Library of Congress
Cataloging-in-Publication Data
Williams, William H. A. (William
Henry Allen), 1937–
'Twas only an Irishman's dream : the
image of Ireland and the Irish in
American popular song lyrics, 1800–
1920 / William H. A. Williams.
p.   cm. – (Music in American life)
Includes bibliographical references
and index.
ISBN 0-252-02246-7 (cloth). –
ISBN 0-252-06551-4 (pbk.)
1. Irish Americans–Songs and music–
Texts–History and criticism. 2. Irish–
Songs and music–Texts–History and
criticism. 3. Popular music–United
States–Texts–History and criticism.
I. Title. II. Series.
ML3554.W77   1996
782.42'089'9162073–dc20   96-4491
                                      CIP
                                      MN

To my children, Bill & Lavinia

CONTENTS

While exploring the Lilly Library on the campus of Indiana University some years ago, I became intrigued by their Starr Collection of sheet music. Had the collection been cataloged, I probably would have done no more than gape at its enormity and pass on. Instead, however, the collection is "sorted" into categories, one of which is "Ireland." A self-proclaimed fiddler with an interest in Irish studies, I thought I might take a look at the material to see what influence, if any, traditional Irish music might have had on sheet music relating to Ireland. I was indeed able to identify some of the melodies but the results did not seem very meaningful. However, I have always believed that when confronted by any body of material the trick is to discover what questions the material can answer. As I went through the songs, I began to realize that they were documents of the evolving images of Ireland and the Irish in America.

It took a while to figure out how to ask the right questions. In 1991 I published an article in *Eire-Ireland* on the image of the Irish in American popular music. The article won the Four Master's Award given by the Irish American Cultural Institute. At that point, I had only dealt with the subject in a very general way, and the IACI's award encouraged me to dig more deeply into the material. This book is the result.

I am deeply indebted to Lawrence McCaffrey and Charles Hamm, both of whom have read a draft of the book. I am grateful to them for sharing their expertise in Irish-American history and the history of sheet music, respectively, and I have benefited greatly from their helpful comments and suggestions. I do, of course, retain the author's exclusive privilege in claiming full responsibility for whatever errors of judgment and editing the reader may find.

I also want to acknowledge the help of my friends Alf MacLochlainn of Galway and Arthur Gribbin of Dundalk and Los Angeles for their assistance on the Irish language. Thanks also to Dr. Kathleen Flanagan of St. Mary's University in Winona, Minnesota, and Dr. Marge Steiner of Bloomington, Indiana. Again, they are innocent of any mistakes that may lurk in the text.

I am especially indebted to the staffs of the Lilly Library and the music department of the Cincinnati Public Library for their bibliographic assistance and their cheerful willingness to keep the supply of songs flowing.

I am particularly grateful to my friend Kenneth Haag for supplying me with lodgings, companionship, and music during my research trips to Bloomington, Indiana.

My thanks also to my wife, Leslie, for helping me with the proofreading and to our daughter, Lavinia, for putting up with two book-writing parents.

I wish to acknowledge the support and encouragement I have received from my colleagues and from the administration of the Union Institute.

Finally, I want to express my appreciation to Judith McCulloh, executive editor at the University of Illinois Press, for her encouragement and advice during the various stages of the preparation of this book. I am also grateful to Theresa L. Sears, Louis Simon, and other members of the Press for their fine work in helping to prepare this book for publication.

'Twas
Only
an
Irishman's
Dream

Introduction

From 1800 to 1920, five million Irish men and women, most of them Roman Catholics, emigrated to the United States. Ironically, they were the largest group of English speakers to arrive in this country during that period.[1] Half inside American culture because of language and a talent for politics, the Irish were also half outside it. Their sheer numbers and poverty, their Roman Catholic religion, their peasant folkways, their almost clannish concentration in urban areas, and, especially after the Famine, their tragic history, all combined to make the nineteenth-century Irish immigrants a highly visible and distinct group.

These Irish Catholics could not, even had they wished, melt into American society, as did the English immigrants, or gradually blend into it, as did the Protestant Irish, Scots, and Welsh. Nor could they easily adjust to American life quietly in small groups or as individuals. Their very visibility meant that their Americanization would be played out, quite literally, upon the national stage with theater and song as key elements in the process.

Irish Catholics were in many respects the first "ethnic" group in America. That is to say, they were the first immigrant group to arrive in extremely large numbers, to gain high visibility by clustering in cities, to retain a strong identification with the old homeland, and to appear sufficiently "different" in religion and culture so that acceptance by native-born Americans was not automatic, and assimilation was, therefore, prolonged. For their part, the Irish immigrants in America came to realize that they shared a uniquely tragic experience and, in the face of Yankee hostility, a common destiny. Unlike other immigrants from Great Britain, the Irish seemed to understand that they would have to succeed as a people, not just as individuals. They would have to construct an image of themselves as Irish *and* as Americans that would gain acceptance in the broad mainstream of American culture.

This would not be an easy task for a group who saw themselves as having been conquered and colonized, whose language had been denigrated, and whose religion had once been driven underground. Added to this was the humiliation of extreme poverty and, with the Famine, the horrors of mass starvation. These were hardly the elements to excite the admiration of success-driven American society.

Yet, for all of their trials, the Irish retained a pride in themselves as a people. The myth of a once glorious past survived in the legends and stories of their oral tradition. Their religion also survived. Beginning with the leadership of Daniel O'Connell, the Irish masses forced England to yield a grudging acceptance of the power of the Catholic Church in Ireland. Although constantly frustrated, hopes for Irish freedom remained alive to inspire the dreams of the Irish in diaspora. Most significantly, in spite of their poverty, in a few generations the Irish Catholics managed to build a parallel social system within America, consisting of churches, schools, hospitals, cultural organizations, and social clubs.

Lawrence J. McCaffrey, in the opening of his essay "From a Land across the Sea," states that "religion, politics, and nationalism combined to define Irish America."[2] There was a fourth factor involved, however, less easy to define but nonetheless powerful. The Irish Catholics did not enter a cultural vacuum when they arrived; their stereotype had preceded them. They got off the boat and found themselves confronting the stuffed effigy of a "Paddy," complete with a "dudeen" in its gob, a club in one fist, a jug in the other, and a necklace of stale mackerel round its neck. "Paddy making" was a Yankee way of celebrating St. Patrick's Day, and it usually caused the trouble intended.[3] However, while the stuffed Paddy could be torn apart and his creators hammered into the ground, the stereotype that inspired the effigy could not be so easily dismissed or smashed. Paddy represented Irish Catholics even before they had an opportunity to create an identity for themselves on this side of the Atlantic; they were Paddies before they could become Irish Americans.

The origin of stereotyping may lie in the human need to simplify the recognition and evaluation of "the Other" – be it in terms of species, gender, ethnicity, economic status, or age. Such psychosocial tendencies may rest upon the way in which the brain processes information. We recognize patterns or *gestalts* even before we can consciously put a label on them. "Stereotypes pare down and simplify reality; too many variations would complicate and confuse," suggests Christopher D. Geist. "Their purpose is to set a group apart from the mainstream."[4] It is, therefore, not mere psychological laziness or ingrained prejudice that turns us toward stereotyping. Gary Hoppenstand observes that we continually negotiate reality every day of our lives: "This negotiated construction results, in part, from there being too much information for the limited capacity of the human mind to process, and, in part, from our need or desire for us to establish a mental grip on the flow of reality." In this sense, stereotyping is, in Hoppenstand's words, one of many " 'tools' in the construction of our reality."[5]

Stereotyping has been the basis for many popular forms of entertainment down through the ages. This is especially true in the theater, where the stereotype enables an audience to recognize and identify a character with minimal effort by playwright and actor. From the stage to the street and back again, stereotypes, especially in ethnically diverse America, were and are powerful forces in our popular culture.

An ethnic group struggles to develop its own identity in the face of its stereotypes. No matter how denigrating, stereotypes cannot be dismissed or overthrown. They can be challenged and faced down, but only slowly and over time. Meanwhile, the group may try to influence its stereotype in positive ways that are still acceptable (or comprehensible) within the mainstream culture. The extent to which the group can participate in the culture determines the amount of leverage it can bring to bear in shaping and directing its own image.

Unable to escape the stereotype that preceded them, the Irish gradually remolded it into something with which they could live – and eventually something they could use to express pride in themselves. In the process, the Irish had to "negotiate" the nature of their image and identity within a largely Anglo-American culture. Arriving with little in the way of skills and urban, industrial experience, most Irish, nevertheless, spoke an Anglo-Irish dialect of English (the "brogue" being a primary characteristic of the stereotypical Irishman). This meant that Irish immigrants could more easily and quickly participate directly in the popular culture of their new nation than could the equally numerous Germans and later arrivals from other parts of Europe. This was important because it was within the realm of popular culture that the Irish stereotype was articulated and where much of the "negotiation" between the Irish and Anglo-America took place.

Stereotypical attitudes about the Irish were expressed through every popular medium: newspaper articles, court reports, school readers, almanacs, political and religious tracts, travel books, novels and short stories, plays, songs, vaudeville sketches, political cartoons, and, eventually, comic strips and films. In terms of cultural "negotiation," the commercial aspects of popular culture are of particular importance. No matter what political, moral, or aesthetic concerns might move popular artists, their primary purpose is always to sell something – a song, a story, a picture, a book. These artists cannot hope to be successful unless they have some genuine understanding of, if not sympathy for, their intended audience. "Since they aim at the largest common denominator," Russell Nye suggests, "the popular arts therefore tend to standardize at the median level of what the majority expects. The popular artist cannot disturb or offend any significant part of his public," and, therefore, the popular artist cannot be primarily concerned with the feelings of a minority, "unless they represent a significant market."[6]

Much of the public discourse about the Irish was the product of Protestant Anglo-Americans talking to each other. However, within the entertainment field the Irish were present, taking an active part. As the Irish became involved in commercial entertainment, as performers, writers, and as audiences, they became part of the calculus for financial success. Eventually, images that threatened to offend either the cultural mainstream or the Irish might have jeopardized sales. Gradually, then, elements of the image of the Irish and Ireland that appeared onstage and in song had to be "negotiated." Therefore, playwrights, songwriters, and performers had to discover what most segments of their market, Irish and non-Irish, would accept. It was, of course, the Irish stereotype that was being "negotiated."

Sometimes Irish organizations brought pressure to bear directly on the process, as when around 1900 the Ancient Order of Hibernians moved from letter-writing campaigns and theater boycotts to riots in order to cleanse the stage of offending images. Most often, however, it was the market mechanism – box-office receipts and song sales – that provided the necessary feedback loops. The increasing role of the market in popular culture had powerful implications for all kinds of cultural "negotiations." As Michael Pickering and Tony Green point out, "The threat of capitalist development in the modern world is the subsumption of all social life into the marketplace." This "universalization of the market" involved not only the emotional life of individuals, but also the social patterns by which groups perceived each other and interacted.[7]

In studying the interplay between commercial popular culture and ethnic stereotyping, sheet music represents a relatively untapped source. In 1800, sheet music was a new cultural artifact in America. Beginning in small printing establishments in the major cities of the eastern seaboard, music publishing had become a big business by the end of the nineteenth century. Therefore, the Irish stereotype in America developed within an area of popular culture that was itself evolving at the same time. This study will look at the evolution of that stereotype, primarily through song lyrics in sheet music published from 1800 to 1920, and, secondarily, through the popular stage (also evolving during these years) from which the songs were promoted. Appearing initially around 1800, the number of popular "Irish songs" increased throughout the nineteenth century and into the first two decades of this century. The study ends with the rapid decline of the production of new songs about the Irish after 1920.

In terms of the cultural negotiations discussed above, sheet music lies at the intersection where several relevant factors come together. First, sheet music helps to focus attention on the interplay between popular culture and market forces. Although not as expensive as books, sheet music was never "cheap" in the sense that everyone could afford it.[8] Moreover, the full enjoyment of sheet music required a piano or a pump organ, accoutrements of, first, the middle class, and, later, the more prosperous working class – the core audiences for mainstream American popular culture in the nineteenth and early twentieth centuries.

Even in antebellum America the songs that appeared in sheet music were never enjoyed exclusively by the members of the middle class who purchased them. A song could be sung by anyone who heard it often enough. If one could not afford the box seats at the theater, there was always the pit or, later, the gallery. Even the most refined of parlor songs could find their way to (or begin life on) a minstrel or vaudeville stage. For those who could not afford sheet music, there were "songsters," cheaply produced collections of popular song lyrics that usually sold for a dime.

Because publishers had little idea which songs would sell, they had to print many different titles in hopes that a few successful songs would bring in the profits. While stories, novels, or plays provide greater depth in portraying an ethnic stereotype, sheet music provides a greater volume of material, a distinct advantage for a study of this type.

Many popular song sheets had illustrated covers, adding an iconographic element to the stereotype of the Irish. The depiction of an Irishman in a tattered coat and old-fashioned knee breeches, jigging about and waving a shillelagh, conveyed a variety of messages to song buyers in America. Moreover, the proliferation of the shamrock on song covers shows the power of popular culture to generate and disseminate symbols of ethnicity.

As a source for studying ethnic stereotyping, however, sheet music has certain limitations. Being commercial items, ultimately intended for musical entertainment in the home, there were certain topics considered inappropriate for songs. Significantly, this meant that the most vicious of anti-Irish (and anti-Catholic) propaganda did not generally appear in the popular song sheets. Generally, the image of the Irish was much less negative in popular songs than in contemporary novels or newspaper articles. At the same time, songwriters virtually ignored certain things that were very important to the Irish but that might have offended, disturbed, or puzzled mainstream audiences. For example, if these songs were our only surviving documents about the nineteenth-century American Irish, we would scarcely know that most of them were Roman Catholic.

Thus, the very attempt to look at the evolving ethnic stereotype of the Irish through sheet music can distort the resulting picture. We see neither the full range of Protestant negativity about Irish Catholics nor are we introduced to the broad spectrum of Irish-American life. What we see evolving, however, is the common cultural currency for Irishness in America; the symbols and images that form the *public* discourse about Irishness.

There are other, more theoretical problems connected with the use of sheet music. For example, not all music that was "popular" was published. For reasons I have already explained, I have focused this study on the commercial side of popular culture. Moreover, as a historian concerned with the evolving stereotype of the Irish, datable material is essential. While dating sheet music before 1852 in America is sometimes difficult (see below), the problems of chronology are not as severe as those surrounding broadside ballads and folksongs. Moreover, a focus on sheet music is not nearly as restrictive as it might seem. We must keep in mind that quite a variety of music did find its way into print and that there was considerable spill-over from one musical medium to another. Some traditional Irish songs, for example, did appear in sheet music, and the lyrics for many nineteenth-century parlor songs turn up in cheap songsters and broadside ballads. Moreover, until recordings, radio, and sound films, the only way to publicize a song was to have it sung from "the stage," which could have been anything from a variety saloon to an opera house.

Another concern, often voiced by sociologists of popular music, is that too great a concentration on sheet music might overshadow the importance of performances and venues, as well as the various cultural "uses" to which "consumers" put the songs. Thus, Richard Middleton emphasizes the importance of placing "historically located" forms of popular music "within the context of the whole music-historical field."[9] In the text, therefore, I have tried to summarize the economic and social history behind the growth of music publishing and of show business. I have also tried to explain the relationship between popular theater and popular song. I have included discussions of minstrel shows and melodrama and have devoted most of two chapters to vaudeville and one to the theater of Harrigan and Hart.

Within necessary limits I have consistently tried to discuss the various contexts in which these songs were sung. Where possible, I have also tried to consider how performances might have helped to control and shape the Irish stereotype. Finally, I have attempted to look at the evolution of the Irish stereotype against the reality of Irish-American experiences from the pre-Famine period to the end of World War I. Therefore, a brief historical summary of Irish immigration, settlement, and adjustment precedes each section.

Within the broad scope of this study I have focused primarily on song lyrics. This is an undoubted limitation, for, as all critics and scholars of popular music maintain, a song is an essential unity, the sum of its lyrics, its music, and its performance.[10] While I have tried to make the reader aware of changes in musical styles, not being a musicologist, I have not attempted the kind of musical analysis that a different type of scholar would bring to the subject.

Focusing on song lyrics also raises questions about what they represent as sources for cultural analysis. While Simon Frith admits that "lyrics give songs their social *use*," he also argues that song lyrics reflect not so much popular culture as "popular culture confusion" concerning the values of a constantly changing society. He reminds us of David Riesman's point that "the same or virtually the same popular culture materials are used by audiences in radically different ways and for radically different purposes."[11] Song lyrics, then, are not historical windows that open directly onto some objective reality about the past. As Pickering and Green warn, "we should not assume that we can simply read off song content as an inscription of the social values, attitudes, norms and beliefs of particular groups. Indeed, song content may in part or in whole be discordant with the moral community, but of value precisely because it offers a symbolic self-legitimating counterpart to that community."[12] Song lyrics, then, do not reflect "reality" but the public *discourse* about reality, the process of cultural negotiation, enabling people, in Richard Middleton's words, to "enjoy and valorize identities they yearned for or believed themselves to possess."[13]

The bricks and mortar of these identities often consist of clichés. One of the problems of studying any aspect of popular culture is that one inevitably ends up searching for meaning amidst an apparently meaningless rubble of words. Yet the effect of clichés is to "defamiliarize the familiar," as Middleton suggests, "to invest the banal with affective force and kinetic grace, to draw out of the concrete world of denotation some sense of those human generalities translated by musical processes."[14] Therefore, if in architecture God dwells in the details, then in popular music God dwells in the clichés. Repetition of the familiar is, after all, a foremost characteristic of popular culture. While homely and familiar words linked effectively to their music may ignite unexpected vitality in an individual song, it is clichés in the aggregate that carry the power to both reflect and influence our ability to create and sustain stereotypes.

Far from being meaningless, then, it is virtually impossible for a popular song, no matter how hackneyed, to lack meaning, especially if we trace the song to its various "uses" – the social contexts in which the song is performed and consumed. There is no such thing as a song completely innocent of some cultural baggage. The baggage can be quite complex, however. What does it mean, Middleton asks, for us to say we like one song rather than another? "Clearly such questions do not have disinterested answers; neither pleasure nor value can appear except through the operation of *ideology*." Ideology imposes a "false universality" upon songs, made up of supposedly natural, innocent, and obvious qualities.[15]

Middleton's argument, insightful as it is, threatens to carry us into the realms of intellectual arrogance, however. To imply that we must squeeze all human expression through the tube of ideology is simply to remain tethered to the old Marxist hierarchy of the "base" and the "superstructure" – economic "reality" and the cultural facades built upon it.[16] Without losing the insights that the more sophisticated Marxist critics have given us, it might be more useful to move from a hierarchical model to a systemic view of culture and society in which the questions of power continually *interact* with the psychological, spiritual, and aesthetic questions that shape the identities of individuals as well as groups. From a systemic viewpoint, therefore, ideology is no more basic than any other factor. If identity can never be understood apart from ideology, neither can it be fully understood through ideology alone. If everything in culture is influenced by ideology, then ideology itself is influenced by all other elements of culture.

Constant changes resulting from the interactions within culture are, therefore, systemic rather than hierarchic. In the interaction between a dominant culture and a subordinate culture neither survives intact. Both are changed because both are in a systemic relationship with each other. This is not to deny power, advantage, or hegemony to the stronger group, or a continued inferior position to the weaker. It is merely to suggest that cultural change takes place at a level beyond volition, beyond compromise, even beyond unalloyed ideology.[17]

All of this is of particular relevance to nineteenth-century America, an unfinished nation with a protean culture that constantly had to redefine reality in the face of geographical expansion, sectional conflict, commercialization and industrialization, urbanization, and immigration. Coming into this country, the Irish Catholics found themselves in a disadvantaged position vis-à-vis the WASPs. The Irish were strangers, generally poor, lacking industrial skills and urban experience, adhering to a religion held suspect by the Protestant majority, and burdened with a stereotype depicting them as either rogues or clowns. In such a situation, WASP social, economic, and cultural power certainly constrained the Irish as they sought to articulate and assert their own identity in America. However, the dominant culture itself was experiencing so much change that the Irish eventually found room to maneuver, space in which to experiment with their own images of themselves. Inevitably, WASP America shaped Irish America. However, in the process, the Irish helped to reshape WASP attitudes.

METHODOLOGY

For the purposes of this study, a song qualified as an "Irish song" if it met at least two of the following criteria:[18]

1. The title contained an Irish name, an Irish place name, or some other reference to Ireland;
2. Irish or Irish-American characters appeared in the lyrics;
3. The lyrics dealt with a situation or setting characteristic of Ireland or Irish America;
4. The song was a part of a theatrical production that centered on Ireland or Irish America;
5. The song was composed and/or performed by someone who was Irish or Irish American or who was associated with Irish plays, musicals, and so on;
6. The melody was derived from Irish traditional music;
7. The cover carried Irish symbols (shamrocks, harps) or other *visual* references to Ireland;
8. The song became accepted by Irish Americans as a part of their culture, although the lyrics may not specifically mention Ireland (e.g., "I Will Take You Home Again, Kathleen").

This study includes songs that were originally written and published in Great Britain but that were available in America.

Although most songs used in this study qualified on several levels, there were inevitably some gray areas where I had to decide on inclusion or exclusion based on my sense of the context surrounding the song. Take, for example, the songs by Edward Harrigan and David Braham written for their musical plays from the mid-1870s to the early 1890s. Most of these shows featured Irish-American characters within their urban environment. Given the nature of the shows, Harrigan felt little need to label a song with Irish references in the title. Moreover, some songs dealt as much with the urban setting that had come to define Irish America as with the characters themselves. In "Danny By My Side," an Irish-American girl sings about walking with her beau across the Brooklyn Bridge on Sundays. Since the song helped to associate the Irish onstage with the flow of urban life, I included it in the study. On the other hand, even though it was Matt Casey who waltzed with the strawberry blond in "The Band Played On," the tie to Irish America seemed too vague to warrant inclusion.

Most of the songs used in this study come from two sheet music collections, one housed in the Lilly Library at Indiana University at Bloomington and the other in the Cincinnati Public Library. The Starr Collection at the Lilly consists of over one hundred thousand items. It is unusual in that it is not cataloged. It is, however, "sorted" into three major categories: (1) individual composers, lyricists, and performers; (2) topics or themes; and (3) songsters and song books. Within the second category there is a heading for "Ireland," representing songs and instrumental pieces associated with Ireland, the Irish, and Irish Americans. This part of the collection contains some 850 pieces yielding around 500 separate titles, most published in the years covered by this study. Since the Starr Collection is not cross-referenced, to find more songs, I searched the folders assigned to individual composers, lyricists, and performers; for example, Thomas Moore, Samuel Lover, Edward Harrigan, Chauncey Olcott, and Ernest Ball. Consequently, I found an additional 125 songs, bringing the total from the Starr Collection to around 625 titles, which form the core of the database used in this study. For purposes of comparison, I also reviewed songs in other ethnic categories, such as the Scots, the Germans, the Italians, and the Jews.

The Cincinnati Public Library has over ten thousand pieces of sheet music. The collection is cataloged and may be accessed by composer and title. A hand search through the card catalog for the collection added over eighty additional titles to the database. The songs in the database represent only a sample of the popular songs about Ireland and the Irish published between 1800 and 1920. Based on advertisements on the covers of the song sheets and the material in the dime songsters, my database may represent somewhere between one-third to one-half of relevant songs for the years under consideration.

To try to keep track of the ebb and flow of words, phrases, and images, I entered information on slightly more than seven hundred songs into an electronic database. Although I have looked at hundreds of other songs appearing in songsters and music books, and although I have quoted from some of them, I limited the database to only those titles I found in sheet music format so that I could base my analysis on the complete artifact – cover (with artwork and information on performers), lyrics, music, and advertisements. Besides fields for title, lyricist, composer, publisher, date and place of publication, I could also search the database for information on cover art, performers, the type of song (love, comic, patriotic), song topics (emigration, Irish pride), types of music, and key words and concepts in the song lyrics.[19] By organizing the songs in chronological order, and then conducting sorts based on the various fields, I have been able to trace trends and changes within the songs.

The analysis was conducted on a decade-by-decade basis, except for the pieces published before the Civil War, when many songs available in America carried no publication or copyright date. Songs imported from Britain were rarely dated. Songs published in America were seldom dated before the 1820s. It was not until 1831 that music was specifically included in the United States copyright laws. Even then, songs do not appear to have been consistently dated until after the Copyright Act of 1852. Consequently, it is difficult to determine exact dates for songs published before the 1850s. While I have been able to find approximate dates for most of these songs, I have not always been able to assign them to specific decades. For this reason, but also because the songs show little change over the early decades, I have placed all of the songs I believe to have been originally published during the antebellum period in one large group consisting of 114 different titles (including twenty-three instrumentals). The rest of the sample contains twenty-six songs for the 1860s and sixty-one for the 1870s. The decades of the 1880s and 1890s each have eighty-seven songs. The first decade of the twentieth century is represented by 106 songs and the last decade in the study by 248 songs.[20]

The book is divided into four parts. Preceding each part, there is an introduction summarizing emigration from Ireland and developments within the Irish-American community. Part 1, beginning with Thomas Moore's *Irish Melodies*, considers the role of romantic, sentimental songs about

Ireland and the Irish, as well as their place within the popular culture of antebellum America.

Part 2 concerns the comic stereotype of the stage Irishman as it emerged from the Anglo-American theatrical tradition to its appearance in the comic songs up to 1870. The section concludes with a comparison of the songs about the Irish with those associated with the Scots, Germans, and African Americans.

Part 3 concerns the emergence of an Irish-American identity in the popular theater and song after the Civil War. The chapters move from melodrama to vaudeville to the theater of Harrigan and Hart.

Part 4 traces the changes that took place in popular songs about the Irish as Tin Pan Alley presided over a revolution in the production and the marketing of American popular song.

 PART ONE

The Romantic Image

Emigration from Ireland

Irish emigration to America began during the colonial period. Between 50,000 and 100,000 Irish sailed for North America in the seventeenth century, and another 250,000 to 400,000 arrived between 1700 and 1776. Although small by nineteenth-century standards, these numbers were significant, given the populations of both Ireland and British North America. Most of these immigrants were from Ireland's northern province of Ulster, home of most of the country's Protestants. However, a quarter of the eighteenth-century immigrants may have been from southern Ireland and as many as a third may have been Roman Catholics. After 1800 the situation began to reverse itself as Catholic emigration from the South first matched and then overtook that of Ulster. From 1820 to 1840, 260,000 emigrated directly to America, while tens of thousands more re-migrated from Great Britain or Canada to settle eventually in the United States.[1]

Although Americans looked on many pre-Famine immigrants as poor peasants with little knowledge of the modern world, the Irish had already experienced enormous changes. An Anglo-Irish patriotic movement (quietly supported by many middle-class Catholics) had resulted in the establishment of brief legislative independence for the Irish Parliament in Dublin in 1782. This ascendancy parliament was not able or willing, however, to deal with the growing dissatisfaction of small Protestant farmers and Catholic peasants. On the heels of the French Revolution, both groups rose in rebellion in 1798. The largely Protestant United Irishmen were put down with relatively limited bloodshed in the North. The Catholic insurrection in the South, however, savagely initiated, was even more savagely repressed.

Although the English moved quickly to try to depoliticize Ireland by urging (and bribing) the Irish Parliament to dissolve itself and merge with Westminster in the Act of Union of 1800, politics had arrived in Ireland to stay. Even the abortive mini-revolution attempted by Robert Emmet in 1803 could not stave off the shift of political activity from the Protestants to the Catholics. In the 1820s Daniel O'Connell, one of the century's greatest orators and political leaders, organized the Irish masses in demanding Catholic emancipation.

O'Connell's emancipation movement was successful in 1829, after which he then mobilized his followers to demand the repeal of the Act of Union and the restoration of the Irish Parliament. Nipping at O'Connell's heels were the Young Irelanders, whose pens were, unfortunately, mightier than their swords. The repeal movement and Young Ireland's half-hearted attempt at revolution failed, and, out of the confusion and despair that followed the Famine and the death of O'Connell, there emerged the Fenians, who made the cause of Irish revolution an international movement. Meanwhile, a restored Catholic infrastructure was slowly laying the groundwork for the "devotional revolution," which eventually moved Catholicism in Ireland from the realms of a folk religion firmly into the fold of confessional orthodoxy.

Because of all these events, most Irish immigrants after 1820 generally shared some degree of national identity, with an accompanying dislike of England; a sense of patriotism easily extended to embrace America; a strong allegiance to the Roman Catholic faith; and political experience that enabled them to grasp quickly the mechanisms of the American democratic process.

WHY THEY CAME

Ireland after 1815 was a country with an exploding population trapped in a severely restricted economy. The abolition of the Irish Parliament in 1800 had deprived the country of any means of protecting its economic interests against manufacturing and agricultural policies that favored England. Consequently, Ireland gradually took on many attributes of what Oliver MacDonagh has called a "satellite, or rather a backward agrarian segment of an advanced, dynamic manufacturing economy."[2]

As Ireland's population roughly doubled from around four million in 1790 to almost eight million by 1845, the eve of the Famine, Irish farmers and peasants tried to cope by constantly subdividing their leases among their children. Absentee landlords, many of them poor managers of their estates, carelessly expanded their rents by allowing the rapidly growing numbers of peasants to carve up their dwindling plots of land at ever higher rents. Thus, a farm in County Clare that had maintained one tenant in 1793, had ninety-six tenants in 1847. By the eve of the Famine, rural Ireland had an astounding population density that, as MacDonagh suggests, "resembled more closely an equatorial delta settlement than any western agricultural community of the present century."[3]

Even by the 1830s, the deteriorating economic situation in Ireland was obvious to anyone visiting the island. Gustave de Beaumont was haunted by the ubiquitous image of "misery, naked and famishing," everywhere he traveled in Ireland. After describing the dire conditions of a typical one-room mud cabin, he hastened to assure his readers that the dwelling was *not* that of a pauper but of an "Irish farmer and agricultural worker."[4]

With most holdings five acres or less and some family plots only a half, sometimes even a quarter of an acre, by 1840 the potato had become the sole food of one third of the people and an essential element in the diet of many more.[5] Partial failures of the potato crop occurred periodically throughout the first half of the nineteenth century. These, coupled with the iniquitous Irish land system, prompted a Royal Commission in 1845 to warn of impending doom unless something was done. By then it was too late. The potato blight struck in the same year the report was published.

In 1845 enough of that year's good crop of potatoes had already been harvested to prevent widespread hunger. However, in 1846, Ireland's entire crop was lost. Imperial response, which had been adequate for the crisis of 1845, became increasingly inadequate, even punitive, for the calamity that had overtaken Ireland. The blight seemed to ease off a bit in 1847 but returned with full virulence in 1848. Although the worst was now over, by then hundreds of thousands were dead and dying, and hundreds of thousands more desperate and frightened Irish men and women were fleeing the country. Between 1845 and 1851 the country lost about two and a quarter million people, around one million of whom may have died of disease and starvation. The rest emigrated. Many joined already swollen Irish communities in England. Many more, perhaps as many as 1,600,000 came to America during the Famine years, adding between 7 and 8 percent to the nation's population. In a few short years Ireland had lost one quarter of its people. In Kirby Miller's words, "An entire generation virtually disappeared from the land; only one out of three Irishmen born about 1831 died at home of old age – in Munster only one out of four."[6]

During the Famine, the poorest among the peasantry were swept away by death or emigration. Alf MacLochlainn points out that between 1841 and 1851 some 360,000 mud cabins, which had housed two million people, disappeared from the landscape. In Ulster 81 percent of houses literally disappeared, in Connaught 74 percent, in Munster 69 percent. In the wake of death and emigration, land holdings were consolidated. By 1851 the percentage of holdings from one to five acres had already declined from almost 45 to 15.5 percent of all holdings. The social structure along with the landscape of rural Ireland was changed forever.[7]

The cultural impact of the Famine was equally cataclysmic. As Mac-Lochlainn points out, there were more Gaelic-speakers in Ireland in 1840 than any time in the country's history.[8] Although Gaelic was already rapidly disappearing from the eastern counties, the Famine broke the back of the Irish language in the middle counties and set the precedent for the heavy emigration of Gaelic speakers from the West during the later decades of the nineteenth century.

MacDonagh has compiled a composite portrait of the average famine emigrant. More likely to be male, he had few skills, and he spent most of the little money he had in traveling to America. MacDonagh underscores what he calls the "communal" nature of the famine emigration. If not accompanied by some members of his family (or someone from his townland), the emigrant was anxious to start saving money to provide passage for those left behind in Ireland. A Roman Catholic, the average immigrant came from rural Ireland and was accustomed to a low standard of living. Nevertheless, he was probably literate and had some knowledge of or even experience in politics. He also probably spoke English, if only as a second language. Finally, the famine emigrant felt "uprooted." His departure from home and friends had not been planned or even desired. He had been forced out.[9]

The Famine initiated the great emptying of Ireland, a process that would continue into the twentieth century. After losing over two million people during the Famine years, Ireland went on to lose an additional 4.1 to 4.5 million people between 1856 and 1921. Somewhere between 3 and 3.5 million of these found their way to America, most in the half-century following 1870, when large-scale immigration to America resumed after the Civil War. Emigration had become an integral part of Irish life.

Irish emigration to America was eventually overshadowed by the arrival of other European peoples. Yet, given Ireland's population, it remained high until World War I. In the 1890s over 427,000 Irish came to the United States, nearly 419,000 in the 1900s, and 125,000 between 1910 and 1914 – an average of 43,000 per year.[10]

Arriving in America, the Irish immigrants had to adjust to their new country and Americans had to adjust to their new fellow citizens. Although coming to "a land of immigrants," the Irish were in many ways the first "emigrant group," arriving in such numbers that Americans were not prepared to receive them. Americans were, however, prepared to recognize the Irish, thanks to a set of stereotypes that were already part of the Anglo-American culture: a romantic stereotype of the exile in flight from a tragic land of beauty; and a comic stereotype of the wild, irresponsible Paddy.

1. Dear Harp of My Country
The Irish Origins

In 1807 two brothers named Power approached a young Irish poet who was enjoying his first flush of success in literary London. Thomas Moore's translation from the Greek of the *Odes of Anacreon*, dedicated (with permission) to the Prince of Wales, already was very popular. William and James Power, publishers in London and Dublin respectively, wanted Moore to supply words for a collection of traditional Irish airs. Moore agreed, and the first two volumes of his *Irish Melodies* came out in 1808; the tenth and final volume was published in 1834. Moore wrote other song series, along with epic poems, biographies, satires, and a three-volume history of Ireland. Nothing else he wrote, however, has had the survivability of the best of his *Irish Melodies*, which were an immediate success on both sides of the Atlantic. They represent the first important body of popular Irish songs and helped to set the contexts and themes for later material.[1]

The *Melodies*, like Moore himself, was a product of the eighteenth-century Celtic Revival that had provided a cultural basis for Anglo-Irish nationalism. According to Edward Snyder, this revival, which began around 1750, was sparked by a growing romantic interest in novelty, in nature, in "native" peoples and their cultures, in the *idea* of liberty, if not always in its practice, and in a desire to replace the mythology of ancient Greece and Rome as the source for the British poetic imagination.[2] Irish involvement in the revival was propelled by the attempt to wrest back from James Macpherson, the Scottish pretender to Celticism, the provenance of the enormously popular "epic" of Ossian. Contrary to Macpherson's claim, the legends of Finn MacCoul and his son Ossian were Irish in origin. The translations, histories, and exegeses, written in refutation by Anglo-Irish antiquarians such as Sylvester O'Halloran, Charles Vallancy, and Charlotte Brooke, also helped satisfy the desire of both Anglo-Irish Protestants and middle-class Catholics to prove, as Andrew Carpenter suggests, "that ancient Irish culture was not that of barbarians but that of a people superior in at least some ways to the people of England."[3]

This attempt to recover Ireland's lost Gaelic culture greatly influenced

Moore. However, because this son of middle-class Dublin Catholics had studied Greek at Trinity College, not Gaelic, the linguistic wellspring of Ireland's Celtic heritage was as closed to him as it was to most of English-speaking Ireland. Fortunately, Ireland's musical heritage was a bit more accessible.

The traditional Irish harpers, who had once accompanied the bards and serenaded the Gaelic chieftains, had survived the final collapse of Gaelic high culture at the end of the seventeenth century. As itinerant musicians, they eventually found welcome in the homes of the Anglo-Irish aristocracy. Changes in musical fashion had gradually led to neglect, however, and by the end of the eighteenth century, just when the Celtic Revival began to focus on them, there was only a handful of old, mostly blind musicians left. To capture what remained of their art, several harping "conventions" were held, the most important occurring in Belfast in 1792. Dr. James McDonnell, the organizer, engaged Edward Bunting, the young organist at St. Patrick's Cathedral in Dublin, to transcribe the melodies. Bunting became enthusiastic about the project, and after some additional collecting, he published the first volume of harp tunes in 1796. A second volume appeared in 1809 and a third in 1840. Although other collections of traditional Irish music had appeared by then, Bunting's remained the most influential.[4] However, Bunting, like many of the era's collectors of the old Irish airs, neglected or was ignorant of the Gaelic lyrics associated with the melodies. This is why the Power brothers, who had published Bunting's first collection, sought out Thomas Moore.

The Powers were fortunate in their choice. Irish literary success, and thus profit, depended upon acceptance in London. Moore already had powerful Whig patrons with close ties to the Prince Regent. Moreover, while Moore had no direct knowledge of the literary or folk traditions of Gaelic culture, and little formal training in music, he did have an exquisite ear for a musical line. Music was, Moore insisted, "the only art for which, in my opinion, I was born with a real natural love; poetry, such as it is, having sprung out of my deep feeling for music." His genius did not lie in his poetry as such but in his ability to combine text and music in an effective, sometimes stunningly beautiful manner. As poems, most of his pieces lie flat on the page. They were written, however, not to be read, but to be sung. About his lyrics Moore himself said that he was "better able to vouch for the sound than for the sense." Terence de Vere White has suggested that the reason James Joyce had a greater regard for Moore's work than had William Butler Yeats was because Joyce was a singer and Yeats was tone deaf. Moore's ability to wed words to music accounts for much of the impact his work had upon the public. As Patrick Rafroidi asserts, Moore was the "first poet of note, writing in English, not only to take up Ireland's past and present as a subject but, mostly thanks to the old airs which were his source of inspiration, to do so in an entirely new and national mode."[5]

While fitting his words to music, Moore often altered the melodies of his traditional material, which Bunting and other collectors had already forced into conventional musical scales and structures. Then Sir John Stevenson, hired by the Powers to supply the musical settings for most of the *Melodies*, further adorned them with fashionable bravura passages. The results, as Jon W. Finson maintains, were not as distant from the then popular Italianate style as the folk origins of the melodies might suggest.[6] Some contemporary critics argued that Moore and his colleague had taken the strange, moving Gaelic airs and rendered them merely pretty. Henry Hazlitt complained that Moore had turned "the wild harp of Erin into a musical snuff-box," an opinion that still survives. Seán O Boyle is certainly right when he states that Moore's alterations of the old harp tunes, based on already "faulty transcriptions," are "far removed from the elemental beauty of the traditional singing in the Irish language." Being thus removed, however, does not make it impossible to recognize that the best of Moore's songs have a beauty all their own, given the period and audience for which they were produced.[7]

However, in his own performances of the *Melodies*, Moore did not use Stevenson's ornate accompaniments, but, according to Thérèse Tessier, employed simpler harmonies of his own.[8] As a performer of his own songs, Moore was careful to mold the words around the musical line so that they were always singable. Even a tune like the "Garry Owen," destined to become the favorite marching tune of the United States Seventh Cavalry, flows along smoothly with its word-per-note match: "We may roam through this world like a child at a feast / Who but sips of a sweet and then flies to the rest." In tunes that took more kindly to the lyric line, Moore's wedding of words and music was nearly perfect. His ability to achieve the union of lyric and melody at the very opening of a song has led Terence de Vere White to ask, "How many poets have written better *first* lines?" One can almost pick them at random: "As a beam o'er the face of the waters may glow"; "Silent, O Moyle! be the roar of thy waters"; "Oh! The days are gone, when beauty bright, my heart's chain wove."[9]

We can best appreciate Moore's accomplishment, then, if we consider him not as a great poet but, rather, as Charles Hamm has noted, as one of the greatest songwriters of the nineteenth century. He was not only gifted in the way he fitted his lyrics to the music, but he had an innate musical sense that guided him as he altered the tunes to fit his words. As Sir Walter Scott said of him, "He seems to think in music." Moreover, Moore's musical sense had a profound effect upon his poetry. According to Robert Welch, "By fashioning English words to the Irish airs . . . his English rhythm discovered a new resource, a flexibility, stimulating after the long reign of the heroic couplet." Moore's lyrics were an important contribution to romantic metrics.[10] However, were they "Irish?"

Writing in *Blackwood's*, William Maginn complained of Moore's audacity in calling his songs Irish. The music was Irish, "but as for the songs, they in general have as much to do with Ireland, as with Nova Scotia."[11] In fact, only 10 to 15 percent of the songs contain any overt reference to Ireland or things Irish. The bulk of the pieces appears to be love songs, drinking songs full of classical allusions, various odes to music and friendship, and nostalgic laments for past joys – elements that became staples of early nineteenth-century romantic popular poetry and song. Yet, the sentiments of the *Irish Melodies* are much more Irish, even nationalistic, than they appear at first glance. Although "Erin" is mentioned in only twenty-three songs, there are between ten and twenty additional songs that may be patriotic allegories masquerading as love songs. Even so apparently innocent a love lyric as "Lesbia Has a Beaming Eye (or 'My Nora Creina')" may contrast the virtues of Ireland (Nora) and England (Lesbia).[12]

Certainly, Moore, who had a great intellectual as well as emotional commitment to Ireland, considered himself a patriot. He once acknowledged that he had lacked Sir Walter Scott's "manly" upbringing among the peasantry, but added, in growing up, "The only thing, indeed, that conduced to brace and invigorate my mind was the strong political feelings that were stirring around me."[13] Moore also had a deep sense of the tragic aspects of Irish history, which included his own memories of the failed Rising of 1798, which claimed several of his radical classmates at Trinity, and of his friend Robert Emmet's tragic one-man revolution in 1803. His nationalism, however, was complex, being simultaneously antiquarian, sentimental, and political in nature.

Under the antiquarian influence of the Celtic Revival, Moore drew upon the work of O'Halloran and Vallancy, casting a romantic gaze back over the faded glories of ancient Ireland and finding in history and myths inspiration for his songs (as he was careful to point out in the footnotes that accompany them). Of the 124 songs in the complete collected edition of the *Irish Melo-*

dies, fourteen are based on old Irish legends. A little over thirty of the songs are patriotic in theme, although ten of these make no overt reference to Ireland. Half the patriotic songs refer to the past glories (and miseries) of Erin.

> Sing, sweet Harp, oh sing to me *[title]*
> Some song of ancient days,
> Whose sounds, in this sad memory
> Long buried dreams shall raise; (1834)

In some songs Moore gave Ireland a feminine persona. Usually referred to by the ungrammatical name of "Erin," she was often depicted lamenting her lost freedom.[14] The words "chains," "slavery," or "bondage," usually associated with Erin, appear in over twenty songs.

Moore's nationalism is, therefore, most obvious when he is dealing with the tragedies of Ireland's past – the depredations of the Danish and English invaders or the internecine strife among the septs of the Gaels. When he came closer to the revolutionary events of his own time, prudence and politics suggested circumspection. Some of Moore's most deeply felt patriotic songs are opaque to anyone ignorant of their background. For example, "Oh! Breath Not His Name," published in the first series, refers to his friend Robert Emmet, one of the last men to be hanged and beheaded for treason in the United Kingdom.[15]

Moore's dedication to his dead, revolutionary friends helped to give the *Melodies* their particular character. In Robert Welch's view, "His *Melodies* are probably his continued tribute to, or perhaps even his exorcism of, their memory. They seem to haunt the languid musical syntax, and help to give it its perpetual note of melancholy." This quality contributes to what Welch calls one of "the main characteristics of nineteenth-century Irish writing in English: there is a continual remembering of the dead, a keeping faith with their memory." Unfortunately, when mingled with the laments over Ireland's ancient wrongs, the transition from the hope of victory to the memory of fallen dead and their inevitable defeat overwhelms any attempt to give meaning to Ireland's past. The poems contradict themselves by creating and elaborating what Welch calls "a mood of melancholy dwelling on past glory."[16] Leith Davis suggests that these contradictions were the result of a colonial ideology taken up by Irish writers like Moore, who, seeking success in England, had to articulate sentiments compatible with British imperialism. Laments for a lost nation and dreams of Irish independence were acceptable only when cloaked within "Romantic images of Irish defeat and subordination."[17]

Yet, for all of their romanticism, Moore's *Irish Melodies* were very much a part of English-Irish politics of the Regency period and in the service of a very practical goal: civil rights for Irish Catholics. Moore received five hundred pounds a year from his publishers to visit the drawing rooms of the English upper class to sing his songs in person. He was most likely to be received in Whig establishments, any hint of Irish nationalism being anathema among the Tories. Under these circumstances, Moore was intent on selling more than music. Several of his songs contain half-concealed political commentary. In "Sublime Was the Warning Which Liberty Spoke," Moore took a daring, liberal stand by comparing the Spanish rebellion of 1809 with Catholic Ireland's own hopes of emancipation: "Who would ask for a nobler, a holier death, / Then to turn his last sigh into Victory's breath, / For the Shamrock of Erin and the Olive of Spain?" By romanticizing much of the Irish past and subtly, sometimes satirically, commenting on recent events, Moore sought to create a sympathetic attitude toward Ireland and Irish Catholics among the more liberal of the English Whigs. In "Though Dark Were Our Sorrows," Moore welcomed the visit of the Prince Regent to Ireland when it was hoped that he would support Catholic emancipation. When the Prince turned against the Whigs and their Irish allies (ending Moore's hope for preferment and, temporarily, for Catholic emancipation as well), Moore may have worked a rebuke into "When First I Met Thee": "Go – Go – 'Tis vain to curse, 'Tis weakness to upbraid thee; / Hate cannot wish thee worse / Than guilt and shame hath made thee."

Moore's sense of his own role in the campaign for tolerance for Catholic Ireland may be inferred from an essay in his *Corruption and Intolerance* (1808). In it he refers to the minstrels who softened the heart of the Emperor Theodosius by giving voice to the sorrow of the citizens of Antioch. "Surely, if music ever spoke the misfortunes of a people, or could ever conciliate forgiveness for their errors, the music of Ireland ought to possess those powers."[18]

While Moore's contemporaries were well aware of the politics behind his songs, the more subtle aspects of Moore's nationalism might have been lost in distant America. Nevertheless, in the romantic age of democratic revolution, Moore's emphasis on liberty had great appeal in America. Although Moore had a low regard for the slave-holding United States, most Americans admired the poet's liberal sensibilities.

> The Minstrel fell! – but the foeman's chain,
> Could not bring that proud soul under;

The harp he loved ne'er spoke again,
    For he tore the chords asunder;
And said, "No chains shall sully thee,
    'Thou soul of love and bravery!
'Thy songs were made for the pure and free,
    'They shall never sound in slavery."
("The Minstrel Boy," 1813)

The words "free," "freedom," and "liberty" appear in thirty-six of Moore's *Melodies.*

In spite of Moore's involvement in contemporary politics, a powerful sense of nostalgia pervades the *Melodies,* being the principal theme of at least twenty-five songs. Throughout many other songs the sense of joy lost, of time slipping away, and of wanderers longing for home are recurring motifs. Consider some key words that appear in the songs: "dream" in twenty-five songs; "home" in nineteen, "memory" or "remember" in twenty, "time" in twelve, and "youth" or "childhood" in fifteen. In "Let Erin Remember" (1808) Moore conjures up the image of an ancient city that fishermen on Lough Neagh reported seeing in the lake's depths. In the image of the drowned city, Moore found a metaphor for his nostalgic vision of the past.

Thus shall memory often, in dreams sublime,
Catch a glimpse of the days that are over;
Thus, sighing, look through the waves of time
For the long-faded glories they cover!

Thus, even before the great upsurge in migration of the Irish to America, Moore's songs helped to introduce into Anglo-American popular culture a vague identification of Ireland and things Irish with a strong sense of romantic nostalgia. Charles Hamm suggests that it was this general theme of nostalgia that helped make Moore's songs so popular in America.[19]

A cluster of key words underscores the somber mood that haunts so many songs: "dark" in thirty-one songs, "cold" in twenty-six, "death," "die," or "dead" in forty-three, "weep" or "tears" in thirty-seven, and "sorrow" in twenty-one. Tessier calls attention to the "solemn" nature that pervades so much of the *Melodies.* She finds only thirty-four of Moore's tunes "lively" or "sprightly." As Moore himself noted, "The language of sorrow . . . is . . . best suited to our [Irish] music . . . while the National Muse of other countries adorns her temple with trophies of the past, in Ireland, her altar, like the shrine of Pity at Athens, is to be known only by the tears that are shed upon it; *Lacrymis altaria sudant.*"[20]

Nevertheless, Moore knew that there could be no darkness without light. He built an internal tension into many of his songs by contrasting his somber images with a series of words referring to light and joy: "light" in sixty songs, "bright" in sixty-four, "beam" in twenty-four, "shine" or "shining" in twenty-two, "gold" in eighteen, "sun" in twenty-three, "smile" in thirty-five, and "joy" in nineteen. Thus, in spite of frequent classical allusions, Moore's basic vocabulary in the *Melodies* is generally simple. In many songs Moore plays the dark and light images against each other to contrast the conflicting moods he feels for his subject. Thus, in "Though Dark Are Our Sorrows" (celebrating the prince's visit to Dublin):

> And thus Erin, my country, though broken thou art,
> There's a lustre within thee that ne'er will decay;
> A spirit which beams through each suffering part
> And smiles at all pain on the Prince's Day.

This "sunshine and shadow" contrast is so strong that it appears as a major motif in at least twenty pieces and as a minor element in many others. "Oh! Think Not My Spirits Are Always as Light" (1808) speaks of "the tear that enjoyment can gild with a smile, / And the smile that compassion can turn to a tear." Moore makes a similar contrast in "One Bumper at Parting" (1813):

> And oh! may our life's happy measure
> Of moments like this be made up;
> 'Twas born in the bosom of Pleasure,
> It dies 'mid the tears of the cup.

Sometimes Moore states the theme in the title of a song: "This Life is All Chequered (with pleasures and woe)" and "Erin, the Tear and Smile in Thine Eye."

Although a common romantic conceit, Moore's focus on contrasting moods and images – light and darkness, sunshine and shadow – did reflect his own reading of the Irish character. He claimed to find in the music of Ireland: "The tone of defiance, succeeded by the languor of despondency, – a burst of turbulence dying away into softness, – the sorrows of one moment lost in the levity of the next, – and all that romantic mixture of mirth and sadness, which is naturally reproduced by the efforts of a lively temperament to shake off, or forget, the wrongs which lie upon it."[21] Early in their collaboration, Moore suggested to Stevenson that the poet who would follow the sentiments expressed in the Irish airs, "must feel and understand that *rapid fluctuation of spirits*, that unaccountable mixture of gloom and levity, which composes the character of my countrymen, and has deeply tinged their music."[22]

Such statements, of course, tell us more about the poet than about the Irish. According to Robert Welch, Moore saw Irish music and politics as deeply entwined, a characteristic that, Moore himself maintained, "appears too plainly in the tone of sorrow and depression that characterizes most of our early songs." As Welch comments, "the connection he made between a nation's mood and atmospheric identity and its airs was fundamental to the way he thought."[23] Thus, while Moore did not comment directly on the Irish character in his songs, he did connect Ireland, and by extension, her people, to a romantic, mercurial sensibility, tinged with sadness. Moore's "sunshine and shadow" motif became established in American popular songs about Ireland, ending up as a well-worn cliché in the Ireland of Tin Pan Alley.

Moore also helped to establish within Anglo-American popular culture those symbols of Ireland – the color green, the shamrock, and the harp. In "The Origin of the Harp" Moore apparently invented the story of an undersea siren who, in love with a mortal, changed into a harp. Moore claimed that the poem was inspired by a drawing he saw on the wall of the cell of his radical friend, Edward Hudson, incarcerated in Kilmainham Gaol. It was Daniel Maclise's illustration of the woman-turned-harp for an edition of the *Melodies* that helped provide Ireland and the Irish with one of their most important icons.[24]

Finally, many of Moore's songs celebrate the Irish sense of place and the beauty of the Irish countryside, which had already been discovered by English and Anglo-Irish travelers in the eighteenth century.[25] In "Sweet Innisfallen" (1824) (an ancient name for Ireland) the poet, forced to leave his "fairy isle," laments: "Thou wert *too* lovely then for one / Who had to turn to paths of care – ." In "The Meeting of the Waters" (1808), nature combines with friendship to make a paradise of the Vale of Avoca in County Wicklow.

> Yet it *was* not that Nature had shed o'er the scene
> Her Purist of crystal and brightest of green;
> 'Twas *not* her soft magic of streamlet or hill,
> Oh! – no it was something more exquisite still.

> 'Twas that friends, that beloved of my bosom, were near,
>   Who made every dear scene of enchantment more dear.
> And who felt how the best charms of Nature improve,
>   When we see them reflected from looks that we love.

Moore's linking of the qualities of the Irish people to the Irish country-side would remain an important element in the popular songs about the Irish for well over a century.

Most important of all, Moore presented a positive national image of Ireland, characterized by Leith Davis as a highly abstract "spirit of the nation," a concept that did not overtly offend British imperial sensibilities. According to Davis, "Moore's *Melodies* provide a universal prototype for Romantic nationalism in a defeated country"; sentiments he was able to put to the service of other countries in his *National Airs*. Nevertheless, power lurks in abstractions, as Irish history demonstrates, and the "spirit of the nation" had an impact upon the Irish at home and in the diaspora, especially when reiterated again and again in popular poems and songs. It had special meaning for the Irish immigrant because, as Davis suggests, "the new 'spirit of the nation' was conceived of as a feeling, as we see it in 'Tho' the Last Glimpse of Erin'":

> Tho' the last glimpse of Erin with sorrow I see,
> Yet wherever thou art shall seem Erin to me,
> In exile thy bosom shall still be my home,
> And thine eyes make my clime wherever we roam.

The immigrant, then, could not leave Ireland behind, nor cease to be Irish. Ireland and Irish identity became internalized. As Moore himself wrote, Ireland was "the country *of all others*, which an exile from it must remember."[26]

The general role played by Moore's *Irish Melodies* in establishing and developing so many themes basic to the popular romantic poetry and song may have tended to make the *Melodies* seem less "Irish" than they actually were. Yet it was inevitable that when British and American songwriters turned to Ireland, Moore's sentiments of longing, nostalgia, and the dream of the lost home would gather about their visions of Erin like the mists of twilight. Although few writers emulated Moore in his use of Irish legends, ancient heroes, or classical allusions, his *Irish Melodies* inevitably helped establish within Anglo-American popular culture many elements that would be combined to make an "Irish" song: Erin as the female persona of Ireland, the cause of liberty, the longing for home and childhood, the mixture of joy and sadness, the harp and shamrock as important national symbols, the beauty of the Irish landscape, and the exile's ineradicable love of the native land.

American publishers quickly pirated Moore's *Melodies* as each volume appeared. Fellow Irishman Matthew Carey published one of the first American editions of the songs. Pocket-sized collections of the lyrics appeared in the States as early as 1815, helping to spread Moore's songs widely among the American public. His lyrics also appeared in countless "songsters" throughout the nineteenth century. He was, in fact, the leading (if involuntary) contributor to song collections published in the United States between 1825 and 1850.[27]

As the most popular songs in America in the second and third decades of the nineteenth century, the *Irish Melodies* proved a commercial success that was, according to Charles Hamm, an important factor in establishing the music publishing business in the United States. Nor did nineteenth-century Americans' love for Moore's songs fade, even in later decades. As late as 1870, the Board of Music Trade's composite catalog for twenty large music publishers shows that thirty-three of Moore's Irish songs were still available in sheet music. By 1900 over thirty separate editions of the *Irish Melodies* had been published in America.[28]

OTHER IRISH SONGWRITERS

Moore's successful combination of songwriting and performing inspired several of his fellow countrymen, Samuel Lover (1797–1868) being the most important. Lover's talents were even broader than Moore's. His artistic output included plays, criticism, novels, opera libretti (two for William Balfe, including *Il Paddy Whack in Italia*), and paintings (he was an expert miniaturist). As a novelist and playwright, he helped to rejuvenate the stage Irishman for the nineteenth-century theater. Lover also wrote well over two hundred songs, some with English settings (for London's Madame Vestris), but many with Irish themes. Like Moore, he performed his own material; however, his audiences extended beyond the polite drawing rooms of the upper class. Lover, like Charles Dibdin and Henry Russell, presented one-man theatrical entertainments, his specialty being "Irish Evenings" in which he sang his songs and read from his works. Lover offered his "evenings," which went under such titles as "Paddy's Portfolio," "Outlaws and Exiles of Erin," and "Paddy by Land and Sea," to Americans in a series of successful tours between 1846 and 1848.[29]

Although Lover wrote many of his own melodies and accompaniments, providing some of them with a distinctly traditional character, he occasionally followed Moore's example of adopting traditional airs and dance tunes. "I'm Not Myself At All" is based on the venerable "Captain Kidd" tune, better remembered as the air for "The Praties They Grow Small Over Here." In "The Hour Before the Day," one of his best songs, Lover simply borrowed the tune, "The Groves of Blarney" that Moore had already reworked for "The Last Rose of Summer." Other songs Lover set to traditional melodies were "The Beggar," "The Fairy Boy," and "The War Ship of Peace."

Like Moore, Lover also looked to Irish myths and legends for the settings for some of his songs. However, he did not have to go back to the dim antiquarian past of the Fianna or the children of Lir. Lover was close enough to the Irish peasantry to draw upon their still-living legends and stories. He published two series of songs: *Legends and Traditions of Ireland* and *Songs of the Superstitions of Ireland*. Except for some of the tunes, however, the Irish character of many of these songs is minimal. The legend or story appears in a prose summary at the head of a song. The song's lyrics do not narrate a story or explain a situation. Instead they expound on an emotion or sentiment.[30] Lover's songs rarely refer to Irish names or places, and except for his comic pieces, seldom use dialect. Nor do these songs contain images and themes that became associated with a popular image of Ireland. Although the emphasis on legends and superstitions no doubt reinforced a romantic view of Ireland, Lover's more serious songs, such as "The Angel's Whisper" and "The May-Dew," appear to have had minimal influence upon Irish popular song as it evolved in the United States.

As we will see in chapter 3, however, Lover's comic pieces, a genre of which Moore was almost entirely innocent, did help to establish for British and American audiences the popular figure of Paddy in song. Songs like "The Boul'd Sojer Boy," "The Low-Backed Car," "Rory O'More," and "The Widow Machree" remained favorites in America for much of the nineteenth century, while Lover's more poetic (and less characteristically Irish) songs of legends faded away.

A few other Irish musicians contributed their songs to America's stage and parlors. Peter K. Moran was probably born in Ireland. He and his Irish wife settled in America, where they gave concerts.[31] Moran produced only a few songs of an Irish character, the most popular of which may not have been his at all. His "Crooskeen Lawn" (more often "Cruiskeen Lawn," meaning the "full little jug") is a rousing macaronic song in praise of drink. Moore had already used the tune for his "Song of the Battle Eve." The "Cruiskeen Lawn" remained popular throughout the antebellum period, and in 1860 Dion Boucicault used it in his play *The Colleen Bawn*.

Irish-born James Gaspard Maeder (1809–76), husband of the famous actress Clara Fisher, honed his musical talents in London and later emigrated to America. He gave concerts, conducted orchestras, and was quite well known to the musical scene in New York. Maeder wrote a great variety of music and contributed to the growing body of Irish popular song. "The Changeling" (1841) appears to be a manufactured attempt to follow Samuel Lover's "Irish Superstition" series. In fact, Maeder composed his own series entitled "Original Irish Melodies." He also wrote light love songs, such as "Kitty Dean," that featured some dialect expressions. Among his other Irish songs were "Ellen Asthore" (1841) and "Erin Weeps Forsaken" (1852), along with a comic piece, "Teddy O'Neale" (1843).

By the 1840s, Irish songs were no longer the exclusive offspring of Irish poets and musicians. Moore and his fellow countrymen helped launch a genre of popular parlor song to which any songwriters in Britain and America could contribute. As the "Irish song" became a commercial product, as well as an expression of nationality, songwriters were able to draw upon an existing stock of preconceived images, ideas, expressions, and stereotypes.

2. Romantic Irish Popular Songs in Antebellum America

It is characteristic of the colonial experience that cultural dependence may continue long after political independence has been attained. In the early 1800s, many of the playwrights, actors, musicians, and composers active in America had been born abroad. Even the native-born musical talent that began to assert itself after 1820, did so within a largely Anglo-American world of shared tastes and mutual transatlantic borrowing. As the music publishing business became established in the young republic, much of the material these firms handled was of European origin, and had been either imported or pirated, the cheapest form of "import." (It was not until 1898 that the United States copyright laws protected the works of foreigners.) Jon W. Finson estimates that until 1840, 90 percent or more of sheet music published in America originated in Britain.[1]

From virtually nothing in 1800, the music publishing business grew rapidly in America. By 1854 around 650 songs were being copyrighted annually in the United States. The market for sheet music in America grew in tandem with the popularity of the piano. By the 1820s, the piano in the parlor had become the musical hallmark of the middle class on both sides of the Atlantic. By 1830, four thousand pianos were sold annually in the country. During the 1860s, the number had risen to thirty thousand. The peak, three hundred thousand per annum, was not reached until the 1920s. During the second half of the nineteenth century, the reed organ, its bellows operated by a foot pump, became popular, especially in working-class homes.[2]

Although one did not have to be wealthy to buy sheet music, at twenty-five cents for a folio or two, it was, as Finson has noted, a "relatively expensive indulgence," not open to the working-class pocketbook.[3] Moreover, the music publishing business depended, as Nicholas Tawa has pointed out, upon an affluent, urban, middle class, which patronized the concerts where the songs got their start and which was ready and able to go out and buy the songs. Music publishers, therefore, had to hope for a stage performance of their songs in order to get them before the public (thus the number of dedications to performers that appear on the song covers). In order to maximize sales, songs had to appeal to as broad a market as possible. Therefore, as Tawa suggests, the songs were "bound to reflect the preferences of a sizeable but generally indiscriminate audience."[4]

Commenting on the commercial nature of the new popular music, Derek Scott asserts that: "The bourgeois 'popular song' was the first product which showed how music might be profitably incorporated into a system of capitalist enterprise. It is in the production, promotion, and marketing of the sheet music to these songs (and the pianos to accompany them) that we witness the birth of the modern music industry."[5] The parlor song was one of the most obvious results of what Richard Middleton has called "the bourgeois revolution" in popular music. By 1840, "most musical production is in the hands of or is mediated by commercial music publishers, concert organizers and promoters, theatre and public house managers. For the first time, most music is bought, not made for oneself."[6]

Sheet music provided a vehicle for recycling many different kinds of music for domestic middle-class consumption, regardless of original purpose. Far from being limited to tear-jerkers, sheet music included comic songs and a variety of dances. As Scott reminds us, "the real target of the sheet-music publication of almost all Victorian song is the middle-class home."[7]

Although many of the sentimental songs were often called "ballads," few were narrative songs, and few of these suggested any affinity with the balladry of the broadside or the oral traditions. The popularity of narrative songs waned rapidly among the American middle class after the end of the eighteenth century. Instead, according to Tawa, most of the parlor ballads were lyrical, non-narrative songs with direct, simple emotional appeal. According to a writer in the *Southern Literary Gazette* in 1851, "Ballads are much oftener the theme of more natural human love and sorrow. A blind child's lament for the glories of the sky – the husband's tender mourning for the departed – the regretful thoughts of brighter and purer days – the half awakened consciousness of sincere affection – all this finds voice in a ballad, a voice that soonest reaches the heart."[8]

Since the ultimate audience for these songs was to be found at home around the piano, the songs were relatively easy to perform; they had simple harmonies, limited vocal range, and easily sung intervals. However, skilled songwriters gradually abandoned the simpler melody lines popular in the eighteenth-century for what Edward Lee calls "the chromatically-based tensions of serious music," which were, in his words, "ideal, in diluted form, for whipping up emotions cheaply."[9]

Songs on certain Irish themes fitted the musical as well as thematic conventions of the romantic parlor songs, making Ireland and the Irish popular subjects. While it is not at all clear that there was an "Irish genre" in terms of musical influences, if we concentrate on the way in which Ireland and the Irish were presented in the lyrics, certain patterns do appear. We will look for those patterns in song titles, then the cover art, the music, and, finally, in the lyrics.[10]

THE IRISH SONGS: TITLES

How did Anglo-American songwriters and publishers identify a song as "Irish"? In the years before illustrated covers became common, the title carried the burden of conveying the nature or theme of any song. Obviously, simply introducing the words "Irish," "Ireland," or "Erin" into the title established the song's identity. If these words did not fit into the primary title of the song, they were often appended to a secondary descriptive title usually carried in parentheses, as in "Away Bonnie Bark (A Popular Irish Melody)." The titles of about half of the pre–Civil War songs in the sample carried a direct reference to Ireland, although often in parentheses.

Titles bearing recognizable Irish names, such as "Kathleen," "Norah," and "Molly," or "Patrick," "Barney," and "Thady," also suggested a Hibernian connection. Before the Civil War, almost half of the titles in the sample carried Irish names. The predominance of women's names in the antebellum titles is striking. They appear in about 66 percent of the titles containing names, 30 percent of all the titles in the antebellum sample. Typical titles are: "Kate Kearney," "Kathleen O'Moore," "Katy Darling," and "Sweet Kitty Neal." Songs with men's names tend to be a bit more descriptive: "Oh, Patrick Fly from Me," "Terence's Farewell to Kathleen," "Paddy Carey's Fortune, or Irish Promotion," and "Mr. Carney, None of Your Blarney." After the 1850s, the proportion of songs with Irish names in the title was never less than 50 percent, remaining an important indicator of the Irish nature of a song through the end of the century.

Following a convention already well established by Irish poets writing in English, songwriters sometimes introduced into their titles anglicized versions of common Gaelic words, such as "mavourneen" (*mo mhuirnín*, "my sweetheart"), "astore" (*a stór*, "my treasure"), "aroon" (*a rún*, "my darling") or "machree" (*mo chroí*, "my heart"). A common type of title was one that links a girl's name with a Gaelic term of endearment, as in "Kathleen Mavourneen," "Aileen Aroon," "Sweet Shylie Asthor," or "Kathleen Machree." Occasionally a title consists entirely of Gaelic (or what was intended as Gaelic) words, such as "Savourneen Deelish" (*a mhuirnín dílis;* "my faithful sweetheart"), or "Gra Gial Machree" (*grá gheal mo chroi;* "bright love of my heart"). Often, simple, obvious dialect clues, such as the use of "o'" for "of," or "ould" for "old," or words such as "blarney," are used in the title to suggest an Irish theme. At least one such linguistic or dialect clue appears in around 25 percent of the titles in the sample published prior to 1860. Their use in titles began to decline after the 1850s.

A well-known Irish place name in a title could also establish the identity of a song. However, because Anglo-American song buyers may not have been very familiar with Irish geography, it took some time for the use of place names to catch on. Before the Civil War, only 7 percent of the song titles in the sample bear references to places such as Dublin, Kilkenny, Limerick, Kildare, and Killarney. Typically, the title relates a girl to a place, as in "Fair Rose of Killarney," "Rose of Tyrone," "Mary of Fermoy," or "Jennie, the Flower of Kildare."

Possibly, song publishers may have been initially uncertain of the audience for Irish songs. Certainly, they went out of their way to identify them. Thirty-four percent of the pre–Civil War song titles in the sample contained at least two Irish signifiers; as in "Savourneen Deelish, An Irish Air." After the Civil War, the use of multiple identifiers in titles declined to about 9 percent in the 1880s and 1890s.

COVER ART

Illustrated covers eventually provided publishers with additional opportunities to reinforce the Irish identity of a song. In the eighteenth and early nineteenth centuries, however, sheet music seldom had covers. Title, composer, lyricist, and dedicatee and/or performer were all printed on the first page above the music. Gradually, engraved title pages or covers began to appear, sometimes with illustrations, but more often only with decorative lettering. Although hand-tinted lithographed title pages first appeared in the 1820s, it was not until the middle of the century that they became the glory of sheet music covers, adding to the "commodity" aspect of the product.[11] For the whole antebellum period, 30 percent of the Irish pieces in the sample have illustrated covers, either engraved or lithographed. The proportion reached almost 40 percent in the years immediately following the Civil

War and then began to decline until the 1890s, when new printing techniques made cover art easier and cheaper to produce.

In the pre–Civil War years, men outnumber women on the illustrated covers in the sample by 44 to 30 percent. However, while most of the women represent the heroines of love songs, one-third of the males represent the comic figure of "Paddy." Women often appear in some type of rural dress, sometimes wearing the famous Irish hooded cloak. Most of the male romantic figures are depicted wearing an Irish costume, which, in the hands of illustrators and dramatists, remained unchanged into the twentieth century: knee breeches, tailed coat, high-crowned tapered hat, and, sometimes, a cloak.

The illustrated covers allow us to see the rapid evolution of the popular iconography of Ireland and the Irish. Occasionally, song covers featured allegorical figures representing Ireland. During the antebellum period one can find a weeping Erin or bearded bards with their harps. In fact, we can begin to see the emergence of the harp as a popular symbol for Ireland. Several covers display that uniquely Irish motif: a harp with the body of a woman.

Other Irish symbols, such as shamrocks and thatched cottages, appear on the covers, along with antiquities associated with Ireland, such as round towers and celtic crosses.[12] While no individual symbol dominates the covers of the pre–Civil War period, some piece of Irish iconography appears on about one-third of the illustrated covers.

Landscapes – mountains, lakes, sylvan glades – or seascapes appear on 26 percent of the illustrated songs in the antebellum sample. Only a few covers suggest a specifically Irish landscape, containing thatched cottages or depicting identifiable places, such as the Lakes of Killarney. However, the significance of the landscapes lies not in their being recognizably Irish but rather in the association of Ireland with the beauties of nature. The use of landscape on Irish song covers increased during the 1860s and 1870s and then dwindled to almost nothing in the less romantic decades of the late nineteenth century. After the turn of the century, landscape recovered popularity and appeared on almost 30 percent of the covers after 1910.

THE MUSIC

While a new genre of Irish popular song was emerging, traditional Irish tunes were also a common part of America's social dance music before the Civil War and were published as instrumental pieces in sheet music form. About one quarter of the titles in the antebellum sample are instrumentals. Some of these contain tunes arranged in medleys; "The New Hibernian Quadrille" (1859), for example, consists of "The Legacy," "Rory O'More," "Gramachree Molly," "The Rose Tree in Full Bearing," "Planxty Kelly," "Believe Me If All the Enduring Young Charms," and "The Gary Owen." Other favorite instrumental pieces in sheet music form were "The Girl I Left Behind Me," "Sprig of Shillelah [sic]," "The Low-Backed Car," "Paddy O'Rafferty," and "St. Patrick's Day."[13]

As fashions in dance changed during the nineteenth century, the jigs, reels, and marches used in the quadrilles gradually dropped out of the popular market for dance music for the piano. However, jigs and, especially, hornpipes, continued to be used by clog dancers in the minstrel and vaudeville stage until the end of the century (see chapter 6).

At least half of the Irish songs in the sample published in America before the Civil War were based on traditional Irish tunes or were composed in the traditional style. For example, Finson notes that the purely pentatonic tune of James G. Maeder's "Ellen Asthore" (1841), is very much in the style of Celtic traditional tunes. In fact, Maeder's tune is found widely in Scottish and Irish folksongs, "Fair Flower of Northumberland" and "I Went to Bed with My Navvy Boots On," being just two examples. The melody for "The Irish Mother's Lament," an unusual crossover into the Irish genre from the early Victorian craze for "Gothick," is surprisingly similar to "The Yellow Rose of Texas," a tune with some likely Irish antecedents.[14] Some tunes may have entered the oral tradition, or, at least, had their position in the tradition reinforced from the stage and from sheet music. To this day, fiddle tunes such as "Barney Brallaghan," "Paddy O'Carrol," "Rory O'More," "Larry O'Gaff," and "Lanigan's Ball" retain the titles of the nineteenth-century songs for which they were used.

In many of the pieces, songs and instrumentals alike, the association of Irish music with jig time is very obvious. Almost 30 percent of the songs and instrumentals in the antebellum sample are in the 6/8 time of the Irish double jig. This does not take into consideration the widespread practice among composers and arrangers of using 3/8 and 2/4 march-time signatures for tunes that are basically jigs. For comic songs especially, jig time helped to establish the Irish flavor of the piece.

The musical influence of Moore's *Irish Melodies* is obvious on both sides of the Atlantic. Charles Hamm, for example, points out that the octave leap that appears in the opening bars of many of the traditional airs used by Moore (as in "The Last Rose of Summer," based on the traditional tune of

"The Groves of Blarney"), turns up in the work of American songwriters. Steven Foster's "Old Folks at Home" is one obvious example.[15] Finson finds Moore's influence in the cadenzas before the penultimate line of each stanza of Foster's "Jeanie with the Light Brown Hair."[16]

However, many songwriters were not content to limit themselves to traditional Irish melodies. Samuel Lover only occasionally used the older Irish tunes based on pentatonic scales. As Scott points out, Lover managed a fusion between the emerging idiom of the drawing-room ballads and his Celtic musical sources. In fact, according to Scott, the composers of parlor ballads gradually established their own Irish "tradition," the most obvious characteristic being a shift from major to relative minor key in mid-section of the song, a trick Tin Pan Alley writers would imitate years later.[17] For the most part, "Irish" music, as it appeared in early nineteenth-century parlor songs, was a combination of traditional harpers' airs, bits of jig tunes, and an emerging "popular tradition" (which middle-class song buyers were prepared to accept as "Irish") created as composers built upon one another's successes. Eventually, popular romantic songs required ever greater ranges of emotions than could be expressed through traditional-style melodies. The presence of traditional tunes in the genre of popular music declined after the middle of the century.

SONG TEXTS: LOVE IS ETERNAL

The lyrics of songs about the Irish reflect many of the themes that were generally associated with sentimental parlor songs. Love songs, for example, represent the single largest category of popular Irish song in the sample; 63 percent before the Civil War.[18] After reaching a peak of 69 percent during the 1860s, the proportion of Irish love songs in the sample drops markedly to 34 percent in the 1870s and down to 23 percent for the 1880s, before recovering their popularity in the 1890s.

Not surprisingly, we encounter Irish examples of all of the types of love songs Tawa has found in the parlor ballads: parting lovers; solitary figures, usually women, awaiting the return of their lovers; separated lovers who have no hope of reunion; the elegy at grave side of the beloved; the rejected lover; also the good-humored love song, sometimes making gentle fun of the over-sentimentality of the era.[19]

In the late eighteenth and early nineteenth centuries, love songs had tended to be impersonal and abstract, given to classical allusions and rather formal declarations of love; or they were humorous, even ironic. Things changed around 1810 as love songs became more earnestly romantic. According to Tawa, Americans of the antebellum era "thought of love as the bond which created enduring personal, family and societal relationships. With it came the emotional security and feeling of permanency they craved, and which they thought were often denied them in the hurly-burly of the outside world."[20]

Although Irish stereotypes are usually associated with comic figures, they are also clearly present in the love songs. The Irish girl matched the ideal sweetheart of the antebellum songs, as described by Tawa. She was of rural background, young, and marriageable. She asked for neither wealth nor position. She was simple but not stupid, naturally sensitive and naturally beautiful. However, she was also characterized by a passive, child-like innocence that seldom suggested the emotions of a mature woman.[21] Above all, she was faithful, a quality evident in William Pembroke Mulchinock's Mary in "The Rose of Tralee," first published in Britain in 1846:

> She was lovely and fair as the rose of the summer,
> Yet 'twas not her beauty alone that won me,
> Oh, no! 'twas the *truth* in her eye ever dawning,
> That made me love Mary, the Rose of Tralee.[22]

What distances songs like these from our own contemporary culture is the fact that the love celebrated in the parlor song was not a sexual love but what Tawa calls "a tender affection for, and a watchful cherishing of, one person by another." Such love was to cheer and bless every moment of life, even the last, at which point it was to accompany the beloved into immortality.[23] Indeed, the faithfulness of Irish lovers, men, as well as women, takes on mythic proportions and becomes their defining characteristic, continuing even in death. Thus, in the song "Yes! 'Tis True That Thy Kate Now Is Sleeping" (1853), the spirit of the deceased Kate speaks directly to Dermot, her surviving spouse.

> For a love like mine declineth never
> Tho' the spirit be freed from earthly clay,
> But unseen at thy side, Dermot, ever
> It lighteneth thy path with its ray.[24]

While songs mourning the death of the beloved, usually female, were popular in American popular song culture, they seem to have been especially important in Irish love songs. Prior to the Civil War, they constitute 22 percent of the love songs in the sample. For example, "Lament of the

Irish Emigrant" (1843), by Mrs. Price Blackwood and William R. Dempster (a British composer who found his way to America) describes the
emotions of a man about to emigrate after burying his wife and child. In
1844, "Answer to the Lament of the Irish Emigrant" appeared. On the cover
a man in knee breeches kneels by a tombstone, while in the sky above him
are images of his dead wife and baby. In the song, the voice of his departed wife reassures him that all will be well in America:

> Though Erin's shores you leave, Willie,
> An angel follows thee;
> Thy baby's spirit linked with mine,
> Shall watch thee o'er the sea;

The song concludes with the hope that "Our triune shade will peaceful seek
/ Its home beyond the sky."[25]

The grave site had special importance within nineteenth-century Anglo-
American culture. Visiting the grave of a loved one promised spiritual insights regarding both the deceased and the living. Finson suggests that
placing the husband at the grave of his wife prior to his emigration allowed
Blackwood to follow the conventions regarding the treatment of death in
Victorian songs.[26] In an Irish context, however, the pain of the Irish emigrant having to leave *behind* the grave of parents or of the beloved, thus
depriving him of the opportunity to commune with the dead, must have
seemed especially moving to Americans. Happily, the theme of the dead
beloved faded rapidly after the Civil War.

The plight of parted lovers is a more common theme, found in 36 percent of the Irish love songs published in antebellum America. Where a song
is narrated by one of the lovers, it is usually in the voice of the male emigrant who recalls the girl he left behind in Ireland. Less frequently, it is
the abandoned girl who laments the departure of her lover for America.
In the years immediately after the Civil War, the theme of lovers parted by
emigration tended to dominate Irish love songs; from 44 percent in the
1860s to 71 percent in the 1870s. The proportion then dropped to an average of 18 percent for the remainder of the century.

There is an account of an Irish girl, serving at a private musical party
in New York, who, upon hearing the great Adelaide Phillips sing "Kathleen Mavourneen," "forgot her plates and teaspoons, threw herself into a
chair, put her apron over her face, and sobbed as if her heart would break."[27]
And why not, given the pathos of the lyrics?

Mavourneen, Mavourneen, my sad tears are falling,
    To think that from Erin and thee I must part,
It may be for years, and it may be forever,
    Then why art thou silent, thou voice of my heart?
It may be for years, and it may be for ever!
    Oh! why art thou silent, Kathleen Mavourneen?[28]

The music was by English-born Frederick N. Crouch and the lyrics are usually attributed to a Mrs. Crawford, although whether this was Mrs. Annie Barry Crawford, an English poet, or Julia Crawford, the composer's County Cavan-born wife, is not clear.[29] The song was published in England in 1838 and in America in 1840. Crouch, a well-trained musician, had a passion for things Irish and wrote several other Irish songs, including "Dermot Astore" – the "answer" song to "Kathleen Mavourneen" (also with Mrs. Crawford) – as well as other songs with lyrics by Desmond Ryan: "O'Donnell's Farewell," "Sing to Me, Nora," "Exile of Erin," "Sheila, My Darling Colleen," "Katty Avourneen," "Eveleen O'Moore," "Gra Gial Machree!," "Minona Ashtore," and "Noreen."

Crouch did not prosper in England and in 1849 he came to America, where he fared even worse, his best songs having already been pirated by American publishers. After serving as a trumpeter in the Confederate Army, he was virtually forgotten. Born in Wiltshire in 1808, the son of a cellist and music tutor to William IV, Crouch died in Portland, Maine, in 1896.

"Come Back to Erin" is another perennial favorite Irish song of parting, also written by a Briton – Charlotte Alington Barnard (1830–69), who published her works under the pseudonym "Claribel." The song came out in 1866 and is an interesting example of how a skilled songwriter of the period could work into one piece so many of the elements that had come to define or signify the Irish genre for the popular market. They are all contained in the opening verse of the song, which then serves as the chorus.

Come back to Erin, Mavourneen, Mavourneen,
Come back Aroon to the land of thy birth,
Come with the shamrocks and the springtime, Mavourneen,
And its Killarney shall ring with our mirth.[30]

In the first line, Barnard uses the poetic expression "Erin," along with an already familiar Gaelic term of endearment. Another Gaelicism, "aroon," appears in the second line, along with the emphasis on "land of thy birth."

The shamrock, not yet all that common in Irish songs, is referenced in the third line, as well as "springtime," thus associating Ireland and Irishness with the beauties of nature. This is reinforced in the last line by the reference to Killarney, already a well-known tourist attraction. In spite of the fact that the heroine is going to England rather than to America, the song was a great favorite in the United States, as were other of Barnard's songs, such as "I Cannot Sing the Old Songs."

EMIGRATION AND LEAVE-TAKING

While the parlor songs explored the extremes of joy and sorrow, there was a limit to the kinds of tragedies with which the middle-class imagination was prepared to be entertained. The Irish Famine (and the subsequent influx into America of masses of poor Irish immigrants) had little immediate impact upon the romantic songs of the antebellum period. Nevertheless, a few songs in the late 1840s and the early 1850s did refer to eviction and famine. Unusual for its willingness to at least confront the fact of starvation is "Give Me Three Grains of Corn, Mother," by Mrs. A. M. Edmond and O. R. Gross (1848). A note on the cover explains that the title is taken from "the last request of an Irish lad to his mother as he was dying of starvation." She finds three grains left in her pocket and gives them to him. "It was all she had, the whole family were perishing from starvation." The lyrics ask the question:

> What has poor Ireland done, Mother,
> What has poor Ireland done?
> That the world looks on and sees us starve,
> Perishing one by one!
> Do the men of England not care, Mother
> The great men and the high,
> For the suffering sons of Erin's Isle,
> Whether they live or die!

The lyrics were widely anthologized in America during the nineteenth century, appearing in many school texts.[31]

During the Famine, the English-born composer George P. H. Loder wrote the "Dying Emigrant's Prayer" (1847), setting words by Henry Plunkett Gratten. The song was dedicated to the Irish Relief Commission. Samuel Lover wrote a song commemorating one of the two American men-of-war that was decommissioned and sent to Ireland loaded with relief supplies. His song,

"The War Ship of Peace" (1847), was set to the tune Moore had used for "The Harp That Once through Tara's Halls" and was dedicated as "A tribute of Irish Gratitude to American Manufacturers." "The Emigrant's Farewell" (1852) fits the Famine into the broad context of emigration:

> Then the famine came stalking with gaunt bony finger;
> And our landlord was ruthless and pitiless sure;
> And sweet Kathleen, our blue-eyed – but why should we linger,
> Recounting our sorrows – who cares for the poor?
> Yes, God careth for us. Then no more repining,
> Though we fly from this desolate country away
> To the free happy West; as each day is declining
> For the land of our fathers we'll fervently pray.[32]

In discussing the ubiquity of leave-taking in Anglo-American parlor songs, Tawa notes that the homes Americans voluntarily left to seek their fortunes were (in song, at least) delightful and idyllic. It was not poverty but ambition that set Americans adrift in the world. In terms of antebellum American popular culture, therefore, the experience of the Irish emigrant, driven out by want or politics, was somewhat exotic, like the African slaves who were stolen from their homes or the Indians who had their homes stolen from them. Thus, just as some Anglo-American parlor songs encouraged people to weep over the plight of slaves and the "noble redman," so they expressed a romantic sympathy for the Irish exile. Such songs satisfied what Edward Lee has identified as the middle-class search for novelty, vicarious glimpses into other lives, other classes.[33]

Something of this quality can be found in "Exile of Erin or Erin Go Bragh," by Thomas Campbell. Set to the traditional air "Savourneen Deelish," this very popular song was featured by James Pilgrim in several of his Irish melodramas.

> Oh, Sad is my fate said [the] heart-broken stranger,
> The wild deer and wolf to a covert can flee,
> But I have no refuge from famine or danger,
> A home and a Country remain not for me.

Campbell (1777–1844), a Scot who eventually became rector of Glasgow University, is supposed to have written this song for his friend Anthony McCann, who was forced to leave Ireland because of his involvement in the Rising of '98.[34]

The exile theme itself, while not dominant, is nevertheless well represented in the antebellum Irish songs in the sample. Around 15 percent of the song titles bear the words "exile" or "emigrant," "lament" or "farewell"; as in "Lament for the Irish Exile," "The Exile's Lament," "The Dying Emigrant's Prayer," "The Emigrant's Farewell," and Lady Dufferin's "The Irish Emigrant."

In "The Emigrant's Farewell" (1852) the evicted couple, forced to flee their roofless cabin, voice their despair at leaving Ireland:

Then Erin Mavourneen, how sad is the parting
Old home of our childhood, forever from thee!
And bitter and burning the tears that are starting,
As we take our last look at thee, Erin Machree![35]

Although the situation described in the song was real enough, the lyrics typically draw the veil of romantic rhetoric, vague in its outlines and distancing in its language, over the tragedy of enforced emigration.

In these songs the themes of death and the parting of lovers fitted all too easily into the emigration theme. In "Mavourneen Machree" (1852), the hero emigrates to save his sweetheart from poverty. He earns money in America but, just as he returns to fetch the girl, she dies. In "The Irish Emigrant" by Lady Dufferin and George Barker (ca. 1845), the man, preparing to emigrate, laments that "There's nothing left to care for now since my poor Mary died." Addressing the deceased, he says:

I'm bidding you a long farewell my Mary, kind and true!
But I'll ne'er forget you darling, in the land I'm going to;
They say there's bread and work for all, and the sun shines always
     there;
But I'll not forget old Ireland, were it fifty times as fair, were it fifty
     times as fair.[36]

The real significance of these songs lies in the easy way in which the singer moves from the lost beloved to the lost land, a characteristic of Irish songs of emigration and parting in both sheet music and the broadside ballads. In "Mary Astore" the emigrant couple pray for Ireland as their storm-swept ship takes them from their beloved homeland. Regardless of the sadness over losing loved ones and home, in many of these songs Ireland itself become a focal point of loss.[37]

The sentiment of nostalgia, so strong in Moore's songs, easily blended with the themes of exile and loss. Nostalgia for the lost home, so prevalent in the songs of Stephen Foster, pervades about a quarter of the pre-

Civil War Irish songs in the sample. William W. Austin, in his study of the musical milieu in which Foster worked, identifies the "dream of home" as one of the all-pervasive themes of European and American songs in the first half of the nineteenth century. As we have seen, Moore was among the first poets to exploit this theme. In fact, one of Moore's last poems was one actually titled, "The Dream of Home."

> Who has not felt how sadly sweet
> The dream of home, the dream of home,
> Steals o'er the heart, too soon too fleet,
> When far o'er lea or land we roam?[38]

Although Moore did not write about emigration per se, the subject of exile, the loss of home and friends, and the love of Ireland pervade his *Irish Melodies*. These linked themes continued in the popular songs about the Irish and were part of what Austin calls a common "public tradition" and "international style" in parlor songs.

Austin suggests that the "home/roam" theme spoke to growing numbers of insecure city dwellers, lured or shifted from their small towns and villages by the industrial revolution. Certainly, as Hamm points out, the nostalgic theme of loss was a most appropriate one for Americans: "All Americans had left homes and homelands and friends and families . . . all Americans – no matter how they might be prospering at the moment or how bright the future might appear – suffered from a sense of rootlessness."[39]

Such themes, of course, legitimately belonged to the Irish and, especially, the Irish-American experience. This sense of nostalgia involved a nexus of home, family, sweetheart, and, that ultimate symbol of romantic purity, childhood. In an age that so loved the song "Home! Sweet, Home," it is not surprising, as Michael Turner observes, "that many songs of travel, exile and yearning for home should be Irish in character, nor that the bulk of them should be American."[40]

While the average American, agitated by an uncertain and ever-changing society, could reflect longingly on a secure dream of home and childhood, the distance that separated past from present for the Irish immigrant was represented by three thousand miles of ocean. In the imagination of the songwriter, the pain of nostalgia could reach a particularly exquisite pitch in an Irish song. Thus, "I cannot call the old times back, old times to me so dear," says the head of a family forced by famine and high rents to emigrate in "The Irish Peasant." On the cover is an illustration of a couple leaving a ruined cottage. In "Aileen Mavourneen" the girl calls after her departing sweetheart, "Friend of my childhood, hope of my youth." The girl in W. Langton Williams's "You'll Soon Forget Kathleen" cries out to her beloved as he is about to emigrate:

> Oh! Leave not the land, the sweet land of your childhood
> Where joyously pass'd the first days of our youth
> Where gaily we wander'd 'mid valley and wild wood
> Oh! These were the bright days of our innocent truth.[41]

Such songs point to a growing perception in Anglo-American popular culture, especially after the Famine, that emigration had become central to the Irish experience. Therefore, in the songs of parting, the loss of the beloved parallels the loss of home and homeland. About 18 percent of the lyrics of the antebellum songs in the sample focus directly on the tragedy of emigration, while another 13 percent refer to parting from home and parents or to a yearning for the old homeland. In all, almost one-third of the songs in the antebellum sample deal with some sense of loss, with Ireland itself often as the focal point. In fact, over one half of the antebellum Irish love songs in the sample deal with either departure or death.

THE EMERALD ISLE

Irish nationalist sentiment was not a dominant theme in the antebellum sample of songs. Excluding Moore's works, only a little over 10 percent of the songs published before the Civil War expressed Irish political or patriotic sentiments. This is not surprising, considering that many of these songs were produced by English or Anglo-Irish songwriters. What patriotic sentiments we do find are usually presented within the context of the exile or emigrant themes. Few suggest anything like the fervor of "The Irish Patriot's Farewell to His Country" (1842), with its echoes of Thomas Moore: "Accurst be the dastards, the slaves that have sold thee / And doom'd thee, lost Erin, to bondage and shame."[42]

An attempt, unusual in sheet music, to suggest a national identity based on religion is "Hail! Glorious Apostle (A Hymn for St. Patrick's Day)" by Thomas Comer (1833), dedicated to the choir of the Cathedral of the Holy Cross in Boston. Set to the traditional tune of "St. Patrick's Day in the Morning," the choral piece concentrates primarily on the story of Ireland's saint. However, the last verse calls for divine blessing on the suffering country.[43]

The Ireland that is presented in most of the popular Irish songs of this period is usually a geographical rather than a political entity, a place celebrated in romantic imagination as possessing remarkable beauty. Derived from British travel books and supplemented by Moore's *Irish Melodies*, the idea of Ireland as a land physically blessed by nature had taken hold of the popular imagination. This is another example of how one of the common characteristics of romantic parlor songs could take on special meaning within the Irish context. What Tawa calls "the rural paradise . . . a prelapsarian arcadia," often situated in the South, was a central ingredient in American popular culture in general and in parlor songs in particular.[44] Although it was a land few Americans had seen, Ireland, too, represented the imagined "rural paradise." In "The Rose of Tralee," Irish nature provides a vivid backdrop for the lovers. The song begins:

> The pale moon was rising above the green mountain,
>> The sun was declining beneath the blue sea,
> When I stray'd with my love to the pure crystal fountain
>> That stands in the beautiful vale of Tralee:

In one of the verses, the beloved must share equal billing with the beauties of the valley.

> The cool shades of evening their mantle was spreading,
>> And Mary all smiling was list'ning to me,
> The moon thru the valley her pale ray was shedding
>> When I won the heart of the Rose of Tralee.

"Kate of Kildare," "Rose of Tyrone," and the "Fair Rose of Killarney" all associate the Irish colleen with the beauties of the Irish landscape. Considering the mythical role that Ireland would assume in American culture, we can see how a series of romantic clichés began to take on special meaning when applied to Ireland and the Irish. If we take into consideration cover art, song titles, as well as lyrics, over a quarter of the antebellum songs in the sample contain some references to Irish landscape.

The most enduring of these songs is "Killarney" (1861) by Edmund Falconer and Michael William Balfe. Balfe (1808–70) was born in Dublin and in his day was one of the most successful composers for the theater in Europe. Falconer, whose real name was Edmund O'Rourke, was an actor/playwright. "Killarney" was originally used in his melodrama *Peep O'Day*.

> By Killarney's lakes and fells
>> Em'rald isles and winding bays;

Mountain paths and woodland dells,
Mem'ry ever fondly strays.
Bounteous nature loves all lands,
Beauty wanders ev'rywhere;
Footprints leaves on many strands
But her home is surely there!

"Beauty's home," the song assures us, is in Killarney. Later verses mention popular points of interest around the lakes, and, indeed, the song reflects Killarney's place as a major Irish tourist attraction.[45]

This idealization of the Irish landscape was a common ingredient in Irish melodramas and even in some comic plays. As James Malcolm Nelson has pointed out, even the comic actor and playwright Tyrone Power helped to propagate the romantic image of Ireland as "an ideal 'never-never land.'"[46]

The sentimental parlor songs helped establish the essential element of the romantic image of Ireland and the Irish: to be Irish was to have experienced a great sense of loss – the loss of loved ones, home, and family were tied up with the even greater loss of the homeland. Ireland, a land of great beauty, was assumed to have had a hold on the Irish heart that had little to do with the politics of nationalism. While such images were part of the romantic conceits of Anglo-American popular song, they also connected, however inadequately, to aspects of the reality of the Irish experience, and had, therefore, continuing meaning for later generations of Irish Americans.[47]

The parlor songs of the antebellum period were dominated, then, by an essentially romantic image of Ireland and the Irish. These images were so powerful that the song market was slow to develop comic songs featuring the stage Irishman, who became a familiar figure in American popular theater by the 1840s. Tastes changed somewhat after the Civil War, when comic songs came to occupy a larger proportion of popular Irish songs. However, the association of the Irish with a deep nostalgic sense of loss and of Ireland as a lost land became permanent elements in Irish popular songs well into the twentieth century.

PART TWO

The Comic Image

The Irish Peasant in America

The America into which the Irish poured before the Civil War was a society trying to cope with increasingly large-scale immigration while responding to enormous internal changes and pressures. Being pulled apart by regional tensions, antebellum America was expanding geographically and economically. Immigration added volatility to an already seething pot. Inevitably, America, born during the religious wars of Europe, wresting its land from one race and enslaving another, displayed a high degree of ethnic awareness and anxiety.

Until the arrival of the Germans in the 1850s, the Irish represented the most numerous of the immigrant groups entering America. Dale T. Knobel has suggested that the extreme negativity of the Irish stereotype in antebellum America was in part a result of a struggle over national identity: "The institutionalization of a specifically ethnic prejudice directed at the Irish suggests that ethnicity became another primary identity for antebellum Americans. Americans drew self-identity from their attitude toward an ethnic minority they characterized as Un-American."

For a while Americans thought that perhaps Paddy, the victim of an oppressive society, would shed his strange ways once he had enjoyed the benefits of liberty. However, as Knobel demonstrates, this relatively optimistic attitude toward the immigrants gave way after 1840 to more racist views, as issues surrounding American nationality became compounded with ethnicity. Paddy seemed born, not made, and would be unlikely to take advantage of life in America to reform himself.[1]

Although the word "immigrant" had negative connotations for nineteenth-century Americans, it was not applied universally to all newcomers. According to Knobel, before the great upsurge in immigration from Germany during the 1850s, references to Germans were generally favorable, as Americans assumed that the German moral character was compatible with Anglo-American culture. English, Scots, and Welsh immigrants seldom attracted attention. In Knobel's words, "The foreigner who 'harmonized' with the native-born was no immigrant at all." In the 1840s and early 1850s the Irish were *the* immigrants, and the frequent coupling of the words "poor Irish immigrant" helped to create a stereotype that embedded itself in American discourse.[2]

In one sense, the fact that most of the Irish immigrants spoke at least some English may have contributed in a peculiar way to the tension. Although the Irishman's brogue signified his foreignness, all Americans spoke with some sort of accent, either ethnic or regional. No language barrier separated (or protected) the Irish from the Yankee. Perhaps because the Irish were so like Americans of English descent in speech and in basic appearance, the Yankees became uncomfortable and even fearful in their encounters with them. How could a people be so similar and yet so different? Many Americans must have thought that the Irish suffered from some failing – their religion, their poverty, their culture, their character.

Contemplating the Irish flocking into his city, the New York patrician George Templeton Strong mused, "Our Celtic fellow citizens are almost as remote from us in temperament and constitution as the Chinese." For all of its snobbish exaggeration, Strong had put his finger on part of the problem. Many of those Irish who had come out of rural Ireland were, indeed, remote from the cultural and social structures that defined Strong's individualistic, capitalistic, urbanizing, industrializing America. Many of the Irish immigrants, especially those of the Famine generation, had their roots in a premodern Gaelic culture. While few of the immigrants may have been monoglot Gaelic-speakers, many did speak Gaelic or had been raised in Gaelic-speaking families. After the Famine, as the pattern of emigration spread to the western seaboard counties where Gaelic remained strong, the proportion of Gaelic-speakers among the Irish immigrants arriving in America during the later nineteenth and early twentieth centuries appears to have been surprisingly high. Kirby Miller estimates that between a quarter and a third of post-Famine immigrants spoke fluent Gaelic, and another quarter were children of Gaelic speakers whose parents and teachers had discouraged the use of the language.[3]

The Irish language was only one element of Gaelic traditional culture. As Alf MacLochlainn has pointed out, the culture of the Irish peasantry was "an intense and distinctive vernacular culture, a culture expressed in music, song and dance, social amusements, shared superstition, marriage and funeral customs, housing styles, seasonal observances, organization of craft work, all these things we now call folk-life."[4] Materially poor, rural Ireland was rich in traditional forms of social entertainment. In discussing pre-Famine peasant society, Gearóid O'Tuathaigh describes a culture in which "music and song were woven into the very fabric of society and the fiddler and uillean-piper were kept busy at weddings and wakes, fairs and markets. There was no shortage of dancing; hurling was popular, as were other tests of strength and skill, such as weight-lifting and bowls." O'Tuathaigh also calls attention to a peculiarly Irish form of entertainment, faction fighting, "in which groups of men would club each other with cudgels, sometimes to settle a feud between families or villages but more often simply as a sort of bravado exhibition of strength."[5]

The nineteenth-century novelist William Carleton tried to capture this addiction to merry wars in his story "The Battle of the Factions": "to be sure, skulls and bones are broken, and lives lost; but they are lost in pleasant fighting – they are the consequences of the sport, the beauty of which consists in breaking as many heads as you can." Transported to America, the beauty of the sport was lost on most Yankees. Earl F. Niehaus reports that the citizens of antebellum New Orleans simply assumed that the Irish were "wild." Even the city's Irish leadership seems to have taken fighting among their compatriots in stride, urging only that their fellow countrymen settle their differences in true Irish style – with fists – and not to resort to knives, thereby becoming as "bloodthirsty as the natives."[6]

Alcohol played a large role in a peasant society mired in poverty. For those who could not afford commercially distilled whiskey, which was fairly cheap in Ireland, there was always the homemade *poitín*. Although Father Theobald Mathew's temperance campaign of the 1830s and 1840s did have an impact upon Irish society, the consumption of alcohol, as well as tobacco, remained high. As Oliver MacDonagh has commented, "It is strange, but commonplace, that so terrible a degree of want should have been accompanied by so relatively large a use of income upon 'luxuries.'"[7]

While frowned upon, fighting and drinking were hardly rare in American society. What set the Irish immigrant apart was the unfamiliar folk culture that provided the context for Irish behavior. By the end of the century, America would receive representatives from scores of southern and eastern European peasant societies, who came into our industrial cities trailing the traditions and customs of their premodern cultures. The Irish peasants, however, were the first numerous representatives from such societies to arrive in America. Without the wall of language to hide behind, the peculiarities and archaisms of the Irish folk tradition were very evident for Yankee bemusement and concern.

Consider the manner in which the Irish responded to death. The traditional Irish wake, with its mixture of solemnity, piety, unrestrained lamentations, uproarious hilarity, wild games, obscene pantomimes, and copious drinking was rooted in Gaelic culture. Even greatly modified to accommodate American urban life, "Paddy funerals" amazed and scandalized native-born Americans.[8]

The sudden shifts and extremes in mood and conduct, which probably were once common to all European societies in the Middle Ages, still survived in Gaelic Ireland. Until the Irish Church was able to take firm control of them, the wakes, along with saints' days celebrations or "patterns," ran the gamut from medieval piety to pagan "divilment." This combination of extremes of behavior appears in Thomas Crofton Croker's description of a pattern on the Eve of the Feast of St. John on June 23, 1813, in remote Lough Gougaun in County Cork. Like many pre-Famine gatherings, the pattern attracted vast numbers of people: "we stood amid an immense concourse of people: the interior of the cells were filled with men and women in various acts of devotion, almost all of them on their knees; some, with their hands uplifted, prayed in loud voices, using considerable gesticulation, and others, in a less noisy manner, rapidly counted the beads of their rosary." Croker, an Anglo-Irish Protestant, goes on to describe the crowds at the holy well, some dipping up the water to pour over sick infants, others plunging diseased limbs into the water.

> We left the scene, so calculated to excite compassion and horror, and turned towards the banks of the lake, where whiskey, porter, bread and salmon were sold in booths or tents . . .
>
> Almost every tent had its piper, and two or three young men and women dancing the jig . . .
>
> All become actors, – none spectators. . . . Cudgels are brandished, the shrieks of women and the piercing cry of children thrill painfully upon the ear in the riot and uproar of the scene.[9]

E. Estyn Evans refers to the old Irish patterns and fairs as "moral holidays . . . a feature of many societies which have not been greatly influenced by urban ways and values." He suggests that their purpose may have been "cathartic" and that they retained elements of "lingering fertility magic," such as the elevation of a male goat who still presides at the annual Puck Fair in Kilorglin, County Kerry. Dale Light Jr.'s point is well taken when he suggests that Irish who arrived in America before the Irish Church standardized religious instruction maintained a wide variety of religious beliefs, ranging from paganism to standard Catholicism.[10] The Roman Catholic Church was one of the principal modernizing forces at work in

Ireland. Gradually, and through strenuous effort, it began to tame Irish rural society during the latter part of the nineteenth century.

Nevertheless, elements of the premodern Gaelic culture remained strong. Even the frequently noted Irish habit of exaggeration can be traced to Gaelic usage and probably medieval habits of verbal elaboration that, when carried over into English, were taken as "blarney." Thomas Crofton Croker complained about the "strain of hyperbole" exhibited by his fellow countrymen. "I have heard the resident of a mud cabin speak with perfect assurance of his *'drawing-room'* – an apartment in the roof, to which he ascended by means of a ladder."[11]

Finally, there is the "particular type of zany humor" that D. K. Wilgus found in English-language folksongs of the Irish. The "grotesque" element in Irish humor is a characteristic of wake entertainments, folktales, jokes, songs, stories, and accounts of rural life. This is, of course, part of the very essence of the Irish stereotype, but, as Wilgus suggests, "behind a stereotype lies a truth being caricatured. And certainly the Irish folk have composed, accepted, adopted, and adapted these songs."[12]

Kirby Miller notes that the culture of many Irish-Catholic immigrants "seemed so premodern that to the bourgeois observers from business-minded cultures, the native Irish often appeared 'feckless,' 'child-like,' and 'irresponsible': inclined to behave or justify behavior in ways which avoided personal initiative and individual responsibility, especially as to livelihood."[13] Such premodern remnants of Gaelic culture may have contributed to the distance that native-born Americans perceived separating them from so many Irish.

3. From Teague to Paddy

The Evolution of the Stage Irishman

There was once a Scotsman, a Welshman, and an Irishman. They met on the stage of Shakespeare's *Henry V*, act 3, scene 2. During the siege of Harfleur, the three representatives of England's Celtic fringe hold colloquy outside the entrance to a sapper's tunnel dug beneath the city walls. The verbose Welshman, Captain Fluellen, tries to engage Captain Jamy, a Scot, and Captain MacMorris, an Irishman, in a disputation on the "disciplines of war." The Scot politely sidesteps the invitation, but MacMorris complains: "It is no time to discourse, so Chrish save me . . . 'tis shame to stand still . . . and there is throats to be cut and works to be done . . . so Chrish save me, la!" When Fluellen starts his rejoinder with "there is not many of your nation – " MacMorris explodes: "Of my Nation? What ish my Nation? Ish a Villain, and a Bastard, and a Knave, and a Rascal. What ish my Nation? Who talks of my Nation?" When Fluellen, taking offense in turn, asserts that he is as good a man as MacMorris, the captain replies: "I do not know you so good a man as myself: so Chrish save me, I will cut off your head."

The trumpet announcing a parley in the larger war breaks off the hostility in the smaller battle of words. Unlike Fluellen, who continues to talk his way through the rest of play with proto-Methodist dedication, we see no more of Captain MacMorris. However, his brief appearance helps us chart the evolution of one of the oldest clichés in the English-speaking theater. This early stage Irishman is already endowed with a brogue of sorts, pious phrases used in impious circumstances, and what Declan Kibred describes as "excitability, eloquence, pugnacity and strong national pride," all of which, especially the latter, the English already found both amusing and disturbing.[1] Given that so much of American culture has its roots on the other side of the Atlantic, it is necessary to review briefly the English origins of the stereotype of the Irish, a stereotype that was part of the cultural baggage of the first English settlers in North America.

Even before Shakespeare, medieval commentators, such as Garaldus

Cambrensis, had initiated the centuries-long accumulation of traits that would eventually limn Paddy. As England pursued its slow conquest of Ireland, begun in 1169, it became essential for the English to maintain the starkest contrasts between the images of loyal settlers and the "wyld Irish" – the term itself going back to the Gaelic resurgence of the fourteenth century.[2] By the time England began its colonization of North America, the image of the wild Irish had become so ingrained in the English psyche that they could understand the "savages" of New England only by comparing them with the savage natives of Old Ireland. Indeed, since Ireland constituted England's original imperial sin, the Irish became the gauge by which all other alien (and, therefore, inferior) peoples would be measured. As David Beers Quinn points out, "The use of the Irish as the standard of savage or outlandish reference" was well established by the mid-sixteenth century. The English compared Indians (American and Asian), Africans, Russians, even Spaniards, to the terrifying figure of the wild Irish. In David Hayton's words, "Early characterization of the 'wild Irishman' as a barbarian and near-beast, a Caliban close to home, helped to legitimize Elizabethan rapacity" and, one might add, the English colonizer's fear of the Irish enemy.[3]

Caliban came close to home, indeed. Irish soldiers, Shakespeare's "rug-headed kerns," sometimes swelled the ranks of the English army, and Irish porters, chairmen, footmen, servants, and beggars swarmed into seventeenth-century English towns and cities. To the English, these refugees from an essentially medieval culture, trying to survive in an alien, early modern society, looked, sounded, and acted most strangely. Things Irish or seemingly Irish took on an exotic as well as comic aspect. J. O. Bartley notes that bogs, once discovered in Ireland by English soldiers, were given odd metaphorical applications. In Shakespeare's *Comedy of Errors* Dromio of Syracuse claims that his Nell is so spherical that he "could find out Countries in her." Challenged to locate Ireland, Dromio replies, "Marry sir, in her buttocks. I found it out by the bogges."[4]

English theaters were closed during the Commonwealth and Protectorate periods. When they reopened with the Restoration of the monarchy in 1660, the character of the stage Irishman had to be reinvented. Both the subsequent popularity and frequent appearances of the character suggest that it is only between the late seventeenth and early eighteenth centuries that the stage Irishman really became established in the English theater. In the process, the Irish stereotype gradually lost much of the encumbrance of the old political and religious bitterness.[5]

With the final subjugation of Catholic Ireland at the end of the seventeenth century and the passage of the Penal Laws, Ireland no longer seemed a strategic threat to England and, for a time, the Irish gradually ceased to engender fear in the English imagination. Although the general image of the Irish was still negative, the emphasis shifted from the barbarism of a feared enemy to the poverty, ignorance, incompetence, and spiritual and physical degradation of a defeated people. As early as the 1680s and 1690s, Hayton finds "clear signs of that process by which dread of the Irishman was being replaced by contempt."[6]

The famous Williamite propaganda song, "Lilliburlero," illustrates the transition.

> Ho brother Teague, dost hear de decree?
>   Lilliburlero bullen a la
> Dat we shall have a new duputie
>   Lilliburlero bullen a la
> Ho, by my shoul it is de Talbot;
>   And he will cut all de English throat
>
> . . . . . .
>
> But, if dispense do come from de Pope,
> We'll hang Magna Charta and demselves in a rope.
>
> . . . . . .
>
> Now, now de hereticks all go down,
> By Creish and St. Patrick, de nation's our own.

The song mocks the Irish for their brogue and their impossible hopes for success. The "Lilliburlero" burden, which also becomes the chorus, was essentially gibberish, the sound of Gaelic to English ears.[7]

According to Hayton, "From the Restoration onwards English attitudes towards Ireland were settling into a more-or-less permanent sneer." In everyday speech the term "Irish" usually made nonsense of the word it modified. Thus, to "weep Irish" was to feign sorrow; to "go to an Irish wedding" meant emptying a cesspool. This became a linguistic habit that continued in England through the Victorian era when "Irish evidence" was false testimony; "You're Irish" meant that one was speaking nonsense; and "to dance at an Irish wedding" was to sport two black eyes. In America an "Irish promotion" was a demotion, an "Irish nightingale" was a bullfrog, an "Irish spoon" was a shovel, an "Irish buggy" was a wheelbarrow, and "Irish confetti" referred to bricks.[8]

Hayton suggests that it was a joke book, as much as any particular play, that may have pushed the English stereotype of the Irish along the path from fear through ridicule to humor. *Bogg-Witticisms, or Dear Joy's Commonplaces* first appeared around 1680 ("Dear Joy" was a form of address associated with Irish characters on the London stage). Although Irish jokes had been rare up to that point, Sir Robert Howard's play *The Committee* (1665), already had established Teague as a comic character.[9]

By the middle of the eighteenth century, a greater variety of Irish character types appeared on the English-speaking stage. In addition to peasants, soldiers, and servants, there was the Irish fortune hunter, venal in intent but comical in his poverty, drunkenness, and blundering. The stage Irishman was so well established by the end of the seventeenth century that Englishmen traveling in Ireland began to look for him under every hedgerow. Joseph Leerssen reports that John Dunton's travel book, *The Dublin Scuffle* (1699), reads in places like a comic Irish play.[10]

During the eighteenth century, as Irish actors began to assume Irish roles, and as audiences became more familiar with the various types of Irish characters, the task of playwrights and actors became easier. Both could fall back upon a recognized and accepted stereotype and theatrical convention. As J. O. Bartley explains: "We can see the audience's reaction to the stage Irishman becoming, as it were, more hair-triggered; it was less necessary to depict your Irishman as such, with any great wealth or accuracy of detail; a broad recognizable outline . . . would, before long, be enough to set the audiences' stock reactions in motion and ensure their acceptance of the character." More than one playwright came to realize, as G. C. Duggan noted, that "an Irish man onstage livened up a dull and correct play."[11]

The names playwrights bestowed upon their Irish characters suggest something of the nature of the stereotype: Captain O' Blunder in Thomas Sheridan's *The Brave Irishman*, 1738; Sir Callaghan O'Brallaghan in Charles Macklin's *Love a la Mode*, 1760; Thady MacBrogue in John O'Keefe's *The She-Gallant*, 1764; Lucius O'Trigger in Richard Brinsley Sheridan's *The Rivals*, 1775; Blunder O'Whack in Reynold's *Notoriety*, 1791; and Thady O'Blarney in Oulton's *Botheration, or a Ten Years Blunder*, 1791. All these names suggest a blundering character who was excitable and emotional. Yet, as Bartley notes, the stage Irishman could also be portrayed as, "good tempered, good hearted, somewhat blundering and stupid but with considerable native shrewdness, loyal, chivalrous, irrepressibly cheerful and humorous."[12]

The playwright's need to entertain superseded the more vicious anti-

Irish prejudices. Duggan points out that playwrights were usually kinder to the Irish than were the political pamphleteers. Certainly, by the middle of the eighteenth century, an important shift took place in the image of Teague. At his first entrance in *The Brave Irishman*, Thomas Sheridan's Captain O'Blunder must have struck the audience as just another Irish fortune hunter. Nevertheless, O'Blunder has only a mild brogue and seldom issues "bulls." Blustering and quick-tempered on the surface, he turns out to be a real gentleman underneath. Leerssen regards O'Blunder as a prime example of what he calls the "Anti-Stage Irishman," a sentimentalized comic figure, an apparent rogue or buffoon who turns out to be a man of honor. In Leerssen's reading, Sheridan's play is less about Irish blunders and more about false English perceptions of the Irish.[13]

Although both English and Anglo-Irish audiences took this more sentimentalized stage Irishman to their hearts, the characteristics that made up the stereotype had not changed; they were now simply seen in a more positive light. The "wild" and "barbaric" traits, which had once called forth loathing in an English audience, now provoked mirth and laughter.[14]

As a medieval saint was identified by the iconographic representations of the instruments of his martyrdom, so Teague appeared onstage surrounded by a host of visual and verbal clues: shamrocks, shillelaghs, whiskey, potatoes, and pigs. His very speech, evolving since Shakespeare's day, betrayed his boggy origins. Of course, as Duggan has pointed out, Anglo-Irish figures onstage spoke proper English while the native Irish characters blundered along in their brogues. The cultural implications of this were clear; the brogue itself, the very manner of native Irish speech in English, was, by definition, humorous.[15] Originally an English conceit, this assumption slid easily into American popular culture.

By the beginning of the nineteenth century, the Irishman on the British stage was moving away from the braggart-warrior, whose great grandfather had been Shakespeare's Captain MacMorris, through various types of Captain O'Blunders and servant Teagues, toward Paddy, the comic peasant. This evolution eventually provided the stage Irishman with the potential to play more important functions in the comedies and melodramas in which he appeared. Although sometimes portrayed as little more than a muddle-head speaking a ridiculous brand of English, the peasant Paddy could be cleverer than his foolish behavior might suggest. This crafty peasant was, in David Krause's view, a more authentic type of stage Irishman than his predecessors. "He had a more flexible nature and an instinctive ability to adapt himself to the insecurities and absurdities of his life." According to Krause, Paddy was based on "the long suffering Irish peasant [who] had been forced to assume a cheerful sense of anarchy which amused and protected him from his careless and indifferent masters, who underestimated him and seldom realized how slyly and outrageously he fooled them."[16]

Like the parasite slaves in the Greco-Roman comedies, the powerless Irish peasants of the nineteenth-century Anglo-Irish playwrights and novelists responded to their situation by fighting back with what Krause considers their only weapons: "ironic attitudes and loaded words." Bit by bit this "mastery of guile and comic rhetoric" becomes characteristic of the stage Irishman as his "only instruments of self-respect and self-preservation."[17] All this suggests some degree of awareness on the part of the Anglo-Irish playwrights concerning the complex relationship between the Gaelic peasantry and their masters. On the one hand, the dramatists acknowledged the ability of the native Irish to outwit the landlord class. On the other, they also assumed a bond of affection between the two groups. The Anglo-Irish aristocracy recognized the "cuteness" of their tenants and had an appreciation of them. The peasantry, for their part, professed loyalty to the "quality," while manipulating them as best they could through flattery and taking advantage of their ignorance of the details of country life.

The character of Paddy was personally loyal (although sometimes politically disloyal). His old war-like spirit had degenerated into a general pugnaciousness, and drinking had become a kind of Hibernian avocation. Paddy was also poor, attested to by references to pigs and mud cabins. He was forever given to blundering in both speech and conduct. The most important nonvisual clue that signified the presence of an Irishman onstage was the brogue and the accompanying combination of verbal exuberance and confusion. Annelise Truniger claims that all stage Irishman share one trait: "They can only face reality when they conceive the world in paradoxical words." To the English and the Anglo-Irish, the brogue was a sign of inferiority. Thus, Jonathan Swift in his essay, "On Barbarous Denominations in Ireland," circa 1728, writes, "What we call the Irish Brogue is no sooner discovered, than it makes the deliverer, in the last degree, ridiculous and despised; and, from such a mouth, an Englishman expects nothing but bulls, blunders, and follies."[18]

Bulls and blunders were assumed to be quintessentially Irish. As Maureen Waters defines them, "The *blunder* grows out of the confusion of the Gaelic speaker who doesn't fully grasp the meaning of English words," while "the point of the *bull*, as has often been said, is its pregnancy; it is a metaphorical statement stressing apparent connections which are not real." "Bulls" resulted either from a misunderstanding of an object or idea or from the multiple meanings of a word.[19]

In addition to acquiring these verbal talents, by the beginning of the nineteenth century Paddy had also become proficient in those other necessary theatrical skills of singing, dancing, and telling jokes. Thus armed, Paddy was already well on his way to becoming, in Stephen Gwynn's words, "the funny man of the Empire." As the novelist Samuel Lever's character Darby-the-Blast observes, the poor Irishman may lack much, but "providence is kind to him in another way and fills his mind with all manner of droll thoughts and queer stories and bits of songs and the like. The quality [the Anglo-Irish ascendancy] has ne'er a bit of fun in them at all, but does be always coming to us for something to make them laugh."[20]

This passage is another reminder that the stage Irishman was not simply the product of English prejudice against the Irish but also of the Anglo-Irish ascendancy's half-condescension toward and half-affection for the Catholic peasant. During the first half of the nineteenth century, Paddy was largely the creation of Anglo-Irish writers, such as Samuel Lover and Samuel Lever, and actors like Tyrone Power and John Brougham. Thus, issues of class, as well as of ethnicity, were always a part of the stage Irish stereotype. It is ironic, therefore, that Americans, who had freed themselves from British colonial rule, would have embraced so readily a stereotype of the Irish that had its roots in British imperialism and undemocratic concepts of class.

THE STAGE IRISHMAN IN ANTEBELLUM AMERICAN THEATER

The stage Irishman was still evolving on the English and Anglo-Irish theater when colonial American audiences got their first look at him. Irish as well as Scottish characters appeared on the American stage as early as 1767 in a piece entitled *The Disappointment, or The Force of Credulity.* In this play, the character of the cooper Trushoop was the first in what was to be a long line of comic Irish immigrants in the American theater.[21]

Paddy was already a favorite source of laughter in American humor. Robert K. Dodge has found that Paddy was the most popular of the comic figures in eighteenth-century American almanacs, in which he appeared in short tales consisting of little more than Irish bulls strung together. The resulting stereotype emphasized poverty, a low regard for law, the mastery of comic repartee, and a ready, rustic wit. However, only a few of the stories and jokes reflected an American environment, suggesting that the stereotype was still largely an import from abroad.[22]

After the American Revolution, American playwrights were busy trying to create a new national theater. William Dunlap's *Darby's Return* (1789) was one of the first post-revolutionary attempts by an American playwright to put an Irishman onstage. Although he borrowed the character from Irish playwright John O'Keefe, Dunlap realized that Darby not only offered comic relief, as in British plays, but, as an outsider, he could effectively testify to the glories of American freedom. Some American dramatists followed Dunlap's lead in using an Irishman to give a special immigrant twist to the inevitable patriotic speech. In John Minshull's comic opera *Rural Felicity* (1801), Patrick praises his new homeland, saying, "I fought for liberty, and have found Columbia's shore, and if you hear me sing a song, hurtful to the feelings of my friend, and benefactors, then never trust a poor Irishman of honor, who is proud in heart, though poor in purse." As Gallagher points out, the mixture of the comic with the sentimental was characteristic of the theater of the early republic, which assumed that even Irish immigrants could mend their Old World ways in America's beneficent environment.[23]

The stage Irishman became a standard ingredient in American melodrama, appearing more frequently than Indians. Before 1828 no fewer than twenty-two American plays featured Irish characters.[24] Paddy's primary role onstage, however, was still that of the buffoon. According to Gallagher, "the Irishman more than any other national stage type caused American audiences to break into unrestrained laughter." Earl F. Niehaus, in his study of the Irish in New Orleans, notes the almost insatiable demand for imported British plays with Irish comic characters. "The Irish immigrant theme would remain popular as long as audiences considered Paddy's deviations from American cultural patterns amusing." Like all comic stock characters, Paddy tended to oscillate between grandiose visions of self and narrow concerns for his physical well-being. "Sure, what Irishman ever sprung from the green sod," exclaims a character from James Pilgrim's *The Limerick Boy*, "would think of living without the enjoyment of these illigant accomplishments, eating, drinking, loving, and fighting." By the 1830s Paddy had already supplanted Jonathan, the indigenous Yankee character, as the principal comic figure on the American stage.[25]

Paddy also appeared in blackface in minstrel shows. According to Robert C. Toll, minstrelsy provided many Americans with "one of the only bases that many of them had for understanding America's increasing ethnic diversity." "Understanding" may be too optimistic a term. Eric Lott sees minstrelsy as a kind of battleground for control of American cultural expression: "one sees a constant struggle for control – encompassing black, white, immigrant Irish, and other cultures – within blackface forms themselves."[26]

In his history of the American minstrel stage, Carl Wittke noted a number of performers with Irish backgrounds, including Daniel Decatur Emmett, an Irish American from Mount Vernon, Ohio, who was one of the founders of minstrelsy. Although best known for the songs about blacks and the South, Emmett also wrote Irish dialect songs, such as "The Offish Saiker" ("Turn ivery foiriner out, an' put the Irish in!"). Among Irish-born minstrels were Edwin Kelly of Leon and Kelly's Minstrels, R. M. Hooley, who organized several troops, and J. W. Raynor. George H. Primrose, whose real name was Delaney, was born in London. Irish-American Dan Bryant, founder of one of the most famous troops, had been christened Daniel Webster O'Bryan. Other prominent Irish and Irish-American performers on the minstrel stage were Matt Peel, Barney Fagan, Frank McNish, and Sam Devere.[27]

Many performers who eventually specialized in Irish roles in vaudeville or in melodrama got their start in minstrelsy. Dan Bryant washed off the burnt cork in 1860 and successfully played leads in Irish plays, such as *Handy Andy, Rory O'More, The Irish Emigrant,* and *Pat Malloy.* John Murphy of Murphy and Mack's Minstrels eventually left the troop to perform solo as an Irish comedian. Joseph Murphy also left minstrelsy to play Irish roles in *Kerry Gow* and *Shawn Rhue.* John Collins got his start singing Irish songs from the minstrel stage. Among the better known performers who started in minstrelsy were Irish-born Patrick Sarsfield Gilmore and American-born Edward Harrigan and Chauncey Olcott.[28]

Robert Toll notes that in the early days of minstrelsy songs about the Irish tended to be very negative. However, by the 1850s there were enough Irish and Irish Americans active in the business (as well as in the audience) to soften the images presented in the songs and jokes and to make them more positive and sympathetic. Moreover, the Irish tenor became a staple of the minstrel lineup. Irish songs such as "Home Rule for Ireland for Evermore," "The Irish Regiment," and "The Land of St. Patrick," often sung in blackface, became popular with audiences containing Irish and Irish Americans. In the 1860s, the Christy Minstrels sang "The Bonny Green Flag" to the tune of "Sprig of Shillelagh."

> Here's to the bonny green flag, and long may it wave,
> With the stars and stripes in the land of the brave,
> And at no distant day, it will once more float free
> On that dear little Island over the sea. . . .[29]

THE PADDY ACTORS: TYRONE POWER

By the 1830s the Irishman was becoming a familiar figure in the American theater. In that decade, however, the combined talents of two men in London helped move Paddy from the periphery to center stage on both sides of the Atlantic. In 1836 Samuel Lover's *Rory O'More*, a song turned into a play, was among the first comedies to have an Irish peasant character as the hero. The play's success was guaranteed by the superb acting of the man who created the title role, Tyrone Power.

As mentioned earlier, Samuel Lover was an Irish artist, playwright, novelist, songwriter, and occasional performer who helped to complete the evolution of the stereotypical Irishman from the soldier and servant to the comic peasant. In the process he emphasized the basic decency of his character. Lover's Paddies are more loveable than most of their predecessors in British theater and fiction. Yet, their brogues and blunders leave little to the imagination. Although Lover added many genuine folk elements to his Irish characters, Maureen Waters argues that by emphasizing their intimacy with pigs at a time when *Punch* cartoonists had also discovered this alleged symbiotic relationship, Lover helped to cement the public's association of the Irish with a poverty depicted as both intentional and humorous.[30]

Lover, of course, intended no harm. As Sally E. Foster points out, he actually thought of himself as a patriot of sorts, revealing the truths of Irish peasant life to the British public. He went to great efforts in his novels, stories, and comic songs to try to duplicate the sound of the Irish dialect and to introduce Gaelic words and Irish customs into the action. Moreover, Lover did provide some variety for his heroes. For example, Rory O'More is handsome and clever and no fool when it comes to love. In fact, Lover believed that he had rescued the character of the Irish peasant as depicted onstage and in song from what he called "expletive oaths, 'whack fol de rols,' 'hurroos,' 'pigs,' pratees, brogues, shillelahs, jewels, and joys"; all this at a time when, according to his biographer, Andrew James Symington, "coarseness and vulgarity were the offensive substitutes for wit." Lover replaced the old savage element of the stereotype with a childlike naivete. According to Foster, Lover cleaned up the stage Irishman and made him fit for respectable middle-class entertainment. In doing so, he did give Paddy a new lease on life.[31]

Tyrone Power was the first great interpreter of Lover's Rory O'More. Power wrote some successful plays himself and commissioned others. Yet the public so associated him with his comic-Irish peasant roles that he became known as "Paddy" Power. Touring the United States in the 1840s, Power himself seems to have sensed the special delight Americans took in ethnic and regional stereotypes. Commenting in his autobiography on the relations between the Germans and the Irish in Pennsylvania, Power draws upon his stage persona: "I have understood that Pat has on occasions of high festivity been known to extend his courtesy so far as to pay his German neighbors a call to inquire kindly whether 'any gintlemen in the place might be inclined for a fight'; but this essence of good-nature appears to have been neither understood nor reciprocated, and, proof against the blandishment, Mynheer was not even to be hammered into contact with 'dem wilder Irisher.'"[32]

William Grattan Tyrone Power was the progenitor of a theatrical dynasty that would eventually include one great-grandson who carried his name to Hollywood and another, Tyrone Guthrie, who gained theatrical fame as a director. Power was born on November 2, 1797, in Kilmacthomas, County Waterford, and, when still a child, his mother took him to Wales. At the age of fourteen Power went to England and began a career in the theater. According to Barney Williams, a later practitioner of Paddyology on the American stage, Power initially found Irish roles "repugnant" and became so incensed at the offer of his first such role ("as he thought it was an intended degradation") that he challenged his manager to a duel. However, Power went on as a last minute substitution as Dr. O'Toole in *The Irish Tutor* and was an immediate success. Power already had a great reputation in London and Dublin by the time he reached the United States, where he debuted as Sir Patrick O'Plenipo in Kenney's *The Irish Ambassador* at the Park Theater in New York City on August 28, 1833.[33]

Maureen Waters claims that Power exploited the stereotype of the rollicking stage Irishman. The hero of his farce, *Paddy Carey, or The Boy from*

Clogheen (1833), bubbles over with blunders and malapropisms. Power's playing of the main character in his most successful play, *O'Flannigan and the Fairies, or a Midsummer Night's Dream, Not Shakespeare's,* was so full of pigs, whiskey, and such that it angered some Irish, who sent their complaints to the newspapers. George Potter summed up Power's typical stage character as an "improvident, happy-go-lucky, a buffoon, lacking nothing but a pig tied to a string."[34]

Yet Power himself seems to have preferred roles in which his character was a comic hero who helped to resolve the plot and who even showed some admirable traits. In his *Paddy Carey*, Paddy is a resourceful fellow who uses his talents to prevent an eviction. In *The Irish Attorney: or Galway Practice*, a piece written for Power, his character of Pierce O'Hara drinks too much, but is, nevertheless, superior to the smug English attorney he must defeat. James Malcolm Nelson describes Lover's Rory O'More, a favorite Power character, as "an easy-talking clever resourceful, resilient, and loveable agent for good." Both as actor and playwright, Power seems to have helped the stage Irishman evolve from the fool on the periphery into a comic hero whose actions were central to the play.[35]

Over the years, Power left a great impression on those who had seen him. Joseph N. Ireland's reminiscence is typical: "His mercurial temperament, his genial refined humor, the merry twinkle of his eye, the rich tones of his voice, his skill in music, the grace and heartiness of his dances, his happy variations of *brogue* to the different grades of character he presented . . . combined to make him the most perfect comedian of his class ever known to the American Stage." As Walter Meserve suggests, Tyrone Power probably did more to stimulate interest in the stage Irishman than any other individual.[36]

Power held his final farewell benefit as Gerald Peppers in *Morgan Rattler* on February 10, 1841. He then sailed for England on the *President* on March 21. The vessel never arrived; its passengers and crew were lost at sea.[37]

JOHN BROUGHAM (1810–80)

Of the various Irish character actors in America who tried to take Power's place, many contemporaries agreed that John Brougham was his most legitimate successor. Brougham was born into a Protestant family in Dublin on May 9, 1810. According to the American critic William Winter, who knew him, the actor was from a well-reputed and prosperous French-Huguenot family. Brougham, however, went into the theater and debuted in *Tom and Jerry*, July of 1830, playing around a dozen parts. He was a member of Madame Vestris's famous London company for twelve years. He later claimed joint authorship with fellow-Dubliner Dion Bouci-cault of the great hit *London Assurance*, although the latter insisted that the work was entirely his own.[38]

Brougham came to the United States in 1842, returned to England in 1860, and then settled permanently in America in 1865. During his first trip, he opened at the Park Theater in New York City as O'Callaghan in the farce *His Last Legs* with his second wife, Emma Williams, as Lady Tea-zle. He tried his hand several times as an actor-manager, even attempting to run his own theater, Brougham's Lyceum, in New York City, but failed in all such enterprises.[39]

Brougham was much more than the sum of his Paddy parts. In Ameri-ca he did one-man shows, which included impersonations of the great Irish orators such as Daniel O'Connell and Father Theobald Mathew, as well as renderings of songs and stories.[40] He played a variety of non-Irish roles and, most importantly, was a prolific playwright. He wrote over 126 dramatic pieces, more than any other playwright of the period, with the exception of Dion Boucicault.

Brougham's place in the history of American drama remains assured by his successful burlesques of some of the more pretentious serious dra-mas of his day. By making fun of Indian melodramas such as John Augus-tus Stone's *Metamora*, lampooned in *Metamora; or The Last of the Polli-wogs* (1847), Brougham helped drive the noble red man from the American stage. He introduced Scottish, Irish, and German songs into his Indian bur-lesques, "playing off," as Deane L. Root suggests, "the associations of the tunes – their ethnicity, previous textual reference, characteristic rhythms, melodic type, instrumentation – against the humorous parodying context of the burlesque." The singing and dancing, as well as his ludicrous story lines, prefigure some of the basic elements of the later American musical.[41]

It was his Irish roles, however, that most impressed those who saw Brougham perform. *The Spirit of the Times* recalled that he was "all the genuine Pat, without the strong whisky and shilelah [*sic*] rancor which disfigures so many of the best actors of his class."[42]

BARNEY WILLIAMS (1823–76)

Perhaps the actor who tried most self-consciously to fill the void left by Power's death was Barney Williams, born Barnard O'Flaherty in County Cork. According to Laurence Hutton, after his family emigrated to New York City, Williams started out in the 1830s as a young blackface song-and-dance man, trying to support his widowed mother. Acclaimed for his minstrel dancing, he quickly took on Irish roles. He began by playing heroes in romantic Irish plays and then added the comic parts for which he became famous. His first hit was as Pat Rooney in *The Omnibus* in July of 1840.[43]

Naturally enough, Williams began working with Power's repertory, and by 1847 critics seemed prepared to grant him what one called "a portion of that ubiquitous mantle of 'poor Power,' that has been divided into so many shreds since the death of the original possessor." According to Joseph Ireland, Williams was inferior to Power in the "gentleman" roles, "but in the conventional stage Irishman of low life, the ranting, roving, blarneying blade, or in the more dull and stupid grade of bogtrotters, he has gained a popularity on our stage unequaled by any rival."[44]

Something of Barney Williams's own facility with the blarney comes across in an interview published in *The Spirit of the Times* in 1874. A few days earlier, the Lord Mayor of Dublin had visited Booth's theater, where Williams and his wife were performing: "It's the Lord Mare, is it? Be gorra, if they cheered whin he cam' into the house, didn't they hurray whin I cam' on? Tell me that, will ye? An' whisper, me lad, if they threw up their hats at the blayguard, didn't they yell wid deloight whin Mrs. Williams danced her jig? G'wan now, g'wan me gossoon. The Lard Mare indeed! Faith, it was Mr. and Mrs. Barney Williams who filled the house."[45] It should be noted that Williams was apparently able to suppress his native Cork accent enough to craft for the American stage an all-Ireland brogue that one critic found "rich," but "difficult to establish what particular county of Ireland could lay claim to its paternity."[46]

OTHER PADDY ACTORS

Writing just after the turn of the century, the critic William Winter listed those he considered the consummate representatives of the stage Irishman in the nineteenth-century American theater; in addition to Barney Williams, Winter named John Drew (1827–62) and William J. Florence (1831–91). John Drew (the *first* John Drew, a progenitor of the famous Drew-Barrymore dynasty) was born in Dublin, September 3, 1827. Theater manager, Joseph Jefferson III claimed that "since Tyrone Power there has been no Irish comedian equal to John Drew."[47]

In 1844, Thomas Dunn English, the American doctor, journalist, and composer of "Ben Bolt," adapted Samuel Lover's novel *Handy Andy* for the stage. This became a vehicle for Barney Williams's chief competitor (and brother-in-law), W. J. Florence (born Conlan). Lacking a substantial plot, *Handy Andy* still furnished, according to Walter J. Meserve, "good Irish dialect, farcical stupidity and a few interesting observations," such as, "If a gintleman drinks till he can't see a hole in a ladder, he's only fresh – fresh mind ye's – but drunk as a baste is the word for a poor man!"[48]

In an 1875 interview in *The Spirit of the Times*, Barney Williams mentioned Teddy Leonard, Redman Ryan, and James Hudson among Irish comedians who were famous at that time. Williams regarded George Mossap and John Collins more for their singing than their acting, although New Orleans critics found Collins's more genteel characterizations preferable to Williams's "vulgar buffoonery." As a singing actor, Collins helped introduce Americans to some of Samuel Lover's most popular comic Irish songs, such as "The Widow Machree," "The Low-Backed Car," and "The Bould Soger Boy."[49]

By 1849 there were so many Irish plays onstage in New York City that the *Irish American* rejoiced that "the largest number of Irish actors ever assembled together, are at present amongst us." These included Brougham, Mossap, Collins, John ("Rascal Jack") Dunn, Mr. and Mrs. Thomas Barry, John Drew, and the Williamses.[50] It was the presence of a sufficient number of talented Irish comic actors that helped to induce playwrights to give the stage Irishman more substantial roles.

The vogue for Irish plays in America began around 1840 and lasted through the 1860s. However, in most of these plays the Irish characters had, at best, only a limited relationship with America. According to Walter Meserve, 90 percent of the plays written in America between 1829 and 1849 were by actor/playwrights and theatrical journeymen, few of whom were native born. American drama was still more reflective of Europe than the United States. Thus, at mid-century, Paddy onstage was still an Irishman. Even when cavorting in an American setting, he was an immigrant with a brogue, rendered comic by the very alien nature of his dress, speech, and conduct. It seems as if it was Paddy's alleged Irishness that fascinated antebellum Americans, instead of his potential as a fellow citizen. Neither playwrights nor audiences could yet conceive of the Irish American.[51]

COMIC SONGS, 1800–1870

Considering the number of skilled Irish character actors playing Paddy roles in America, I have found fewer distinctly comic songs (as opposed to light love songs) published before the 1870s than might be expected. Of the songs in the sample published between 1800 and 1870, only around 10 percent were comic in nature. There are several possible reasons for this. For one thing, the father of popular Irish song, Thomas Moore, had little affinity for comedy. Then again, many of the songs used by the Paddy impersonators came from the folk and broadside traditions, which had limited appeal to the middle-class purchasers of sheet music. Finally, the genre of comic songs only began to grow in America after 1840 with the emergence of the minstrel show.

In those comic Irish songs that did appear, however, Paddy looms large; there is an almost animal vitality associated with him in these songs. He is ever ready to prance in our presence, full of energy and mischief. He is also a charmer, a slippery ladies' man, blessed with the luck to usually come out on top. This is the theme of "Paddy Carey's Fortune or Irish Promotion." In the song "beautiful Paddy" is slipped the king's shilling by the recruiting sergeant but ends up with a captaincy in the army and the admiration of the ladies.

> His heart is made of Irish Oak
> Yet soft as streams from sweet Killarney,
> His tongue was tip't with a bit o' th' brogue,
> But the deuce a bit at all of blarney![52]

These comic songs often associate Paddy with poverty, usually presented as more a part of his character than simply as a part of his environment. Far from being a source of pity, his poverty was an object of humor. Consider John Brougham's "Fine Ould Irish Gintleman" (1845), a parody of a well-known British song, "The Fine Old English Gentleman." The "gintleman's" walls are plastered with "fine ould Irish mud," which is also "well acquainted" with his back. He has no desire for wealth, for his clothes are "well ventilated" in summer and, having no shoes, he has no corns.[53]

Another happy Hibernian pauper inhabits Matt Peel's "The Irishman's Shanty" (1859). The cover shows a piper and a tattered group of men before an ill-thatched house. Under the illustration is the caption, "Now then boys, one for the pig," who is also present in the illustration. The song describes Paddy's poverty but assures the listener that "No king in his palace is prouder than he." The song also includes a vocal imitation of the bag pipes, a device that must have made Peel's Paddy seem even more ludicrous to American audiences.[54]

"Teddy O'Neale" (1843) also refers to pigs. In this song, Paddy has already emigrated, but, in a parody of the romantic emigration ballads, his sweetheart visits his now empty cabin.

> I've come to the cabin he danced his wild jigs in,
> As neat a mud palace as ever was seen;
> And, consid'ring it served to keep poultry and pigs in,
> I'm sure it was always most elegant clean.[55]

Even when Paddy was well-off by Irish standards, he might seem poor enough to Americans. In "Barney Brallaghan" (1830), the hero tries to entice his beloved (who remains asleep in her cottage) with a list of his possessions, starting with nine pigs, a sow, and a one-eyed cat.

> I've got an acre of ground, I've got it set with potatoes,
> I've got tobacco a pound, I've got some tea for the Ladies;
> I've got the ring to wed, some whisky to make us gaily,
> A mattress feather bed, and a handsome new shillelagh.[56]

"There's Monny a Shlip," also makes fun of Paddy's poverty masquerading as plenty.

> My shanty I plashtered wid mud,
>   An shtop't all the howles that I could,
> Thin my blankets I shpread,
>   Wid new straw in my bed,
> And the matther so pleasantly shtood.

The object of all of these efforts at home improvement is the pretty, but also extremely useful, Kittie.

> Ah, Kittie was nate as ye plaze,
>   Faith she could make butther and chaze,
> She minded the pig,
>   And the praties she'd dig,
> In sich illegant lady-like ways.[57]

Whatever Paddy's faults, vaunting ambition, Yankee-style, was not among them. Take, for example, "Larry O'Gaff." After a picaresque series of adventures spanning hod carrying and battling Napoleon, Larry retires to a Paddyesque utopia.

Singing didro whack at my ease,
    Living just as I please,
With a wife, spend my life,
Sport and play, night and day,
In Ould Ireland so glorious, now landed victorious.
Long life and success attend Misther O'Gaff.[58]

Drinking and fighting were traditional pastimes long associated with the Irish peasant. The simple-hearted girl in "The Poor Irish Boy" (1854), tries to think through the problem of her lover's drinking habits.

Though the pledge in pure Whiskey too often he's drinking,
Though he idles his time singing *"cush la ma chree"*;
Yet they cannot be mighty great faults, I am thinking
When the glass and the song are both sacred to me.[59]

The hero of Samuel Lover's "Rory O'More" assures his beloved:

Arrah Kathleen my darlint you've teaz'd me enough,
And I've thrash'd for your sake Dinny Grims and Jim Duff,
And I've made myself drinking your health quite a baste,
So I think, after that I may talk to the Priest [to name the wedding day][60]

On the cover of an illustrated edition of "Rory O'More" we see the classic depiction of Paddy in knee breeches, carrying a shillelagh. The cover clearly places Paddy in an Irish setting. In the background are some thatched cottages amid a rural landscape.

The hero of "Paddy Reilly's Pledge" also cavorts on the cover of his song, brandishing his shillelagh. However, the demands of love have forced him to take the teetotaler's pledge, and, as he complains, " 'Twixt woman and water I'm kept in a fayver."[61] Of course, such *comic* temperance songs, along with other Irish songs in praise of drink, appeared in America at a time when serious temperance songs formed a subgenre of morally uplifting and hortatory parlor ballads. In this context, the comic Irish songs only served to strengthen the link already forged in American popular culture between the Irish and alcohol.

Brougham's "The Fine Ould Irish Gentleman" turns into a precursor of "Tim Finnigan's Wake," that classic music hall song of boozy death and resurrection. The "Gintleman" goes out on a spree. As a result, "His senses was completely mulvathered," and his friends, thinking him dead, waked him in proper Irish fashion.

(Spoken)   But when the whiskey bottle was uncorked he couldn't stand
                it any longer so he [the corpse]
(Sung)   riz right up in bed,
(Spoken)   and when sich mighty fine stuff as that is goin' about says he
                you don't think I'd be such a soft headed
(Sung)   fool as to be dead,
                Oh this fine Ould Irish Gintleman was mighty hard to kill.[62]

Brougham's hero also had "the mighty curious knack, Of flourishing a tremendous great shillay [*sic*] in his hand and letting it drop down with a most uncompromising whack." "Birth of Green Erin" (1866) inquires into Paddy's propensity for drink and fighting. A dispute between "Veynus" and Neptune leads to the simultaneous birth of Ireland and of whiskey: "Hinse how can yez blame us, That Erin's so famous, For beauty an' murthur an' whisky an' love?"[63]

"Lanigan's Ball" (1863) is the classic Irish celebration of good fortune turned to riot. Lanigan inherits a farm and throws a party for his friends. Everything is fine until Terence McCarthy puts his foot through the hoops of Miss Flaherty's gown. Then chaos ensues.

Oh, boys, there was a ruction,
    Myself got a kick from big Phelim M'Cue,
But soon I replied to this kind introduction,
    And kicked up a terrible Phillabooloo;
Ould Casey the piper was nearly being strangled,
    They squeezed up his pipes, bellows, chanters, and all;
The girls in their ribbons were all entangled,
    And that put an end to Lanigan's ball.[64]

From the 1870s until well into the 1890s, this theme, the Irish celebration-turned-Donnybrook, when transferred to an American urban setting, would become the most prominent feature of the comic Irish songs written in the United States.

In "Father Molloy" (1861) the theme of the pugnacious Irish man gets a clever twist from religion. Paddy on his sickbed tries to gain absolution from the priest, a rare figure in these songs, who insists that Paddy must first forgive Mickey Malone. After many attempts to evade this stricture, Paddy agrees, but with conditions.

> But since I'm hard press'd and that I *must* forgive,
> I forgive if I die – but, as sure as I live,
> That ugly blackguard I will surely desthroy,
> And now for yur blessing sweet Father Molloy.[65]

This type of naivete bordering on craftiness was a feature of several of Lover's comic peasant songs, such as "The Guide's Song."

> The miles in the counthry much longer be –
> But that is a saving of time d'you see,
> For two of our miles is aiqual to three,
> Which shortens the road in a great degree.

The song ends by claiming, "But along with sivin sinses we have one more – . . . / 'Tis nonsense, spontaneously gracing our shore." It is little wonder that, as J. S. Bratton observes in reference to British music hall songs, "There is a traditional association between the Irish and nonsense humour and the misue of language."[66]

It is interesting to compare the comic stereotype of Paddy to the image of Patrick, the romantic Irishman of the serious songs of love and exile we examined in chapter 2. Paddy is in some respects a parody of the handsome Patrick, who is brave in adversity and faithful in love. In Patrick, these qualities are taken for granted. Poor Paddy has to work hard to stake his claim as a fighter and a lover. It is his bragging about his prowess in these areas that forms an essential part of his stereotype.

The stereotype of the romantic Irishman is linked to his baser although much more vivid and entertaining Paddy-self by a reckless passion, which comes through in both the comic songs and the romantic parlor love songs. Eliza Cook's "Fair Rose of Killarney," with music by Stephen Glover, contends that "the wild sons of Erin can love till they die." In "Beautiful Erin" the exile proclaims that "I'll sing amid the dark woods wild, The songs of my own green land." "Green Hills of Erin" depicts the Irish as brave, liberty-loving people who live for the moment.[67]

An interesting example of the way Anglo-American romantic sensibilities manifested themselves in popular culture is illustrated by the linguistic distinctions made between Patrick and Paddy. Sixteen percent of the song lyrics in the sample before 1870 contain either dialect, linguistic clues, such as "blarney," or bits of Gaelic, such as "Aileen mavourneen acushla machree." All but one of the songs with Gaelicisms (most of which are terms of affection) belong to Patrick and his love songs. On the other hand, *all* of the dialect songs belong to Paddy's comic domain.

Moreover, the titles of almost half of the comic songs contain Gaelic surnames: "Barney Brallaghan," "Biddy McShane," "Larry O'Gaff," "Rory O'More," and "Teddy O'Neale." By contrast, only four of the fifty-eight love songs have titles with Gaelic surnames. Clearly, the Anglo-American world was finding humor in the very sound of native Irish names.

Yet, some songwriters, such as Samuel Lover, seem to have intended something more than humor in their depictions of Paddy. Lover's biographer, A. J. Symington, suggests that some of Lover's comic songs "depict the Irish peasant *as he is*, with his keen relish for a joke and innocent delight in its own absurdity, his tender pathos and racy humour, the comical twists in his reasoning, his quick-sightedness, warm-heartedness, and droll arch-impudence."[68] Paddy, it would seem, was supposed to be real. It was going to be difficult for both Americans and Irish Americans when it came to sorting out the "real" Irishman from the stereotype – assuming anyone would try.

4. Ethnicity and Parlor Songs
Paddy Compared

As we have seen, the writers of Anglo-American parlor ballads responded to middle-class fascination with the exotic by producing songs about Indians, Africans, and the denizens of the Celtic fringe. The parlor songs also provided limited opportunities to sample the glories of European high culture, as represented by Italian opera or German lieder. This kind of cultural curiosity did not take place in a void, however, as the United States became increasingly aware of its growing ethnic diversity. The presence of African Americans began to impress itself upon the national popular culture at the same time that large numbers of European immigrants flooded into the country. To appreciate the unique character of popular songs about the Irish we must compare them with songs about other ethnic groups such as the Scots, the Germans, and the African Americans.

THE SCOTTISH SONGS

Until the end of the Civil War, the Scots appear in the parlor songs about as often as the Irish.[1] Songs about the Scots had been around for a long time. What passed for Scottish songs became well known in England around 1680 and remained popular for two hundred years, while Irish songs did not gain popularity until Moore's collections began to appear after 1808.[2] After the Union of Crowns in 1603, numbers of Scottish Lowlanders moved to London, carrying with them a certain longing for home. Perhaps it was their presence, combined with the fact that the Scottish Lowlands were more accessible than Ireland, that produced a fad in seventeenth-century England for Scottish tunes and songs. John Playford, and later his son Henry, used Scottish melodies in the various editions of the *English Dancing Master*, beginning in 1651. By the early eighteenth-century, a "Scottish" style of popular song, based partially on traditional elements, had already emerged. Collections, such as William Thompson's *Orpheus Caledonius* (1725) and James Johnson's *The Scots Musical Museum* (1787), consisted of both popular and traditional material. Johnson's collection contained some genuine lowland ballads contributed by Allan

Ramsey, Robert Burns, and Walter Scott, collector/poets who frequently rewrote lyrics (often to expunge startlingly explicit sexual references) and who even set their own verses to traditional tunes. Unlike Moore, these Scottish collectors tried to stay close to the language and style of the traditional songs.

Most of the "Scotch" material intended for the parlor songs was not produced by these proto-folklorists, however, but by middle-class songwriters, many of them women. Since most of these Lowland women felt that anonymity became them, much of their work was published without attribution and was often mistaken for genuine Scottish folksongs. Even when traditional melodies were used, much of the flavor of the originals was "refined" out of them. Some of the most popular songs, such as "Annie Laurie," were largely modern compositions in both lyrics and melody.[3]

Songwriters and publishers used titles to establish the identity of their Scottish songs, although in ways that differed from their methods for labeling Irish songs.[4] It is in the songs' settings and themes, however, that the contrast between the Scots and Irish genres is most striking. The Scots, like the Irish, had suffered defeat at the hands of the English. Like their Irish counterparts, Scottish peasants endured poverty and faced the pain of emigration. Yet the Scottish popular songs seem much sunnier; they conjure up a more settled, more satisfying, even idyllic existence. There is only one song reflecting the exile and emigration theme in my sample of Scottish songs.

There is a greater proportion of love songs in the Scottish sample; 65 percent as compared to 45 percent for the Irish in the antebellum sample. Significantly, only 7 percent of the Scottish pieces in the sample deal with parted lovers, as compared to 18 percent of the Irish material. Similarly, only 5 percent extol the dead beloved, while 18 percent of the Irish songs cherish this morbid theme. The Scottish songs better lent themselves to what Jon W. Finson identifies as one of the most common themes in nineteenth-century popular songs: "love that endures into old age."[5] Since they could not stay at home with their loved ones, the Irish depicted in popular songs could hardly look forward to or backward on a lifetime of continuous domestic bliss. Although the lyrics in Irish songs also placed great value on home and hearthside, the Scottish songs celebrated the enjoyment of domesticity while the Irish songs mourned its loss. Unlike so many of the Irish parlor songs, the Scottish pieces are bound to the homeland; *all* of the songs in the sample are about Scots in Scotland, while 18 percent of the Irish songs in the antebellum sample dealt with exiles and emigrants.

These differences reflect the contrasting images of the Scots and Irish within Anglo-American popular culture. In the hands of poets and lyricists, the Scots had emerged from the eighteenth century clothed in the Romantic, genteel image of what might be called the "acceptable Celt." By 1800, Scottish nationalism had become a thing of poetry and romance and Scottish poverty a sentimental pastiche of "hame" and "bairns." Within Anglo-American culture, the Scots represented "good" peasants – healthy, happy (presumably Protestant), and contented with their lot. Theirs were the simple pleasures of morally pure love, home, and hearthside. Burns's rewriting of frankly sexual songs such as "John Anderson, My Jo," greatly aided the process.[6] Unfortunately, his prickly sense of democracy became lost in the parlor ballads' vision of a pre-industrial, rural, homogeneous society, which the economic policies favored by those who owned the pianos had done their best to destroy. Derek Scott refers to an 1852 article in *Eliza Cook's Journal* that praised Scottish songs as "morally healthy," emphasizing, in Scott's words, "contentment with one's lot" and abounding "in pictures of domestic peace and comfort" amid "the beauties of nature."[7]

In other words, the Scots of the parlor songs represented what Richard Middleton calls a bourgeois vision of "organic social harmony," a comforting counterpart to industrial England and industrializing America. Middleton states that the middle-class fascination with Celtic songs can be seen in the way peasants were romanticized in the parlor ballads. By "exoticizing" them, the peasants' own cultures and even, to some extent, their economic and social problems, were rendered invisible. Naturally, it would have threatened this rural idyll, and the ideology that helped create it, to populate it with clowns. There appear to be few Scottish counterparts to Paddy in the Scottish genre of parlor songs.[8]

The American music-buying public seems to have taken these Anglicized Scottish songs to their hearts. Songsters published up to the Civil War were just as likely to carry Scottish as well as Irish songs.[9] Perhaps American song buyers found in the simple virtues of Jock and Jeannie echoes of a rural, Jeffersonian value system that was already under siege in the decades before Lincoln's election. Moreover, by 1840, compared to the Irish, there were far fewer actual Scottish immigrants on hand to disturb the myths presented by the songs.

In spite of their early popularity, however, the American market for Scottish songs did not survive the Civil War. Few new songs about the Scots appear after 1860 in my sample. Although songs such as "Annie Laurie,"

"The Blue Bells of Scotland," and, of course, "Auld Lang Syne," continued to be popular well into the twentieth century, the Scottish genre of
popular songs did not become, as did the Irish songs, an integral part of
American popular culture.

German songs were also well represented in American sheet
music during the nineteenth century. The Germans were, of course, the
one antebellum immigrant group whose numbers matched and eventually surpassed those of the Irish. However, initial American interest in German songs preceded the great wave of immigration from Germany that
began in the 1850s. In the 1830s George Reed of Boston began publishing
the *Gems of German Song* with English words in place of the German texts.
The series was intended, and was accepted by the American public, as a
welcome departure from the relatively simple strains of the British parlor
ballads that had come to dominate American music up to that time. Not
as florid as pieces drawn from Italian opera, the German songs were, nevertheless, generally more sophisticated than the usual Anglo-American
songs. Relatively simple melodies were carefully integrated with their piano accompaniments, in imitation of the high-culture influence of lieder.
German immigrant composers, such as Franz Abt, were successful in adopting the German "chromatic" style of piano accompaniment to the talents
of the average American parlor pianist.[10]

The popularity of German songs in America is evident in the Lilly Library's Starr collection. Out of an estimated 300 pieces in the "Germany"
category, I sampled 122 titles; 16 instrumentals and 106 songs.[11] Of these,
ninety-five were published in the nineteenth century, most between 1850
and the 1870s. This suggests that the sudden presence of hundreds of thousands of German speakers significantly augmented the initial interest in
German songs. Over three-quarters of these songs had titles in German,
as well as in English, on the cover and most of the others carried the German titles inside, above the music. By including German titles on the covers, publishers did not have to use additional signifiers to identify the nationality of the songs. Therefore, there are few German proper names,
geographical place names, or national references in the titles.[12]

With few exceptions, the song lyrics tend to reflect the high seriousness
of German poetry and lieder, focusing on romantic love, on *heimat* or home,
on nature, and on a morbid fascination with an ill-defined but all perva-

sive *Weltschmertz*. Although most of these pieces were published in America, they were written by Germans living on either side of the Atlantic and represent the types of songs popular among the middle class in the *Vaterland*. Therefore, it is not German ethnicity but what we might call a German *sensibility* that is communicated through these songs, a sensibility that seems to have both reflected and reinforced a certain tendency in nineteenth-century Anglo-American society to associate things German with high culture and moral seriousness. For example, the Rev. H. R. Haweis, author of *Music and Morals*, found German music superior to French and Italian because of its "essentially moral, many sided and philosophical character."[13]

For whatever reason, German characters generally fared better than the Irish in the multiethnic theater of minstrelsy. There were jokes about their fondness for beer and food, but, according to Robert C. Toll, the minstrels usually depicted Germans as practical and hardworking. "Because they fit so well into white American values and world-view, Germans seemed model immigrants."[14] Perhaps for this reason, Hans was not as tempting a target for comic songwriters as was Paddy.

Although vaudeville songs about German Americans increased after 1870, the number of romantic German songs published in America appears to have begun to decline considerably after the Civil War. While twenty-one German titles in the sample were published in the 1860s, only twenty-seven appeared during the next three decades, and only a few of these songs suggest an American setting or a German-American identity.

To some extent, the very conditions that helped to make songs about the Scots and Germans popular in America limited their ability to survive in nineteenth-century American culture. Both genres were already well established in Europe by the tine they arrived in America. Already "fixed" in their countries of origin, the genres had less flexibility to continue to evolve within an American context. German songs, especially, may have come too richly encumbered with cultural baggage. The language of Schiller, Goethe, Beethoven, and Schubert, associated with the glories of European high culture, may have been a barrier to easy integration into American popular culture. By comparison, the popular genre of Irish song, which barely existed before Moore, was still in the process of developing during the antebellum period. With a weaker exportable cultural basis in the Old World, it was much easier for the Irish genre to be adapted to the American environment.

In terms of stereotypes, as well as the socioeconomic positions they shared, the ethnic group with which the Irish had most in common was the African Americans. The stereotypes of both groups were not invented out of whole cloth but had evolved out of interactions based on multilayered inequality – not the least of which mandated that the object of the stereotype did not, could not, communicate directly to the world. Other voices from other cultures spoke for them. From Samuel Lover to Somerville and Ross and John Millington Synge, Paddy, the Irish Catholic peasant, was often presented onstage and in fiction by people who were neither peasants nor Catholics. Similarly, Sambo, the comic representation of the African American, was essentially the creation of white plantation owners and Northern song-and-dance men.

Paddy's relationship with Sambo was fairly complicated. From the earliest days of minstrelsy through vaudeville they shared the same stage, even on many occasions the same interpreter. A blackface performer, singing at one point in the entertainment of his "Lubly Lou" back on the plantation, might later extol the glories of Erin or elaborate on the follies of Paddy. When the black makeup came off at the end of the performance, it might have well been an Irishman or Irish American underneath. To some extent, Paddy and Sambo were brothers under the burnt cork; both, of course, being white. As Eric Lott notes in his study of American minstrelsy, "When one notes . . . that those who 'blacked up' and those who witnessed minstrel shows were often working-class *Irish* men, the complex picture of the blackface institution and its audiences is complete."[15]

Up to a point, Paddy and Sambo were very much alike. Many of the traits ascribed to Sambo were also part of the burden of the stage Irishman. According to Sam Dennison in his study of the image of blacks in American popular music, "A central theme of songs about the black concerns the myth of the happy, indolent slave, bound to his master by strong ties of devotion." As we have seen, the image of the Irishman, inherited from the British stage, was also that of a lazy, happy-go-lucky rogue whose one good trait was often an irrational loyalty to his hapless employer. Or consider Christopher Geist's summation of Sambo: "Indolent, faithful, humorous, loyal, dishonest, superstitious, improvident, and musical." Each of these traits attached themselves to Paddy as well.[16]

Both Sambo and Paddy had the characteristics of children. Referring to Sambo, Joseph Boskin suggests that his "entertaining grin was just one aspect of a large notion, the presumption that Sambo was an overgrown child at heart." In Tyrone Power's play, *The Omnibus* (1833), the hero, Pat Rooney, is described by his mistress as "a little too familiar, but he does not mean to be impertinent; he's as simple and unsophisticated as a child, and honest as he is light-hearted."[17]

Again, just as Paddy's boundless good humor seemed to make him impervious to the pain of his poverty, Sambo's laughing, clowning, and dancing belied the pain that "normal" people would associate with slavery. One antebellum visitor to a southern plantation marveled at how the plantation Negroes he encountered "seem a happy race of beings & if you did not know it you would never imagine they were slaves."[18]

In Anglo-American culture it was assumed that anyone who was black or Irish was an endless source of fun. At the end of the seventeenth century, Englishman John Dunton promised his readers that "as an Irishman is a living Jest," the accounts of his travels in Ireland "'twill be merry and pleasant." Around a century and a half later, S. S. Cox proclaimed in a lecture at the Smithsonian Institute that "an Irishman is a lump of humor, and it is impossible to divest himself of it, as it is to live without eating. He may be steeped in misery, but he is always over head and ears in fun."[19] Concerning the image of Sambo, Boskin maintains, "To make the black male into an object of laughter, and, conversely, to force him to devise laughter, was to strip him of masculinity, dignity, and self-possession. Sambo was then, an illustration of humor as a device of oppression, and one of the most potent in American popular culture."[20] The same thing could be said about Paddy.

That the two stereotypes occupied the same plane of humor can be seen in the following story, told by a New Orleans slave owner (in the hearing of his black servants). After settling in the Mississippi area, an Irishman had acquired six children and nine slaves. Not prospering, Paddy decided to head for better opportunities upriver. Writing to his abandoned wife, he consoled her: "and so, my darlin', I'll lave you; but I'll do my best for you. I'll lave you the dear, nate, pretty little childer, and I'll take the nine nasty dirty negroes." In another story, a doctor, in telling how his slave managed to talk him out of a new coat, allowed as how the slave's argument was worthy of an Irishman. John Bernard, an English comedian and theater manager insisted that "the negroes [are] the greatest humorists of the Union, and in many respects I have thought them like the lower Irish: with the same confusion of ideas and difficulty of clear expression, pouring words out of their mouths on the high tide of natural drollery."[21]

Even the same romantic formulas applied to both the Irish and the African-American stereotypes. For example, Dennison points out that the typical sentimental songs about the "happy" plantation slave consisted of three nostalgic elements: recollections of happy childhood; separation from home and family; and the longing to return to the old childhood home as life draws to a close. As we have seen, many Irish songs had a similar structure, reflecting antebellum popular, romantic tastes and class hegemony as much as racial bias. To the extent that some Americans were embarrassed, or at least unsettled, by both black slavery and Irish immigrant poverty, Dennison's comment that "the black seen onstage represented an escape from the black seen in everyday life," might apply to the stage Irishman.[22]

Dennison ascribes to white racism factors that characterize the bourgeois Anglo-American approach to all "lesser" peoples, regardless of color. For example, Dennison condemns as racist the tendency of whites who, in trying to use the real music of African Americans, recast it into the mold of formal European music. Yet the same spirit of bourgeois cultural appropriation applied to the traditional music of the Scots and the Irish. "In each case," as Van den Merwe points out, "musical indebtedness went along with social hostility," revealing a mixture of condescension and affection "appropriate to subject peoples."[23]

Paddy, like Sambo, was a creature of his superiors, a situation Declan Kibred describes as "a classic example of the tendency of all repressive regimes to sentimentalize their victims."[24] At the center of both stereotypes was the same "natural," "irresponsible," "irrepressible" *joi de vivre* that the disciplined and businesslike Anglo-American culture has always held suspect, but longed to possess. In Paddy and Sambo, white, Anglo-Saxon protestants could enjoy the antics of characters whose lack of inhibitions they envied, all the while accepting their exuberance as proof of inferiority. Inevitably, both Irishmen and African Americans were encouraged to play, as a means of survival, the roles constructed for them.[25]

The creation and evolution of the stage Irishman into the rollicking Paddy figure was the product of English and Anglo-Irish society, resulting, as Vivian Mercier notes, "from the observation of Gaelic folk ways through the lenses of a different culture."[26] Since this was the culture of the colonizer, the image of Paddy takes on an ideological cast, which, according to Ned Lebow, is very common in imperial relationships. To the *colon*, the "natives" were always "indolent and self-complacent, cowardly but brazenly rash, violent, superstitious and incapable of hard work. On the more complimentary side, they were described as hospitable, good-natured, and curious but incapable of prolonged attention."

Only through this formula of contradiction can the *colons* account, to their satisfaction, for the economic and social gap that separates them from the quaint but apparently feckless natives. Unfortunately, in Lebow's view, the stereotype eventually imposes a kind of reality upon its victims. "We can speculate that the image of the Irish, propagated for seven centuries, gradually became ever more a reality," evolving into "a perceptual prison, a closed image through which information about Ireland was structured and given meaning."[27]

THE RALE PADDY: STEREOTYPE AND REALITY

Dale T. Knobel argues that the popular image of the Irishman in pre–Civil War America was largely a negative one. Certainly, many of Paddy's alleged characteristics as depicted on the stage and later in song – the drinking and fighting, the lack of self-discipline, the emotional extremes, the laziness, and so on – were not highly regarded by native-born Americans. Yet Paddy onstage was a comic figure instead of the frightening, or at least, disturbing, drunken Irish pauper many Americans saw or thought they saw on their streets. Moreover, as depicted by the best Irish actors with their fluid singing, graceful dancing, and infectious good humor, the image of Paddy occasionally rose above clownishness toward a sort of apotheosis of geniality. Critic George Daniels, recalling the Paddyesque presentations of Tyrone Power, maintained that in the midst of the clowning, "some kind-hearted trait; some dash of *genuine* feeling, had suddenly come across us and made us long to take him [Power] by the hand and claim acquaintance." Concerning Power's characterization, a British correspondent for *The Spirit of the Times* claimed that it was something "every Irishman knows to be just and every Englishman perceives to be amiable."[28] In a similar spirit, William Winter admired John Brougham's comic Irish roles, claiming that "no performer could ever have embodied them with *closer fidelity to the Irish nature*, with rosier humor, or with more felicitous art."[29]

In 1853, *The Spirit of the Times* maintained that Barney Williams, "*as a representative of the Irish character*, excels chiefly in the impersonation of the rustic peasant: poor in pocket, yet rich in humor, with a smile for his own troubles and a sigh for another's grief." A reviewer for the *New Or-

leans Picayune in 1854 claimed that "in the presentation of the *genuine* Paddy, the *true Irish peasant*," Barney Williams gave his audiences "the broad, unmistakable, wide awake 'broth of a boy,' alike ready to fight or shake hands, equally at home with the girls or the boys." In 1858 the *Cork Examiner* stated that Irish themselves regarded Williams as a "*real Paddy*, and a *true son* of the sod." While the stage Irishman often appeared as a cross between a buffoon and a savage, the *Examiner* claimed to see in Williams's impersonation "the *genuine Irishman of humble life* – brave, honest, warm hearted, up to all kinds of fun, with no conscientious aversion to 'a drop of the native,' a decided taste for getting into scrimmages, and a willingness to go any and every length for a friend."[30] Even Samuel Lover was perceived in positive Paddyesque terms when he visited America. "How his black eyes twinkle, and what fun there is in his face!" marveled one reviewer. "He seems brimful, and running over, with good humour, and looks as if care never had or could touch him. . . . Hurrah! we have Rory O'More amongst us."[31]

James Malcolm Nelson argues that there has been too much emphasis placed on Paddy as the blundering fool to the exclusion of the "lively, resilient and resourceful Irishman who so often emerges from the plays."[32] This observation throws into question Knobel's insistence that Paddy, as envisioned by the average American, was primarily a "verbal construct" as opposed to a visual one. Knobel's concentration on the content analysis of editorials, sermons, political pamphlets, as well as printed plays, may miss the positive elements, especially in nonverbal form, of the stage-Irish stereotype.[33] The reviews quoted above suggest that by the middle of the nineteenth century American audiences were responding to the more positive side of Paddy. In this sense, the good-humored aspect of the stereotype might have mitigated some of the more negative traits associated with the Irish.

Moreover, the reviews quoted above suggest something else. It seems clear that many Americans took Paddy, as depicted by the likes of Power, Brougham, and Williams, as *true* representatives of the Irish character. Americans admired the performances of Power et al. because they thought they provided an accurate portrayal of Paddy at his best. Knobel suggests that the tendency for critics to attack any actor who did not seem genuine in his rendition of the Irishman demonstrates that they believed that a properly delineated Irishman onstage revealed truths about Irish character.[34] As an illustration of the resulting confusion between stage Irish and real Irish, Niehaus relates how New Orleans court reporters made explicit connections between the Irish farces that entertained them in the evenings and the conduct of Irish miscreants brought before the law the next day. One reporter claimed that he was not sure whether an offender before bench was copying Lover or Brougham. Another claimed that one Irish drunk "smiled in a most bewitching manner, *a la Power*, and said, he allowed, that he might have been a little tight."[35]

This confusion between the stage and reality burdened the Irish in America with a stereotype that was embarrassing, annoying, and even damaging. Yet, as I have tried to suggest, the stereotype was not universally negative. Americans came to like some of Paddy's characteristics. Even if celebrated with more laughter than sympathy, they formed the basis for more positive qualities that Irish Americans themselves would both respond to and try to refine.

Therefore, by the end of the Civil War, there was, besides the negative aspects, a more positive side to the stereotype of the Irish. As we have seen, the parlor ballads, based on romantic images of the exile and the lost homeland, were highly sympathetic to the Irish. And, as suggested above, even the comic songs, when produced within the context of the acts of the best performers, presented a somewhat benevolent portrait of Paddy. True, the impetuous, irrepressible, and irresponsible Paddy did not quite correspond to the Yankee's ideal citizen; the very things that audiences liked about Paddy rendered him less efficient and effective at the American game of getting ahead. However, neither the images of soulful Patrick, the romantic exile from Erin, nor good-humored Paddy disturbed Americans as much as the hoards of Irish drunks, lay-abouts, criminals, and paupers whom Knobel has found crowding the shadows of the national imagination. While the negative side of the stereotype might have predominated for much of the nineteenth century, the positive aspects provided a kind of beachhead within the popular culture, in song and on the stage, which the Irish themselves would gradually expand.

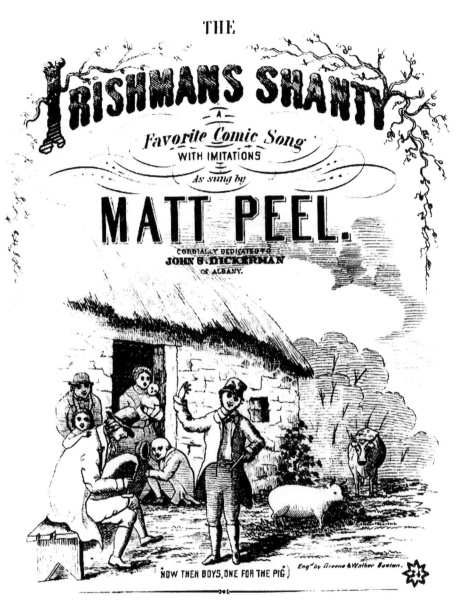

Poor but happy: Paddy with piper and pig.

(All illustrations courtesy of the Lilly Library, Indiana University, Bloomington, Indiana.)

THE FINE OULD

IRISH GINTLEMAN.

Written and Sung by

JOHN BROUGHAM,

AND BY HIM DEDICATED, TO HIS FRIEND

OLIVER C. WYMAN,

OF BOSTON.

Price 25 cts net

BOSTON
Published by GEO. P. REED, 17 Tremont Row.

Here, Paddy closely resembles his minstrel counterpart, Sambo.

Leaving home and the graves of loved ones.
Note the deceased wife and child, transformed into angels.

J. E. McDonough as Shaun the Post, from Dion Boucicault's Arrah Na Pogue.

When Erin shall stand 'mid the Isles of the Sea.

MUSIC BY S NOURSE

SUNG WITH GREAT SUCCESS JAS PERRY

ROBERT EMMET,

As he appeared leaving the Marshalsea Lane Depot on the night of the 23rd July 1803.

Published by J. L. PETERS New York.

T.A.BOYLE. DOBMEYER & NEWHALL. M.GRAY. C.J.WHITNEY & CO. R.MORGAN.
SAINT LOUIS. CINCINNATI. SAN FRANCISCO & PORTLAND. DETROIT. QUEBEC.

Entered according to Act of Congress in the year 1874 by J.L. Peters in the Office of the Librarian of Congress at Washington.

Irish patriots were relatively rare on American song covers.

Edward Harrigan and Tony Hart, the latter in one of his "skirt" roles.

Irish history meets the Broadway musical.

"Coon" in this context means "Ragtime."

An Irish-Jewish fantasy.

Paddy with Squaw, another ethnic romp. Not even the pipes are authentic.

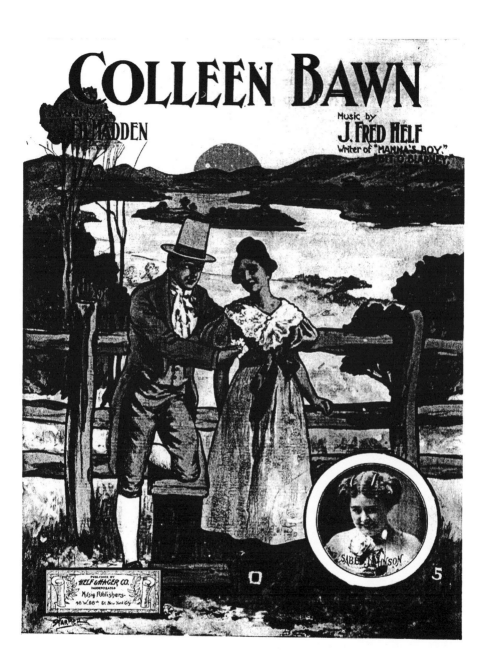

Irish love in an Irish landscape, as seen from Tin Pan Alley.

The Irish know how to have a good time.

PART THREE

The Image in Post–Civil War

Popular Theater

The Irish in Urban America

Perceiving America as a land of opportunity, many Irish immigrants were able to find jobs in a society that, after 1820, had embarked on the task of building an infrastructure of roads, canals, railroads, and cities. There was a certain grimness to this match of grand engineering projects and unskilled Irish labor, often called "Yankee ingenuity and Hibernian brawn."[1] According to Ira Rosenwaike, the Irish were over-represented in the lower paid jobs in New York City. In 1855, 20 percent of the employed Irish worked as laborers, compared to 3.5 percent for all other immigrants. In fact, the Irish accounted for 87 percent of foreign-born laborers in the city, evidence, as Robert Ernst has noted, of the limited options available to them. Another 26.4 percent worked as domestic servants. Those Irish women who were unable or unwilling to enter domestic service accounted for almost 70 percent of those employed in the "needle trade."[2]

Working conditions on the roads, canals, and railroads were abysmal; the cold in winter, the heat in summer, the swamps, the poor food and housing, the lack of sanitation in the Paddy Camps, the bad whiskey that contractors offered as part of the pay – all combined to produce broken bodies and early deaths. Mile by mile, unmarked Irish graves were left behind as crews pushed the roadbeds and canals westward. A broadside ballad commemorating the digging of the New Orleans New Canal in the 1830s has this stark memorial:

Ten thousand Micks, they swung their picks
To dig the New Canal.
But the choleray was stronger'n they,
An' twice it killed them all.[3]

Whiskey often was offered to, even forced upon, an Irishman as partial payment for his wages. "Paddy on the Canal" finds a young greenhorn overwhelmed by the hospitality provided by his ganger.

I being an entire stranger, be sure I had not much to say,
The boss came round in a hurry, says, "Boys, it is grog time a-day."

We all marched up in good order, he was father now unto us all,
Sure I wish'd myself from that moment to be working upon the canal.[4]

As Joseph Curran puts it, "For men suffering from cold, fatigue or sickness, whiskey was a tonic, a restorative. To men desperate and despairing, it offered a temporary escape. Many Irish males (and some females) drank to endure their miserable lot or to forget it. Their hard drinking was noticeable because they were noisy, convivial and often belligerent."[5]

Bad whiskey was a poor substitute for money or food, and it soon took its toll. Theodore Parker, the New England reformer, once remarked that he seldom saw a gray-haired Irishman. As Carl Wittke notes, the death rate of the Irish in America was twice the normal rate of those who stayed at home. Even after the Civil War, from 1880 to 1900, the Irish mortality rates in New York City were generally above those for the average of the population. As late as 1920, it was still 25 percent higher than that of other well-established groups in the city.[6]

Few Irish brought an urban experience with them when they emigrated. At the time of the Famine, only 5 or 6 percent of the population of Ireland lived in areas of more than ten thousand people; most of the country's population explosion had occurred in the rural areas. Yet, a predominantly rural people at home, the Irish became an urban people in the United States. Most of the Irish immigrants, being spade farmers, had limited agricultural skills. Most lacked the knowledge, even if they had the means, to go into farming in America. After the Famine, few even had the inclination to seek a living on the land. The industrializing cities, on the other hand, offered jobs for men and women with no means or skills. Exclusively Irish neighborhoods in cities like Philadelphia and New York began to appear by 1830. The later influx of the 1,600,000 Irish into the United States during the famine years was so great that for a generation this group constituted much of America's urban proletariat.[7]

Strange and alien as they must have seemed to many Irish immigrants, American cities also gave them opportunities to cluster together as they had in Ireland. In pre-Famine Ireland, many Irish peasants lived in clachans, villages of jumbled mud cabins. The surrounding land was parceled out on the ancient rundale system, the Irish version of the medieval in-field, out-field system. Although modern Gaeltacht settlements in the west of Ireland appear today as a scattering of houses across the landscape, before the Famine the clachans were filled with people. One clachan, called Blackstaff in Farney, contained over two hundred cabins as early as 1798. Another near Galway city in 1845 numbered around two thousands inhabitants.[8]

For a people used to the densely populated clachans, life in rural America held few attractions. An Ulsterman, who had been successful in farming in Missouri, wrote home in 1821 to complain that he still missed life in rural Ireland: "I could then go to a fair, or a wake, or a dance . . . I could spend the winter's nights in a neighbor's house cracking jokes by the turf fire. If I had there but a sore head I would have a neighbor within every hundred yards of me that would run to see me. But here everyone can get so much land . . . that they calls them neighbors that live two or three miles off."[9] Even before the Famine, Irish immigrants tried to reinstitute the ramshackle and gregarious clachan in America. Kirby Miller quotes an English visitor who, upon observing the Paddy Camps that lined the new canals, was amused to see how much they resembled the peasant villages of Ireland, complete with "those sterling Irish comforts, a cow, a pig, and a 'praty garden.'" Sir Horace Plunkett, viewing the Irish urban slums, attributed them "to the fact that the tenement house, [for] all its domestic abominations, provided the social order which [the emigrants] brought from Ireland."[10]

Whatever benefits there were to be had in numbers, the Irish emigrants in the nineteenth-century American city enjoyed them to the fullest. Even before the Civil War, slum densities in American cities were high. According to Dennis Clark, the density in New York City rose from 94.5 per block in 1820 to 163.5 in 1850. In the Tenth Ward it was 170 per block as early as 1840. After the war, the ward grew in density from 432 per acre in 1880 to 747 in 1898, making it perhaps the most crowded district in the world by the turn of century. The true nature of the situation becomes apparent only when it is recalled that urban residential structures in the nineteenth century did not rise above seven or eight stories and that the average was four.[11]

As the Irish began clustering together in American cities, inhabiting some of the worst slums the country has ever seen, they certainly must have felt the need for the comfort of their own numbers. However, they may have paid a price for the social and psychological benefits gained by swarming together in the cities. According to Lawrence McCaffrey, ghetto life tended "to exaggerate and perpetuate ethnic and racial vices and stereotypes," nurturing as it did, "Irish failure much more than it encouraged Irish ambition by cultivating the paranoia, defeatism, and feelings of inferiority planted by the past."[12]

Clark has called attention to the way in which the Irish used the "folk networks" of the homeland to adapt to the new urban environment. "Family ties, fellowships based on specific locales and interests in Ireland, and ingenious reproduction in the American context of Irish customs and activities formed a cultural substructure for the group."[13] At its best, the Irish community in American cities offered support for the young greenhorn seeking aid and friendship.

Harsh as the urban industrial environment was for the Irish, it held some advantages for them in the post–Civil War years as American cities expanded rapidly. Drawing upon church, political influence, family contacts, a variety of nationalist and benevolent societies, and a few key Irish-dominated businesses, such as saloons and contracting, the Irish community in America developed its own economic infrastructure to provide jobs and help to the incoming greenhorns. The Irish built the horse and streetcar lines and then drove the cars themselves. They built city halls, police stations and fire stations, and, in some cases, virtually monopolized the positions within them. In fact, they built almost everything in post–Civil War America. As early as 1870, one-fifth of the nation's building contractors were Irish born, and they naturally tended to hire Irish workmen.[14]

It was in the industrial cities where they were most numerous that the Irish began to reap some of the rewards of power in Gilded Age America. Having served a long apprenticeship in the rank and file of Tammany Hall, "Honest John" Kelly, former congressman and brother-in-law of John Cardinal McCloskey, became the first Irish Catholic leader of New York City's Democrats after the fall of Boss Tweed. In 1880, William R. Grace became the first Irish-Catholic mayor of the city. Two years later, Hugh O'Brien established the precedent in Boston. A new era and a new brand of urban politics had arrived in America.[15]

During the Gilded Age, however, there was little inclination within Yankeedom to lighten the psychological burden upon the Irish. Organized anti-Catholicism, which first erupted within the Know-Nothing movement of the 1850s, reappeared in the 1880s with the formation of the American Protective Association. Political cartoonists, like Thomas Nast, who hated the Democratic party and Tammany Hall almost as much as he hated the Roman Catholic Church, pictured the Irish as ape-like barbarians, given over to rum and Romanism, if not outright rebellion. In the unfriendly environment maintained by Yankee suspicion and economic competitiveness, McCaffrey asserts: "Irish ghettos served as psychological havens, preserving traditions and values and perpetuating a sense of community among people who could have disintegrated in an oppressive situation."[16]

Therefore, it was not only their clannishness and poverty that helped to isolate many of the Irish in the cities where they settled most heavily. Facing external hostility, the Irish communities turned inward upon themselves. WASP suspicion begot Hibernian reaction in various ways. The myth of Anglo-Saxon superiority produced what L. Perry Curtis Jr. has called "Celticism," the counter-myth of Celtic superiority. Moreover, the demands for support by both the Roman Catholic Church and Irish nationalist groups – the need to build an infrastructure of hospitals, charities, schools, nationalist and cultural associations – occupied much of their attention and helped to isolate the Irish from the larger society.[17]

Of all of the forces that tended to pull the Irish community in upon itself, perhaps the most powerful was the very thing that made life in America so unique and full of promise: individualism. Grasping this strange prize seemed to require the immigrants to cut themselves free from the very ties that provided identity and to risk the loneliness of the brave new Yankee world. In David Doyle's words, the Irish immigrants "feared the isolation of a certain psychic fragmentation which in America seemed the very concomitant of the best adjustment, of the well-conducted and the successful."[18]

For many, the pull of family and neighborhood was a strong counterforce to capitalist individualism. So were the teachings of the Roman Catholic Church, which feared the threat of a materialist Yankee culture upon the spiritual health of its communicants. Nevertheless, the Irish came to America to better their lot, and they were not opposed to success when it came within their grasp. Francis Walsh has found a "lace curtain literature" produced by and for Irish Americans. A survey of sixty-three novels and short stories written for Irish Americans between 1840 and 1873 reveals a significant concern with issues of success.[19] In spite of the chaos that threatened them, the Famine Irish were laying the basis for survival and, for their children, eventual success.

5. "To the Land We Left and to the Land We Live In"

On the subject of Irish melodrama, Barney Williams once told an interviewer for *The Spirit of the Times* that "no other class of dramas appeal so tenderly to the imagination. They are full of poetry and romance, for there never was yet an Irish play written where virtue was not rewarded, vice punished, and heroism, in some phase or other, exhibited." Along with the "sweet melodies of Erin," they were, he said, bound "to enlist the sympathy of a spectator, awaken his imagination, and excite his humor."[1]

Melodramas helped provide a context for sentimental songs about Ireland. While comedy mixed with heroics in these essentially ritualistic portrayals of good versus evil, the semi-serious tone of the Irish melodrama encouraged the use of songs about love, patriotism, and a longing for the lost homeland. Most Irish dramas featured at least one song. Dion Boucicault used an average of four in his most famous Irish plays.

Early historical dramas, such as John Daly Burk's *Bunker Hill* (1797), Antrim-born James McHenry's *Hearts of Steel* (1824) and *The Usurper* (1827), and George Pepper's *Kathleen O'Neill* (1829), usually were set in Ireland's glorious past, providing a context in which American audiences could see Irish characters in something other than comic circumstances or dire poverty. While some plays were imported from Britain, between 1860 and 1892 Irish and Irish-American playwrights produced twelve nationalistic Irish melodramas for American audiences.[2] Some, such as John Brougham's *Temptation; or, The Irish Immigrant*, (1849) or Dion Boucicault's *Pat Malloy* (1861), featured the Irish immigrant in America. Most Irish melodramas, however, continued to focus on life back in Ireland.

John Brougham's Irish characters provoked sympathy, as well as laughter, and were generally more realistic and well-rounded than most, for the Dublin-born playwright displayed some genuine understanding of the plight of his fellow immigrants. In *Temptation* O'Bryan asks two working-class Yankees, Tom and Polly, for shelter. When told to look for work, "Anywhere – everywhere," O'Bryan answers: "Faith, sir, that's exactly the place I've been looking for the last three weeks, and there was nobody at home. I hunted the work, sir, while I had the strength to crawl after it." Yet, for all of Brougham's sympathy for his fellow countryfolk, his Anglo-Irish background may have limited his vision. As Pat M. Ryan points out, Brougham's characters were largely content with their lowly status.[3]

Barney Williams and his wife, Maria, were among the first of the Irish man-and-wife teams in America, and one of few such teams to have their own company.[4] They hired the British immigrant playwright James Pilgrim (1825–77) to write plays for them that mingled typical Paddy farce with melodrama. Pilgrim's most successful play was the comedy *Irish Assurance and Yankee Modesty*, written for the Williamses in 1853. Although Carl Wittke has described some of Pilgrim's plots as "so preposterous that it strains both the patience and credulity of the modern reader," the playwright knew how to churn out lines that would appeal to Irish-American audiences. In *Shandy Maguire*, another vehicle for the Williamses, the hero, struggling to defeat the ubiquitous evil landlord, reminds the audience, "there are hearts across the big waters, in the New World, that have stretched forth a helping hand to poor Ireland, and will do it again."[5]

According to Bruce A. McConachie, some of the plays Pilgrim wrote for the Williamses suggest an attempt to "modernize" the traditional Irish comic character for American middle-class audiences who might have been put off by Paddy's normally unrestrained roistering. For all of his blundering in *Irish Assurance and Yankee Modesty*, Pat does manage to advance the fortunes of a hardworking Yankee businessman. In Pilgrim's *Ireland and America*, the tricky peasant Jimmy Finnegan leaves his irresponsible ways behind him to become James Finnegan, a successful New York businessman, sober and industrious, as adept at making a fortune as at rescuing colleens in distress. Pilgrim's attempt to combine the clean-cut, go-ahead American hero with the traditional comic Paddy must have stretched the limits of mid-century melodrama, however. As McConachie points out, it was Dion Boucicault who found a way to make a hero out of Paddy by pairing him with a genteel Irish aristocrat.[6]

Boucicault was born in Dublin around 1820. Destined to spend most of his life outside of Ireland, he nevertheless received the most indelible gift that city can bestow – its accent. It remained with him all of his life, making it difficult for Boucicault, the actor, to play convincingly any but Irish roles. The exceptions must have proven the rule. When he donned the feathers and buckskins of the faithful Wah-no-tee, the old Indian in his own play *The Octoroon,* he must have played the role, as David Krause suggests, with a rich brogue.[7]

Boucicault got his theatrical start in London as both actor and playwright (one of his first roles was that of Lover's Rory O'More). He came to America in 1853, but spent much of the sixties touring abroad with his Irish plays. In 1870 he returned more or less permanently to America, where he died in 1890. If he was not exactly an Irish-American playwright, he wrote with a firm knowledge of Irish-American audiences.

Depending on where one looks in the histories of the nineteenth-century theater, Boucicault appears to have had many careers. He was a clever and popular actor, a prolific playwright and skillful adaptor for the stage, an innovator in everything from dramatic structure and character development to stage mechanics and theater safety (he helped spur the adoption of the fire-proof curtain).

As a playwright, Boucicault also provided a bridge that would lead from the stage Irishry of Lover to the sophisticated comic-dramas of John Millington Synge and George Bernard Shaw. At least part of the character of Synge's Christie Mahon in *The Playboy of the Western World* owes something to Boucicault's clever comic heroes, and Shaw played Boucicault the compliment of modeling the trial scene in *The Devil's Disciple* on the trial of Con in *Arrah na Pogue.*

In *The Colleen Bawn* (1860), *Arrah na Pogue* (1865), and *The Shaugraun* (1874) Boucicault sought to transform the traditional stage Irishman from a mindless buffoon into a comic hero. Indeed, Boucicault announced that he had declared war on Paddy: "The fire and energy that consists of dancing around the stage in an expletive manner, and indulging in ridiculous capers and extravagances of language and gesture, form the materials for a clowning character, known as the 'Stage Irishman,' which it has been my vocation to abolish."[8]

The extent to which Paddy continued to haunt Boucicault's creations is a matter of ongoing debate. Most critics seem to agree with David Krause, who maintains that Boucicault did manage to alter the image of the traditional stage Irishman as a hard-drinking blunderer

> by making his Irishman the clever and attractive central character in a play set in Ireland, in which the absurd Englishman, or Anglo-Irishman, makes a fool of himself among the Irish. . . . To be sure [Boucicault's hero] is a blathering rogue, a cheerful liar with a powerful thirst, but he is also a literate playboy who cavorts outside the ordinary restraints

of society, a picaresque clown who ingeniously rights all wrongs with an instinctive sense of justice and bonhomie.[9]

What Boucicault created, according to Heinz Kosok, were "characters *with* rather than *at whom* the audience will laugh." Laugh it did at the exposure of stuffy, snobbish, and prudish Victorian values personified by the English in Boucicault's plays. Referring to Boucicault's hero Myles-na-Copaleen in *The Colleen Bawn*, Krause observes that for all of his being a cheerful rogue, Myles "gave the inhibited Victorians a chance to find vicarious release from the solemn and righteous standards by which they tried to live."[10] For all of their nationalistic sentiments, Boucicault's plays were more threatening to Victorianism than to Victoria and her reign over Ireland.

While Irish and Irish immigrants flocked to these plays and took pride in the nationalist sentiments on display (about which their author seems to have been sincere), only Boucicault's *Robert Emmet* came close to upholding the rebel cause. For the most part, Boucicault's plays presented, in Kosok's words, a "romanticized, sentimentalized and largely falsified image of Ireland." Most of the plays end with what Stephen Watt calls "the myth of reconciliation": the hope that the Irish and English could peacefully coexist in Ireland.[11]

Boucicault gave Irish melodrama a new lease on life. According to Joyce Ann Flynn, after the appearance of *The Colleen Bawn*, "Irish-American dramatists embarked upon a new style of drama, the nationalist melodrama with comic ethnic touches, portrayed against a specific Irish locale." Edward Falconer, who created the role of Danny Mann in *The Colleen Bawn*, produced his own play, *The Peep O' Day Boys*, which boasted sensational scenes closely patterned on Boucicault's. James A. Herne wrote *Garry Owen* for Tony Farrell and Maggie Cline in the 1890s, and Bartley Campbell wrote *My Geraldine* and *Friend or Foe*, the last for William J. Scanlan.[12]

The changes that took place in Irish melodrama "were not the result of a higher artistic evolution among playmakers," Flynn maintains, "but of a new and homesick audience much interested in viewing plays about Ireland: the famine immigrants." According to Flynn, the main function of these plays was to address the needs of the Irish in America, not those left behind in Ireland. She suggests that, because of the close relationship between audience and playwright in nineteenth-century American theater, a kind of "partnership" emerged that allowed Irish-American audiences to influence what the playwrights put on the boards. "The theme of emi-gration and its relationship to the ultimate destiny of the Irish people was consistently introduced into dramas in which issues of nationalism and an unjust land system were raised." Flynn also suggests that by depicting ru-ral scenes and by referring to nationalist sentiments, the plays gave to the immigrant audience a "semblance of the familiar" and helped to mitigate the sense of alienation that they might otherwise have felt.[13]

Yet, by anchoring part of the Irish-American identity so solidly upon images of the old homeland, the melodramas also made it imperative for the immigrants to find an emotional and psychological link to the Ameri-can side of their identity. The conventions of the melodramas limited their ability to provide this link. For example, Flynn observes that in many plays the hero's emigration could be avoided if only some sort of pardon could be obtained. Or, if he had to emigrate, he would be able to return to Ire-land to be restored to legitimacy.[14] Such plots weaken the connection be-tween Ireland and America. Moreover, a return to Ireland was not some-thing that many Irish could afford, even assuming they wanted to go back. Yet, so strong was this theme of return in the melodramas that it became a standard feature in the popular songs after 1900.

Adhering to the idea that the roots of Irish-American ethnicity lay in Ireland's colonial experience, Flynn sees the melodramas as presenting "patterns of values, images and plot structures that suggest continuity of a deeper sort between the Irish identity in Ireland and that in the new world." The plays showed the Irish in America that they were part of a great di-aspora. This helped to reinforce for the Irish-American community, as well as for the Yankees, the fact that a whole people had been forced to leave their homeland because of poverty and injustice to seek asylum in Amer-ica. Moreover, the presentation of heroes of common birth helped a work-ing-class Irish audience to see itself in a positive light.

THE SONG THEMES

Emigration

The theme of homesickness continued to be popular among songs written after the Civil War. One of the best examples is Thomas P. Westendorf's famous "I'll Take You Home Again, Kathleen" (1876), in which the man promises to take the woman back "to that dear home be-yond the sea." The fact that there is no mention of Ireland in the lyrics made little difference to many Irish Americans then or since. The name of "Kathleen" in the title and the longing for the home over the sea was enough to make it Irish.[15]

Yet after the Civil War there appears to have been a decline in the proportion of songs that touched on the immigrant experience (songs about emigration, home, and the loss of Ireland): in my sample the proportion of such songs declined from 32 percent before the Civil War to 20 percent in the 1860s and 1870s down to 16 percent in the 1880s and 1890s. These changes reflect in part the dramatic growth in comic songs (36 percent of all songs in the 1880s and 1890s), as well as the gradual decline in popularity of the sentimental parlor ballads. Recalling that many of the songs about the Irish had been written on the other side of the Atlantic, the proliferation of comic songs set in the American city may be seen as a step in the process of "Americanization" of the Irish stereotype. Nevertheless, laments for the loss of home and homeland continued to be an important element in non-comic songs about Ireland. In comparison with the Germans, their immigrant partners in numbers and in time, Irish theatrical routines and songs were more likely to cast a sentimental eye back to the old homeland.[16]

Although the proportion of songs touching on emigration declined, the new ones that were produced reveal a different character after the Civil War. Less likely to be composed by Anglo-Irish and English songwriters, Irish songs for melodramas, as well as for vaudeville, were no longer addressed to a predominantly middle-class audience. Although still highly sentimental, compared to their antebellum predecessors, the postwar songs are less often cloaked in romantic conceits about parted lovers or noble "exiles" lamenting their tragedies in language imitating high poetry. The sense of loss is more basic, simple, even elemental in expression. In their very lack of pretense a hint of the raw emotions of the uprooted sometimes comes through. Some songs, for example, depict the immigrant's sense of loss as represented by some physical symbol of home and homeland, as in "A Handful of Earth from the Place of My Birth" (1884).[17]

The new songs of emigration were written for the popular theater, where Irish and Irish-American performers sang before audiences containing many of their fellow countrymen. Jon W. Finson notes that post–Civil War songs about immigration began to idealize the promise of the New World as much as the lost glories of the Old. He cites the title song from Dion Boucicault's *Pat Malloy* (1865) as an example of this transition. Beginning with the words, "At sixteen years of age, I was my mother's fair-haired boy," the song tells in simple language a fairly realistic tale. The singer, one of fourteen children, explains that he went first to England and then to America to make some money to send home.

> From Ireland to America across the sea I roam,
> And every shilling that I got, ah sure I sent it home;
> My mother couldn't write, but on there came from Father Boyce;
> "Oh, heaven bless you, Pat," says she – I hear my mother's voice!

Each verse ends with the line, "For ould Ireland is me country and me name is Pat." On the song's cover the actor Dan Bryant poses as the character of Pat, dressed in knee breeches and a "caubeen," or brimless hat, and sitting on an immigrant's trunk. In an answer song, "Mary of Fermoy" (1866), Pat's sweetheart, left behind in Ireland, describes how he was forced out by landlords and high rents to Columbia's "bless'd land of liberty," where Erin's sons would not be slaves of lord or queen.[18]

An even simpler, almost naive example of the post–Civil War emigrant song is "Maggie, Darling, Now Good Bye" by C. A. White (1872). The piece is a duet for "Barney," who is about to emigrate to America, and "Maggie," who is supposed to remain behind to look after the old folks. In alternating verses the mawkish dialogue sets forth the facts: the farm will not support them; there is no work in Ireland; Barney must go off to find a new home in America. In the encore verse Maggie refuses to be left behind and sings, "With God's help we'll work and strive hard, To make a home on Freedom's shore."[19]

"The Haleys from Mullingar," sung by the vaudeville duo of Grogan and Farrel, depicts the typical "greenhorn" type of characters played by vaudeville song-and-dance teams.

> We are two Irish emigrants, Just from across the sea:
> In the steamship "Adriatic," Of the White Star line, came we.
> At the Battery Park we landed, Bag and baggage here we are –
> Dan Haley and his wife Buddeen – From the town of Mullingar.
>
> We were forced to leave our neat little home,
>   It was poverty drove us away!
> They deprived us of our piece of land
>   When the rent we could not pay!
> They took our pig and praties,
>   And our cow sold at the fair!
> Which grieved and almost broke the hearts
>   Of the Haleys from Mullingar.

To seek a living we find it's hard,
  In this free and distant land,
Without a friend or relative,
  To lend a helping hand.
The old woman can wash and iron in style,
  While I can handle a spade or crow-bar;
So if you hear of a job just please to inform
  The Haleys of Mullingar.[20]

The appeal of this type of song lay in the shock of recognition it must have provided many in the audience, recapitulating their own experiences as greenhorns.

As famine and evictions returned to Ireland in the late 1870s and early 1880s, songs grew sharper in their depiction of the situation. "Sad-Fated Erin" (1882) is unusually stark for a popular song.

Come, sit down beside me and listen, mavourneen
  Come listen while Erin's sad fate I deplore
A cry of distress has come over the ocean,
  The heart-rending wail of the famished, asthore!
While comfort and plenty around us are smiling
  While neither the cold nor the hunger we dread
The shadow of famine lies dark over Erin;
  Her sons and her daughters are wailing for bread
. . . . . .
And pitiless landlords, unheeding their wailings,
  Hard-hearted and deaf to their miserable cry,
The hunger-starved tenants thrust out their dwellings,
  And shelterless leave the poor creatures to die.

CHORUS:

Oh, God help the children of sad-fated Erin;
  From cruel oppression soon may they be free;
For Oh, they are dying with cold and with famine;
  The wail of their sorrow comes over the sea.[21]

In "The Irish Emigrant's Return" (1881) an Irishman comes home from America only to find his family and his sweetheart dead. No one helped them because no one had anything to give. In J. F. Mitchell's "The Exile's Lament, or Lay Me on the Hillside" (1886) it is the emigrant himself who is dying. "Eviction, foul and cruel, sent Him far across the foam / From that sweet spot which Irishmen, Where e're they be, call home."[22]

What Kirby Miller has called the "image of exile" is obvious in these popular songs, as it is in the countless broadside ballads of the era. These songs reinforced the sense, prevalent among many Irish emigrants, of having been driven out of Ireland, as opposed to having chosen a better way of life abroad. Even Yankees could sense this feeling. Edward Everett Hale commented that "Every Irishman who leaves Ireland for America seems to be as really driven thence . . . as if he had made a stand in fight at the beach at Galway, and had been driven by charged bayonets into the sea."[23]

"Must We Leave Our Ould Home (or Queenstown Harbor)" (1890) is about an old couple who, having been evicted from their cabin, must emigrate. The song goes on to try to set the sufferings of the Irish within a context that Americans might understand.

> Still the Irish year by year, flock in thousands to our shore
>> To escape cru'l England's law forever more,
> They are fighting for their rights, dear friends,
>> Did we not do the same?
>> 'Twas Paddy then, that help'd us win our fame.
> So don't look down on the Irish, but lend them a helping hand,
> And pray to God that dear old land to free.[24]

"The Poor Oppressed in Ireland," a vaudeville song sung by Harry Osborne and Fanny Wentworth (to the air of "Slavery Days") was in the form of a dialogue between a father and daughter. The girl wants to marry Teddy, who could help the old man on the farm. The father gives her some realistic advice:

> Go tell the news to Teddy, that your father gave consent,
>> And tell him that he is free to name the day;
> But let him seek another land, for he cannot earn the rent!
>> Sure, he'll find a home in dear America.[25]

Irish Character

The Irish were sensitive to the fact that they had failed to gain freedom for their country and that they had "fled" Ireland in hunger and desperation. This may help account for the success Frank Wilson had with his song "There Never Was a Coward Where the Shamrock Grows" (1880), performed by Harry and John Kernell.

Pat may be foolish and very often wrong,
    Pat's got a temper which don't last very long;
Pat is full of jollity as ev'rybody knows,
    But there never was a coward where the Shamrock grows.[26]

While there was no getting away from Paddy's faults, it was, neverthe-less, possible to present certain aspects of the Irish stereotype in a posi-tive light. Harry Clifton's "Where the Grass Grows Green" (ca. 1856–67) claims:

Poor Pat is often painted, With a ragged coat and hat
His heart and hospitality, Have much to do with that;
Let slanderers say what they will, They cannot call him mean,
Sure a stranger's always welcome, Where the grass grows green.

Although poor and sometimes foolish, Pat is not vicious.

'Tis true he has a weakness for a drop of something pure
But that's a slight debility that many more endure
He's fond of fun – he's witty – though his wit is none too keen
For there's feeling hearts in Erin, where the grass grows green.[27]

In songs such as this we can see how the positive qualities, which critics thought they had seen in the characterizations of the Irish by performers such as Power, Brougham, and Williams, were finding their way into pop-ular song.

The Cult of the Shamrock

American popular song was obviously a more suitable vehicle for depict-ing the emotional impact of Irish emigration than for exploring its political and economic causes. Given the increasingly formulaic approach to song-writing after the Civil War, it was very convenient to focus on symbols that could link the immigrant to the lost land and the abandoned family. Thus, the lowly shamrock began to come into its own after 1870. As a visual sym-bol of Ireland, its appearance on song sheet covers increased from 9 per-cent of illustrated covers in the sample before the Civil War to 18 percent in the 1870s. Following a decline for 1880 to 15 percent, the shamrock appeared on 37 percent of illustrated and/or decorated covers by 1890.[28]

The typical role of the shamrock in emigration songs can be seen in "Dear Little Colleen" (1877). An immigrant in America, whose sweetheart in Ireland is about to join him, sends her a request.

Oh bring me my darling to bless and to cheer me,
　　One sweet bit of shamrock from over the sea,
　　Fondly 'twill whisper when you are near me,
Whisper dear Colleen of home unto me.[29]

In Westendorf's "Good Bye Mavourneen" (1877), this time the doctor turned songwriter actually set out to produce a "real" Irish song, ringing all the changes on Erin, love, home, the Shannon, and, especially, the shamrock. The boy, about to emigrate, promises his girl that he will return to fetch her.

Here in my bosom this pledge I will keep,
　　'Tis but a leaf of the Shamrock so green,
And ev'ry night when I lay down to sleep,
　　I'll kiss it and think of my Colleen.[30]

In "Dear Little Colleen" the shamrock stands for the distant homeland. In Westendorf's song it symbolizes the pledge of love between the boy and the girl. In "Three Leaves of Shamrock" by J. McGuire (1889) the plant represents family ties, even from beyond the grave. In the song, a girl hands some shamrocks to a friend about to emigrate with these instructions: "Take them to my brother, for I have no one other / And these are the shamrocks from his dear old mother's grave." The song was popular enough to find its way into broadside ballads.[31]

In J. F. Mitchell's "The Exile's Lament" (1886), the dying emigrant asks, "Let a bunch of Shamrocks green be planted o're my grave." Linking the shamrock to Irish character, J. K. Emmet in "The Love of the Shamrock" (1879), claims that the plant's three leaves stand for "love," "valor," and "truth," characteristics shared by all true Irish men and women. The "Dear Little Shamrock" (1870) explains that the herb's three leaves reveal a lesson for Irish self-help and solidarity.

That dear little plant that springs from our soil,
　　When its three little leaves are extended;
Denotes from the stalk we together should toil
　　And ourselves by ourselves be befriended.[32]

In "The Emblems of Ireland," Will H. Morton ("America's Comique") managed to work in not only the harp and the shamrock, but also "the wolf dog resting calmly / Near the round towers of our land."[33] By 1887, when this song was printed, the basic iconography of Ireland was so well known it could be rattled off from a vaudeville stage. If a Hoosier like Westendorf could spin out the shamrockery, it is clear that these symbols and the sentiments they called forth had already reached the stage of being acceptable and endlessly repeatable elements in the common currency of American popular culture. Yet it is also clear that these popular songs were no longer being addressed only to a Yankee middle class over the heads of the Irish. Songwriters had to assume that immigrants, first and second generation, were part of the audience.

Irish Nationalism

Sheet music publishers, who had to aim more broadly in hopes of large sales, must have found songs focusing on Irish nationalism too parochial. In the 1860s and 1870s only about 16 percent of the songs in the sample even alluded to political and patriotic sentiments; in the last decades of the nineteenth century the proportion declined to around 13 percent. Nevertheless, there were a few full-blown sheet music ventures into Irish nationalism. "Viva Hibernia" by M. A. Gilsinn (1873) was dedicated to the members of the Irish Catholic Benevolent Union of the United States. The song is full of the kind of poetic patriotism that was part of the popular culture of nationalism in the nineteenth century.

> Erin, oh Erin, Ocean's fair queen,
>> Proudly thy children kneel before thee,
> With joy they greet thee in thy robes of green,
>> And harps of sweetest tone adore thee.

However, as if it was somehow extravagant to bestow such sentiment upon a nation that had not yet gained its independence, the sheet music also carried an additional set of words: a "Lyric Ode to Marquette," commemorating the two-hundredth anniversary of the discovery of the Mississippi.[34]

More to the point was "When Erin Shall Stand Mid the Isles of the Sea" (1874). The title is a reference to Robert Emmet's famous speech from the dock, and the lyrics paraphrase parts of that speech. "Home Rule for Old Ireland" (1878) contains a litany of modern Irish heroes and leaders, including Daniel O'Connell, Emmet, "plane old Isaac Butt," and the Fenian hero, John Martin.[35]

Some of the most rousing nationalist songs appeared as supplements in Sunday papers, very cheap productions in terms of paper quality and design. One example is Artane and Gerald O'Brien's "Ireland's Freedom" (1880). The song is dedicated "to the Irish Member of Parliament, Mr.

Charles Stewart Parnell." However, although it starts out with a big "Hurrah for Parnell" and the Land League, it soon gets lost in misty dreams of serried ranks assembled and ancient Gaelic war cries. "Dear Ireland, When You're Free" was given away with an edition of the *New York Sunday World*. The red and green cover features a large shamrock with Emmet in one leaf and Parnell in another. The song, one of many on both sides of the Atlantic written to commemorate the centennial of the Rising of '98, carries a popular version of the rebel tradition that Patrick Pearse would soon turn into a revolutionary ideology – each new generation must be prepared to renew the sacrifice for Ireland.[36]

Compared to the post–Civil War emigration songs, which maintained some basis in reality, the songs of Irish nationalism tended toward vague, overblown romanticism. A few songs, however, drew more convincingly from experience and passion. "Leaving Old Ireland and Thee" (1884) tells the story of a young man forced out of Ireland by famine and eviction. In the song he recalls his father, a Fenian killed by soldiers in Derry. He hopes to see his father's last wish fulfilled when the Saxons are finally driven from Erin. The song also makes an important link between Irish nationalism and American patriotism. The emigrant son, bound for America, says to his mother:

> Then give me your blessing dear mother;
>   A neat little home soon you'll see;
> Where the star-spangled banner floats proudly
>   O're the beautiful land of the free.[37]

The most famous Irish nationalistic song was written, or at least rewritten, in America. Dion Boucicault worked "The Wearing of the Green" into his play *Arrah na Pogue*, first produced in 1865. The song in one form or another went back to the year just after the Rising of '98. For his version, Boucicault claimed that he had drawn upon some half-remembered verses sung by his mother. This may be true of the first verse, but the second and third verses certainly carry an Irish-American sentiment.

> O Erin, must we leave you, driven by a tyrant's hand?
> Must we ask a mother's blessing from a strange and distant land?
> Where the cruel cross of England shall never more be seen,
> And, where, please God, we'll live and die still wearing of the green.

> But if at last our colour should be torn from Ireland's heart,
> Her sons with shame and sorrow from the dear ould soil will part;

I've heard a whisper of a country, that lies beyant the sea,
Where rich and poor stand equal in the light of freedom's day.

These verses were probably Boucicault's own, and were considered inflammatory, offending Queen Victoria, and were supposedly banned from the British stage. Needless to say, the song was a great hit in America.[38]

Making It in America

If one pier of the identity of the Irish immigrants rested in Ireland, then the other had to be firmly planted in America. The Irish had to somehow put down roots and earn their livings in what they hoped would be a land of opportunity. The songs of vaudeville and melodrama gave voice to these hopes. "Give an Honest Irish Lad a Chance" stated an ambition shared by thousands of immigrants. In a song with all the trappings of a vaudeville piece, the singer, promising "I will try to do what's right, I will work both day and night," proclaims his plans to get a job and "bring out" his mother and sister.[39]

Although "Dora Dooley" (1899) has no specific Irish references in the lyrics, the last verse provides an unusually realistic hint of the immigrant struggle to survive.

> She works hard down town each day,
>> The work is large, but small the pay,
> At home she helps to pay the way,
>> Does my Dora Dooley,
> She has younger brothers three,
>> Her father's just "gone blind" while he,
> Was looking for prosperity,
>> So says Dora Dooley.[40]

In one of the more successful Irish songs of the late nineteenth century, "Bridget Donahue" (1882) by Johnny Patterson ("The Irish Clown"), we see the more optimistic side of emigration to the States.

> I sent her home a picture, I did upon my word,
>> Not a picture of myself but the picture of a bird;
> It was the American Eagle, and I says Miss Donahue,
>> Our eagle's wings are large enough to shelter me and you.[41]

Among the realities of Irish immigrant life were the many friends and relations who might follow a husband, son, or daughter once they had established a toe-hold in America. Many Irish men and women worked hard to achieve the goal of reuniting the family in the United States. Potter notes that in spite of what might appear to be a haphazard disarray in the spectacle of thousands of individual Irish men and women flooding into America, there was a "deep foundation of order, even logic" based on the "complex of intricate family relationships" that imposed duties and responsibilities on the immigrants. Each individual had the potential for creating a small beachhead upon which friends and relations might later arrive. In the 1880s a priest in Ballyhaunis estimated that nineteen of every twenty girls going to America joined uncles and aunts or other near relatives.[42]

The tangible link between the newly arrived in America and the folks back home was the remittance – money saved out of scant wages and sent back to Ireland. This was a great burden on men and women who earned the pay of unskilled laborers and domestics, and Kirby Miller has found evidence of resentment on the part of some of those sending money back home. Nevertheless, according to Lawrence McCaffrey, although they were at the bottom of the social-economic ladder, between 1848 and 1861, Irish immigrants sent $60 million back home through money orders. This figure does not include cash remittances. In "Goodby Johnnie Dear" (1890) a young emigrant remembers his mother's parting words: "Write a letter now and then, *send me all you can.*" When Johnnie lands in America, he gets work and hospitality from his friends and does, indeed, start sending money back home to his poor old mother.[43]

The Day We Celebrate

The Irish were proud of their achievements, and every St. Patrick's Day they marched to demonstrate that pride. In "The Day We Celebrate" (1875) Edward Harrigan lists the assemblage for the great New York St. Patrick's Day parade:

The Ancient Order of Hibernians, Fr. Matthew's [*sic*] Temperance men,
The Sprig of Shamrock and Fenians too, on the seventeenth of March fall in.
The longshoremen are next in line, all hardy, stout and tough,
Their hearts are made of Irish Oak, Although their hands are rough,
The music blaring sweet "Garry Owen" or "Killarney's Lakes" so fair,
To the City Hall we make a call, To be review'd by the Mayor.[44]

Although an American invention, the St. Patrick's Day Parade was an occasion for emigrants and their children to experience a sense of belonging to an Irish nation. Batt O'Connor, a homesick emigrant from east Kerry, walked in a St. Patrick's Day procession in Providence, Rhode Island, in 1893: "and in the emotion I felt, walking as one of that vast crowd of Irish emigrants celebrating our national festival, I awoke to the full consciousness of my love for my country." O'Connor eventually returned to Ireland to take part in the 1916 rising.[45]

Very few real revolutionaries came from among the ranks of the St. Patrick's Day marchers. The parade was, however, an Irish-American festival. Behind the marching and celebrating (and "green" and "orange" rioting that occasionally marred "The Day"), lay an Irish-American ideology consistently repeated in speeches, toasts, and editorials from the time of Daniel O'Connell's agitations to the World War I era. One part of the ideology tied the cause of Irish freedom to the situation in which the Irish emigrants found themselves in the United States. Michael Davitt, a Fenian and founder of the Irish National Land League, underscored this theme, telling his emigrant audience in America: "You want to be honored among the elements that constitute this nation . . . aid us in Ireland to remove the stain of degradation from your birth . . . and [you] will get the respect you deserve." A letter to the *Irish World*, January 1, 1876, stated the case with stark simplicity. "We are slaves in the United States and . . . the reason for such a state of things is plain: Because we haven't an Irish nation."[46]

The problem was that many Americans looked askance at what they regarded as the immigrants' obsession with Irish nationalism and the anti-British agitation that accompanied it. As Thomas Brown put it, "Perhaps the single most important theme in Irish-American literature is that devoted to justifying immigrant loyalty to Ireland and reconciling it with their loyalty to the United States." Thus, the second thrust of Irish-American ideology, was stated as early as 1814 by Thomas O'Connor, editor of *Shamrock and Hibernian Chronicle*. O'Connor urged his readers to understand that, as refugees from British tyranny, Irishmen were *already* Americans. They differed from the native-born Americans only in place of birth; "in terms of political purpose, they were alike." An "Irishman by birth [was] an American by adoption." Many St. Patrick Day banquets concluded with the toast, "to the land we left and the land we live in."[47]

According to Victor Greene, it was this welding of Irish identity with American destiny that made the St. Patrick's Day celebrations so important to the Irish community. "By so honoring their patron saint, they complemented their identity as Americans." "The Day" was an essential ritual for the Irish "partly because it reminded them of the compatibility and basic similarity of being both Irish and American." The Irish, like the eighteenth-century Americans, struggled against English imperialism. In this context, St. Patrick was a national hero, as well as a saint, "one who gave his people a religious identity separate from that of the English and thereby welded together the Irish and American national struggles."[48]

According to Irish-American spokesmen, both Irish nationalists and American patriots shared a republican identity maintained in the face of British royalism. Each year the speakers at the St. Patrick's Day celebrations would look forward to the time when Ireland would emulate the United States and win its freedom. In seeking to accomplish this goal, the Irish were acting as Americans. As early as 1784, President McKay of the Boston Charitable Irish Society, raised the toast: "May *our friends, countrymen in Ireland*, behave like the brave Americans till they recover *their* liberties."[49]

The Civil War and Dual Patriotism

Obviously, the concept of dual loyalties and dual identities for the Irish in America had been fully articulated well before the Civil War. By the 1850s, Irish-American nationalists had envisioned an ideal revolutionary strategy that would remain unchanged into the twentieth century. Somehow, the United States, by providing money, weapons, trained fighting men, or at least political pressure, would help liberate the old homeland. After the Civil War, the Irish weeklies in the United States focused on Irish-American patriotism in their articles and short stories. Irish-American writers not only stressed Irish allegiance to the United States but sought to build the conceptual bridge from the American Revolution and the Civil War to the struggle of Irish freedom. The Irish, having fought and died for American freedom, claimed a right to link their American patriotism to the cause of Ireland.[50]

Participation in the Union armies provided the Irish with a great opportunity to proclaim their loyalty to their adopted land, as well as their pride in being Irish.

> On the twenty-first of July, Beneath a burning sun,
> McDowell met the Southern troops, In battle at Bull Run;
> Above the Union vanguard, Was proudly dancing seen,
> Besides the starry banner, Old Erin's flag of green.[51]

Their participation in the Union ranks provided an opportunity for the Irish to present themselves as a part of American society while stressing their Irish identity. "The Irish Are Preferred" contrasted Irish service during the Civil War to anti-Irish prejudices: "But now on every side a different cry is heard, / And the public feeling is – an Irishman preferred."[52]

Even during the Civil War, at least one song tried to sort out the questions of loyalty and allegiance once the Irish immigrant became a citizen. In "The Irish Volunteer" (1862), the Irish boy tells his girl as he goes off to fight for the Union,

> The land that has bless'd us With love and protection,
>> Is smitten with peril, Beleaguer'd with foes,
> The brave and true hearted, With loyal affection,
>> Must march where the banner Of liberty goes.
> The emerald island Away in the ocean
>> With white breakers kissing, Its murmuring shore,
> America's armor Will someday be needing,
>> That British oppression May curse her no more.[53]

The Fenian dream of an Irish-American army of liberation is found more often in the Irish songsters than in sheet music. An example is "Pat Murphy of Meagher's Brigade" (sung to the tune of "Think of Your Head in the Morning"). Published in *Delaney's Irish Song Book No. 4*, the song appears to have begun life as a comic piece to which some more serious verses were later appended. By the end of the song Poor Pat is dead and the singer comments:

> Then surely, Columbia can never forget, While valor and fame
>> hold communion,
> How nobly the brave Irish Volunteers fought, In defense of the flag
>> of the Union,
> And, if ever old Ireland for freedom should strike, We'll a helping
>> hand offer them freely;
> And the star and stripes shall be seen along side, Of the flag of the
>> land of Shillelagh![54]

We find the same hope voiced in another song entitled "St. Patrick's Day."

> When I think of her plains, Where tyranny reigns,
>> And despotic landlords carry their sway,

I wish for the time, when with the Sixty-Ninth,
　　To land on old Ireland on St. Patrick's Day.[55]

This dream (and it was little more than a dream) of the American Fenians died hard. A song entitled "The Irish-American Army" by "Corporal Barney" appears in *Stephens' Fenian Songster*. Although the style is closer to the broadside tradition than to that of popular sheet music, it is a clear statement of the hope that Ireland would be liberated by an army of returned Yanks.

　　When comes the hour to fight the Power,
　　　　That tramples Irish freedom,
　　Columbia, then, will give us men,
　　　　A Grant, too, if we need him?
　　Then raise a cheer, Ye despot hear,
　　　　And surely 'twill alarm ye,
　　For soon you'll see Ould Erin free,
　　　　By the Irish-American Army.[56]

Francis Leiber, visiting America from Prussia, was struck by both the clannishness and the nationalism of the Irish in America. "They, in fact, openly retain their name, and often, in the very moment that they make use of the highest privileges of citizenship which any country can bestow, they do it under the banner of Irishmen." Leiber recognized that the Irish wanted to become Americans while still clinging to their particular identity, but he warned that such "serving of two masters will not do"; all of which goes to show how much a German knew about the Irish – or America.[57] The Irish themselves saw no contradiction to the claim of dual loyalty. Consider, for example, Harry Pierce's "The Flag of Ireland Free" (1884).

　　Although I am now in the land of the free
　　　　And a citizen true to the core,
　　Old Erin will ever be dear unto me
　　　　As the day when I left the green shore.

As usual, the singer assures his listeners that he will one day return and fight to free Ireland.[58]

One of the most careful attempts to articulate this sense of dual patriotism can be found in "That Sweet Bunch of Shamrocks" (1890). The song begins when the singer receives a bunch of shamrocks from his mother in Ireland.

> Columbia, queen of nations, don't be angry with me dear,
>> If I praise this bunch of shamrocks Which I proudly wear;
> For I know you treat me kindly, I love you all the more,
>> But I can't forget old Ireland, and that dear old harp of yore.
> The good son loves his mother, tho' devoted to his wife.
>> And he will defend them, Even with his life;
> So, I, America darling, would as freely die for thee;
>> Though cherishing still old Ireland, And my mother o'er the sea.

Patrick Collins, editor of the Boston *Pilot*, also used this conceit to explain his dual allegiance when he described himself as "loving mother Ireland" and his "wife, America."[59]

In the context of American popular culture, then, the dual identity of the Irish American was cobbled up out of such symbols and metaphors. Concatenations of sweetheart, mother, Ireland, shamrocks, and allegiance to America, all presented within the metaphor of a marriage, provide an insight into the ways songwriters, some Irish, some not, tried to make sense of Irish allegiance to both the old homeland and the United States. How could the Irish love America *and* Ireland? The logic of the case remained a Hibernian mystery to almost everyone except the Irish. It took the Yankees a long time to understand that the answer to this question ultimately lay in emotions, sentiment, and identity rather than in politics and that the question was, therefore, not one about which they had to worry.

Nevertheless, the task of establishing a dual identity was a particular challenge to the American-born Irish, who, although they had no firsthand knowledge of the Emerald Isles, were called upon to feel the hurt of Ireland's wrongs. In his St. Patrick's Day address to the Irish of Worcester, Massachusetts, a young man named John Turner showed that an American birth did not excuse one from loyalty to Ireland: "Though I have never breathed the invigorating air of the land of happiness, or witnessed the recreation which so many experience in the land of virtue, yet, sir, from my infancy my father has instilled in my mind and impressed it so deep on my heart, that for his sake and in detestation of the wrongs inflicted by the hand of tyranny, it shall never be erased from my memory."[60]

Behind Turner's pledge of loyalty to Ireland there seems to have been another pledge – to the memory of his father and his father's generation. For the American-born Irish, Ireland and the Irish cause was an emotional tie, not only back to a homeland they had never seen, but to their parents and the trials and tribulations they suffered in coming to America. This sentiment was captured by T. D. Sullivan in his poem, "The Irish-American," written, perhaps, after his visit to America in 1890.

> Columbia the free is the land of my birth
> And my paths have been all of American earth;
> But my blood is as Irish as any can be,
> And my heart is with Erin afar o'er the sea.[61]

What of the other side of the "hyphen"? Eventually, the immigrants from Erin had to articulate the American side of their complicated identity. This involved weaving ties between the two ends of their fragmented experience separated by the broad Atlantic. Some of these ties were very concrete, such as remittances home or tickets sent to bring loved ones in Ireland out to America. Other efforts were political, such as membership in the American branch of the Irish Land League or in the Clan na Gael. There was also a complex web of words and metaphors that explained how one could be passionately both Irish and American; how one could claim to yearn for Ireland, yet never return. The biggest problem of all, however, was how one could take the stereotype of the Irish and turn it into something acceptable to Irish immigrants and Yankees alike. We can see the process at work if we look at the comic songs of the era.

6. The Irish and Vaudeville

Vaudeville was much more fecund than melodrama as a source for popular songs about Ireland and the Irish. It was a different kind of theater altogether. It not only provided more opportunities for singing and dancing, but it also represented a series of cultural conventions that shaped and framed the songs as well.

Vaudeville was the product of several changes that took place in American show business, beginning with the evolution of the minstrel show. By the 1850s the minstrels' original "plantation" jamboree, formalized into the semicircle of performers with end-men and an interlocutor, had become confined to the first part of the entertainment. The show often concluded with a burlesque of a popular play or opera. Sandwiched in between was the "Olio" or variety segment, vaudeville in miniature.[1]

Unfortunately, even the three-part minstrel show still lacked women, a serious drawback as minstrelsy began to face competition after the Civil War, when *The Black Crook* (1866) opened at Nibloe's Gardens in New York City. The show consisted of a series of extravagant musical set pieces, strung together on the most slender of plots. Its main appeal, however, was its large cast of young women in short skirts and flesh-colored tights. The American musical was born, and with it, eventually, the American show girl.

At around the same time, big city saloons, into which no "respectable" woman would venture, were offering entertainment – comedians, clog dancers, and singers of both sexes. By 1872, there were between seventy-five and eighty concert or variety saloons in New York City, where the entertainment, rough, boisterous, and varied, was by and for the working class. The saloons offered performers, many from poor immigrant backgrounds, a chance to earn a living at something other than harsh physical labor, domestic service, or prostitution. What Minnie, mother of the brothers Marx, said about vaudeville also applied in a more modest way to the concert saloons: "Where else can people who don't know anything make so much money?"[2]

For those performers just getting started there were the "dime museums" that mixed curiosities and freaks with circus and variety acts. Tony Pastor started as a child performer in Barnum's Museum and then moved on to minstrel shows and circuses, before becoming manager of his own theater. In 1865, Pastor recognized the box-office potential of having women in the audience as well as on the stage. When he closed off the bar in his New York variety theater, cleaned up the acts, and began handing out bags of flour to ladies at his matinees, the road to respectable variety and vaudeville was open. Beginning with a theater at 201 on the Bowery, Pastor gradually moved uptown, until he acquired his famous theater on Fourteenth Street on Union Square, next to Tammany Hall.[3] The names of performers who got their start at Pastor's reads like a roster of the great vaudevillians and musical comedy stars of the late nineteenth century. Among them were Irish-American performers such as Harrigan and Hart, Maggie Cline, and the Four Cohans. Pastor himself performed most evenings. He had a number of Irish songs in his repertory, praising Irish participation in the Civil War and decrying no-Irish-need-apply prejudice.

In the decades that followed the establishment of Pastor's, there were ample opportunities for performers of all kinds to find work in variety shows, wherever the venue. From the 1860s through the 1880s, Irish, blackface, and "Dutch" or German were the most popular ethnic comedy acts, with Irish acts predominating.[4] There were song and dance singles by the likes of Kitty O'Neal, John W. Kelly ("The Rolling Mill Man"), and Tim Rogers. Pat Rooney was a comic as well as a popular dancer, as was Sam Ricky. An early partner of Ned Harrigan, Ricky's was, according to Joe Laurie Jr., the first famous Irish comedy act. Laurie also notes Maggie Weston as the first "biddy," or comic Irish female in variety and Maggie Cline as the first single woman Irish comedy singer.[5]

There were Irish double acts, featuring two comedians, rather than the comic-and-straight-man combination that became popular in the twentieth century. The first Irish double, McNulty and Murray, "The Boys from Limerick," was followed by Clooney and Ryan, Needham and Kelly, and Kelly and Ryan – the "Bards of Tara." Slapstick comedy was the staple of the knock-about Irish "four acts," such as the Four Shamrocks and the Four Emeralds. There were even Irish family acts such as the Four Mortons, McCoy and McEvoy and their two daughters, and the Four Cohans. Jerry Cohan, the father, even organized a "Hibernicon," an all-Irish version of vaudeville. It was Jerry's son, George M., who was destined to become the most famous member of the Cohan family and one of the foremost Irish Americans in show business.[6]

In her study of male-female comedy teams, Shirley Staples lists several Irish or Irish-American duos who were popular in the 1870s and 1880s. Fred and Annie McAvoy performed their own original musical sketches, such as "The Emigrants" and "Pat's Frolic." The Collinses, perhaps in imitation of Barney Williams and his wife, did "Barney's Courtship." John and Maggie Fielding had successes in 1873 with "O'Connor's Child, or the Harp of Tara" and "The Emerald Isle."[7]

As Robert Snyder has observed in his history of vaudeville, "Irish acts – performed either by Irish people or people pretending to be Irish, according to nineteenth century theatrical conventions – were a striking presence on the vaudeville stage." As Arthur Loesser noted, "In show business the words 'Irish comedian' were the name of an effect, not necessarily of an essence. It was a trade name." Writing from New York in 1877, Dion Boucicault claimed, "We [Irish] are more popular in the theater than ever. Young actors and singers take Irish names for the benefit of the fashion." Therefore, while Irish and Irish Americans, like Harrigan and Hart, sometimes played in blackface or did "Dutch" characters, members of other ethnic groups returned the favor. Joe Weber and Lew Fields, who eventually became famous for their German-Jewish comedy act, used Irish song, dance, and comedy in their early routines at Duffy's Pavilion in Coney Island, where they started in 1877, and later at the Windsor Theater on the Bowery.[8]

ALL SINGING, ALL DANCING

In vaudeville, to be Irish was to dance. Irish immigrants brought traditional step dancing to America, where it became a part of theatrical dancing. Solo Irish step dances, such as the double jig and the hornpipe, are still performed with the upper body stiff and the arms held at the sides. All action is in the feet that beat out the rhythm. The contrast between the immobility of the upper body and the movement of the feet could be accentuated by balancing a glass of water on the head of the dancer or an egg on each shoulder.[9]

Irish step dancing provided the start for more than one twentieth-century tap dancer. George M. Cohan began his career with the same Irish steps his father had used when he started in the theater. Ruby Keeler, the first film star noted for her tap dancing, learned her earliest steps at her Catholic school on New York's East Side, where a woman came in weekly to teach flings, hornpipes, and jigs. Her first job was in Cohan's *The Rise of Rosie O'Reilly* in 1923. Gracie Allen, partner of comedian George Burns, picked up Irish step dancing from her father and, as a teenager, appeared with her sisters as one of the "Four Colleens." While she and George were courting, they would visit Jimmy Cagney's house to trade steps. Cagney himself eventually played George M. Cohan in the film *Yankee Doodle Dandy*, in which he recreated Cohan's inimitable stiff-legged, proscenium-to-proscenium dancing style.[10]

Dancing, in soft shoe or in clogs, was an integral part of many Irish acts. When they were not knocking each other around the stage, Irish double acts invariably broke into jig or reel steps, even if dancing was not the primary talent on display. In his descriptions of Needham and Kelly, Kelly and Ryan, and Bradford and Delaney, Gilbert notes the reel dancing and walk-arounds between song verses and the mandatory dance at the end of a song. The Irish family acts all combined dancing with songs and comedy.[11]

The team of Andy and Annie Hughes provides an example of how dancing was worked into the typical couple act. Between the verses of their introductory song, the Hugheses would go into a chorus that featured their dance breaks:

> Oh, watch the movement of our feet, (Break.)
> In execution we'er so neat, (Break.)
> We'll try to plase yees one and all –
> The collywobbles we can cure –
> Kape your eyes on us now,
> And watch us welt the flure. (Dance.)[12]

The Hugheses later billed themselves as "The Happy Irish Couple," and Andy Hughes wrote a dance song that seems to include a physical description of the pair (they probably alternated the first four lines and did the last two together):

> Are you looking at me Katy, you see I'm dancing mad,
> Sure I also time with you, for sure I'm just as bad,
> But you're so very small, and you know I'm tall and lean,
> We're always on the move, as plainly can be seen,
> Oh Katy, Oh Micky, to dance it is no trouble,
> For we are known by everyone as the Happy Irish Couple.[13]

There were many variations built on traditional step dancing. There was the sand jig, for example, as exemplified by Kitty O'Neill, who performed in both variety saloons and in vaudeville in the 1870s and 1880s. The most popular kinds of dances on the vaudeville stage were those performed in clogs, special dancing shoes that had wooden soles. Near the end of the nineteenth century, before tap shoes replaced clogs, some dancers inserted pieces of iron rods in the heel and toe of their clogs. There was no "Irish clog" as such. Clog dancing does not appear to have been a dominant feature of Irish indigenous folk or working-class culture. In fact, dancing in wooden-soled clogs seems to have been a British, particularly a Lancashire, contribution to American show business. However, Irish step dancing, especially the double jig with its "battering step," and the vigorous solo hornpipe, was easily adapted to the use of clogs. Irish and Lancashire steps, mixed with African-American dance styles, created the intricate footwork upon which theatrical clogging and later tap was based.[14]

With such attention paid to the art, it is only natural that among a hoard of dancers the work of certain individuals stood out. Minstrel dancer George Primrose, whose real name was Delaney and who performed into the twentieth century, was renowned for the soft-shoe style he helped to develop. The two most famous clog dancers associated with Irish acts were both named Pat Rooney – father and son, each very famous in his day (there was a third Pat Rooney, a grandson, who also danced). Patrick James Rooney, the patriarch, was born in Birmingham, England, in 1844 and emigrated to America. By the 1880s he was a top comic Irish song-and-dance man. A few of his own songs were successful, such as "The Day I Played Base Ball," "Pretty Peggy," and "Is That Mr. Reilly." In spite of moments of burlesque when he would sing "Biddy the Ballet Girl" and then clog around on his toes dressed in a tutu, Rooney was apparently a graceful dancer, very much in keeping with the new respectable audience that vaudeville managers like Pastor, B. F. Keith, and E. F. Albee were trying to attract.[15]

Later, Rooney danced with his son, who was born in 1880. After his father's death, Pat Rooney *fils* became one of the greatest clog dancers in vaudeville. His specialty was a very elegant form of the waltz clog that he would do, hands in his pockets, to the tune of "The Daughter of Rosie O'Grady." W. C. Fields said of the younger Rooney that one would think he was floating over the stage, were it not for the sounds of the taps. Rooney, who performed with his wife, Marion Bent and, after her retirement, with his son, kept comedy as part of his act. He had a long career and appeared in the original production of *Guys and Dolls* in 1950. He died in 1962, and when the third Pat Rooney died in 1979, a century-long family tradition of Irish-American song and dance men came to an end.[16]

THE IRISH VAUDEVILLE COMIC

By the 1880s, the Irish comedy acts had been around long enough that critic John J. Jennings could complain about the Irish comic:

"immutable in his makeup and unmindful of the hoary age of the jokes with which he tortures the intelligent portions of his audiences." Jennings described the various guises of the classic Irish comedian: "A gorgeous plaid suit with baggy trousers and short coat topped by a high white hat, and the outfit completed with a cane; or a wardrobe consisting of a semi-respectable thin-sleeved, square-tailed frock coat and high water broadcloth pants, with polished and towering stove-pipe hat; or a hod-carrier's rig; or any half-idiotic attempt to duplicate a workingman's get-up."[17] Irish comics frequently wore side whiskers called "dinegals" or all-round chin whiskers generally known as "Galway sluggers." Red wigs were common and the more decadent versions of the character sported green whiskers. The canes, however, were standard. According to Jennings, "the canes are used for thumping the floor of the stage, and the stove-pipe hats for banging each other in the face, for this class of comedians always travel in pairs." In addition there was lots of falling and tumbling.[18]

The vaudeville version of the stage Irishman did not please some Irish, who were annoyed by the strange clothes and exaggerated makeup. "The Fine Irish Gents," published in one of Pat Rooney's songsters, issued this rebuke:

> It's a shame on the stage, how they mimic our race,
> In a style that's a mystery to me,
> How the people in front, will stand such insult;
> Receiving such blockheads with glee.
> If they went to old Ireland they'd find their mistake,
> For our boys and our girls are well dressed,
> In manners as well to you I will tell,
> For they stand in the land with the best.[19]

The song has all the earmarks of a vaudeville piece, including a patriotic non sequitur at the end, calling for Irish freedom and "the green with the red, white and blue." In all likelihood this song was performed cheek-by-jowl with the kind of acts it appeared to protest.

Outrageous as some of the vaudeville characterizations were, it is important to remember that by the 1870s and 1880s the urban types they represented were replacing the traditional comic Irish peasant. In fact, the American vaudeville stage exported the new urban Irish comedian back to Ireland. The American comic team of Furgeson and Mack visited Dublin in the 1880s and introduced the new urban slapstick Irish comedy to the music halls there.[20]

Naturally, many of the routines exploited the alleged Irish propensity for drinking and fighting. A Pat Rooney songster published in 1878 carries a routine, attributed to Johnny Roach, entitled "The Cobbler." The song is about a cobbler tormented by a tyrannical wife, whom he eventually shoves into the river, after which he "cautiously bid her good night!" The performer's monologue patters on in between the verses. One part describes the cobbler and his wife getting into a fight: "And thin, without waitin' for any one to tell her what to do, she'd up with a brick and let's drive at me. I can dodge it aisy enough 'cause I'm used to it; but another poor divil there standin' by, an' not sayin' a word to anybody, he got it plump in the mug. Up comes the police, and walks the three av us off for assault and batthery, an' d_____n the one got batthered but the poor divil who had nothin' to do wid it. But that's the way of it – evil communications corrupt good manners."[21]

Vaudeville demanded a new style of humor. As Gunther Barth points out, the new urbanites, strangers to each other, lacked the older, more relaxed American approach to language and humor. Given the rapidly changing format of the typical vaudeville show and an audience conditioned to the faster tempo of urban life, there was no longer time for the slowly building story of traditional rural humor.[22] A double act, for example, might start with a monologue by one of the partners until he was joined onstage by the other, at which point the jokes came in rapid two- and three-liners.

> Pat: Did you hear about the explosion down at the gas works?
> Mike: No. Anybody kilt?
> Pat: Forty Eyetileians and one Irishman.
> Mike: Oh, the poor man.

Until near the end of the century, when the Roman Catholic Church and nationalist organizations succeeded in protesting the caricature that passed for Irishness in some of the vaudeville acts, a certain grotesque quality hung around the comic Irish character. The long-suffering John Jennings, while claiming to abhor the stuff, gives ample evidence of the strangeness of the comic Irish routine, circa 1880s: "The other mornin' I intered a friend's salune. There war grape shkins on the flure, an' I sez to him, 'How do ye do Mr. Cassidy? I see you had a party last night.' 'What makes you think so?' sez he. Because I see the grape shkins on the flure, sez I. 'Thim's not grape shkins,' sez he; 'thim's eyes. Some of the b'ys hed a fight here lasht noight an' you're now surveyin' the battle-field.'"[23]

Even more than the songs, the jokes and patter of vaudeville routines pared down ethnic stereotypes to their essential elements in order to get them across quickly to an audience made up of a variety of nationalities. In *Writing for Vaudeville* (1915), Brett Page provides a quick lesson in how to dress up a joke in Irish costume. In the process of showing how to string jokes together around a particular character, Page first gives a joke "straight," without any characterization. A gentleman dines at a Chinese restaurant where he encounters a dish featuring a delectable sort of meat. Wishing to know the nature of the meat, the diner asks the Chinese waiter who, unfortunately, does not understand English,

> . . . so I pointed to a morsel of the delicious dark meat and, rubbing the place where all the rest of it had gone, I asked:
> "Quack, quack?"
> The Chink grinned and said:
> "No. No. Bow-wow."

The story is then adopted to an Irishman named Casey:

> "Mither av Moses," says Casey, "this is shure the atein for ye; but what's thot dilicate little tid-bit o' brown mate?"
> "I don't know" says I.
> "Oi'll find out," says Casey. "Just listen t'me spake that heathen's language."
> "Here, boy," he hollers, "me likee, what you call um?"
> The Chink stares blankly at Casey. Casey looks puzzled, then he winks at me. Rubbing his hand over the place where the rest of the meat had gone, he says:
> "Quack-quack?"
> A gleam shot into the Chink's almond eyes and he says:
> "No. No. Bow-wow."
> It took seven of us to hold Casey, he felt that bad.[24]

What makes this story Irish? First, it is set solidly within the language of the urban, working-class with just enough Irish dialect to support the ethnic label. Then, there is the Irishman's supposed volubility and loquaciousness, which give the story and dialogue a bit more color. The ethnic lines are sharpened and at the same time comically mixed ("Mither av Moses"). Finally, the Irishman, unlike the unnamed and undifferentiated character in the original story, is given to extreme reactions ("It took seven of us to hold Casey . . .").

John Higham has observed, "While coming to terms with the city . . . the immigrants were also forging an urban mass culture to replace the traditions they could not transplant intact. It is hardly surprising that heterogeneous people, cut adrift from their past and caught up in the machine process, should have found the substance of a common life in the stimuli of the mass media."[25] It is not surprising that first- and second-generation immigrants helped to pioneer the new mass media such as vaudeville and Tin Pan Alley.

It was largely because vaudeville was very much at the center of the new mass culture of multi-ethnic, urban America that it was not for the greenhorn right off the boat. Newly landed immigrants seeking entertainment would have had to work their way from the ethnic periphery toward the mainstream. Desperate for some contact with the culture they had left behind, the Irish just off the boat might have patronized Irish variety saloons, such as Kerrigan's Pleasant Hour on West Forty-second Street. There they might have heard the great uilleann piper Patsy Touhey playing traditional jigs and reels. As the greenhorns settled into life in America, they might have attended an Irish melodrama such as "The Rambler from Clare" or "The Ivy Leaf" (both productions of Power's Ivy Leaf Company in the 1880s and 1890s) and again encountered Touhey's stupendous piping. However, from the turn of the century until the piper's death in 1923, anyone who wanted to hear Touhey would have had to catch his comedy act with his partner, Charles Henry Burke, at one of the large vaudeville theaters.

Patrick J. Touhey was born near Ballaun in the Loughrea section of County Galway in 1865 into a family of pipers. His parents emigrated to America when Patsy was three. For all practical purposes, he grew up an Irish American. Even the pipes he played reflected the American experience. They were made in America by Billy and Charles Taylor, who had emigrated from Drogheda, County Louth. Tuned to concert pitch and made with a narrow bore, they were designed for a brighter and louder sound that would carry in the large saloons and vaudeville halls of the United States.

Once out of the Irish pubs and into mainstream vaudeville, however, virtuoso renditions of traditional Irish music were not enough. Touhey's act mixed puns and slapstick business with piping and step dancing (by Touhey's wife May Gillen). Although most of the music and dancing was Irish, one of their most popular encores was "Turkey in the Straw." Even a great performer on a uniquely Irish instrument found himself pulled toward the mainstream of American entertainment.[26]

One encounters the same phenomenon among the recordings the great Sligo fiddler James Morrison made in New York between 1921 and 1936. Along with traditional reels, jigs, and hornpipes, Morrison recorded popular American two-steps such as "The Wreck of the 99" and "Oh Dem Golden Slippers," as well as such nontraditional Irish-American favorites as "When Irish Eyes Are Smiling" and "My Wild Irish Rose." Like Touhey, the most talented of Irish traditional musicians found themselves pulled to some degree away from their roots just by virtue of performing in a multi-ethnic environment.[27]

Facing no language barrier, the Irish quickly found their way into vaudeville, both as performers and as audience. One patron of the Bowery variety theaters admitted that while Germans were certainly in attendance, "there is an unmistakenly Irish stamp on most of the faces of those present." The Germans, after all, had their own theaters and beer gardens.[28] Yet, while there were plenty of Irish in vaudeville, onstage and in the house, vaudeville was not Irish theater. A form of entertainment well suited to the multiethnic industrial city, vaudeville could not cater exclusively to one group. The Irish, Dutch, Jewish, and blackface acts had to appeal to the different members of the working class and the rapidly growing white-collar class that patronized the shows. Poles, Italians, Slavs, and Greeks also had to see something of their own experiences onstage, even if their ethnic groups were not represented on the bill. What they saw were characterizations, often comic and grotesque, of people whose original homes and homelands lay far beyond the boundaries of the city, all striving, not just to survive, but to "make it" in an environment that was at once alien and mesmerizing, grim, dirty and, at the same time, glittering with promise.

Perhaps the best way to understand the role of vaudeville in American popular culture is to analyze it as a "social ritual," which Christopher Small has defined as "an act which dramatizes and re-enacts the shared mythology of a culture or social group, the mythology which unifies and, for its members, justifies that culture or group." According to Small, the ritual involves the specific setting – the building, the stage, the arrangement of space within the hall, the attitude of the audience – as well as the actual performance itself.[29]

Exploring the ritual nature of vaudeville, we can begin with the progress of a member of the audience, coming out of the noise and confusion of the city street into the relative opulence, quiet, and order of the theater lobby. Experience, backed up by ushers enforcing management policy, has taught him that a certain decorum is required – there *are* ladies present! Yet there is a certain democracy at work as well. There are no reserved seats and the patrons quietly find their own places, for, with the onset of the "continuous performance," the show is already in progress. The members of this audience of equals, all facing the stage, do not interact with each other directly but spontaneously join each other in laughter and applause. A limited, momentary community of strangers has been created.

In the city, of course, communities of spectators were constantly forming and dispersing hundreds of times a day to view fires, accidents, fights, parades, and so on. It was part of the ritual of vaudeville, however, to formalize aspects of urban existence and to present them to the audience in controlled forms of entertainment. The continuous performance mimicked the flow of urban life. Members of the audience came and left; the show went on. Onstage, the procession of unrelated acts paralleled the fragmented nature of urban existence; a hodgepodge of people and events, ever in motion, producing brief encounters and then dissolving. However, vaudeville allowed the audience to do the one thing that was so difficult to do out on the streets. It enabled the spectator to concentrate on one thing at a time, to grasp it, to understand it and enjoy it.

Also, just as a certain order lay behind the willy-nilly movement of people and goods through the city, so the vaudeville bill was carefully planned to provide pleasure, build expectations, and then help shift the old audience out to make room for the new. The bill would invariably begin with a "dumb" act, acrobats, jugglers, or trained animals. The noise of incoming patrons would not disturb it and, as the cycle of acts came round, it served as a good "chaser," following as it did the "final" act, a big musical number or short play with a well-known star.[30]

In the song-and-dance acts and in the comedy acts and sketches, the audience saw a variety of urban types and ethnic groups. It was a case of the city watching and discovering aspects of itself. Moments of pathos for the poor and unfortunate were followed by raucous spoofs of German, Irish, blacks, or Italians. Edward Harrigan was right when he once complained that the newer style of humor of the 1890s was based on laughing *at* rather than *with* someone.[31] He did not appreciate, however, that in laughing at the stereotypes presented onstage, members of the audience were laughing *with* each other. Thus, among the mythic experiences that the ritual of vaudeville provided was that of a momentary equality among unequals; a brief community of strangers united in their enjoyment of being entertained; a collection of individuals made to feel, even if only for an hour or so, that they somehow were a part of the city whose tempo, sense of change, style, and culture they shared and understood.

As Albert F. McLean Jr. pointed out in his study of vaudeville as ritual, the institution was for "the New Folk," the primarily rural peoples of Europe (and America) who found themselves facing the challenge of the polyglot, industrial city. Thus, the roots of vaudeville lay in the experiences of those peoples "who sought images, gestures, and symbols which would objectify their experience and bring to their lives a simple and comprehensive meaning." To McLean, vaudeville was one means by which "the disruptive experience of migration and acclimatization was objectified and accepted. In its symbolism lies the psychic profile of the American mass man in the moment of his greatest trial."[32]

In Stephen Steinberg's view, the immigrants, uprooted from home and past, embraced American culture, not out of self-hatred but out of a need for some rootedness, some sense of belonging to their adopted country.[33] Part of the myth of vaudeville, then, was that there *was* an American culture to which the immigrants and their children could attach themselves. This helps us place into some perspective the ethnic comedy that was so central to vaudeville from the 1870s into the early years of the twentieth century. Onstage, ethnic differences were not being celebrated, nor were they simply being satirized. Joke by joke, the more extreme manifestations of ethnicity were being rendered unimportant by being made ridiculous. They were the differences that ultimately made no difference, providing they were eventually shed. For underneath their variegated exteriors, all urbanites shared the same goal – to survive and, if possible, get ahead. According to Barth, vaudeville not only entertained "but it also stimulated aspirations for an ampler life that transformed downtrodden men and women into rising people and convinced ambitious people that they were indeed on their way up."[34]

This is why the greenhorn was the butt of so many jokes; and it is also why most newly landed immigrants were not ready for vaudeville. Vaudeville could not help initiate the newcomer into American life until the greenhorn was ready to surrender his or her attachment to the Old World and its ways. Indeed, its message for the newly arrived was, according to Steinberg, "a powerful message from the larger society, which was that the 'greener' was destined to remain on the periphery of the society and its system of rewards."[35] This was vaudeville's most powerful myth: that one could become an American to the extent that one could shed the trappings and habits of the Old World.

Up to at least World War I, vaudeville was a theater of assimilation – assimilation to America, to the industrial city with its frantic pace, to one's fellow migrants and immigrants, and to the opportunities for individual success. Sitting in the audience, the assimilating immigrants could see their former greenhorn selves, stumbling over dialect or brogue, lost in a wilderness of strange words and customs, beset by sharp hustlers of their own group, but still, somehow, surviving. Or the immigrant would see sketches in which fully assimilated American-born children demonstrated their superior grasp on American urban reality, far ahead of anything their old-fashioned, Old-World parents could manage. And then there were the performers, themselves immigrants or children of immigrants, representatives of success, even if the glamour of the theater was mostly glitter that disguised a schedule of two or three shows a day.

It is this theater of assimilation that provides the context within which all of the ethnic jokes and songs were presented. The proscenium arch was truly a frame within which the acts onstage took on a very special and very limited meaning. It was as if the performers said to the audience: "This sentimental song we just sang about Ireland may bring tears to your eyes. But while the tears are real, the Ireland I sing about is not. And while we sing about returning, I am not returning, and neither are you. We sing these songs and tell these jokes because we are in America and because we are a certain kind of American."

Maggie Cline, who included a lot of Irish material in her act, had just finished "Don't Let Me Die Till I See Ireland," when a man in the gallery yelled, "Well, why don't you go there?" "Nit!" Cline called back, as she swaggered offstage. "It's too far from the Bowery."[36] Robert Snyder, in recounting this incident, suggests that it illustrates the limits to which performers could identify themselves and their acts with one ethnic group. Cline's rejoinder, however, could be taken as a fine bit of reality therapy. Reality for her, and for everyone in her audience, Irish and non-Irish, was out there on the streets of New York, not on some Emerald Isle of the imagination.

The ethnic stereotypes, which formed the basis for so much of the comedy, were another part of vaudeville's ritual of assimilation. "Stereotypes," Snyder suggests, "provided simple characteristics that roughly explained immigrants to native-born Americans and introduced immigrant Americans to each other."[37] But what did members of the various ethnic groups think as they looked into the distorted and comically cracked mirror held out to them from the stage?

David Grimsted has noted the tendency of the American working class to tolerate stereotypes of themselves as depicted in the nineteenth-century low-comedy theater. "Perhaps the amorphousness of American life made persons with no particular social status eager to watch characters who were simple, naive, and imperfect but who at bottom had a wealth of practical good sense and wholesome good sentiments. And the exaggeration of the stereotypes' naivete and quaintness enabled even the least sophisticated people in the audience to feel safely superior, comparatively worldly wise."[38]

Much depended on the amount of control or at least the extent of participation of the ethnic group in the rendition of its own stereotype. African Americans could have found little of themselves in the grotesque antics of white men in blackface, or, for that matter, black men playing white men in blackface. Irish comics onstage, however, could expect to play before Irish in the house. What, then, could Pat in the audience learn from the green-whiskered Paddy on the other side of the footlights?

A hint may be found in a brief comic bit that Pat Rooney *fils* did with his wife, Marion Bent. Although noted for their expert and elegant dancing, Rooney and Bent kept some of the traditional patter associated with the Irish couple performances. In one of their acts, Rooney would be in a workingman's costume while Bent would be dressed to the nines. At one point this exchange took place:

Rooney: What's your favorite stone?
Bent: Turquoise
Rooney: Mine's a brick.

Commenting on the passage, Snyder suggests the more obvious layers of humor involved in the joke: "For an Irishman with calloused hands, it was a wry confirmation of working life; for others, the difference between a hard-working man and an acquisitive woman; for non-Irishmen, a humorous look at how the other half lives."[39] The joke may have run deeper for the Irish in the audience than Snyder suggests, however. Rooney was playing with the Irish stereotype. Here was one of the best dancers of his day, a second generation theatrical success, accompanied by his beautiful, well-dressed wife, pretending to be a hod carrier, making a joke about a brick. Micks with bricks – the very rhyme found its way into dozens of songs. However, this was not the old stereotype of the redoubtable Paddy jigging about with his shillelagh, ready to take on all comers. This was the new American, industrial-strength Irish stereotype of the unskilled laborer who, like the hero of "Tim Finnegin's Wake," could *only* rise in the world be-

cause he carried a hod. This was where stereotype and reality merged. Some Irish did rise, of course, and for those Irish, Rooney's joke invited a self-satisfied glance back over the hard path they had traversed to whatever success they (or their parents) had achieved. For the mick whose only stone really was a brick, however, whose whole universe was a brick, who would be buried, figuratively, by a brick, the joke approached gallows humor. Under such circumstances, was laughter at Rooney's joke an assent to self-loathing, or a psychological smashing of the brick – a liberation from the brickyard of the soul?

Of course, laughter at one's stereotype was not initially laughter at one-self. J. S. Bratton asserts that humor "can be used most effectively in a disturbed and fragmented society to preserve community of feeling by laughing at things together, and to defend individuals against confusion and disintegrating pressures by uniting them with their fellows and attacking outsiders."[40] One began, then, laughing at one's neighbors, at one's surroundings, at the situation one was in, and only then, by an act of inclusion in the community of sufferers, at oneself.

On the connection between suffering and humor, David Krause maintains, "Ironically and necessarily . . . the awareness of one's misery, one's original sin, precedes and provokes the most antic comedy." In his study of the Irish comic style, Krause observes, "Unlike the form of most works that pass by the name of comedy, the mainstream of Irish comedy is non-corrective and nonromantic. Irish comedy does not reform its outrageous clowns or allow them to live happily ever after." Certain aspects of this Irish comedy seem to have found their way into vaudeville, where a kind of toughness and resilience emerged in the stage-Irish character during the late nineteenth century. Often depicted as a fool, he also could be what Krause calls "a resourceful clown," who is "a formidable figure . . . nimble and cunning."[41] It was this kind of figure who could embrace the brick with all its varied layers of meaning.

Finally, we must recognize that laughing at one's stereotype was part of the process of assimilation. David Doyle has noted "the fashion in which Irish emigrants seem to have been ready to caricature their own past, and to mock incoming 'greenhorns,' by exaggerating the outlandish or the peculiar." He suggests that this apparent acceptance of Paddy-Whackery "seems to bespeak a certain good humored readiness to change. . . . They abandoned or caricatured gently what could mean little to them anymore."[42] This did not mean, however, that one ceased to be Irish. It meant that one had to find an Irish identity that was compatible with being an American.

In the stereotype of the stage Irishman as presented in vaudeville sketches and in songs, the Irish found a transitional figure who could help them link their Irish and American identities.

7. The Irish American in Post–Civil War Song

In the process of being adapted to vaudeville and its song styles, the character of the stage Irishman evolved into the stereotype of the Irish American. Admittedly, the American Pat was often merely the old Paddy dressed up in the garb of an urban workingman. Nevertheless, even this adaptation was important for three reasons. First, it suggested an *American* ethnic type who was part of the urban scene, in contrast to a transplanted European peasant trying to adjust to an alien environment. Second, the transition from Paddy to Pat implied that some of the stereotypical traits identified with the Irish peasant would be inherited by his urban children. That is, there was such a thing as "Irishness" that survived even in the American-born generations; an idea accepted by Irish and non-Irish alike, although for different reasons. Finally, the Irish and Irish Americans on the stage and in the audience, writing as well as buying songs, participated in the negotiation and even manipulation of their own stereotype. The result was a transitional figure, a character that, while still reflecting some of the old Anglo-American prejudices, also began to take on characteristics with which the Irish immigrant community could identify.

The basic elements of this more positive image can be seen gradually taking shape in vaudeville songs from the 1870s into the 1890s. Moreover, for all of the antic comedy that surround these songs, the comic songs of the Gilded Age reflected, no matter how grotesquely, part of the reality of the life of the urban Irish. It is this limited connection between vaudeville comedy and reality that helps to account for the willingness of many Irish Americans of the period to accept the comic Irish songs as part of their entertainment.

The evolution of the Irish-American stereotype was closely tied to the increase in comic Irish songs in the post–Civil War period. From 13 percent of the songs in the sample published before the war, comic songs grow to 23 percent in the 1860s, 30 percent in the 1870s, and remain at an average of 36 percent in the samples for the 1880s and 1890s. Many of these songs are set in urban America. In the 1870s, the American city is the setting for 25 percent of all of the songs in the sample, a situation rare before the Civil War. In the 1880s and 1890s, half of the songs, many of them comic, are about urban Irish Americans.

It is these songs that document most clearly the Americanization of the Irish stereotype. Still full of blarneying, blundering, fighting and whiskey, Paddy gradually sheds his knee breeches and peasant ways to take on the trowsers, vest, and derby of the urban workingman or the coat and top hat of the "solid man" on the rise. Indeed, most of these comic songs are about men. In spite of the many magazine cartoons and the comic parts in vaudeville sketches and plays for "Bridget," Paddy's female counterpart has only a minor role in the comic songs. There are a few comic widows and a few heroines of the social *faux pas*, such as Mistress Murphy, the inadvertent perpetrator of the pants-in-soup incident chronicled in "Who Threw the Overalls in Mistress Murphy's Chowder?" (1898). There are also some comic songs given over to Irish-American girls, such as "Biddy, the Ballet Girl" and "Bridget Maguire, the Typewriter Girl." For the most part, however, the comic business belongs to Pat. He increased his appearance in comic songs from 42 percent in the antebellum sample to around 60 percent in the 1860s and 1870s to reach a peak of 88 percent in the 1880s.

We can see this process at work by looking at the names used in the song titles in the sample. The proportion of titles with Irish names grew moderately after the Civil War; from around 44 percent before the war to an average of 52 percent afterward. From the antebellum period through the 1860s, around 66 percent of the names in the titles were feminine. In the 1870s, male and female names were about evenly balanced. Then in the 1880s, males suddenly predominate, appearing in 66 percent of the titles using names, with the proportion dropping to 53 percent in the 1890s.

Simultaneously, there is also a shift in the titles away from first names toward the use of Irish surnames, anglicized versions of Gaelic patronymics. In the 1880s and 1890s, over 80 percent of the titles with names used either full names ("Roderick O'Dwyer") or, most often, just the surname by itself ("Swim Out O'Grady"). This replacement of first names in song titles with the Gaelic patronymic correlates with the increasing prominence of the comic Irish song. Before 1860, only 20 percent of the songs with names in the title were comic. This changed to 35 percent in the 1860s and 1870s, and almost 60 percent in the 1880s, declining to 47 percent in the 1890s.

In effect the Gaelic surnames became a sort of advertisement for comedy. Songs with titles such as "Mike McCarthy's Wake," "McGonigle's Led Astray," "Reagan's Evening Out," "Let Her Go Gallagher," "Murphy's Boarding House," and any song featuring the name "McGinty" carried the promise of comedy. This, coupled with the dramatic shift in the titles away from feminine to masculine names, leads to the inescapable conclusion that during the Gilded Age in vaudeville and in popular songs the Irish male was a comic figure.[1] Only African Americans suffered from a more demeaning stereotype.

There was much greater scope for material in comic pieces than in songs about love, emigration, or Irish patriotism. Although many of the comic songs ran to formula, there was still room in the comic format for passing commentary on a wide variety of topics. Therefore, we find expressions of Irish pride as well as satires on Irish economic mobility in the comic songs of the late nineteenth century. In this chapter we will look at examples of vaudeville songs about work, success, the police and politicians, Irish fighting and drinking, but also Irish fun and geniality.

DRILL, YE TARRIERS, DRILL

Given the working-class orientation of the Irish stereotype in vaudeville, it is not surprising to find occasional comic songs on the subject of work, or the denial of work. For example, in "No Irish Need Apply" (ca. 1860) an Irish immigrant inquires after a job, in spite of the employer's notice that Irish are not wanted. When the Yankee reiterates his anti-Hibernian policy, Paddy feels his "dandher rising."

> I couldn't stand it longer; so, a hoult of him I took,
> And I gave him such a welting as he'd get at Donnybrook.
> He hollered: Millia murther! and to get away did try,
> And swore he'd never write again: No Irish need apply.
> He made a big apology; I bid him thin good-bye,
> Saying: Whin next you want a bating, add: No Irish need apply.

Unperturbed that in turning to violence he has acted according to type, our hero philosophizes:

> Sure, I've heard that in America it always is the plan
> That an Irishman is just as good as any other man;
> A home and hospitality they ne'er will deny
> The stranger here, or ever say: "No Irish need apply."
> But some black sheep are in the flock: a dirty lot, say I;
> A dacint man will never write: No Irish need apply!

Although in the comic vein, Thomas J. Curran suggests that this type of song actually reflected a new sense of confidence among the Irish after the Civil War, as those who began to move up the economic ladder felt they could voice their resentment toward anti-Irish sentiment.[2]

Generally, for a song about workingmen to get into sheet music, there had to be a strong comic hook, be it ever so gruesome. Some songs made grim jokes out of the real-life dangers encountered on the job, as in Thomas Casey's "Drill Ye Tarriers, Drill" (1888). The song tells about Big Jim Goff, who is blown high in the air when a blast goes off prematurely.

> When pay day next it came around,
> Poor Jim's pay a dollar short he found,
> "What for?" says he, then came this reply,
> "You were docked for the time you were up in the sky."

"Poor O'Hoolahan" (1898) chronicles the gradual deterioration of another "tarrier," the poor mick who got to hold the fuse when blasting time came round: "I'll bet yer he lost his nose! Poor O'Hoolahan, / I'll bet yer he lost his toes! poor O'Hoolahan."[3]

Such comic songs offered a grimly humorous perspective on a basic realty in the lives of Irish laborers. As one Irishman noted at the time: "How often do we see such paragraphs in the paper, as an Irishman drowned – an Irishman crushed by a beam – an Irishman suffocated in a pit – an Irishman blown to atoms by a steam engine . . . and other like casualties and perils to which honest Pat is constantly exposed, in the hard toils for his daily bread."[4]

THE SOLID MAN

Some of the songs of the 1870s and 1880s, while still in the comic vein, voiced pride in the fact that the Irish working class was getting ahead, as in "It's the Irish, You Know" (1885).

> On St. Patrick's Day we parade,
>> And work every day at our trade,
> At carrying the hod, turning the sod,
>> And find in the end it has paid.

J. J. O'Grady combined satire with an acknowledgment of Irish success in "The Men Who Come Over from Ireland" (1896).

> If you listen a while, I will try to explain, of
>> The Men Who Come Over From Ireland;
> They are not often wealthy, the truth I'll maintain,
>> When the men first come over from Ireland;

They come to this country with only their fare,
       But soon of America's wealth they've a share,
Then they work like a horse 'till they're in with the Mayor,
       The Men Who Come Over From Ireland.[5]

Other songs focused on the "mick on the make" – the Irish workingman who became a foreman, a policeman, or a politician. These were the "solid men" who were making a name for themselves and for their people. One of Edward Harrigan's most popular songs was "Muldoon, the Solid Man." Another song in the same vein is "Dan Maloney Is the Man," circa 1880.

Sure he is no day laborer, his debts he'll always pay,
He hires all his men himself at five dollars a day;
Now when the politicians they need a helping hand,
They send for Dan, for well they know,
Dan Maloney is the man.

In the same ambitious vain is J. P. Skelly's "The Gintleman from Kildare" (1879), who proclaims, "Now I'm going into politics and swell my reputation." Once in Congress, "I'll be a friend to all the boys, They'll always find me square."[6]

Songs about the rising Irish usually teetered between the expression of pride and satire. In 1883 Pat Rooney published the very popular "Is That Mr. Reilly?" The song's chorus praised the "Mr. Reilly they speak of so highly." The verses present an outrageous spoof on Paddy ambition, which, nevertheless, probably struck a responsive chord among the Irish in Rooney's audience.

I'll have nothing but Irishman on the police
       Patrick's Day will be the Fourth of July;
I'll get me a thousand infernal machines,
       To teach the Chinese how to die,
I'll defend working men's cause, Manufacture the laws,
       New York would be swimming in wine,
A hundred a day will be very small pay
       When the White House and Capitol are mine.[7]

COPPERS

One way up the ladder was to join "the force." However, while a job behind the copper shield was one way out of immigrant poverty, it was not necessarily a path to respectability; at least not until police reform professionalized the force. Ned Harrigan's "Are You There Moriarty?" (1876) presents the happy, charming Irish cop, "quick witted, always ready to welcome you with joy," whose primary interest lies in charming the ladies rather than in catching criminals.[8]

Unfortunately, there were stronger temptations than the opposite sex to take a policeman's mind off his work. In New York City at mid-century a policeman might have earned $500 a year, out of which he had to pay $40 to his precinct captain and from $150 to $200 to the politician who got him the job. In 1899, an Albany commission, looking back over the past half century, concluded that "the New York police force was . . . an association of criminals who each paid for their posts and received in return carte blanche to plunder the people in any fashion their ingenuity could devise."[9]

We find the idea of using the policeman's beat as a springboard for something better in "McGinty, the Ladies' Pride" (1889). Officer McGinty, who got his job through political pull, claims:

> I'm fond of my work and I love my profession,
>   but soon I am going to retire.
> Then I'll get an office, a paying position,
>   And out in my carriage, with coachman I'll ride.
> A blue blood I'll be, with a fine pedigree,
>   and in a big house I'll reside.[10]

During the latter half of the nineteenth century, the Irish dominated New York City's police force. The close ties between the Irish cops and the Irish pols was long an open joke, belatedly immortalized in the song "Tammany" by Vincent Bryan and Gus Edwards (1907), one verse of which begins, "Fifteen thousand Irishmen from Erin came across, / Tammany put these Irish Indians on the Police force," and concludes, "Tammany, Tammany, your policemen can't be beat, / They can sleep on any street."[11]

Looked down upon by the middle and upper classes, whose property and sense of propriety they were supposed to protect, the police were not always highly regarded even within their own working-class communities. When Pat puts on the copper shield in "He's On the Police Force Now" (1890), the singer comments, "I hear he has stopped drinking, but I know he has stopped thinking, / He's on the police force now." Another vaudeville song, "Oh, Gilhooley You're a Lad!" by Harry Burns portrays a "sacret savrice offussur" who seems to have turned his part of the force into a branch of organized crime. "My min they hev a faro bank, On the corner of Siventh and Pinn, / Just give three taps upon the dure, The byes will let you in."[12]

In cities like New York, Boston, and Chicago, politics eventually became one of the surest ladders out of working-class poverty for the Irish. Commenting on Tammany boss George Washington Plunkitt's theories of *real politique*, urban style, Arthur Mann notes, "Tammany was equal to the Catholic Church's hierarchy as an engine of social mobility for gifted, ambitious Irish-Americans." In both institutions careers were open to talent. Plunkitt was one of the last of the great old-time Irish bosses within the Tammany system. From his dais on Graziano's boot-black stand in the old New York County Court House, Plunkitt ran his barony and, when the spirit moved him, conducted a pro-seminar on urban political science for the benefit of William L. Riordon, a fellow Irish American and a journalist. Plunkitt's explanation of the connection between Tammany and the immigrants of New York City, especially the Irish, is breathtaking in its clarity and candor. Concerning the gratitude an Irish immigrant would show to his new hometown, Plunkitt explained, "his friends here often have a good place in one of the city departments picked out for him while he is still in the old country. Is it any wonder that he has a tender spot in his heart for old New York when he is on its salary list the mornin' after he lands?" Plunkitt is best remembered for his Solomon-like ability to distinguish between dishonest and honest graft. The former involved outright theft, such as embezzlement of funds; this he deplored. The latter consisted of "opportunities" and as Plunkitt suggested for his own epitaph: "He Seen His Opportunities, and He Took 'Em."[13]

Many lesser lights also found or hoped to find opportunities in politics. The hero of "When Our Dinner Hour Comes 'Round" (1888) dreams of a successful career in politics, and, in the process, defines the meaning of success in immigrant terms. Once he becomes mayor, our hero predicts:

> And then I'll shine in judicial line,
>   Wid men of great renown,
> In a brown stone flat and a high plug hat,
>   You bet I'll own the town.[14]

In a vaudeville song by Tim Rogers, Mike McNally, "The Sound Democrat," brags:

I own the Eighth Ward and population,
　　My influence there they are very great,
The people say at the next election
　　They will put me up for candidate.[15]

In New York City, a seat on the Board of Aldermen was akin to a being handed a blank check, drawn upon the taxpayer. (Not for nothing was the city's Common Council known in the 1850s as the Forty Thieves.) In Edward Harrigan's *The Mulligan Nominee* (1880), Dan Mulligan seeks a seat on this august body. In the song "Oh, He Promises," Harrigan paints the easy path to political rewards as Dan harangues his followers.

I promise you employment, But you must keep it dark;
I'll have you count the sparrows, boys, Flying in Central Park.

CHORUS

He promises, he promises, bold Daniel Mulligan,
Ye'll all be sure of a sinecure from our next alderman;
He promises, he promises, he never told a lie;
We'll live at ease, do as we please and labor we'll defy.

In the play, Mulligan entertains the board with whiskey; too much, as it turns out. "Whatever will I do," Dan's wife, Cordelia, laments, "The Aldermen are all sound asleep." Dan's response must have brought down the house. "Lave them be. While they sleep, the city's safe."[16]

There were occasional hazards for playing fast and loose with the city's funds. In "McGonigle's Led Astray" (1883), a ward heeler ends up in the penitentiary for trying to rig an election. In "Reagan's Evening Out" (1883), the protagonist tends bar "where all our city's laws are made." He promises:

And when I'm nominated, You'll all be finely treated,
　　Just let me get a start and watch me sprout.
You'll never say I blundered, For the city's brave one hundred
　　[a reform group],
Might put me where I'll have no evening out.[17]

Even for those who were too free and easy with the public purse, there was a residue of affection from poor New Yorkers who benefitted from a highly inefficient and corrupt process that was, nonetheless, the nearest thing urban America had to a welfare system. "The Hodman's Lament" memorializes Boss Tweed: "Tho' you robbed the rich you fed the poor, And never acted mean" and hails him as "poverty's best screen."[18]

Harrigan provided one of the best portraits in song of the Irish political boss in "Old Boss Barry" from *Waddy Googan* (1888).

> There's a quiet little room at the back of a saloon
> That stands on the top of Cherry Hill,
> Where the men from the tenement hold lengthy arguments
> On every thing besides the liquor bill.
> The owner of the place has a Conamara [*sic*] face,
> A leader, you hear me, thru and thru,
> When he comes in the door, we all bow to the floor
> With Old Boss Barry, how d'ye do.
> Then the men fall in line, round about election time,
> Yes, all from the top of Cherry Hill,
> Sure it's he could colonize and really parnallize,
> The party that would vote against his will.[19]

By the 1870s the association of shady politics with the Irish was already so ingrained in American popular culture that when a songwriter named A. G. Weeks sought to attack women's suffrage by suggesting that political wives would simply become the pawns of shiftless working-class husbands, he cast his satire in an Irish dialect. Writing under the pseudonym of Dennis McFlinn, Weeks produced "Rights of Ladies" in 1876. Looking forward to coed politics, the singer dreams of his life as the husband of an office holder.

> Wid four or five dollars a day
> It's meself twould vote to elect her
> An put in me pocket the pay.
>
> . . . . . .
>
> An' whin all the votin' is over,
> An' Biddy's elected, shure thin
> I'll live like a pig in clover
> Wid Honorable Misses McFlinn.[20]

TO RISE IN THE WORLD

Ye can find them now in public life, in private life as well,
Ye can find them raising buildings, ye can find them raising hell.[21]

Comic songs about contractors, police, and politicians were only part of vaudeville's satire of urban Irish types. Those Irish reaching for middle-class respectability were also considered fair game. Andrew Greeley has argued that there was a steady growth in the Irish middle class from 1865 to 1895, but it barely kept pace with the arrival of more immigrants who reinforced Irish poverty. Yet, when measured by the situation in which the Famine immigrants had found themselves upon arrival, they, and those who followed them, did better than is often realized. Many men and women arrived as adolescents with little in the way of money or skills. While striving for economic independence, a family, and a home, they sent money back to Ireland, and, simultaneously, supported the creation of an extensive urban Catholic infrastructure of schools and hospitals. In spite of these burdens, some were able to move into the middle class.[22]

Although the spectacle of a growing Irish middle class generated the inevitable Yankee sneers, Irish-American songwriters and performers exploited the theme as well. As we will see, Ned Harrigan made the rising Paddy the centerpiece of several of his plays. In the 1880s, satirical songs about Irishmen trying to climb their way up the social ladder accounted for a third of the comic songs in the sample.

Much of this satire was aimed at the working-class family attempting to put on airs, as in C. F. Horn's "Miss Mulligan's Home Made Pie" (1885).

> As I sat at my rosewood peanny one day,
> > Making chords that were solemn and grand,
> Mr. Mulligan's footman came over the way,
> > With a big billy doo in his hand.
> As a neighbor and friend I was asked to attend,
> > A party at Mulligan's social and high,
> And I found by the way 'twas the very first day,
> > That Miss Mulligan tried to bake homemade pie.

The pie, once the crust is chiseled off, turns out to be a disaster.

> Mr. Fogarty tumbled and groaned on the floar,
> > With the pleurissy pains in his chest,
> Maloney cried out, "I don't want any more,"
> > As he tried to unbutton his vest,
> John Michael Dupree kept calling to me,
> > "Gilhooly I'll lave you my debts if I die,"
> While Gerald McCann said he pitied the man,
> > Who would marry that girl and her homemade pie.[23]

This formula, the Irish party that ends in chaos, is most assiduously applied to those situations when Pat throws a party to celebrate a successful step up the socioeconomic ladder: a move to a new flat, a promotion, or election as alderman or state senator. Even something as simple and domestic as a christening could lead to a debacle, as does "Mrs. McCarthy's Party" (1888), where the progression is from supper to dancing to whiskey to fighting.

> They fought 'till they were tired,
> And poor Patsy Flynn was fired
> Through the parlor window out into the street;
> Delia Clancy's nose was broken,
> And Pat Ryan was a-chokling
> Tom Grady who was stretched out at his feet.[24]

Any attempt by an Irishman in a song to ape the ways of his betters causes trouble. In "There Goes McManus" (1889), the hero goes to a ball in pants he rented from a Jewish tailor. The pants split and the enraged McManus returns to beat up the tailor. Hauled into court, he must pay a fine because "he tried to be a swell." The lesson in "Learning McFadden to Waltz" (1890) is a cruel one for his partner. "Sure, the poor girl went round for two weeks on crutches" for trying to teach the bricklayer how to dance. Opening night at "Casey's Social Club," by Ned Harrigan, starts out with dances but ends in a riot when Casey falls into the spittoon and starts a fight.[25]

The willingness of Irish Americans to be entertained by these satires may be evidence of class tensions within the Irish community. They may represent a reverse class bias – working-class suspicion of rising too far, too fast; of embracing the lace curtain at the expense of community values.

THE IRISH JUBILEE

A common feature of many of the comic songs was a propensity toward exuberance, exaggeration, and excess, not merely in terms of drink and violence, but as exhibited by incessant rhymed lists of names, dances, and food. Songwriters exploited the easy way they could rhyme Irish names, although few went beyond the heroic efforts of "John James O'Reilly" by Flora Moore (1890). The occasion of a wedding produced the inevitable guest list: "They'll be the Casey's, and the Tracy's, the Clancey's, DeLacy's / Hoolihans, Monahans all will be there."[26]

"The Irish Jubilee" (1890) describes a mammoth wingding to celebrate the rise of a local Tammany politico. When Doherty is elected to the Senate, he decides to celebrate. He throws a banquet, sending out invitations in twenty different languages. The feast would have staggered Pantagruel.

> There was pigsheads and goldfish, mocking birds and ostriches,
> Ice cream, cold cream, vaseline sandwiches
> Blue fish, green fish, fish heads and partridges,
>
> . . . . . .
>
> Red herrings, smoked herrings, herring from Old Erin's Isle,
> Bologna and fruit cake, and sausages a half mile.[27]

Other songs like "Mullaly's Groc'ry Bill" (1897), "The Irish Christening" (1877), and "McCarthy's Boarding House" (1878), consisted of little more than rhyming lists of foods and/or names.

For many immigrants this indiscriminate mixture and superabundance of foods was part of what America was about. However, these songs also suggest something else. According to Mark Slobin, similar material appeared in Yiddish popular songs published in New York a decade or so later, reflecting a fascination in mixing vast quantities of American and European foods – ice cream with *kreplach*, for example. In Slobin's view, however, the "linguistic variety and hyperbole [in these songs], along with cultural excess, reflect the disarray of immigrant life."[28] To some immigrants, American abundance, which was often something that they might see but not touch, was fascinating but also grotesque. By associating a people of poverty, such as the Irish, with these rhymed catalogs of excess, songwriters were exploiting the anarchy implicit in immigrant dreams as well as immigrant life.

ROWS AND RUCTIONS

The alleged propensity of the Irish for violence was an increasing feature of the comic Irish songs until the very end of the nineteenth century. While references to fighting appear in only 2 percent of the antebellum songs in the sample, the proportion rose to an average of 9 percent in the 1860s and 1870s and jumped to 18 percent in the 1880s, before declining to 10 percent in the 1890s. This incidence of violence in songs is a direct result of the increase in the number of comic Irish songs after the Civil War. In the 1880s, 38 percent of the comic songs about the Irish made reference to fighting.

Perhaps the most outrageous example in song is "The Irish Spree" (ca. 1880). The song depicts an Irish gang breaking up a bar.

Smash went the windows, and smash went the furniture,
Then on the fire we put it for to burn it sure!
Then in the bar we turn'd the rum and whisky on,
That's what the boys and the girls got so frisky on;

The arrival of the police only supplies cannon fodder for the rioters.

Privates, Detectives, Sergeants, and more of them.
They were no use for soon we had the best of them;
When they went down we danc'd on ev'ry chest of them;

The narrator brags that "We left sixty dead upon the floor, we did." While there are plenty of Donnybrooks depicted in songs of the period, none of them come close to "The Irish Spree" for sheer ferocity.[29]

More typical is "Reagan's Evening Out" (1883).

Then up jumped Shamus Mooney, And made a pass at Rooney
    And hit old Owney Flynn a fearful clout.
This angered and it vexed me, And many a head next day
    Bore witness that 'twas Reagan's evening out.

Some songs reflected the Irish workingman's violent reaction to unwelcome (and un-Irish) intrusions into the family circle. William J. Scanlan's "If I Catch the Man" (1882) expresses the father's instinctive reaction when a daughter takes up dancing.

If I catch the man who taught her to dance,
    The la-de-da dance, the tra-la-la-dance,
On top of his nose I'll make my fist prance
    And the twist of the both of his legs, ha ha.[30]

Sometimes Pat was the hapless victim of the random violence of the universe, as depicted in "Down Went McGinty" by Joseph Flynn (1889), and introduced in the minstrel travesty, "McGinty in Town" by the Carncross minstrel troop in 1889. Dan McGinty bets five dollars that Pat McCann cannot carry him up to the top of a high wall. When it appears that Pat can scale the ladder easily enough, McGinty, to win the bet lets go, "Never thinking just how far he'd have to drop."

Down went McGinty to the bottom of the wall,
    And tho' he won the five, He was more dead than alive,
Sure his ribs, and nose, and back were broke from getting such a fall,
    Dress'd in his best suit of clothes.

At the end of the song, the hapless McGinty drowns himself and his ghost haunts the docks, "Dress'd in his best suit of clothes." However, in the answer song, "McGinty's Wake" (1889), the ghost has to fight to preserve McGinty's famous suit from thieves, seeking to rob the corpse. There was a flood of "McGinty" songs, the ultimate answer to which was "I'll Paralyze the Man That Says McGinty" (1890). The singer, tired of reports that McGinty has been found, resorts to violence.

> Yor oughter seen me lick him, And stick him and kick him,
> Yor oughter seen me grab him, And stab him to the floor.
> I'll stand a joke of any kind, no matter what it be,
> But I'll paralyze the Man that Says McGinty.

The cover shows a simian-faced Paddy brandishing an axe and gun.[31]

In an era when most prizefighters were Irish, another popular song about Irish pugnacity was John W. Kelly's "Throw Him Down, M'Closkey" (1890). A prize fight is arranged between an African American and the Irish champion, M'Closkey. However, just prior to the match, the black man decides that he might not get fair treatment in an Irish ward and so declines the honor. McCracken volunteers to step in to take his place, providing M'Closkey does not bite, which, of course, he does.

> The friends of both the fighters that instant did begin
> To fight and ate each other the whole party started in,
> You couldn't tell the diff'rence in the fighters if you'd try,
> McCracken lost his upper lip, M'Closkey lost an eye.

The chorus made the song famous.

> "Throw him down M'Closkey" was to be the battle cry,
>   "Throw him down M'Closkey," you can lick him if you try,
> And future generations, with wonder and delight,
> Will read on hist'ry's pages of the great M'Closkey fight.

Maggie Cline bought the song from Kelly for two dollars and made it one of her specialties. She would cue the stagehands to throw down bricks, sandbags, or anything at hand every time she sang the line, "Throw him down M'Closkey." The stagehands grew weary as Maggie went back out onstage for encore after encore. When Maggie sang the song in bars, the patrons obliged by throwing their mugs and glasses to the floor.[32]

For political purposes, anti-Irish publications, such as *Puck*, with its cartoonist Thomas Nast, exploited the association of the Irish with violence.

Indeed, the image of the fighting Irish permeated American popular culture. Although the depiction of Irish violence and the culture's attitude toward it would change over the years, to this day the phrase "to get your Irish up" refers to a temper rapidly approaching the boiling point. By the 1870s, Americans associated Irish violence with Fenian revolutionaries, Molly Maguire–type labor strife, urban crime, and urban riots, such as the Orange parade battle in New York City in 1871 that left thirty-three dead and ninety-one wounded.[33] Not for nothing was the police van of the day called a "paddy wagon," a peculiar vehicle in which Paddies as cops hauled off to jail Paddies picked up as drunks and brawlers.

Such violence must be seen in the context of urban poverty. In New York City and Boston, the poorest Irish were part of an urban underclass crowded together in the worst slums in American history. Only the Irish squatters in sections of Harlem and what is now Central Park escaped the tenements by reinstating in New York City something like the traditional medieval Irish clahan. Charles Dickens, visiting the tenements of Five Points in the Sixth Ward, described a nightmarish scene: "Where dogs would howl to lie men and women and boys slink off to sleep, forcing the dislodged rats to move away in quest of better lodgings. . . . all that is loathsome, drooping and decay is here." At the time of the Civil War, Five Points held 3,435 Irish families. The next largest ethnic group, the Italians, numbered only 416 families. Conditions in the American slums were terrible and the physical and mental health of those in them deteriorated. In 1850, 85 percent of those admitted to Bellevue Hospital in New York City were Irish born. In 1858, of 2,000 prostitutes in Penitentiary Hospital, 706 had been born in Ireland.[34]

In the slums, only crime seemed to flourish. As early as the 1820s, the Sixth Ward in New York City had already earned its name, "Bloody Ould Sixth." Many of its gangs, such as the Kerryonians, the Plug Uglies, the Roach Guards, and the Shirt Tails, were Irish. The Bowery gangs consisted of employed workers and artisans who followed the fire wagons and provided muscle when needed for their political patrons. According to Luc Sante, however, the Irish gangs of the Sixth represented the true underclass.[35]

Over the decades, other ethnic gangs formed in the city, but even in the late nineteenth century the Irish gangs were still prominent. The Irish make up of the Whyos in the 1880s is evident in the roster of its members: Hoggy Walsh, Fig McGerald, Bill Hurley, Googy Corcoran, Baboon Connolly, Slops Connolly, Dorsey Doyle, Red Rocks Ferrell, and Piker Ryan. It was on Piker Ryan that the police found the gang's rate sheet for jobs, ranging from two dollars for a simple punch, to fifteen dollars for chewing off an ear, to one hundred dollars and up for "Doing the big job." One of the gang, Dandy Johnny Dolan, was particularly admired by his peers for his invention of a copper eye gouger, designed to be worn on the thumb, and for imbedding sharp axe blades in the soles of his fighting boots. In 1887, Dr. P. O'Connell of Chicago lamented to Archbishop Croke of Cashel, "Let who will scan the dockets of our police courts and he shall see no end of Irish Names." When looked at from the bottom up, the violence described in "The Irish Spree" seems no more exaggerated than what might have appeared on a police blotter of the period.[36]

THE CREATURE

The most conspicuous characteristic of the Irish stereotype was the consumption of alcohol. The stereotype of the drunken Paddy was so all-pervasive that when the *New York Times* reported that one hundred thousand Irish had taken the pledge at a temperance gathering in 1890, the reporter noted that *few looked Irish;* "all looked like substantial American citizens." In the twentieth century, the association of Irish with alcoholism has been so accepted by sociologists that Andrew Greeley asserts that it represents an anti-Irish bias among some researchers.[37] Even today, drink and Irishness are still standard items in comedians' repertories. In 1992, television comic Mark Russell, commenting on the attempt of gays to march in New York City's St. Patrick's Day parade, suggested that the combination of homosexuality and Irishness must be heavy ethnic burdens. "What do they do?" Russell asked, "stagger out of the closet?"

As with fighting, the association of the Irish with drinking increased in the songs until the 1890s. The proportion of songs in the sample containing references to drinking increase from 9 percent before the 1860s to 15 percent in the 1870s and to 24 percent in the 1880s. Again, many of the references to drinking occur in comic songs, although the situations presented in some of the songs hardly seem funny in our more sensitive age. Although intended as a comic piece, "Och! Paddy, Is It Yerself?" is unusual in that it represents the woman's point of view. The wife, dreaming that she is finally free of her drunken husband, awakes to reality as he stumbles in: "I knowed yer drunken footstep and yer rummy voice." Why, she wonders, did he come home?[38]

The hero of "Larry Mulligan" (1894) gets so drunk that his wife beats him up. Yet, by the end of the song "Larry Mulligan he is full again, Staggering along the street as happy as can be." In "McCarthy's Widow" (1887) the widow's newly acquired second husband boasts that he intends to get drunk and then tear the house apart to prove who's boss: "McCarthy wasn't hearty, Now she's got a different party, / Oh! she might have lick'd McCarthy, But she can't lick me." Will H. Barry's parody of "The Sidewalks of New York" depicts a night on the town:

> This side, that side, staggering 'round the town,
> We won't go home 'till morning, London bridge is falling down,
> Out on a bum together, me and Rummy Rouke,
> Slipped and spoiled our faces on the sidewalks of New York.[39]

Several songs, such as "Mick McCarthy's Wake" and "McGinty's Wake," repeat the old saw about the "corpse" who resurrects himself when the whiskey bottle is opened. While some of these songs seem to celebrate drunkenness, many carry the barbs of irony and satire that, as J. S. Bratton has observed, helped songwriters, performers, and audiences deal with topics and emotions, which, while common, might otherwise have been embarrassing.[40]

Ned Harrigan made frequent use of drinking in his sketches and songs. "The Mountain Dew" (from *The Blackbird*, 1882), a song in praise of *poitín*, became well known in Ireland and, having gone through the folk process, can still be heard there. In "Taking in the Town" (from *Reilly and the Four Hundred*, 1890), McGuinnes drinks so much whiskey during his visit to New York City that, when he turns on the gas, he is blown back out of town. "John Riley's Always Dry" (from *Mulligan's Silver Wedding*, 1881) deals with a peculiarly Hibernian phenomenon.

> His father often told him, When John was but a youth,
> That ev'ry mortal Riley, All died from whiskey drouth;
> Of course it is a failing, The poor man can't deny,
> 'Tis but a freak of nature, boys, John Riley's Always Dry.[41]

However, Harrigan also presented drinking as a kind of social sacrament within the Irish community, as in his song "The Pitcher of Beer" (from *The Mulligan Guard's Christmas*, 1880):

> Oh the child in the cradle, The dog at the door,
> The fires so cheerful and bright,
> Old folks at the table with plenty galore,
> For to welcome you in with delight,

Their blessings they give, it's "long my you live,
And so gaily glide o'er each year":
Then they hand you a glass for to let the toast pass.
And we drink from the pitcher of beer.[42]

From the hearthside, the communal warmth of alcohol spread out to the bars to envelop Irish-American male society, where it cemented the bond of both friendship and clientship. "Drinking with Daniel Maloney" by M. J. Cavanagh (1884), provides a glimpse of the "solid man" whose "heart and pocket's open to assist a fellow man. . . . Have the best on the bar, aither wine or cigar, When drinking with Daniel Maloney." William Scanlan's "Irish Potheen" (1882) points up the connection between drinking and friendship: "Should a friend I chance to meet, I never fail to treat; / To that sparkling drink the Irish call 'potheen.'"[43]

Denis Clark points out that operating illegal stills and drinking houses or "shebeens" was one of the few small business opportunities available to Catholics in the small villages and rural areas in Ireland. Moreover, Irish Catholics did not look down upon publicans, as did many Protestants. Back in Ireland, "successful pub keepers became the models of affluence and leadership in a land where only the priest had stood out among Catholics as a leadership figure." Getting into the saloon business in America seemed a natural step for many of those immigrants who could scrape up the money to invest in a couple of bottles of whiskey.[44]

As early as 1820 in Philadelphia, one-fifth of the liquor licenses granted that year by the Quarter Sessions Court went to those with recognizably Irish names. By the 1890s, the proportion was around one-third. In a city that, within living memory, suffered through "dry" Sundays, the Irish "drinking club" of Philadelphia must have been an especially welcome amenity. The situation in Worcester, Massachusetts, was even more striking. In the 1880s two-thirds of applicants for liquor licenses were Irish, although only one-third of the city's population was Irish. Moreover, while only one-sixth of the city's population had been born in Ireland, one half of 1880 saloon keepers were Irish born and another 10 percent were Irish Americans.[45]

The nineteenth-century saloon was a kind of social club for workingmen. Hull-House researcher Ernest C. Moore acknowledged the social value of the saloon, noting that it was often cleaner, warmer, and better appointed than the average patron's home. The better ones provided food, drink, entertainment, and companionship. Saloons also served as employment centers for Irish immigrants. Below the most minimal level of civilization, however, the saloon became a sink of vice and squalor. Some of the Irish bars of nineteenth-century New York City earned reputations as being the worst and most dangerous dives in the city. Among these were Billy McGlory's Armory Hall, Owney Geoghegan's Hurdy Gurdy on the Bowery (headquarters for Geoghegan's Gas House Gang), McMahon's Haymarket, Boiled Oysters Malloy's Ruins, Paddy Martin's Milligan's Hell, Diamond Dan O'Rourke's, and, worst of them all, McGurk's Suicide Hall, patrolled nightly by its bouncer Eat-'Em-Up Jack McManus.[46]

As we have seen, Irish songs of the Gilded Age presented two aspects of alcohol. In the urban Paddy songs it was the catalyst that set off the comically destructive "rows and ructions." But it was also depicted as an integral part of community life, both domestic and public. There is certainly nothing remarkable about songs celebrating the social aspects of drinking. Other ethnic groups, such as Germans and Italians, placed alcohol in the center of their culture as well. The Irish themselves, however, along with their critics, saw alcohol as a problem. Noting that the Irish outranked all other ethnic groups in arrests for drunkenness in nineteenth-century American cities, Richard Stivers has stated, " 'Irish' and 'drunkard' became synonymous in nineteenth-century America." In 1881, Henry C. Lea of Philadelphia published an anti-Irish satire as part of a campaign against municipal corruption. The book, *Solid for Mulhooly,* was republished in 1889 with cartoons by Thomas Nast. One, entitled "His Paddy-gree" shows baby Mulhooly in a pigsty, brandishing a bottle of whiskey. A 1911 cartoon in the Harvard *Lampoon* entitled "The Glorious 17th of March," showed a man stretched out on a couch, dead drunk.[47]

In his inquiry into the nature and cause of Irish drinking habits in nineteenth-century Ireland and America, Stivers looks at the Irish stereotype within the contexts of Irish and Irish-American culture: "My contention is that early in the nineteenth century a negative identity of drunkard was fostered upon the Irish by a cultural stereotype and related institutionalized practices. Later in the nineteenth century, however, the Irish stereotype converged around a more positive image of the Irish drunk – the 'happy drunk,' a stage caricature Irishman."

What had been a negative identity – drunkard – evolved into a positive group identity. In Andrew Greeley's words, "The happy Irish-American drunk has been imposed on the Irish Catholic culture in the United States every bit as much as the 'Stepin-Fetchit' stereotype has been imposed on black culture." Just in looking at the songs, it is clear that the happy Irish drunk was present from the days of Tyrone Power right through to the end of the century. However, the shift in emphasis from the Irish peasant to the Irish-American workingman gave the stereotype a greater impact within American popular culture.[48]

Stivers argues that in post-Famine Ireland, hard drinking among bachelor males was a form of "cultural remission." The male bonding through alcohol compensated for the inability of young men and old bachelors to be economically independent (no jobs, no farm), and, thus, unable to marry and to engage legitimately in sex. Male group drinking, therefore, helped to maintain the stability of a society characterized by unattached males with very limited horizons. When transplanted to America, the context of drinking shifted from maintaining a social system to proclaiming an ethnic identity. "In Ireland drink was largely a sign of male identity; in America it was a symbol of Irish identity." As such, drinking was no longer limited to males. It could, and did, involve the whole Irish-American community.[49]

As a result, the Irish in America during the last half of the nineteenth century may have drunk more than their countrymen who stayed at home. Elizabeth Malcolm suggests that the temperance movement had a much greater impact upon Ireland than the United States. Tracking per capita consumption of spirits, she notes that after 1860 Irish consumption declined. Slightly less than the rest of the United Kingdom, Irish consumption was only half the level of the United States in 1860. America's gradual decline in spirit consumption did not bring it down to Ireland's level until 1890. Malcolm points out that while some Irish drank a lot, many did not drink at all. Recent studies on Irish drinking habits at home and in England suggest there might have been a phenomenon of immigrant drinking that greatly exaggerated the more modest levels of consumption by the Irish at home.[50]

It is, therefore, possible that Irish-American drinking habits in the nineteenth century were more American than Irish. Yet, because the stereotype of the Irish American identified him with drink, drinking, according to Stivers, "made one more Irish; it distinguished one from other ethnic groups. Hence in the act of drinking, in the affirmation of a life-style, one was truly nationalistic. Ultimately drink – even more than it had in Ireland – acquired a spiritual value; it had become sacred."[51]

Unfortunately, as Stivers points out, the negative and positive aspects of the Irish stereotype regarding drink existed so closely together that the shift from one to the other was little more than a matter of context. Too often in real life, Pat of Harrigan's "The Pitcher of Beer" and Pat of "The Irish Spree" could be one and the same. The cup that cheered could turn into the berserker's potion. It is little wonder that Irish Americans called whiskey "the creature." Widow Nolan in Harrigan's *Squatter Sovereignty* (1882) kindly offers a tired Italian worker, Pedro, a drink of whiskey: "'twill do you good, hammering away at the last in the quarry. You need a drop of the *creature*."[52]

A MERRY PEOPLE

What was so insidious about the role of drink in the Irish-American stereotype was the close connection between drinking and those traits and behavior that define the positive side of the stereotype. Late nineteenth-century songs and vaudeville sketches depicted the Irish as a merry, uproarious group. "The Irish Wedding" (1872) suggests the sheer exuberance of this image: "Jumping, thumping, tittering, blathering, rollicking, frolicking, chocking with laughter and bursting with fun." As in so many songs, just reeling off the names of the celebrants suggests the merriment. Other songs depicted the raucous joy of an Irish party.

> We sing the whole night long, with voices loud and strong,
>   When Miss Maloney sings she is a howler;
> There's always lots of fun with glasses round each one,
>   When drinking out of Miss Maloney's growler.[53]

That things sometimes got out of hand did not necessarily have to spoil the fun.

> For that was the way with the Flaming O'Flannigans,
> They were the terrible boys of the name,
> For kissing, and courting, and filling the can agin',
> They were the boys for to keep up the game.[54]

The association in the songs of drinking, fighting, dancing, singing, and general exuberance with the Irish character grew steadily to reach a peak of 25 percent of the songs in the 1870s and 1880s. Even when reduced to a hard-luck tramp, the "happy" element of the Irish character seemed to shine through. "Happy Hooligan," a 1902 song based on Frederick Burr Opper's comic strip hobo, maintained the stereotypical attitude of the Irishman without aid of dialect or specific Irish references.

> He means to do good, but is misunderstood,
> He must have been born on a Friday!

Tho' chuck full of pluck, he plays in hard luck;
His face and his clothes are untidy.
So drink to this man, with glass or with CAN,
Poor Hooligan, lowly in station,
In appearance a sight, his heart seems all right
He's the happiest man in the nation.[55]

No pigs, mud, whiskey, or shillelagh; yet, Hooligan stands in direct line of descent from Tyrone Power's and John Brougham's happy, poverty-stricken Paddies of the pre–Civil War era.

Carried over from the stage Irishman to the stage Irish American, the resulting stereotype had a powerful influence, not only on the way the Yankees viewed the Irish but on the way the Irish in America viewed themselves. Witness the testimony of Dr. P. O'Connell of Chicago. In 1887 Dr. O'Connell wrote a long letter to Archbishop Croke of Cashel, urging him to take action to stop the latest wave of Irish emigration to America: "It is with poignant sorrow that I see the Irish once more rushing to the United States where they are fast going to rot." In the course of a long diatribe on the evils into which the poor Irish immigrants fall when they arrive in America, Dr. O'Connell relates the following incident in order to clinch his argument that they should stay in Ireland.

An Irish funeral party undertook to transport the body of their friend to the Roman Catholic cemetery in Peoria, Illinois. During the course of the journey, the mourners were too drunk to notice that, while crossing a muddy passage in the road, the coffin fell out of the wagon and rolled down the side of an embankment, where it then sunk into a ditch. The funeral party did not miss the coffin until the mourners had traveled some distance. Dismayed and disgruntled, bereft of both corpse and whiskey, the companions turned back, dreading the disgrace that would be heaped upon them when they returned home. As luck would have it, however, they soon encountered another funeral party, this one complete with a coffin, possession of which the first party immediately demanded. Upon being refused, they attacked. After a short battle, the first group won its prize, which they victoriously conveyed to Peoria and planted proudly in their comrade's grave. The original designee for that honor was not discovered until some months later, after the summer sun had done its work.[56]

Now, Dr. O'Connell, a man who does not seem to have been burdened with a great sense of humor, did not claim any firsthand knowledge of this incident. He tells his tale with great seriousness and with a proper sense of outrage. Nevertheless, one must wonder if the good doctor, in his deep concern for the morals of his less fortunate fellow Irish men and women, was not unwittingly repeating some early piece of urban folklore, more suited to the saloon or vaudeville stage than to high ecclesiastical correspondence. The story is a classic Paddy tale, wild, funny, and grotesque. The theme of the corpse that got left behind is well known in song and story. In "The Night that Paddy Murphy Died" the mourners leave the body in one of the many bars they visit en route to the cemetery; "And when we came to the graveyard, we found we'd left the corpse behind."[57]

Whether true or false, Dr. O'Connell's tale of the lost corpse is well within the tradition of Paddology – incredible blunders followed up with antic responses – and illustrates Paddy's appeal within the popular culture. Such escapades represent a momentary triumph of unreason, but also of uninhibited creativity, over the formal structures of society, thus subverting the sanctioned order of things. Mary Douglas reminds us that "whatever the joke, however remote its subject, the telling of it is potentially subversive. Since its form consists of a victorious tilting of uncontrol against control, it is an image of the levelling of hierarchy, the triumph of intimacy over formality, of unofficial values over official ones."[58] Perhaps Paddy's popularity in American culture was ultimately due to his power to demolish periodically the highly disciplined structures of the Anglo-Saxon's *Weltanschauung*, providing a momentary vision of an anarchy that was as bracing as it was frightening.

There is no way to tell whether Dr. O'Connell's story was true or not, and this is precisely the problem. The stereotype of the Irishman was so entangled with the reality of his life in America that even the most sympathetic observers might not easily have separated one from the other. There was great tragedy in this. An Irishman taking a drink, getting into a fight, or just generally having a high old time was not like other men who might drink, fight, or celebrate. He was acting an elaborately scripted role. He was fulfilling a grimly comic prophesy. He was playing the stereotype of *himself*.

For people living on the edge, selling the labor of their bodies on the cheap, surrounded by strangers, and often dying young, perhaps the difference between the stereotype and reality was somewhat blurred, perhaps, even unimportant. If one was to be a Paddy, condemned to a life on construction sites, down in mines, or in rolling mills, then being a hard-drinking, hard-fighting ladies man who was the life of the party offered a special glint to life. For such a person living on the edge, laughter was a special commodity, not so readily available that one would insist on academic scrutiny as to the correctness of its source.

The stereotype of the vaudeville Paddy did not look as bad from the working-class perspective as it did from that of the middle class. The Irish of the stereotype were funny and fun-loving, ready to sing and dance. The inner demons of drink and violence became mere foolishness and comedy onstage and in the songs. Moreover, for all of his continuity with the traditional anti-Irish stereotype imported from Britain, the stage Irishman had become an American. In the songs and vaudeville sketches, an Irish-American persona, which had not existed before the Civil War, was being born.

Therefore, while Catholic priests and concerned laity churned out stories and novels designed to protect the Irish immigrant from the temptations of Yankee materialism, and while the Irish-American newspapers strove to stoke the fires of Irish nationalism, the image of the Irish American was being cobbled together willy-nilly in songs and gags, sketches and dance routines, nightly in concert saloons, variety halls, and vaudeville houses all across the country. The results were by no means primarily negative. As we will see in the next chapter, in the hands of an artist such as Edward Harrigan, the stereotype could be molded to reveal the strengths and pride of the Irish urban community.

8. The Theater and Songs of Edward Harrigan

While many Irish songs of the late nineteenth century accentuated the more grotesque aspects of the Irish stereotype, a smaller proportion suggested the more positive qualities of Irishness: generosity, a sense of community, loyalty and courage, and a simple pride in being Irish. At least 11 percent of the songs in the 1860s and 1870s provide positive comments on Irish pride and on the Irish character. In the last two decades of the century, the proportion rose to about 16 percent. One person who was very effective in developing the more positive side of the Irish stereotype was Edward Harrigan of the team of Harrigan and Hart.

Ned Harrigan was born in 1844 on "Cork Row" in the Corlear's Hook section of New York's Lower East Side. His father, William, was second-generation Irish, the Harrigans having come from Cork by way of Newfoundland.[1] Growing up in New York City, Harrigan showed an early interest in music and performing. However, it was not until he found himself in San Francisco in 1867, after several years of following maritime jobs, that he began his theatrical career. The fact that he got his start as an entertainer in San Francisco might have been an important factor in the development of his brand of satire, which allowed him to make fun of the Irish while celebrating them. His satiric distance, as well as his own sense of ethnic confidence, may reflect the experience of the West-Coast Irish, who did not suffer from the discrimination and hostility encountered in the East. Without a ghetto mentality, they were able to cultivate a positive Irish identity within the context of San Francisco's developing cultural pluralism.[2]

Solo song and dance routines led Harrigan to try out various partners until he teamed up with young Anthony J. Cronin in Chicago in 1871. Cronin took the stage name of Tony Hart and remained Harrigan's partner until 1885. The team had their first big success at Tony Pastor's theater in New York City during the 1872–73 season. Although Hart specialized in skirt or "wench" parts, he appears to have been a good all-around comic performer, especially in Irish roles.

Of all of the performers associated with the comic stage Irishmen in nineteenth-century America, Harrigan and Hart were by far the most famous. Hart confined his talent to performing. Harrigan, however, was also a prolific writer. In addition to thirty-six major plays, there are records of some eighty sketches written between 1870 and 1879. Although Harrigan experimented with melodramas throughout his career, including several set in Ireland, he was at his best and most successful when he focused his comic genius on New York City. The city returned the favor; from the mid-1870s through the early 1890s, most of Harrigan's plays were very successful. Twenty-three of them ran for more than one hundred performances – an unprecedented achievement in those days.[3]

Both Harrigan and Hart played a variety of ethnic characters, including Irish, "Dutch," Italian, and blackface roles. The two performers created their acts out of a blend of minstrelsy, burlesque, and variety. Harrigan's most famous plays, the *Mulligan Guard* series, had their origin in a vaudeville sketch, first staged in July of 1873. Harrigan gradually expanded the scope of these musical plays to encompass much of urban, working-class New York. As the sketches developed into musical plays, Harrigan, along with Charles Hoyt, helped to develop the farce comedy so popular in the late nineteenth century. Harrigan's string of *Mulligan Guard* comedies was, however, unique, and several historians have cited them as forerunners of contemporary situation comedies.[4]

Carl Wittke once noted that in the exaggerated comic presentations of urban ethnic diversity after mid-century, "we have the beginnings of a certain realism in the American drama, for they were based on actual observation of life experiences." Harrigan's type of comedy, relying as it did on recognizable urban character types, was a part of this movement toward realism in the American theater. Nineteenth-century critic Cecil Smith recognized that Harrigan was among the first to attempt to present on the New York stage "quasi-realistic local color by employing as characters familiar Bowery figures, whose manners and locutions were fairly accurately produced . . . with broad satire and travesty."[5]

There were, of course, scores of performers doing ethnic, especially Irish, characterizations in the post–Civil War theater. What made Harrigan special, both as performer and writer, was his ability to appear to individualize the various stereotypes he brought to his theater. It was characters, not plots, that fascinated him. He once confessed, "I wish a fellow could make a play without a plot." While Harrigan's characters have more than a touch of caricature in them, "At the same time," suggests Gerald Bordman, "there was a truthfulness and compassion to Harrigan's portraits that constantly raised them above caricature and made them a rarity on contemporary stages."[6]

Harrigan, Hart, and many of their company went out of their way to model their characters on people whom they saw on the streets of New York. E. J. Kahn describes Harrigan at work, sitting on a park bench, taking notes on the passersby. "If some uncommonly appealing individual passed by – a tramp, say, or a minor politician – Harrigan would leap to his feet and take off after him, scribbling notes as he went." Harrigan, Hart, and members of their troop would even meet immigrants at Castle Garden. Looking for authentic additions to the company's wardrobe, they would literally buy a shirt off a man's back.[7] Harrigan and Hart's comic blending of ethnic stereotypes – African Americans, Jews, Italians, and Chinese, as well as Irish – with individualized characterizations taken from the city streets, gave life and vitality to their performances. Harrigan once said, "I have sought above all to make my plays like pages from actual life." When he built his own theater, Harrigan had inscribed on one of the walls the words from *Hamlet*, "to hold, as 'twere, a mirror up to nature."[8]

By the late 1870s Harrigan began to phase out variety acts and sketches and turn to full-length plays, most of them featuring highly realistic sets depicting the Lower East Side. According to Richard Moody, it was as if the "back wall of the theatre had been cut way, opening to a view of Corlear's Hook, Cherry Hill, Baxter Street, or Five Points. The shops, alleys, and tenements, the men and women who raced in and out, were strikingly familiar." Critic William Dean Howells, commenting in 1886 on the setting of *Dan's Tribulations*, noted: "the illusion is so perfect that you lose the sense of being in the theatre; you are out of that world of conventions and traditions, and in the presence of the facts."[9]

Part of Harrigan's success, therefore, lay in his ability to put the city itself on the stage and then people it with a variety of recognizable urban types. "Though I use types and never individuals, I try to be as realistic as possible. . . . Each drama is a series of photographs of life today in the Empire City." In Harrigan's case, "realistic" applied to character types, settings, costume, dialect, and recognizable action, rather than to plots.[10]

As suggested in the chapter on vaudeville, by seeing onstage recognizable characterizations, even stereotypes of themselves, denizens of the rapidly changing industrial city felt somehow validated and better able to structure and order their world. Details of behavior, dress, even character were suddenly pulled out of the amorphous mass and held up for observation, as if to say, "Yes, this *is* real. It is a part of your daily life." In this respect, Harrigan's work was part of the well-established tradition of all urban popular entertainments: to reveal the city to itself. Just as eighteenth-century Romantics carried small frames around with them through which they viewed, and, thus, "revealed" Nature, so from the seventeenth century onward, woodcuts, engravings, broadside ballads, songs, sketches, and eventually plays "framed" the city and its people for those who lived and worked in it.

Harrigan's urban theater must have owed something to John Brougham and especially Benjamin A. Baker and Dion Boucicault. All three men had written plays during the pre–Civil War era that focused on the city. One of the most famous was Baker's *A Glance at New York* (1848). The play was notable because of the performance of Francis S. Chanfrau as Mose, the Fire B'hoy. As characterized by Chanfrau, Mose was the first truly American urban type to be depicted on the stage. The "b'hoys" were members of urban gangs that followed various fire engine companies, as well as serving particular political patrons. Arriving at a fire, rival gangs were more likely to fight each other than the flames.

Born on the Bowery, Chanfrau had been a b'hoy himself. With Mose's first line, "I ain't gonna run wid dis machine [engine] no more," the audience, which contained many b'hoys, went wild with the exciting shock of recognition. Baker and Chanfrau had produced the ultimate "frame." As David L. Rinear points out in his study of the character, "Chanfrau's Mose involved the tripartite phenomenon of an actual Bowery b'hoy playing a fictitious Bowery b'hoy to audiences composed largely of Bowery b'hoys."[11]

Mose was one of the first characters on the American stage to speak with the immigrant-tinged patois of the city. "I'm bilein' over for a rousin' good fight with someone somewhere . . ." Both the term "b'hoy" and Mose's dialect strongly suggest an Irish ancestry. Laurence Hutton believed that Harrigan's characters were the "legitimate descendants of Mose." Richard Moody agrees, suggesting that Mose could have served as a model for Harrigan's Dan Mulligan.[12]

Harrigan also may have been influenced by Dion Boucicault, who, as we have seen, sought to transform the traditional stage Irishman from a buffoon into a comic hero. Dan Mulligan and his tribe share with Boucicault's characters the same ready wit mixed with sentimentality, as well as the same desire to puncture respectability and live life on the "aisy" side. Boucicault once told Harrigan, "You have done for the Irish in New York what I have done for the Irish in Ireland." In a way, Harrigan did translate the Dubliner's comic heroes in terms of Irish America. Like Boucicault, who placed his comic Irish characters within Irish settings, Harrigan, by having a variety of Irish Americans onstage, avoided the accusation of libeling Irish Americans.[13]

Whatever the sources for his inspiration, Harrigan focused on the city as no other American playwright had before him. He even produced the kind of urban epiphany that Baker and Chanfrau had achieved with Mose. Some hint of the sort of magic that Harrigan could create between the Lower East Side on his stage and his audience may be found in the record of the opening night of *Reilly and the Four Hundred*, the production that inaugurated his new playhouse in 1890. In the play, Harrigan introduced a new urban type into his company in the form of two teenage "chippies" or tough girls. Maggie Murphy and Kitty Lynch were figures known on the street but new to the stage. When Kitty (played by Ada Lewis) appeared in her scruffy clothes and tight, ill-fitting sweater and rasped out to the pawn broker, "Say Reilly, gimme me shoes!" she stopped the show.[14] For a brief moment, Harrigan had recreated the shock of recognition that an older New York audience had enjoyed when Chanfrau introduced his Mose onstage in 1848. Harrigan had "framed" another bit of the city.

While uptown liked to see what downtown looked like onstage, Harrigan and Hart were careful to make sure that downtown could afford to see itself. When they rented *The Comique* in 1876, they cut prices, dropping the gallery seats from twenty-five to fifteen cents.[15] Harrigan had to raise the price back up to twenty-five cents when he opened his own theater in 1890. However, Harrigan designed his theater to insure an intimate atmosphere connecting actors and audience across the footlights. It was a family theater and a people's theater. As one patron wrote, recalling a matinee of *Cordelia's Aspirations* (1883): "My gracious, I never ran across a noisier audience. There was a man right back of us continually eating peanuts and scattering the shells right and left. I found one in my bonnet when I got home. Every other minute, he'd shriek ouuuu . . . look at Harrigan! Oh, lor' he takes the cake, he do! – and then a peanut shell would lodge in his windpipe and he'd set up such a dreadful coughing that we couldn't hear a word that was said on the stage. And the babies! They must all have been teething that afternoon!"[16]

HARRIGAN'S SONGS

In addition to writing plays, Harrigan was also a successful songwriter. He formed a musical partnership with his father-in-law, David Braham, who served as his composer and musical director. Each play had four to seven major songs, the choruses of which were usually picked up by everyone onstage and many in the audience. The two men turned out more than two hundred songs over a twenty-year period. Indeed, Harrigan and Braham's pieces were among the first popular songs from musical shows (as opposed to the vaudeville and minstrel stage) to find success in sheet music.[17] Their songs helped contribute to what Timothey E. Scheurer calls the "colloquial or vernacular style" of Tin Pan Alley. They also anticipated the approach to songwriting that would characterize Broadway songs of the early twentieth century. Charles Hamm suggests that their songs "represent the beginning of urban popular song, and thus anticipate what song was to become in the following decades." However, Hamm's assumption that the songs were so much a part of New York that they did not travel much beyond the Hudson is open to question. Harrigan's company toured almost every year and his popularity held up longer in San Francisco than in New York. In fact, the songs may have been more popular than the shows themselves, judging from the number of Harrigan and Hart songsters that were published.[18]

Harrigan went to great efforts to bring the city into his songs, as well as onto his stage sets. In "It Showered Again" (1886), a courting couple seeks shelter from the rain under the awning of Murphy's Saloon. There, between showers, and amid the clatter of horse cars, buggies, and wagons, not to mention Murphy's strangulated renditions of "The Last Rose of Summer," (all described in the song's lyrics), he proposes and she accepts.[19]

In "Going Home with Nelly after Five," from *The Mulligan Guard's Picnic* (1883), the boy sees himself and his girl as part of the great urban throng.

> Oh Broadway is a thorough fare for both the high and low;
> There side by side just like the tide it's up and down we go;
> It's laboring men and working girls like bees out of a hive;
> Among the crowd, I'm going home with Nelly after Five.

In "Danny By My Side," from *The Last of the Hogans* (1891), the Brooklyn Bridge is the setting for urban working-class recreation.

> The mother's [sic] with the children, Go out to take the air
> From tenement and alley, A pleasure oh so rare;
> It's there the poor and lowly, All watch the river glide;
> What joys to me such sights to see, With Danny by my side.

In 1932, when Al Smith was asked for a song on the occasion of the fiftieth anniversary of the Brooklyn Bridge, the former governor obligingly croaked out "Danny By My Side."[20]

Harrigan was among the first to recognize that within the crowded tenements of New York something like community could exist in spite of the poverty and ethnic tensions. Some of his best songs found something to celebrate in the rough urban culture coming into being around him. They recognize working-class Irish America as a community, which, amid overcrowding and poverty, could take pride in its ability to survive and occasionally even prosper.

"Babies on Our Block," from *The Mulligan Guards* (1879), recites the (Irish) names of the children in Murphy's tenement. Inspired by Harrigan's encounters with mobs of Irish kids on his daily walks through New York, the song's chorus consists of brief paraphrases from two of the children's favorite singing games: "Little Sally Waters" and "Green Gravel."

If you want for information, Or in need of merriment,
Come over with me socially To Murphy's Tenement;
He owns a row of houses In the First Ward, near the dock,
Where Ireland's represented By the Babies on our Block.
There's the Phalens and the Whalens From the Sweet Dunochadee,
They are sitting on the railings With their children on their knees,
All gossiping and talking With their neighbors in a flock,
Singing "Little Sally Waters," With the Babies on our Block.

Even the appearance of the slum landlord does not disturb Harrigan's idyll of Irish togetherness.

It's good morning to you, landlord; Come, now, how are you to-day?
When Patrick Murphy, Esquire, Comes down the alley way,
With his shiny silken beaver, He's as solid as a rock,
The envy of the neighbors' boys A-living off our Block.
There's the Brannons and the Gannons, Far-down and Connaught
    men,
Quite easy with the shovel And so handy with the pen;
All neighborly and friendly, With the relations by the flock,
Singing "Little Sally Waters," With the Babies on our Block.

The song, another great favorite of Al Smith, is typical of Harrigan's skillful blend of the gentle satire and sentimentality that enabled his audience to recognize, celebrate, and also laugh at themselves. The litany of Irish names, already standard in Irish-American comic songs, suggests the sense of community that Harrigan sought to depict.

Although Harrigan sentimentalized Mulligan's Alley, he did not pretend that it was utopia. In "Down in Gossip's Row" (1880), where numerous Irish names come up for discussion, there is precious little privacy.

> Good evening Misses Dooley, Oh, did you have you your tea,
> I had a glass of lager beer, Just now with Missis Fay,
> She wants to be a Yankee, I'll let the neighbors know,
> She lived in County Connaught [*sic*] 'for she moved in Gossip's Row.[21]

Most of Harrigan's characters were working class, and many were poor. Gotham Court, one of the worst of the city's tenements, was one of the sources for "Mulligan's Alley." However, Harrigan was an entertainer, not a reformer, and his plays were comedies, not tragedies. His depictions of Irish working-class life in New York were sunny, good-humored, and sentimental, yet, not necessarily unrealistic. Often the scenes onstage provided some reflection of immigrant life in New York City. "Mulberry Springs," from *The O'Reagans*, (1886), saluted the "Neighborly people from Cork and Kerry," who crowded together even while they sought relief from the summer's heat on the roof of one of the notorious tenements in the vicinity of Spring and Mulberry Streets.

> The heat is intense, and the crowd is immense,
> > All praying and whistling for wings,
> To get up and fly to the clouds in the sky,
> > The Boarders of Mulberry Springs.

Harrigan's recognition and celebration of the Irish urban community was perhaps one of the most important aspects of his work, for it presented a positive picture of one of the essential realities of Irish-American life. The Irish immigrants found comfort and support in being surrounded by their fellow countryfolk. They resisted attempts by leaders, such as Archbishop John Ireland, to settle them in rural areas for what Lawrence McCaffrey calls their "preference for community living among their own religious and ethnic group."[22]

Not that togetherness was something the Irish inhabitants of the slums could easily avoid. Yet, in song after song, Harrigan delineates the qualities of the urban, working-class Irish American with gentle humor – and also with great affection, as in the second verse of "Maggie Murphy's Home," from *Reilly and the Four Hundred* (1890):

> Such dancing in the parlor, There's a waltz for you and I,
> Such mashing on the stairway, and kisses on the sly,

God bless the leisure hours, The working people know,
And you're welcome every evening, At Maggie Murphy's Home.

CHORUS:

On Sunday night is my delight and pleasure don't you see,
Meeting all the girls and all the boys that work down town with me,
There's an organ in the parlor to give the house a tone,
And you're welcome every evening, at Maggie Murphy's Home.

The affirmation of the working-class family was a quiet theme that Harrigan returned to again and again in his plays. In *Cordelia's Aspirations* (1883), Dan Mulligan, sadly packing for the move out of Mulligan's Alley to a posh uptown flat, comes across his dad's old lunch bucket, and sings "My Dad's Dinner Pail."

Preserve that old kettle, so blacken'd and worn,
It belonged to my father before I was born,
It hung in a corner, beyant on a nail,
'Twas an emblem of labor, was Dad's dinner pail.

The pail also doubled as a growler.

There's a place for the coffee, and also for the bread,
The corn beef and praties, and oft it was said:
"Go, fill it wid porter, wid beer, or wid ale,"
The drink would taste sweeter from Dad's dinner pail.

While the image of a little kid rushing the growler for the old man would have appalled WASP reformers, it was apparently an appealing one for Harrigan and his audience, for he used it in another song, "My Little Side Door," from *Dan's Tribulations* (1884). The song is sung by Dan Mulligan as the proprietor of a store-cum-bar, equipped with a side entrance.

When the supper is spread with corn, meat and bread,
It's "Take down the pail and go buy,
A pint of buck-beer, oh, the poor man to cheer
A'toiling all day makes him dry,"
A sweet little boy, his father's own joy,
Comes running right into my store,
He says "How are you, Dan" with growler in hand
As he enters my little side door.

In Harrigan's songs the family ties spread down through the generations, represented by some object, the very survival of which symbolized a triumph over the pressures of immigrant poverty, such as "The Old Featherbed" from *McSorley's Inflation* (1882).

> In the county Mayo, long, long ago,
> Me father himself took a wife,
> 'Twas all understood he would do what he could
> To provide for me mother through life.
> His father, old Dougherty, Gave all the crock'ry
> His table to eat of their bread;
> Her mother, God save her, Said all she could lave her
> As a token of love was her old featherbed.

There would have been some Irish among Harrigan's audiences who retained childhood memories of their working-class neighborhoods, even if they, like Harrigan himself, had moved beyond them. "Paddy Duffy's Cart," from *Squatter Sovereignty* (1882), was typical of many American popular songs in its nostalgic memory of boyhood fun and "Where-are-they-now" recollections of lost companions. Yet, for an immigrant community the litany of those who "made it" and those who did not must have had a certain poignancy.

Harrigan also had his own satiric versions of the rising Paddy. Placing his Irish working-class characters in contact with, or even in the position of the upper class had great comic potential. *Reilly and the Four Hundred* opened in 1890, shortly after Ward McAllister, intrepid discoverer of New York City's "Four Hundred," published *Society As I have Found It.* Harrigan had earlier allowed his characters to pursue the lace curtain in *The Mulligan Guards' Surprise* (1880) and in *Cordelia's Aspirations* (1883).[23]

Harrigan himself had moved "uptown" and so had some sympathy for his characters. Referring to Cordelia's aspirations for the lace curtain, Harrigan once said that they "gain what value they have because they are couched in the dialect of the poor emigrant and flavored with the aroma of want. A cultured, refined, and beautiful millionaire Cordelia, aspiring to be numbered among the billionaires, talking faultless English, would excite not the shadow of a smile, but simply pity and disgust."[24]

In spite of Harrigan's own economic success, there was an ambiguous class element in his comedy. He once explained that "polite society, wealth, and culture possess little or no color and picturesqueness" and, thus, served as "a foil to the poor, the workers, and the great middle class."[25] Thus, one of Harrigan's broad themes was that the centripetal force of the tenement community was more powerful than the centrifugal force of individualistic social mobility. Cordelia's ambition to move out of Mulligan's Alley is turned against her, and Reilly's ventures among the Four Hundred are the stuff of satire. In *Cordelia's Aspirations*, Dan Mulligan tries to explain why he is unhappy in his new uptown flat: "Cordelia, I know you saved my money and I know you're trying to elevate me, but I can't forget me neighbors. There's no one up here to sit out on the front stoop and have a glass of beer wid me. There's no barber shops open of a Sunday morning where you could hear the daily news of the week and never fish can I buy from a peddling wagon on a Friday."[26]

Harrigan's message to the working class seems essentially conservative. In Alicia Koger's words, Harrigan "suggests that those who foolishly wanted to overstep their prescribed social and economic boundaries should expect ridiculous failure. His message to his lower East Side neighbors was: 'Be content with the blessings you have and do not risk them in lofty ambitions.'"[27] It was a strange message from a man who had himself moved up and out of the ghetto. Yet it parallels attitudes that were very common within nineteenth-century Irish-Catholic culture in America. In novels and tracts, clergy and lay writers alike urged the Irish to stay together and not give in to the materialistic individualism of the Yankees.[28] At the same time, there was an element of realism in Harrigan's advice. For every one who managed to climb up the ladder, several more would fall and languish. When Dan Mulligan proclaims in *Dan's Tribulations*, "Better contentment with a plate of porridge than to be down hearted at a feast," there must have been a nodding of heads in the audience by those who could look forward to few feasts. The play ends with Dan and Cordelia, still devoted to each other, returning to Mulligan's Alley, having to start all over again. As Maureen Murphy suggests, this aspect of Harrigan's art underscored the attractive qualities of the Irish and "reinforced the growing image of the Irish in America as not only high spirited, but also responsible and trustworthy."[29]

An important element in the Harrigan and Hart plays and sketches was the multi-ethnic makeup of their cast of characters. Germans and African Americans (played in blackface) were standard throughout all of the Mulligan Guard series. Jews and Italians, and even Chinese (also played by white men) appeared in other plays.[30] Harrigan's New York Irish lived cheek by jowl with all of the other ethnic groups in the city, as illustrated in "McNally's Row of Flats" from *McSorley's Inflation* (1882).

The great conglomeration of men of every nation,
A Babylonian tower 'O, it could not equal this
Peculiar institution where Brogues without dilation,
Were rattled off together at McNally's Row of Flats.

CHORUS:

It's Ireland and Italy, Jerusalem and Germany,
O Chinamen and Nagers and a paradise for cats,
All jumbled up together in snow and raging weather,
They represent the tenants of McNally's Row of Flats.

Such assemblages were hardly unusual. As Harrigan once said, "Below Fourteenth Street, after eight o'clock at night, the U. S. Language was a hard find." When someone asked Harrigan if all the ethnic groups in New York really lived "sort of thick an' mixed like the innards of a mince pie," Harrigan assured the man that they were even thicker, and with "more spice in 'em." When criticized for having so many immigrants and blacks in his plays, he responded, "Whoever votes the Republican or Democratic ticket in the United States must be an American, no matter what may be his mother tongue or color."[31] A microcosm of New York's Lower East Side, McNally's flats represented the evolution of a particular kind of American cosmopolitanism, so central to the emerging Irish-American culture, combining assimilation – "We're all Americans" – with strong ethnic identity – "We're Irish, as well."

As pointed out in the last chapter, Harrigan's plays and songs also reflect the growing political role the Irish were assuming within this ethnic stew. "My district is the town of Babel," says one of Harrigan's aldermen, "and the Irish flag floats from the top."[32] While the Irish and blacks in Harrigan's plays were quick enough to thump each other all over the stage, his Irish politicians were eager to seek alliances with them against the Germans. In "Hang the Mulligan Banner Up," from *The Mulligan Guard's Nominee* (1880), Dan Mulligan, running for alderman, tries for a broad ethnic coalition of Irish, African Americans, Italians, and Scandinavians that would "leave the Dutch behind."

The plots of the *Mulligan Guard* series revolve around two sets of ethnic tensions: Irish versus German and Irish versus African American. The domestic tensions are usually between the Mulligans and the Lochmullers. Inevitably, the second-generation members of the families intermarry. Koger suggests that Harrigan's sketches and plays reveal a "natural"

Irish-American bias against Germans. His plots usually favored the Irish, and his Germans generally lack depth and humanity.³³ Considering that the German characters were seldom played by Germans, while the Irish Americans in the cast played themselves, it is not surprising that the Irish came off best.

There was also the larger tension between the Irish and the African Americans, represented by their respective target companies: the Mulligan Guards and the Skidmores. The Skidmores' sole *raison d'être* revolves around attempts to triumph over the Irish. While Harrigan's stereotype of blacks is largely negative, they are at least allowed to be proud and disdainful of whites.³⁴

Almost every one of the Mulligan plays contained at least one "melee," as Harrigan called them in his stage directions, carefully choreographed battles between the Mulligan Guards and the Skidmores. Yet, as Koger describes them, these were "loud and violent, yet good natured and fair-mindedness usually restored peace. Above all, Harrigan wanted to depict harmony of the races who lived and worked closely together on the lower East side, so he always tempered the battles and insults with humor. Thus he made the racial problems seem less serious."³⁵

Koger shows that there is a progression in the Mulligan Guard series in terms of race relations. In the early plays, Dan's prejudices against other races are very much intact. By the last play, *Dan's Tribulations*, we find that he has mellowed and the play ends on a chord of domestic and racial harmony. When Dan proclaims at the end of *The Mulligan Guard Picnic* that "We are all family" he meant not only the Mulligans and their friends but *all* the neighbors of Mulligan's Alley. Dion Boucicault once told a reviewer for the *World* that Harrigan waved two banners, one inscribed "Erin Go Braugh" and the other "E Pluribus Unum."³⁶

Although Harrigan's plays and songs contributed to Irish pride, he did not hesitate to satirize some of the sacred cows of Irish nationalism. *The Major* includes an immigrant who had brought with him eighteen shovelfulls of Connaught earth. In another play, Cordelia's FNA (Florence Nightingale Association) secretly knits ear muffs for the Fenians in case they decide to try to invade Canada again.³⁷

While Harrigan's Irish are more individualized than the other ethnic characters who appeared in his plays, they are still stereotypes. Yet he used his stereotypes to accomplish two things in his delineation of the Irish. First, while retaining some of the stage Irishman's traditional character, he accentuated Paddy's positive side. Arthur Hobson Quinn underscores this in his description of Dan Mulligan, the grocer and ward politician who had fought in the Civil War in New York's 69th Regiment: "He is honest courageous, loyal, impulsive, irrational, likely to become drunk and disorderly at slight provocation and while irascible and quarrelsome, is forgiving and generous even to his enemies."[38]

Second, Harrigan convincingly adapted his Irish characters to the American urban environment, an achievement also recognized by his contemporaries. One critic, Lewis C. Strang, compared Harrigan to Thomas Q. Seabrooke, who impersonated the traditional stage Irishman. Strang praised Seabrooke's Paddy: "Happy-go-lucky, improvident, and bubbling over with rollicking jollity and uncultivated mirth, he accepts with ready compliancy whatever fate has in store for him. . . . Yet one likes him, loves him for his impulsiveness, his heartiness, his simplicity, and his honesty, for the rich burr in his speech and for his mother wit, that is irrepressible and irresistible." Strang seems cooler to Harrigan's Irish Americans, finding them "all New Yorkers. They have cleansed their boots of the sod, have ceased to look upon the hod as a natural means of livelihood, and have turned toward politics, in which they thrive and flourish as the green bay-tree. They are sophisticated in the ways of the world, and they have a keen appreciation for the main chance."[39] They were, Strang said, less the "Celts of romance" and more Americans, which is exactly what Harrigan intended.

In 1890, Harrigan seemed at the height of his powers; he was in his own theater with a hit. Yet *Reilly and the Four Hundred* turned out to be his last success and by 1895 he had to rent *The Harrigan* to Richard Mansfield, who renamed it *The Garrick*. Harrigan took to the road and even went back into vaudeville. Even with pared-down productions of his plays he was still popular in his old base, San Francisco. However he could no longer connect with New York City, rapidly changing under the impact of massive immigration from southern and eastern Europe. "There's been a great change in the sense of humor in New York," he grumbled to an interviewer, "It isn't native, it isn't New York. It's Paris, or Vienna, or someplace."[40]

On May 9, 1909, Harrigan was onstage for the Lamb's Gambol at the Old Met. He was still a performer's performer and he received a ten-minute ovation. Once backstage, however, he suffered a stroke. Eddie Foy, one of the new breed of Irish-American entertainers who did not need Irishness in his act, helped put Harrigan in a wheelchair.[41] Harrigan remained an invalid until his death in 1911.

Ned Harrigan's great achievement had been to Americanize and urbanize Paddy. He created Irish-American comedy in an urban setting. He offered his fellow Irish an identity based on the reality of their lives in America's cities. Yet, with the passing of the Harrigan Era, the urban nature of the Irish-American image in popular culture, especially in song, began to slip. A new generation of Irish and non-Irish would find the Emerald Isle across the sea a more satisfying source for "Irishness" than Mulligan's Alley.

PART FOUR

The Image on Tin Pan Alley

The Post-Famine Immigration

While Ned Harrigan's songs remained popular with the generation that grew up on them, neither Harrigan's theater nor his approach to Irish-America was in tune with the changes taking place as the nineteenth century came to a close. Although these changes were occurring broadly throughout American culture, they are particularly pertinent to popular music. Consequently, the nineties was a pivotal decade in terms of the image of the Irish and Ireland in American song.

Many of the elements of the old Irish stereotype were still in place. One writer in the nineties maintained that "a Celt is notoriously a passionate, impulsive, kindly, unreflecting, brave, nimble-witted man; but, he lacks the solidity, the balance, the judgment, the moral staying power of the Anglo-Saxon." Nevertheless, as Kathleen Donovan points out, Yankee attitudes toward the stereotype were changing. "Celtic" traits, it was agreed, were not all bad, and some Yankees thought they could discern among the Irish signs of progress and assimilation. At a deeper level, as Dale T. Knobel suggests, the Irish benefitted from a change within Anglo-Saxon ideology that shifted "The Celt" from a racial to an ethnic category, thus implying that differences between Yankee and Irish might be largely cultural after all.[1]

Thus, a rising tide of immigration had raised the Irish in Anglo-Saxon eyes. As one Yankee in Lowell, Massachusetts, commented, "generally speaking [the Irish] . . . do not bring habits or institutions differing greatly from those of the Americans themselves." As Ellen Skerrett has noted, "Not only did new immigrants push the Irish up the economic ladder, but by comparison, they made the Irish appear more American and less foreign."[2] In return, the newcomers, encountering Irish policemen, Irish politicians, Irish bureaucrats, Irish saloon keepers, Irish contractors, and Irish teachers could be excused for thinking that "Irish" equalled "American."

Dublin's Lord Mayor, Sir James Power, visiting the United States in 1903, was impressed by the progress his fellow countrymen had made in America. "The Irishman in America [is no longer] merely a hewer of wood and a drawer of water." Such tasks were now done by the Italians, the Poles, the Chinese, and the blacks, while "Irishmen are universally respected, and found occupying many of the respectable positions in the country."[3] Part of the success of Irish America at the turn of the century was measured against the newcomers from southern and eastern Europe, Asia, and from the southern United States. Compared to the "new immigrants" and peoples of color, the Irish – white, Christian, English speaking, and more than familiar with urban, industrial life – did not look so bad to Yankees who, a generation earlier, had compared them to apes.

It was no accident that the term "lace curtain" was coined in the 1890s. So many Irish were moving up the ladder from the working class to the lower-middle and middle classes that the satires of Harrigan, Finley Peter Dunne, and Thomas Beer found an easy and obvious mark. By 1900, American-born Irish were over-represented in lower-middle-class positions, such as clerks, salespersons, teachers, and bookkeepers, and were under-represented in the poorer jobs. True, compared to the accomplishments of Germans, Scandinavians, and the recently arrived Jews, Irish success was, as Timothy Meagher has pointed out, unspectacular and fragile. The Irish tended to "slip" more than other groups. Yet, based on the economic distance they had to travel and the vast numbers that had crowded the bottom of the ladder, the Irish in America had turned a corner. Even among the great numbers of working-class Irish, the majority was now skilled or semi-skilled. In many factories the Irish had moved into the foreman class.[4]

Andrew Greeley regards the "success story" of the Irish Americans as having taken place in the years between 1890 and 1930, particularly during the twenty years after 1900. It was in these years that they entered the mainstream of American life. For example, young Americans growing up around World War I had about a fifty-fifty chance of ending up in a white-collar occupation. For Irish Catholics, however, the chances were two to one. According to Timothy J. Meagher, "the analyses of family life at the turn of the century frequently focus on [the Irish] as the principal examples of immigrant adjustment to an urban industrial world."[5]

In most cities where the Irish were concentrated, therefore, Irish social mobility and geographical dispersion accelerated after 1900. Moreover, the Irish population was dominated increasingly by those born in America.[6] Inevitably, American popular culture began to reflect the interests of the second generation, who may have occasionally hummed "The Old Bog Road" but whose feet were firmly planted on Broadway.

Yet it is too easy to forget that fresh emigrants kept on coming from Ireland, primarily from the western seaboard counties: 390,179 from 1891 to 1900 (down from 655,482 in the previous decade), 339,065 from 1901 to 1910, 146,181 from 1911 to 1920, and 220,591 from 1921 to 1930.[7] Although small in proportion to earlier waves of Irish immigrants and dwarfed by the arrivals from other parts of Europe, many of the late post-Famine immigrants settled in the traditional Irish centers of New York, Philadelphia, Boston, and Chicago, as well as the smaller industrial cities of the East Coast and Midwest. As a result, there were strong Irish-born enclaves in many cities in the early decades of the twentieth century. In turn-of-the-century Lowell, for example, 40 percent of the Irish were foreign born.[8]

The post-Famine immigrants differed in several ways from their predecessors who had fled the terrors of the "Great Hunger." Better educated, thanks to the national school system, they were also a bit better prepared for emigration. No longer desperate and unplanned, emigration had become something that many Irish boys and girls were raised to expect. The old pre-Famine habit of subdividing lease holds among all of the married children was gone. In its place was a fierce desire to keep land intact and, as peasant ownership became instituted, to expand holdings whenever possible. With the nonpartible inheritance going to one son, there was also a dowry for only one daughter. As a result, only one boy and girl from a family could usually expect to marry. The rest would either have to remain in an unmarried and, therefore, subordinate and dependent state, enter the church, or emigrate. Many chose emigration.

Many of the post-Famine immigrants enjoyed one singular advantage over many other immigrants of the period, and, to some degree, over their Irish predecessors. Many could count on the help of family or, at least, friends when they landed in America. Also, the post-Famine emigrants were more conventionally religious than their predecessors had been. Through the "devotional revolution" pushed forward by the church, Irish Catholicism was gradually purged of many of its "folk" elements. Religious practice was standardized and a powerful sort of piety, focused on church and family, was institutionalized within Irish life.[9] Therefore, in spite of all the problems and hardships the post-Famine generation faced, they enjoyed some advantages: their youth, their family ties to American Irish, their faith and their church, and a parity of males and females that made marriage in America a practical goal. All these factors provided a stability that the earlier immigrant Irish communities had not known.[10]

Nevertheless, the members of this generation of immigrants needed all of the structure they could get. The mean age, which had been 22.5 for men and 21.2 for women, dropped below 20 for both sexes after 1890.[11] Thus, many of the emigrants had to negotiate simultaneously the transitions involved in both emigration and the shift from adolescence to adulthood. As for their economic potential, few of them brought either money or marketable skills. Therefore, even though most of them were literate (and few among the Gaelic-speakers lacked English), most had to enter the American economy at the bottom. For those who succumbed to bad fortune or despair, there was still a large, chaotic urban underclass awaiting to devour them.

In his book *Emigrants and Exiles*, Kirby Miller, commenting on the post-Famine exodus, notes that for the first time most Irish immigrants came from the western seaboard of Ireland, the last bastion of Gaelic traditional culture.[12] Therefore, the post-Famine emigrants represented the most traditional and conservative elements of Irish society. They had clung to the land even during the Famine, but socioeconomic changes had finally overtaken them and had driven them out.

A strong part of the cultural baggage of this group was what Miller has called the "culture of exile," rooted in traditional Gaelic culture and sustained by a Roman Catholic worldview. From the time of the early Irish monks, who accepted missionary work abroad as the "white martyrdom" of voluntary exile, the leaving of Ireland was portrayed in the Gaelic tradition as a tragic event. Taking as their model the "wild geese," those members of the Gaelic, Catholic nobility forced to flee English conquest in the seventeenth century, many Catholic peasants, especially those from Irish-speaking enclaves, tended to look upon emigration as exile. They expressed and, thus, reinforced these feelings in song and story, in everyday language, and in the custom of the "American wake." The majority of Catholic immigrants was either too Anglicized to take up this burden or they were able to lay it aside once they arrived in America. However, Miller argues that a significant minority, especially among the post-Famine emigration, carried this burden with them to their graves. In his study of the letters this post-Famine generation of immigrants sent back to Ireland, Miller claims to have found a "pervasive dissatisfaction with urban-industrial life." Although American-born Irish began to disperse themselves throughout the industrial cities in which they worked, the last wave of immigrants from the western seaboard counties remained clumped together in their own neighborhoods well into the 1930s. Thus, at the very moment when Irish Americans were moving up and out of the ghettos, becoming in some respects more American than the Yankees, there was a solid core of recently arrived Gaelic speakers who found comfort primarily in each other's company, the bits and pieces of Irish culture and habits they brought with them, and their memories of home.[13]

The traditional Gaelic tendency to cast emigration in a somber light had appealed to the romantic culture that produced the first popular songs about Ireland. It had also been useful for the propagandistic thrust of the Young Irelanders and the Fenians. However, as we have seen, it remained a minor theme in the popular songs of the post–Civil War era. As the writing of Irish songs in America was taken over by Tin Pan Alley, much of the anger and anguish of this sense of exile was transformed into a highly sentimentalized sense of nostalgia for the old sod, itself depicted in ever-more fantastic terms until, remade into the Emerald Isle, it dominated many of the songs written after 1900. Although the new songs were probably aimed more at the second and third generation, they were far from being simply frivolous conceits of Alley songmongers. Their nostalgia was a translation of the "culture of exile" into the language of American popular culture, into a series of images about a nonexistent Ireland that enabled Irish Americans to portray themselves in ways that both they and the rest of America could appreciate.

This reinvention of the image of Ireland in American popular culture coincided with the emergence of a new, complex sense of nationhood back in Ireland. A relatively young generation of Catholic and Protestant poets, dramatists, language enthusiasts, and assorted visionaries took up the cause of Irish nationalism in the wake of the vacuum created by the fall of Parnell. For a time this new Ireland seemed to be more a state of mind than a political entity. Forces, however, were moving behind the scenes to reinvigorate Irish nationalist politics and push it in a revolutionary direction. The belated passage of the Home Rule Bill in 1912, bringing in its wake the disdain of separatists and the threat of Civil War from the Ulster Unionists, did little to quiet the island. World War I, far from putting nationalist issues on the back burner, provided the opportunity for revolution in 1916. Events followed each other at a confusing pace. The execution of the rebels, the success of Sinn Féin in the elections of 1918, and the party's creation of an underground parliament, Dáil Éireann, the Anglo-Irish War of 1920–21, the creation of the Free State and the subsequent Civil War and partition – all of this was too much for most Americans and many Irish Americans to absorb. Somehow, a real Ireland had emerged, exciting, bloody,

and confusing, which had virtually nothing to do with Irish-American identity. Independent Ireland and Irish America would go their own separate
ways. The remainder of this study will chart the Irish-American path into
the early decades of this century.

9. Paddy on the Alley

According to Richard Middleton, the nineteenth century witnessed the culmination of one revolution and the beginning of another in western popular music. The first, the "bourgeois revolution," was marked by "the spread of the market system through almost all musical activities," producing new types of music such as the parlor ballad. By the 1890s, the second revolution was well under way, based on the emergence of a mass culture, shaped by "monopoly-capitalist structures" and a new "American hegemony" in popular music. In America, this music featured new dance forms, beginning with ragtime and rapidly evolving into jazz. The new popular music was characterized, according to Middleton, by "new methods of mass production, publicity and distribution," resulting in the consolidation of the modern American music publishing industry in New York City. Of the sixteen songs published in the decade from 1892 to 1903 that sold a million or more copies, all but two were published in New York. Historians refer to this in-gathering of popular music publishers and songwriters as Tin Pan Alley. The Alley initially coalesced around Union Square, which boasted Pastor's, as well as Harrigan and Hart's *Theatre Comique*, among other houses. For a brief time the proximity of theaters and song publishers made Union Square the entertainment capital of America. As the theater district moved uptown from the Square on Fourteenth Street, so did the song publishers. The Alley briefly reassembled itself on Twenty-eighth Street, after the new, successful firm of Witmark and Sons moved there in the early nineties. Then, between 1903 and 1908 it moved to West Forty-second Street. By the 1920s the Alley extended from Forty-second to Fifty-sixth Streets.[1]

Whether considered as place or state of mind, Tin Pan Alley represented a revolution in the writing and publishing of popular music. First, unlike established music publishing firms, whose catalogs contained dances, piano solos, sacred music, opera, and classical selections, Tin Pan Alley firms specialized exclusively in popular songs. Under these circumstances, it is not surprising that the way to Tin Pan Alley was pioneered by newcomers to the field rather than by the old established firms. Some Alley founders were former "drummers," or salesmen, who had carried sheet music as a sideline to their other goods. In contact with the grass roots, these men thought they understood the audience for popular music, as well as the music business itself. A few decided that they could write songs as good as those they were selling. Some of these salesmen-composer-publishers, such as Charles K. Harris, Will Rossiter, and Jerome Remick, founded very successful houses.[2]

Because they had few preconceptions about either American popular music or the music business, first- and second-generation immigrants also played an important role on the Alley. The house of Witmark and Sons was started by teenage brothers in 1886, who, being underage, had to have their immigrant father sign the papers for them. By the 1890s theirs was the first major popular publisher with a national market. Because they published the scores of shows by Victor Herbert, Chauncey Olcott, and George M. Cohan, there were many new Irish songs in their catalog.[3]

But which songs to buy? Which songs would sell? Although the element of mystery remained at the heart of the music business, the Tin Pan Alley firms did their best to minimize the uncertainty. Publishers still employed the old reactive strategies. Firms still did their best to hitch a ride onto popular hit songs or important events. Some of the new firms, however, decided that it was better to be proactive; to scan the news of the day for emerging personalities or upcoming events about which they might write a song. Among the various innovations credited to the Witmarks, none was more important than their decision to write and publish "Cleveland's Wedding March" to coincide with the president's nuptials. According to Kenneth Aaron Kanter, it was the Witmarks who introduced the practice of writing songs about front page events.[4] The new technologies that began to clutter American life around the turn of the century also served as a launching platform for successful songs, such as "Come Josephine in My Flying Machine," "In My Merry Oldsmobile," and "Hello Central, Give Me Heaven."

By approaching songwriting with the same manufacturing mentality that other businessmen brought to making shirts and skirts, the Alley revolutionized the production of popular song in America. As David Jasen points out, it was only after the emergence of Tin Pan Alley that songs were written on demand, either for performers who wanted particular kinds of songs to fit their acts or for publishers who wanted a "cover" of a competitor's recent success. As early as 1890, composer-publisher Harry Von Tilzer found that a songwriter had to think of his work as "a commodity with a cash value and in order to augment the value he must subordinate his own personal tastes to those of the music-buying public."[5]

In marketing the product, the song sheet cover became more important than ever. The new rotary press, along with the techniques for mixing photographs and multicolor art, added eye appeal to the songs. In the sample for this study, the percentage of illustrated covers grows from a low of 23 percent in the 1880s, to 40 percent in the 1890s, 58 percent in the 1900s, and 63 percent in the 1910s. From 1900 to 1920, around one-third of the song sheet covers pictured performers, either in cameo or, for stars such as Chauncey Olcott and Blanche Ring, in full portrait. While attaching a picture of a performer to the cover was not new, by the end of the nineteenth century the performers were a part of vast vaudeville circuits that criss-crossed the nation. Therefore, as Jon W. Finson points out, "the variety circuit on which a single performer could present a composition several times a day in several cities over a period of weeks raised the level of exposure [of songs] exponentially."[6]

Nowhere is Tin Pan Alley's adaptation of modern business methods more obvious than in its creative attempts to solve the old problem that had bedeviled sheet music publishers from the beginning: how to get a song before the public. The old-line firms had paid little attention to marketing a song, apart from putting a dedication on the cover to the particular artist they hoped would sing it. In David Ewen's words, "song hits happened. Publishers themselves did little or nothing to create them."[7] The realization that hit songs could be *made* to happen was the secret to the Alley's success. And so, the art of song "plugging" was born.

Plugging was aimed at both the performer and the audience. Performers might get free cigars, drinks, dinners, train tickets, and even have their room and board paid. There were less expensive ways, however, for publishing houses to induce performers to adopt their songs. Part of the reason for the Alley's continued proximity to the theater district in New York City was to make it convenient for artists and managers to drop into an office to hear a firm's latest wares. If "dropping in" left too much to chance, there were always the "pullers-in" (a feature borrowed from the garment trade) stationed on the sidewalk to induce, cajole, or push a passing singer, agent, or theatrical manager into the front offices. Inside, there would be pianos, rehearsal rooms, and perhaps a convivial glass or two.[8]

Getting a performer to sing a song was one thing; getting the patrons to take notice of the song and eventually to buy it was quite another. Thus, the true art of song plugging had to involve the audience, as well as the performers. The venues were the saloons and the theaters, with appropriate plugging techniques adopted to the specific environment.

Although publishers sometimes used whistlers, especially in saloons, in theaters they preferred to employ a "stooge" or "boomer," usually a clear-voiced boy soprano planted in the gallery. The stooge would wait until the performer had completed the song to be plugged. He would then stand, as if inspired, and the spotlight, by prearrangement, would pick him out. Then in sonorous tones he would repeat the chorus. The hope was to get the members of the audience to join in, thus reinforcing the song in their memories. Among those who got their start in this bargain basement of show business were Gus Edwards (who inspired "A Song in the Gallery"), Al Jolson, Fannie Brice, George Jessel, and Eddie Cantor.[9]

By whatever means, a song that made its way to the vaudeville stage and musical theaters of New York gradually found its way across the country as performers toured the circuits. Before the popularity of recording discs, more Americans heard their songs from the vaudeville stage than from any other medium of professional entertainment. At the same time, traveling salesmen carried the song sheets out to the cities and small towns throughout America. As Maxwell Marcuse suggests, songs gained national popularity slowly, week by week, month by month. The marketing of a successful song was at least a two to three year process at best. However it was accomplished, getting the songs out of New York was the key.[10]

Since the city was also the home of most of the large vaudeville circuits, the New York stage was the keystone in the arch that connected the composers and publishers of Tin Pan Alley to the widely dispersed song-buying public. By the turn of the century, vaudeville had become respectable, less of a working-class and more of a middle-class form of entertainment. This meant that men could take their wives and daughters to the shows. Indeed, matinee audiences were largely made up of women. During the early years of the century there were between two and three thousand vaudeville theaters in the country. New York City originated over 310 shows a season. The feedback loops provided by performers and audience helped the Tin Pan Alley publishers to determine not only the content but also to shape the style of their songs.[11]

Questions of marketability also affected the musical structure of popular songs. Charles Hamm notes the shift in the relationship between verse and chorus. Tin Pan Alley gave the chorus to the solo voice instead of to a quartet, as had been done from the Civil War to the early 1880s. Eventually, the chorus carried the main melodic material and, in fact, "sold" the song. As an ad on the back of one of Witmark's songs in 1900 stated, "hear the chorus once, and you've got it." Where formerly the title might have been buried anywhere in the song, after 1890 it invariably came from the first or last line of the chorus. As a result of this evolution, the verse became little more than a function of the chorus.[12]

To be successful a song had to have a "punch"; it had to be "catchy." As Felix McGlennon (a very successful songwriter who alternated his career between New York and London) put it with an unusual bluntness, "I would sacrifice everything – rhyme, reason, sense and sentiment, to catchiness. There is, let me tell you, a very great art in making rubbish acceptable."[13]

It was within this sales-driven environment of Tin Pan Alley that Irish songs began to change significantly toward the end of the nineteenth century. Certainly, the Alley's song mills were as adept at turning out Irish songs as any other type. While the sample for this study contains 87 songs each for the decades 1880 and 1890, there are 106 songs for the 1900s, and 248 for the 1910s. The increase in the number of Irish songs in the new century reflects the tremendous overall growth in the Alley's output. However, it also suggests that the Alley's tunesmiths recognized a popular and profitable genre.

The Alley exploited the well-known propensity for Irish names to rhyme – even in song titles: "Arrah, Come in out of the Rain, Barney Mc-Shane" (1909), "I'm On Agen with Monaghan (And Off Agen with You)" (1910), "Come Kiss the Blarney, Mary Darling" (1911), "Blarney Barney Finn" (1914), "Rafferty's Chimes (Dugan, Degan, Donlin, Egan)" (1914), and "Arrah Go On, I'm Gonna Go Back to Oregon" (1916). Internal rhyming had always been a feature of Irish comic songs, an adaptation from the Irish broadside style and even traditional Irish song. It is possible, therefore, that one of the sources for Tin Pan Alley's infatuation with rhyming might have derived from the evolution of the Irish popular song.

A NATION ONCE AGAIN – ALMOST

In the early years of the century, there were still some songs being written for patriotic Irish melodramas. "Remember the Boys of '98," written for the play *Robert Emmet, the Days of 1803*, is based upon the melody Moore used for "Let Erin Remember the Days of Old." The cover shows the writer-performer Brandon Tynan in a green uniform, flanked by soldiers and the green flag. The musical play also included such traditional favorites as "Savourneen Deelish."[14]

While this kind of song still appealed to many Irish in America, it was a bit parochial for the larger market that writers and publishers on Tin Pan Alley sought to capture. For Irish nationalist sentiment to find a place in sheet music and on the vaudeville stage, it would have to be presented so that all Americans could understand it. For example, within the American context Irish nationalism could be simply an issue of ethnic fairness: everybody had a flag and a national anthem, why not the Irish?

> Let the Germans sing their "Wacht am Rhein,"
> The French the "Marselesez" [*sic*],
> Let the Scotsman sing their "Auld Lang Syne"
> John Bull his Navy Praise,
> But a heart of Erin's Isle will cling,
> That's sixty or sixteen,
> And will raise his voice and proudly sing,
> "The Wearing of the Green."[15]

The stereotype of the Irish as a race of fighters receives a patriotic dispensation by Tin Pan Alley in "Ireland's Flag of Green" (1907), which announces that "The Irish have a world-wide reputation / As warriors who are both brave and bold," and promising:

> Some bright day you will see them get together,
> In a battle much the greatest ever seen,
> After it they'll have home rule for ever,
> And independence on their flag of green.[16]

With the changes in the British constitution removing the House of Lord's power to block legislation, the Home Rule Bill finally passed the House of Commons in 1912 and was due to take effect in 1914. This resulted in some renewed interest in that old Gladstonian ghost. "Independence Day in Dublin Town" (1914) announced that "Home Rule has come to Stay." The seriousness of this song may be sensed by its subtitle, "A Novelty Song," and the line about giving an "Irish Tango Tea," a plug for another song by the same publisher. The performer of the song, Emma Carus, appears on the cover, leading a parade with a green banner emblazoned with "Home Rule." The big-voiced Emma must have had some success with the song, for two years later she was singing an updated, "What's the Matter with the Irish? (They're Getting Better Every Day)" (1916): "Tho' their fight for Home Rule seems in vain, / You can bet your life they'll try again." On the cover of this song Carus is flanked by two harp-emblazoned green flags.[17]

In 1916, with the Great War in its second year and President Wilson urging "preparedness" for the country, at least one song, "Keep a Place Down in Your Heart for Ireland," tried to tread the fine line between Irish and American loyalties, admonishing second-generation Irish to

> Keep a place in your heart for Ireland,
>   But in Uncle Sam put your trust,
> Work and Pray for him, march away for him,
>   To help him fight his battle if you must,
> This is where your father made his home, sweet, home,
>   'Tis your own dear heart's desireland,
> So take a stand in Yankee land but
>   Keep a place down in your heart for Ireland.[18]

Some songs kept alive the old "Irish-American Army" theme of the post–Civil War era: "All Aboard for Ireland and over the sea, / Come Murphy, Maloney, O'Brien and McGee; / We are heading for Dublin to set Ireland free."[19] This survival of the old Fenian dream of an Irish-American army of liberation in a Tin Pan Alley song shows the extent to which something that had once been a genuine part of Irish-American nationalism had become a popular-culture cliché. It is all the more surprising, then, to find it echoed in a line of "A Soldier's Song": "Soldiers are we whose lives are pledged to Ireland, / Some have come from a land beyond the wave." Written in Ireland, the song became the Irish national anthem. It was published in America in 1917. The cover displays the Irish tricolor as the only illustration. None other than Victor Herbert provided the musical setting. Although he had spent relatively little time in his homeland, the grandson of Samuel Lover was an ardent nationalist and, during these years, enthusiastically lent his name and presence to various Irish causes in New York.[20]

During the heady year of 1919, in the aftermath of the 1916 Rising, the Armistice, and the opening of the Versailles Peace Conference, there was a flurry of songs intended to cash in on the anticipation of Irish independence. Some, such as "God Made Ireland a Nation" (1919) with its tricolor and shamrock-emblazoned cover, offered strong nationalist statements. In "I'm Coming Back to Old Ireland (When It's a Nation of Its Own)" (1919), the singer vows to return to an independent Ireland where there will be no king or queen "but an Irish President." The cover of "Strike the Blow for Independence" (1919) shows a man riding a horse and carrying the Irish tricolor while Uncle Sam doffs his hat in salute. The song is dedicated to "The President of the Irish Republic, Eammon De Valera," then on tour in America.[21]

One of the most impassioned pleas for Irish independence appeared in "When Ireland Comes into Her Own" (1919). Hoping that the postwar world would create an independent Ireland, the songwriters add their voices to those calling on President Wilson to pressure Britain on the Irish Question.

> Alsace is as free as the Holyland,
>> And so is her Sister Lorraine,
> The Slavs everywhere are as free as the air,
>> And Belgium's unshackled again,
> For each State that's given her liberty,
>> A new star up yonder is shown,
> What a beautiful scene, Sure all heaven will gleam,
> When Ireland comes into her own.[22]

If only Wilson had hummed a few bars of that at Versailles.

As the Irish and other European immigrant groups mounted their campaigns to use American influence on behalf of their old homelands, grumblings about divided loyalty were heard. However, as Timothy Meagher points out, the Irish could agitate for Irish independence during this period, "not as undigested hyphenates fighting for a foreign cause, but as patriotic Americans pursuing a logical extension of America's basic beliefs."[23]

As we have seen in previous chapters, the Irish had long before learned how to explain their dual loyalty to America and Ireland. One way was to emphasize the parallel between American independence and Irish freedom. "Let's Help the Irish Now, (An Appeal to the World)" (1919) argues that since the Irish had helped free other nations, Ireland itself deserved independence. Even as late as 1920, Charles Lawlor, the composer of "The Side Walks of New York," could trot out the old doctrine of dual Irish-American loyalty with "Irish Liberty" (sung by Emmett Moore in *Ireland A Nation*).

> An Irish boy in Yankee land sailed across the sea,
>> To fight for Uncle Sam and France – for home and liberty,
> He fought the fight and victory won – for freedom took his stand,
>> And freedom now is what he wants for his own native land.[24]

Some of the Tin Pan Alley songs about Irish nationalism were written by Irish or Irish Americans who seriously intended to help the cause. Their songs may have played some small role in garnering a broader sympathy for Irish independence. However, Tin Pan Alley songs also reveal the extent to which the sentiments of Irish-American nationalism had become so many clichés that could be hauled out and rearranged whenever some performer or songwriter decided it was time to try to whoop up the Irish for a big round of applause or a decent sale of sheet music. Noticeably absent from these songs is the old enemy, Perfidious Albion, suggesting the degree to which these songs were tailored to WASP Anglophilia, as well as middle-class Hibernian tastes.

During the 1890s, the Irish comic song was in a state of transition. Some of the urban Paddy songs, so popular in the 1870s and 1880s, were still being written in the late 1890s and early 1900s. In 1904 there was an attempt to revive the McGinty craze of earlier years with "Come Down McGinty." Other comic Paddy songs from Tin Pan Alley were "Mike McCarthy's Wake" (1894) and "Swim Out O'Grady" (1894). "King Gilhooly" (1899) is of interest mainly for the relatively late appearance of the simian-faced Paddy who appears on the cover, enthroned in red and green, and accompanied by the ancient symbols of Paddydom: a dudeen, shamrocks, a shillelagh, and a harp. Davis William Cahill and Charles B. Lawlor's "The Mick Who Threw the Brick" (1899) also sported a Hibernian apeman on the cover.[25]

However, the old knock-about Paddy songs were passing in favor of "novelty" songs, which were comic, but in a very special sense. They embraced the new, the improbable, the eccentric, the nonsensical, and the unexpected, what Richard Middleton calls the "thematizing of shockingly ebullient, vernacular, everyday *noise*."[26] The fact that "telephone," itself a novelty to many people, rhymed with an Irish name, was enough to generate "Cordelia Malone" by Billy Jerome and Jean Schwartz (1904). Similarly, there is "Nora Malone, Call Me by Phone" (1909), which includes an example of Tin Pan Alley Gaelic: "Mushawurra, wurra, wurra, wurra, / Old Erin's Isle could not make me smile, / Without Nora Malone." Another attempt to juxtapose the Irish label with technological innovation was "In My Irish Aeroplane" (1917), in which the aviator hero promises to fly off to Sligo for his Irish bride, after he finishes "shootin' Teutons."[27]

Some of the most successful novelty songs were written by the team of Billy Jerome and Jean Schwartz. Jerome came from upstate New York, while Schwartz was a Hungarian Jew whose family had emigrated to America while he was a youngster. Schwartz and his sister had studied piano in

Budapest (she had been one of Liszt's many "pupils"), but he quickly picked up the American idiom just as ragtime was becoming popular. His first success was a ragtime piece entitled "Dusky Dudes" (1889).

Although Jerome and Schwartz wrote all kinds of songs, as a team they turned out some of the most popular of the new type of Irish pieces. Their "Mister Dooley" (1902) had little to do with Finley Peter Dunne's famous bartender, but a lot to do with the newly discovered power of popular culture to capitalize on the success of a person or an image and shift it from one medium to another. Although Dunne's photo is on the cover, the Dooley of the song turns out to be an early version of Mel Brooks's "Two-Thousand Year Old Man."[28]

A look at a few of Jerome and Schwartz's successes will illustrate the way clever writers could make a song "Irish." The team's first big success was "Bedelia" (1903). This was followed by an even bigger hit in the Irish genre, "My Irish Molly O" (1905). Both "Molly" and "Bedelia" are typical of Jerome and Schwartz's approach to Irish songs, Tin Pan Alley style: internal rhymes sung to a catchy melody with a syncopated rhythm and marked by sudden shifts from minor to major modes, and back again. If at times the results sometimes sounded more *klezmer* than Hibernian, no one seemed to mind.

Jerome's lyrics for the two songs show how a master of the art of song manufacturing fabricated an Irish song. The first line of "Bedelia" contains one of the words, "roguish," frequently used by Tin Pan Alley to limn an Irish lass: "There's a charming Irish lady, With a roguish, winning way." The next line contains the internal rhymes that long helped to characterize an Irish song: "Who has kept my heart *a-bumpin'* and *a-jumpin'* night and day." Jerome then throws in the two Irish place names that appear most frequently in songs: "She's a flower of Killarney with a Tipperary smile." Then, of course, there is the inevitable mention of the "isle," sometimes "Emerald," but here

> She's the best that ever came from Erin's Isle,
> And I find myself a-singing all the while.
>
> CHORUS:
>
> Bedelia, I want to steal ye, Bedelia, I love you so,
> I'll be your Chauncey Olcott, If you'll be my Molly O;
> Say something, sweet Bedelia, Your voice I like to hear;
> Oh, Bedelia-elia-elia.
> I've made up my mind to steal ye, steal ye,
> Bedelia dear.[29]

The internal rhyming in "My Irish Molly, O" is a bit more imaginative and less compulsive. There are a few Gaelicisms sprinkled around and the chorus also manages a nod at the traditional Irish bull.

> Molly – my Irish Molly – My sweet acushla dear,
> I'm fairly off my trolley – my Irish Molly, when you are near,
> Spring time you know is ring time,
> Come dear, don't be so slow,
> Change your name g'wan, be game,
> Begorra and I'll do the same,
> My Irish Molly O.

Blanch Ring, "The Irish Queen," helped make "Molly" a big hit. It was recorded by mainstream bands, as well as Irish groups such as the famous Flanagan Brothers.[30]

The productivity of Tin Pan Alley can be measured by the way in which a hit song begot offspring. Maude Nugent's "Sweet Rosie O'Grady" (1896) was blessed, some years later, by "The Daughter of Rosie O'Grady" (1918). In the same year, "The Sister of Rosie O'Grady" turned up, dedicated to the Goldwin Pictures star, Mabel Norman, whose photo appears on the cover. By including a musical paraphrase from the original "Rosie," "The Sister" uses a trick that was already well established during the time of Harrigan and Braham.

While it did not require a lot of knowledge about Ireland to write an Irish song on the Alley, creative license occasionally ran away from any semblance of realty. "Kerryanna" (1910) was intended as one of the era's trans-ethnic romps, in this case an Irish-Japanese song. However, the Irish place names in the song get confused with those of Scotland, and on the cover a man in a Scottish tartan and glengarry gazes into the eyes of a Japanese girl.[31]

Although the most successful Irish pieces of the era were generally waltz songs, such as "Sweet Rosie O'Grady," the shifting dance crazes of the period also offered opportunities for all kinds of variations on the Irish theme. For example, "The Irish Tango" (1914) asks the unlikely question: "Paddy Dear, say can you do, the Tango up and down? / O Paddy Dear, don't you know, the craze of Dublin town?" The cover shows Pat, dressed in his traditional knee breeches and a shamrock-speckled hat with a tapered crown, doing the tango. On the other hand, the "Dublin Rag" (1910) cries out: "Play me that Dublin rag, That Irish troublin' rag / Kiss me like you would the Blarney stone."[32]

The incongruity of an Irish rag was not lost on some of the songwriters. In John and William West's "Everything at Reilly's Must Be Done in Irish Style" (1899), Reilly is outraged when a black piano player hired for his party breaks into a rag. Reilly declares, "There'll be no coon cake walking, . . . no ragtime talking," and he summarily ejects the piano player.[33]

Of course, one of the best ways to churn out an Irish song was to recycle bits and pieces of old Hibernian hits. "My Irish Song of Songs" (1917) managed to work in all the great Irish songs of the prewar era (titles are italicized):

> Sure you have all the charms of my *Mother Machree,*
> You're *my Wild Irish Rose,*
> You remind me of *old Kilkenny,*
> *Where the River Shannon flows,*
> When your *Irish eyes are smiling,*
> I know where my heart belongs,
> You're *a Little Bit of Heaven,*
> You're my Irish Song of Songs.[34]

Part of the humor of the Irish novelty songs lay in playing off an old, well-established genre, with its clichés and stereotypical characters and situations, against the innovations of the "modern" twentieth century – its dances, its technology, its slang, and its dedication to fast-paced change. Although Irish themes were adapted easily to the novelty craze, the juxtaposition of Irishness with technological innovations and popular fads suggests that "Irish" stood for something that already seemed old-fashioned. Simultaneously, the novelty songs' jarring absurdities (Paddies in knee britches doing the tango), helped to erode whatever attachment to reality the nineteenth-century Irish song had enjoyed. On Tin Pan Alley there was neither time nor place. There was only a continuous "now," jangling to the incessant demands of the market.

ABBIE'S IRISH INDIAN

One particular kind of novelty song that frequently involved the Irish capitalized on the incredible ethnic mix and the resulting heightened ethnic consciousness of early twentieth-century urban America. Tin Pan Alley churned out a series of comic songs that depended for their humor on improbable ethnic combinations. These songs account for a surprisingly large proportion of the comic Irish songs in the sample: 44 percent for the 1900s and 39 percent for the 1910s.

Admittedly, some of these songs were simply continuations of the well-established Irish-German feuds. In "Ha-Le Ha-Lo or That's What the German's Sang" (1901), Dan Sweeny cannot stand the singing of the "Dutch" in the tenement. The resulting riot lands them all in jail, where the Germans continue their yodeling. "It's the Irish" (1905) assures us that the "Irish and Dutch they won't rhyme" as a way of explaining the inevitable interethnic fighting. In "McElwee" (1909) the singer confesses that Irish names were better "than Krausmann any day, / For the Germans never did amount to much." When an Irish girl marries a German in "A Little Bit of Irish" (1911), the singer reassures her that "Leana Herman is decidedly German, But your style and smile is from the Emerald Isle."[35]

"Arrah Wanna (An Irish Indian Matrimonial Venture)" by Jack Drislane and Theodore Morse (1906) started a brief craze for Paddies with squaws.

> Arrah Wanna, on my honor, I'll take care of you,
>> I'll be kind and true, we can bill and coo,
> In a wigwam built of shamrocks green,
>> We'll make those red men smile,
> When you're Mrs. Barney, heap much Carney, of Killarney's Isle.

With typical Tin Pan Alley disregard for detail, the cover shows an Indian maiden and a tepee with an Irishman playing the continental-style bag pipes instead of the Irish lap pipes. Crowded onto the cover are harps and shamrocks. A peace pipe replaces the traditional "dudeen." The only good joke in the song is the use of "Arrah," a common stage-Irish expression that Boucicault had turned into a name for his play *Arrah na Pogue*. By the early twentieth century it had become a key word in American popular culture, denoting things Irish.[36]

Not surprisingly, with a hit on their hands, the team of Drislane and Morse wasted little time in bringing out "Since Arrah Wanna Married Barney Carney" in 1907. This time a chief, decorated with shamrocks, joins the happy couple on the cover. The union was a success, because "Instead of Powwow dances, it's the Irish reels entrances."[37] There were a few other songs of this breed, such as "My Irish Prairie Queen" (1909) and "Be My Tipperary Bride" (1912).

The Hiberno-Hawaiian connection was forged with "O'Brien Is Tryin' to Learn to Talk Hawaiian" (1916). The song's gibberish Gaelic-Hawaiian carries echoes of the seventeenth-century "Lilliburlero," evidence of the historic Anglo-American habit of making fun of "exotic" languages.

With his "Arrah Yaka Hula Begorra Hicki Dula"
And his Irish "Ji-ji-Boo,"
Sure O'Brien Is tryin' to learn to talk Hawaiian
To his Honolulu Lou.

"Since Maggie Dooley Learned the Hooley Hooly" (1916) looks at the Hawaiian phenomenon from the Irish perspective.

Since Maggie Dooley learned the Hooley Hooly,
Ireland's Fading away
The Sweeney's and Daley's have sold their Shillelaghs
and bought Ukelelees [sic] to play,

The inevitable musical reaction came in "Sing a Good Old Irish Song for Me" (1917), which urges Irishmen to "Forget your Ukulele's [sic] and mention the Shillalie's [sic], When you praise the Emerald Isle, you can't go wrong."[38]

Tin Pan Alley clearly thought it funny to put an Irish man or woman in exotic surroundings. In "Mister Pat O'Hare" (1910) the hero knocks on the door of a harem asking for a tour. "Arrah-Arabia" (1908) tells the story of Maggie Brophy, a belly dancer "who never saw the Nile but came from Erin's Isle." The most popular song of this ilk was "I've Got Rings on My Fingers" (1909). Jim O'Shay a castaway in India, is made a nabob by the natives, who like his Irish smile. He sends for Rose McGee to join him, promising:

Sure, I've got rings on my fingers, bells on my toes,
Elephants to ride upon my little Irish Rose,
So come to your nabob, and next Patrick's Day,
Be Mistress Mumbo Jumbo Jijjiboo, J. O'Shay.[39]

Part of the humor of these songs lay in playing with the cliché about the ability of the Irish to charm their way into any situation. However, behind this good-humored joke stood a less attractive comic assumption; the American Irish were so associated in popular culture with the working class that once relieved of their picks, hods, aprons, and brooms and placed in unexpected settings they were rendered ridiculous.

A second comic stratum had more to do with race than with class. As an immigrant's immigrant, gatekeeper for the WASP, and buffer between the Yankee middle class and the hoards of "non-Anglo-Saxon" newcomers pouring into America, it was considered funny to fling Paddy into the melting pot. Thus, the humor of "Kelly's Gone to Kingdom Come" (1910). Reported missing in "Has Any One Here Seen Kelly," the search took on an international scope in this answer song, introduced by Maude Lambert, in which we learn that Kelly's full name is "Pat O'Hara Connamara Palistine O'Guggheim Li' Hung Dooley Ballyhooly J. Columbus Kelly." The missing Irishman finally turns up in "I'm the Man They're Looking for, Kelly, That's My Name" (1910), as sung by Carrol Johnson of Lew Dockstader's Minstrels.[40]

The most significant ethnic combinations in these Tin Pan Alley pieces were between the Irish and the Jews, which began appearing in songs after 1910. One of the first was "It's Tough When Izzy Rosenstein Loves Genevive Malone" (1910). This was followed by a hit from the *Ziegfeld Follies* for 1911, "My Yiddisha Colleen." The same year saw "Yiddisha Luck and Irisha Love (Kelly and Rosenbaum, That's Mazeltoff)" (1911): "Corn beef an' Gefilte fish; Mixed together, that's a dish." At the wedding the band played "Mazeltoff" and the "Wearing of the Green." "Moysha Machree" (1916) involves the offspring of an Irish-Jewish marriage. Ever seeking to balance the two sides of his family, Moysha drives a "Jewick [Buick] and a Catolic [Cadillac]," and "'Tis on Sunday he sings the Rosary, / And on Friday night to make things right, / He sings 'Jerusalem, Jerusalem' [musical paraphrase]."[41]

Although most of these songs were good humored, the ethnic stereotyping was generally at the expense of the Jews. In "There's a Little Bit of Irish in Sadie Cohen" (1916), concerning a Polish girl who married an "Irisher," we learn that, "Even with her Jewish face, she's a credit to the Irish race." "My Yiddishe Colleen" reverts to the traditional stereotype of Jews and money.

> Darlink come and mingle, won't you marry me,
> Then we'll have a Hebrew honeymoon,
> Bring the jingle, jingle, right where I can see,
> The wedding march will have a money tune.[42]

While intermarriage between Irish Catholics and Jews was a popular cultural fantasy, cooperation in business, entertainment, and politics was not. Praising Johnny Ahearn, who ran the third district that was half Irish and half Jewish, Tammany's George Washington Plunkitt explained his protégé's success in being popular with both groups: "He eats corned beef and kosher meat with equal nonchalance and it's all the same to him whether he takes off his hat in the church or pulls it down over his ears in the synagogue."[43]

There was, then, at least some basis for cooperation between the two groups, providing a rational for "If It Wasn't for the Irish and the Jews" (1912), by the team of Jerome and Schwartz.

> Talk about a combination, Hear my words and make a note,
> On St. Patrick's Day Rosinksy, Pins a shamrock on his coat,
> There's a sympathetic feeling, Between the Blooms and McAdoos,
> Why Tammany would surely fall,
> There'd really be no hall at all,
> If it wasn't for the Irish and the Jews.[44]

Crazy as these songs were, they reveal the fascination with the ethnic stew that urban America had become. The songs themselves were a harbinger of plays and films about the Irish and the Jews.[45]

It is interesting to compare these Irish "ethnic" songs with the Tin Pan Alley pieces about Italians and Jews that begin appearing after the turn of the century. Like the Germans, but unlike the Irish, both groups had their own sheet music. Songs in Italian were imported from Italy. Songs in Yiddish were published in New York City.[46]

When Tin Pan Alley turned to the Italians, the negative ethnic stereotyping is obvious even in some of the titles: "The Dago Banana Peddler," "Down in Spaghetti Row," "I'm Going Back to the Land of Spaghetti." While a few of the Italian songs are romantic, most fall into the comic/novelty category and are redolent with heavy stage-Italian accents. While the Italian girls who appear on the covers of the Tin Pan Alley pieces are usually dark-haired and pretty, the men, based on existing stage stereotypes, are exotics, either sinister or comic in their depiction, but seldom suggestive of a good citizen, much less a next-door neighbor. The organ grinders and banana peddlers who populate these songs find their girls have left them for an Irishman or German or, as in "My Mariuccia (Take a Steamboat)" (1907), for some "Tough Tony" who will take them back to Italy. Some Italians are depicted as lazy and shiftless. Others, if they work without monkeys and bananas, do menial tasks. The denizens of "Tony Spagoni's Cabaret" (1907) (where one can "hear them eating macaroni") are described as "the wops with the mops who manicure the boulevard."[47]

References to stilettoes and "The Black Hand" exploited popular symbols of supposed Italian criminality. The "Dago Banana Peddler" brags that his father was a brigand and that he keeps a stiletto where the police cannot find it. The cover of "Go On, Good-a-bye" (1910) depicts a swarthy Italian in soft hat, neckerchief, earring, and fierce black mustache brandishing a stiletto in one hand while giving the two-fingered salute to a mob, which is shouting "Dago, Dago."[48]

Some of the Tin Pan Alley songs about Jews followed the "Arrah Wanna" model by imagining Jews in improbable settings: "I'm a Yiddish Cowboy (Tough Guy Levi)" (1918); "Big Chief Dynamite" (1919) – a Jewish Indian; "Mosha from Nova Scotia" (1915) – he cannot talk or his hands will freeze. The songs alternated from celebrating unlikely Irish-Jewish nuptials to emphasizing Jewish exclusiveness. In "Marry a Yiddisher Boy" (1911), her Jewish boyfriend tells Sadie to drop the "Irishe Goy" and marry him: "I'm a good yiddishe button-hole finisher."[49]

There is some good-humored fun with Yiddishisms – "Isch Ga Bibble (I Should Worry)" (1913); Jewish high spirits – "Becky Do the Bombashay" (1910); and the incessant Tin Pan Alley fascination with rhymes – "Issie Get Busy." However, negative ethnic stereotyping is rife in these songs. While they avoid some of the worst Christian stereotypes of the Jews built up over the centuries, there are few songs that do not contain some reference to money, business, pawn shops, or sly deals. "My Rose of the Ghetto" (1911) is serenaded with: "Rosie Kohn, I groan and moan . . . / My heart's a pawn ticket you can keep." On the song covers and in the songs, Jewish physiognomy is a subject for racial humor, as in "My Yiddisher Blonde" (1912), where we are assured that "mit a different nose she'd be a Lillian Russell."[50]

The half century from the 1880s through the 1920s was probably the most race-conscious period in American history. The influx of immigrants from every national and linguistic group in Europe added to the racial tensions already existing along the color line between whites and African Americans (and, in the West, among whites, Asians, and Hispanics). In such a situation, ethnic stereotyping was inevitable. By 1900, the Irish had been through the worst of it. Irish stereotypes were still present in the culture, but, as we have seen, they were in the process of changing. Comparing the "ethnic" songs emanating from twentieth-century Tin Pan Alley, it is clear that the Irish fared much better than the Italians and Jews, relative newcomers to America. In songs about Irish Indians and Hiberno-Jewish couples the previous emphasis on Irish drinking, fighting, and blundering is muted; sometimes it is not even present. Accounting for 7 to 10 percent of the post-1900 songs, pieces like "Arrah Wanna" were hardly damaging to Irish-American reputations. In some sense, these songs are take-offs on the older Irish stereotype – the bragging b'hoy going off and charming the natives, even the Jews. The racism that colors the turn-of-the-century songs about Italians and Jews, not to mention African Americans, no longer characterizes the Irish stereotype.[51]

While the Irish were working their way up the economic ladder, the influx of "new immigrants" helped push them up the social ladder as well. Thomas J. Curran suggests that it is the shift in WASP prejudices away from Irish Catholics toward Italians and Jews that helps ease the Irish into the American mainstream. And if the Cabots and the Lodges still looked down upon the Kennedys and Murphys, the La Roses and Rosenblatts sometimes had a hard time telling the difference between Yankee and Hibernian. Harry Golden, growing up on the East Side of New York City during World War I, recalls that Irish policemen defined "American" for many of his neighbors. "Many of the newly arrived immigrants [from eastern and southern Europe] believed that the Irish and American were synonymous terms."[52]

Almost, but not quite. Why was it considered funny to have an Irishman visit a harem or become a nabob or Indian chief? Why was it funnier to have an Irishman instead of a Yankee marry a Jew? The comic songs of the Tin Pan Alley era show the extent to which the Irish were still in the "immigrant" category within American popular culture – still outside of the WASP center. Although no longer considered threatening, Irish men, like Jewish men, Italian men, and black men, could still be considered comical.

Yet, in the ethnic songs of turn-of-the-century Tin Pan Alley, we can see the vague forms of a certain kind of assimilation taking shape. The Irish-Jewish songs in particular were forerunners of the "Abie's Irish Rose" approach to ethnicity that became popular onstage and in films after World War I. Lester D. Friedman, in *Hollywood's Image of the Jew*, has put it very succinctly. "According to these films, the easiest way to become Americanized is to marry a Catholic girl, enter into a partnership with an Irishman, or adopt a Gentile baby." As Friedman contends, the result of the comic amalgamation of ethnic groups was to cast into absurdity the very concept of immigrant ethnicity and exclusivity, upheld by the first generation in the face of second-generation Americanization. He describes these Jewish-Irish romance films "as the assimilationist films par excellence," which lampooned old world ways, extolled the shift from the traditional to the modern, and celebrated "those who consign custom to the history books in their headlong dash to become true Americans."[53] In their article on the Irish in American film, Dennis J. Clark and William J. Lynch underscore the method by which assimilation was achieved in the cinema. In the "Cohen and Kelly" films of the twenties, both the first-generation Irish and Jewish immigrant characters are depicted as "boorish, loud, stubborn, crude, and given to humorous mishandling of the English language," while the assimilating and intermarrying offspring lose all trace of ethnic identity. Invariably, however, in most of these films, it is Irish-American cultural determinates that come out on top, since the Irish were closer to defining "Americanism" than any other immigrant ethnic group.[54]

The ethnic and other novelty songs suggest the situation Irish Americans found themselves in during the early decades of this century. They were no longer at the bottom of the heap; no longer despised and ridiculed. Like "honorary whites" in South Africa during the days of apartheid, the Irish by 1920 were close to becoming honorary Yankees. In both cases, the titles were hollow. Successful Asians in Cape Town were not white and Irish Catholics in Boston, no matter how wealthy, were not Protestant Anglo-Saxons. Within the popular culture, the Irish were still seen as immigrants, albeit, acceptable immigrants who seemed safely American. Even their nationalist songs were more ardent in their praise of Uncle Sam than of Eammon De Valera. If the Irish Americans were going to embrace the "hyphen," they would have to express their Irishness in ways that would fit easily into twentieth-century American popular culture.

10. Irish America in Search of an Image

By the turn of the century, Irish-American tastes were changing. Many Irish Americans, moving out of the tenements and into stable working-class and middle-class neighborhoods, brought with them a yearning for a higher cultural and social status than their parents had attained. These aspirations had a definite impact upon the entertainment field. Men and women who had escaped from the equivalent of Mulligan's Alley were much less interested than their parents had been in revisiting it in the theater. Moreover, the heightened cultural sensitivity that accompanied the growth of Irish nationalism was increasingly intolerant of the stage Irishman's low comedy. Second- and third-generation Irish were looking for images of themselves and of Ireland that were more compatible with their new bourgeois sensibilities and more acceptable to their Yankee neighbors. They wanted images that would somehow unite the Irish past with the American present; images that could inspire rather than embarrass. For many of the rising Irish, as well as for those who had already risen, the nineteenth-century Irish vaudeville comic was no longer acceptable. For some, he had become an insult.

Cries of outraged respectability were not new to the Irish-American community. Even Harrigan and Hart had come in for occasional criticism. In 1884 the Boston *Pilot* noted an attempt by some Irish in the city to organize a boycott of the team's tour. The paper dismissed the idea as ridiculous. "The Irishman who could be offended at *The Mulligans* or *Cordelia's Aspirations* is not sure of himself or his people."[1]

By the turn of the century, however, Irish eyes were not smiling at everything they saw on the stage. In the Irish Kensington (better known as "Fishtown") district of Philadelphia, on March 30, 1903, a riot broke out when two hundred Irishmen disrupted a performance of *McFadden's Row of Flats*. The police had to be called to restore order. The papers noted that a similar shindy had greeted a play called *McSwiggan's Parliament* in 1887. The agitation was eventually laid at the door of the Ancient Order of Hibernians. The AOH was often in the forefront of the nationalist cultural crusade to make the arts safe for the Irish.[2]

The most famous battle in the *Kulturkampf* over Irishness occurred during the first American tour of the Abbey Theatre in 1911, featuring John Millington Synge's *The Playboy of the Western World*. The *Gaelic American* carried a resolution that pledged, if the play was not withdrawn, "to drive the vile thing from the stage, as we drove *McFadden's Row of Flats* and the abomination produced by the Russell Brothers." (By 1907, after a sustained campaign, the AOH helped to banish the Russell Brothers, a vaudeville team that specialized in an outrageous transvestite spoof about two Irish "biddies" or servant girls.)[3]

The antagonism that some Irish Americans displayed toward Synge's *Playboy* and the Russell Brothers' skits did not originate solely in nationalist fears about the old stereotype of the Irish as blundering peasants, unfit for self government. Within American popular culture, Irish Americans already had fantasized an ideal Ireland that Synge's play and the Abbey Players' emphasis on realism threatened. For example, the *Gaelic American* was outraged at the bare feet of the actresses: "And such feet. No such feet ever came out of Ireland before. They were typical Anglo-Saxon feet – big, clumsy and flat . . . Irish women have the daintiest feet in Europe." Joyce Anne Flynn sees in these Irish-American protests a "possessiveness and anxiety concerning Irish subject matter in public performance that reflected the uncomfortable adjustment to urban America from which the grandchildren of the famine immigrants were only beginning to emerge."[4]

The new medium of film also came under Hibernian scrutiny. Thomas Cripps states that in 1915 the Irish in Boston joined the NAACP in demonstrations against *Birth of a Nation*. The Knights of Columbus later forced changes in MGM's *The Callahans and the Murphys*. According to Cripps, the trade papers, staffed heavily by Irish Americans, were on the lookout for ethnic slurs, going as far as to evaluate films with Irish themes for their appropriateness for Irish neighborhood theaters.[5]

These Irish reactions coincided with the onset of a decline in ethnic humor that, according to Paul Distler, had been the dominant form of vaudeville comedy from 1875 to 1905. In a sense, then, Irish Americans succeeded in cleaning up their stereotype partly because American popular culture in general was less dedicated to maintaining the old image of Paddy. Yankee attitudes toward the Irish were beginning to mellow. Kathleen Donovan argues that during the 1890s, while some mainstream magazines continued to denounce Roman Catholicism and Irish-dominated political machines, others such as *The Forum* and *Atlantic Monthly* were taking a more positive, if still condescending, view of the Irish. As John J. Appel's study of *Puck* reveals, the Irish began to look better once the Yankees compared them to the "new" immigrants from southern and eastern Europe. As early as 1887, *Puck* admitted that Pat was more "energetic" and less radical than the "inferior" Bohemians and Russians who were making their way to America.[6]

Along with Donovan, Francis Walsh notes the changes taking place in cartoons of the Irish after 1900. Even within the pages of *Puck*, where Thomas Nast's simian-faced Paddies had once terrified decent Protestant Americans, the image had softened, especially after the death of its anti-Catholic editor, Joseph Keppler, in 1894. By the end of the century, the violent Irishman was rare in *Puck*'s pages. Frederick Opper's cartoons for *Puck* became increasingly friendly in humor. In 1904 he created his "Happy Hooligan" cartoon in which, according to Appel, the Irish violence is gradually transformed into more wholesome "Irish scrappiness." Opper eventually produced the drawings for Dunne's *Mr. Dooley* books. Like the English before them, the Yankees had not abandoned the stereotype of the Irish; after the turn of the century they were simply beginning to see it in a different light. Appel notes that the cartoons and jokes were still condescending, but not necessarily negative. "What counts is the meaning imparted to stereotypes, whether they are seen as menacing, harmless or neutral."[7]

Changing Yankee attitudes reflected changing Irish realities, as it became clear that both a respectable Irish-American working class and middle class were rapidly emerging from the industrial chaos of the post–Civil War years. The Irish themselves responded to the new combination of political and cultural clout to assuage their nagging sense of inferiority, demanding a new image of themselves in American entertainment. One response was to produce Irish entertainment exclusively for Irish Americans. As we saw in an earlier chapter, Irish melodramas had established themselves after the Civil War. Dennis Clark documents the emergence, beginning in the 1870s, of parish drama societies and theatrical groups associated with Irish organizations. These groups staged renditions of Boucicault's melodramas, as well as Edmund Falconer's *Eileen Oge*, James Pilgrim's Irish musical reviews, such as *Robert Emmet* and *The Irish Tiger*, and Henry A. Jones and Henry Herman's *The Silver King*. After World War I, plays with romanticized Irish settings or upwardly mobile Irish-American themes were favorites among the Irish audiences in America. In vaudeville, the Irish insistence on more respectable representations of themselves also began to bear fruit. In 1903, for example, *Variety* applauded the team of Mark Murphy and his wife for offering "the essence of real Irish humor that is a thing apart from the spurious imitations of the ordinary witticism of knockabouts wearing green whiskers and talking with an insistently rolling 'R.'"[8]

The shift in taste is also clear in the sheet music produced during the late nineteenth and early twentieth centuries. The proportion of comic pieces in the sample declines from an average of 36 percent of the sample for the 1880s and 1890s to 24 percent for the first decade of the new century, down to 18 percent for the 1910s. Moreover, the importance of Paddy as a comic figure also declines in popularity. He dominates the comic songs of the late nineteenth century, appearing in 88 percent of such pieces in the 1880s and in 71 percent in the 1890s. By 1900, however, he is a minor figure in the comic songs: 24 percent for the 1900s and 32 percent for the 1910s. Indeed, satires on the rising Paddy, which accounted for about one-third of the comic songs in the 1880s, virtually disappear after the turn of the century, although the theme remained popular for a while in vaudeville sketches and in the early cinema.

Even more striking is the decline in the negative traits associated with the stage Irishman. The proportion of comic songs that featured some kind of violence decreased from 38 percent of the sample for the 1880s to 19 percent for the 1890s, to 16 percent for the 1900s to 7 percent for the 1910s. Similar changes can be seen in the words used to describe the Irish in the songs. Over the four decades from 1880 to 1920 references to drinking decline from 24 percent, 9 percent, 3 percent, to 2 percent respectively: fighting from 18 percent and 10 percent, down to 2 percent after 1900. The clusters of words referring to the combination of drinking, fighting, dancing, and singing – all part of the stereotype of the stage Irishman – decline from an average of 26 percent of the songs for the last two decades of the nineteenth century to an average of 8 percent for the first decades of the new century. It appears. then, that Paddy peaked in American song in the 1880s and started to decline in the 1890s.

THE NEW URBAN IRISH

The most powerful force driving the change in their image was the Irish-American community's search for respectability, the yearning for the "lace curtain," which, according to Timothy Meagher was "less an occupational status than a state of mind." Francis Walsh believes that the term "lace curtain," which emerged in the 1890s, was more than a symbol for prosperity for the Irish middle class: "It also connoted a self-conscious, anxious attempt to create and maintain a more genteel life style . . . the need to separate themselves from their hard drinking, lower class predecessors. The net result was to foster a mania for respectability."[9] Nothing threatened respectability quite as much as a buffoon with a jug, tripping over feet and tongue with equal abandon. By the end of the 1890s, vaudeville performers and songwriters were busy scraping off Paddy's rougher edges. "Who Threw the Overalls into Mistress Murphy's Chowder?" (1898) reflects the transition in taste. The first verse of the song is directly from the mold of the older Irish celebration-run-riot vaudeville song:

> Mistress Murphy's gave a party just about a week ago,
>> Everything was plentiful the Murphy's they're not slow,
> They treated us like gentlemen we tried to act the same,
>> Only for what happened well it was an awful shame.
> When Mrs. Murphy dished the chowder out,
>> She fainted on the spot,
>> She found a pair of overalls at the bottom of the pot.
> Tim Nolan he got ripping mad, his eyes were bulging out,
>> He jumped up on the piano and loudly he did shout.

CHORUS:

> "Who threw the overalls in Mistress Murphy's chowder?"
> Nobody spoke so he shouted all the louder,
>> "It's an Irish trick that's true,
>> I can lick the mick who threw
> The overalls in Mistress Murphy's chowder."

A few years earlier, the song might have ended true to form in a fight. However, when Mistress Murphy revives she remembers that she had done the laundry earlier that day and left the pants in the pot. Nolan apologizes and, rows and ructions avoided, everyone joins in on the chorus. The song works on several levels. While a jibe at the one-pot working-class family trying to put on airs, it is also a take-off on the old Paddy song, with the expected riot lost in the joke. It is also a glimpse of the new Irish who can take a joke and join in on the fun instead of breaking each other's heads.[10]

Still, Paddy, like Bram Stoker's Dracula, was a creature to be staked into his coffin, and, like that other Irish-conceived monster, Paddy refused to stay dead. Even in his decline he haunts the humor of the 1890s and early twentieth century in his doomed resistance to the lace curtain as it inexorably closes around him. Finley Peter Dunne was the foremost humorist to have fun with Paddy's futile struggle against deadening respectability, as related by the fictional barkeeper, Mr. Dooley. In one piece, Mr. Dooley recounts the time Hogan wanted to name at least one kid after his father, Michael, or his mother, Bridget. Hogan's upwardly mobile wife refuses: "'D'ye think I'm goin' to sind th' child out into the' wurruld,' she says, 'with a name' she says, 'that'll keep him from anny employmint,' she says, 'but goin' on th' polis for-rce.'" She proposes the name "Augustus." "'An' be hivins,' says Mr. Dooley, 'twas Augustus th' priest give it. Th' poor, poor child!' "[11]

Dunne continued Ned Harrigan's satire on the rising Irish. In one episode, he has Mr. Dooley describe Mr. Donahue's losing battle with gentility. Entertaining an old crony, Donahue urges his sophisticated daughter to play a few "chunes" on the piano. The guests suggest various jigs and reels, none of which Molly knows. When someone asks for "The Wicklow Mountaineer," Mrs. Donahue takes charge: "'She'll play no "Wicklow Mountaineer"'... If ye want to hear that kind iv chune, ye can go down to Finucane's Hall,' she says, 'and call in Crowley, th' blind piper,' she says. 'Molly,' she says, 'give us wan if them Choochooski things,' she says, 'They're so ginteel.'"[12]

By the time the Molly Donahue sketches began appearing in the late 1890s, the lace-curtain theme had already become a well-established feature of American humor. Just after the turn of the century, Will M. Cressy began turning out his "Mag Haggerty" vaudeville playlets for Thomas Ryan and Mary Richfield. In *Mag Haggerty's Father*, an Irish bricklayer comes into wealth when his daughter marries a millionaire. The ordeal of the curtain turns out to be almost as bad as Mr. Dooley had intimated, as the daughter tries to make a gentleman of the old man.[13]

Although old Paddy struggles against nouveau Patrick in these sketches, Ryan himself was anxious to portray "a type of Celtic character that would in no wise offend the members of the race." This meant no green whiskers, slapstick, and exaggerated makeup. The brogue was authentic but quiet, not boisterous. Thus, the old Paddy was kept in check and, as Shirley Staples has pointed out, Ryan's Haggerty reassured his Irish audiences that there was no need to be ashamed of old habits, as long as new ones ultimately prevailed. At a time when the older, more knock-about working-class Irish acts (such as Favor and Sinclair's *The Maguires* and their classic sketch *Hogan's Flat*) were dismissed as "old fashioned," the Haggerty plays gained in popularity.[14]

It was not merely Ryan's quieter Irish character that caught on. According to Staples, Mary Richfield's characterization of Mag, as a "graceful colleen who moved effortlessly into higher social circles," displayed the kind of traits people wanted to see in the new generation of Irish Americans. The *New York Mirror* claimed that Richfield also generated a "remarkable following among the women who are fond of vaudeville in its best form."[15]

Staples notes that the popularity of Ryan's Haggerty character was rather like that of George McManus's Jiggs in the comic strip *Bringing Up Father*. The strip first appeared in 1913 and began syndication in the Hearst chain in 1919. McManus claimed that the strip had been inspired by a play, William Gill's *The Rising Generation* (1893), which he had seen as a boy at the St. Louis Opera House, managed by his Irish-born father. McManus's comic strip had a strong Irish following.[16]

Haggerty and Jiggs, through no fault of their own, became rich, and, for all of their Irish wit and working-class resourcefulness, were trapped in shoes, collar, and tie. Although McManus's Jiggs inherited the simian upper lip of his nineteenth-century cartoon ancestors, his Paddyness, crushed under the plug hat his wife Maggie forced upon his head, was reduced to dreams of Dinty Moore's corned-beef and cabbage or an occasional night out on the town. The best poor Jiggs could manage was to sneak out to a poker game with the boys. His greatest hope was to avoid Maggie's rolling pin when he staggered home late. As Kathleen Donovan suggests, Maggie is the traditional comic Bridget evolved from serving maid into domineering housewife.[17]

What makes Edward Harrigan's Dan Mulligan heroic, by comparison, is Dan's refusal to embrace willingly the lace curtain. His Paddyness enabled him to triumph eventually over social-climbing wives, ravenous in-laws, and insistent bill collectors. Harrigan's characters might rise or fall, but they were to some extent captains of their own fate. They could, if necessary, return to Mulligan's Alley and thrive. Haggerty and Jiggs lost the luxury of going back to their working-class roots. What doomed them was the unequal nature of the domestic battle they vainly tried to wage. Ambitious wives were one thing, but daughters-to-the-curtain born were something else. Like Dunne's poor Donahue in the Mr. Dooley sketches, Haggerty and Jiggs had to deal with fully Americanized daughters who had no more attachment to the old working-class life than they had to the ould sod itself. For the Irish father of twentieth-century comics and vaudeville, the lace curtain had finally closed.

While the theme of the risen Irish provided rich material for some vaudeville sketches, plays, and a few George M. Cohan musicals, there is little evidence that it had much influence on Tin Pan Alley. A few early Alley songs did allude to the tensions between the blue-collar father and the pink-collar daughter. One example is "Since My Daughter Plays on the Typewriter," also known as "Bridget McGuire" (1889). The father complains that since Bridget became an office worker she will not take lunch in a basket or drink cold "tay" from a flask, but dines instead at the Bon Ton Cafe. She dates her boss. The worst part, however, is the new culture she brings home.

> She says she's a regular daisy,
>> Uses slang till my poor heart is sore,
> She now warbles snatches from operas,
>> When she used to sing "Peggy O'Moore,"
> Sure she's gone to the devil entirely,
>> She's bleach'd her hair till it is lighter,
> And I'll dance a Can Can on the face of the man,
>> That taught her to play the Typewriter.[18]

In "O'Brien Has No Place to Go" (1908) the father finds he cannot relax in his own home because his girls are courting on the porch, in the parlor, and in the kitchen. He ends up kicking out all the Irish suitors. The pretty, redheaded girl on the song's cover, which contains no other Irish symbols, is typical of the depiction of the turn-of-the-century Irish-American girl. After 1890 the popular culture iconography that identified Irish girls as redheads seems to have contributed to the use of red as an identifying color for Irish song covers, second only to green.[19]

The Irish-American girl began life as the tough "chippie" characterized by Harrigan's Maggie Murphy and as the somewhat gentler girl who sings "Danny By My Side." The street-smart type had a brief life as a Bowery lass, as in Safford Waters's "The Belle of Avenoo A" (1895). This song is unusual for its heavy use of urban dialect. The pretty belle moves in the world of the urban Irish, having as a lover Billy McNeill, who works as a bouncer at Clancy's Bar. The song was Blanche Ring's first big hit, after which she went in for more genteel fare.[20]

Occasionally, the Irish-American girl appears as a good-hearted, selfless slum rose, as in Lew Sully's "The Idol of Donovan's Row" (1898) or Ford and Bratton's "The Sunshine of Paradise Alley" (1895). Although the latter was written for the British music halls, the daughter of Widow Mac-Nally, who nursed the little O'Brien boy and who seems all set to marry Tommy Killeen, fitted naturally into the American vaudeville stage.[21] Yet, although she rapidly moves off the streets and out of the slums, the Irish-American girl is more visible on the song covers than in the cliché-ridden lyrics of the songs in which she appears. She is still essentially the true-hearted, pure Irish colleen of the old parlor ballads but with a bit more up-to-date zip and personality.

Yet, in reality, the Irish-American girl was special. She was the first daughter of immigrants to be accepted on her own terms into American popular culture. There was no accent, no speaking with hands, no dumpling-fattened cheeks, no immigrant mannerisms at all. She was American; yet, with an alleged Irish flavor. To the daughters of more recent immigrant groups, she was barely distinguishable from her Yankee sisters. In 1914 a New York West Side social worker described the newly arrived immigrant girl, scurrying back and forth to work, head covered in a shawl, encountering "the daughters of her Irish and American neighbors in their cheap waists in the latest smart styles, their tinsel ornaments and gay hair bows."[22]

In spite of the popularity of "Sweet Rosie O'Grady" and "My Irish Molly O," however, the twentieth-century song-buying public seems to have had only a minor interest in the Irish-American girl or with the Irish neighborhoods that bred her. Before the turn of the century, the identification of Irish America with urban America had seemed solid, thanks in part to Ned Harrigan's sizeable contribution in plays and songs. In songs about the city, the Irish seemed ubiquitous. Why was it "Casey" who waltzed with the strawberry blond when "The Band Played On?" Why was Albert Von Tilzer's "Take Me Out to the Ball Game" (1908) about the courtship of baseball-mad Katey Casey? And why was it "Down in front of Casey's Old brown wooden stoop" that those boys and girls with Irish names tripped the light fantastic on "The Sidewalks of New York" (1890)? For a brief decade or so before the turn of the century, an Irish name conjured up the American urban scene.

The "comics," a rapidly evolving medium of popular culture in the 1890s, also stressed the ubiquity of the urban Irish. In 1896, Richard Outcault, a former contributor to *Judge* and *Life*, launched a new cartoon based on the denizens of Hogan's Alley. The name was a tip of the hat to Ned Harrigan, whose work Outcault greatly admired. The last verse of "Maggie Murphy's Home" begins, "I walk through Hogan's Alley, At the closing of the day." There were all kinds of ethnic types in the cartoon, but the Irish presence is unmistakable. The next year Gene Myers brought out the sheet music for "Dance of the Hogan Alley Hoboes."[23] What was missing from American popular culture at the turn of the century, however, was a playwright or songwriter willing to do for the urban Irish Americans in the twentieth century what Ned Harrigan had done for them in the late nineteenth century.

Only one person could have followed in Harrigan's footsteps, and that was George M. Cohan. Cohan was raised in a second-generation Irish-American theatrical family. His grandfather was Michael Keohane (O'Caomhan in Gaelic) who, like his wife, was from County Cork.[24] As mentioned earlier, George's father, Jerry Cohan, had started out as an Irish dancer in minstrel shows and then formed his own "Hibernicon." Later, as an actor-manager, Jerry Cohan put on plays with Irish themes such as *The Molly McGuires*. However, as the family troop, "The Four Cohans" (father, mother, George, and his sister Josephine) became established, the strong identification with things Irish began to fade. One of George's youthful successes was in playing the lead in a production of *Peck's Bad Boy*.

Growing up, George M. Cohan had been greatly impressed by Edward Harrigan's plays and songs. He once wrote: "Harrigan inspired me when I applauded him from a gallery seat. Harrigan encouraged me when I first met him in after years and told him of my ambitions. I live in hopes that some day my name may mean half as much to the coming generation of American playwrights as Harrigan's name has meant to me." Cohan's musical tribute to his early idol was the song "Harrigan" (1907) – "It's a name that no shame never has been connected with." Ironically, Cohan used it in a show about suburbia; *Fifty Miles from Boston* (1908) was a long way from Mulligan's Alley.[25]

Cohan continued his father's move away from Irish material, casting a much broader theatrical net. His first big musical hit, *Little Johnny Jones* (1904), had nothing to do with the Irish. He did attempt a Harrigan-type German-Irish combination in *The American Idea* (1908), in which the old ethnic squabbles between the families take place during a vacation in Paris. In the 1920s, Cohan produced a series of plays and musicals with some Irish-American characters: *Little Nelly Kelly* (1922), *The Rise of Rosie O'Reilly* (1923), *The Voice of McConnell* (1918), and *The Merry Malones* (1927). However, the songs from these shows failed to break new ground and they arrived just at the point when the Irish genre of popular songs had passed its peak.

Perhaps the Irish had become so assimilated to the industrial city by 1900 that it became harder to produce a distinctly Irish identity within the urban context, at least within the limitations of popular song. Writing about "Sweet Rosie O'Grady," Jon Finson notes that except for name and urban background, there is nothing particularly Irish about Rosie. "Her ethnicity has been immured in national style . . . and assimilated by this means into the general popular culture to meet the demands of a far-flung market."[26]

Finson is wrong, however, when he extends his analysis to the whole range of Tin Pan Alley songs about the Irish published during the early decades of this century. If the city streets could no longer provide an appealing venue for an Irish identity, there was always the ould sod itself. As we will see in the next chapter, as far as the song-buying public was concerned, the Irish rose bloomed best not in America's cities but back in dear old Ballybeyond in Ireland. In fact, the image of the Irish Americans as an urban people peaks in the songs in the 1880s and 1890s (when 56 and 43 percent, respectively, of the songs in the sample were set in urban America). In the first two decades of the new century, in song after song, Irish eyes were looking less to Broadway and Times Square and more to Erin. In their search for an alternative image for themselves, Irish Americans, with encouragement from Tin Pan Alley, would return in imagination to the Emerald Isles.

11. All That I Want Is in Ireland

An alternative vision of Irishness had already begun to emerge in the 1880s, principally around the figure of William J. Scanlan. As a performer and songwriter, Scanlan was initially skillful in exploiting Paddy roles, as he did with his song "If I Catch the Man." However, he also discovered the formula for taking Irish melodrama and replacing the older, more conventional Irish songs that had accompanied these plays with thoroughly Americanized concoctions that were more in the spirit of the nascent Tin Pan Alley than the Ould Sod.

Scanlan was second-generation Irish, born in Springfield, Massachusetts, in 1856. He began his career as "The Temperance Boy Songster." As a teenager, he came to New York City and played in a double act with Jim Cronin ("that Hibernian wit and comic"). The act played successfully at Dan Bryant's and at Pastor's. When the duo disbanded in 1877, Scanlan toured with Minnie Palmer.[1] While playing the role of an Irishman in Bartley Campbell's *Friend and Foe* in 1882 (in which he introduced the song "Moonlight in Killarney"), Scanlan caught the eye and ear of impresario Augustus Pitou. Pitou was skillful at writing or commissioning vehicles for his leading performers to take on tour. Under his aegis Scanlan starred in *Shane-Na-Lawn* (1885), *The Irish Minstrel* (1886), *Myles Aroon* (1888), and *Mavourneen* (1891).

Like many popular songwriters, Scanlan was not particularly careful when it came to the originality of his melodies. One of his most successful songs, "My Nellie's Blue Eyes" (1883), the only one to survive into this century, echoes the Venetian song "Vieni Sul Mar."[2] The simple melody of "My Nellie's Blue Eyes," innocent of any traditional Irish influences, is a prototype of the modern Irish love song as composed in America. It, along with other Scanlan songs, such as "Scanlan's Rose Song" (1883) and "Remember Boy, You're Irish" (1886), also may have helped propagate that remarkable genetic trait possessed by almost every Irish colleen in song: blue eyes.

The fact that I am Irish, I never will deny,
I love my native country fresh and green;

Where the open hearted laddie, and the pretty blue-eyed lass,
　　The wild flow'rs of her country may be seen.

Soon the dear old harp of Erin from slumber will awake,
　　It's echo's sweet will peal thro'out the land;
To show that still she lies in every heart and clime,
　　Like treasured gems of love both true and grand;

Like the warmth and dew of Spring, which bring to life and strength,
　　The flowers and blades from mother earth so dear;
So from silenced graves of woe, tears of joy will flow,
　　And then from every heart and tongue you'll hear,
Remember Boy, You're Irish.[3]

The song, from *Shane-Na-Lawn*, shows how songwriters were beginning to treat the "Irish" popular song as a framework upon which to hang clusters of key words and images identified with Irishness. In this one song, Scanlan managed to work in "mother," "childhood," the color green, "blue eyes," the beauties of the Irish landscape, the harp, the shamrock, and a tip of the hat to the sorrows of poor Erin. Scanlan's songs were among the first to revive Thomas Moore's smiles-and-tears motif as a kind of shorthand reference to Irish tragedies, the descriptions of which were beginning to seem inappropriate for popular songs. Finally, he also managed to articulate a sense of national pride without evoking either the pain of famine and eviction or the call to take pike in hand and join the Fenians to invade Ireland or Canada, whichever was closer.

Pitou claimed that Scanlan (who, according to press reports, carried a piece of the "ould sod" in his pocket) had a successful tour of Ireland. Yet, Scanlan's efforts as a songwriter went beyond the usual boundaries of the Irish genre. He introduced songs into his performances that had nothing to do, in music or in lyrics, with Ireland: "Peek-A-Boo," "Ring the Bells," "The Little Christmas Tree," and "She's Like the Violets Blue." Extracted from the Irish context of the melodramas, such songs had a good chance of success with a wider audience.

In his memoirs, Pitou hailed Billy Scanlan for his "natural ability . . . his comedy was effective, his pathos convincing, and he was original, creative and magnetic. . . . Having a sweet tenor voice of some power he sang his ballads in a way that reached the hearts of the people." Pitou concluded that, "no actor was ever so idolized by the Irish people.[4]

Unfortunately for the former temperance singer, the child was not father of the man. Scanlan, like many entertainers of his day, including Tony Hart, indulged in excesses of various kinds. In addition to being a heavy drinker, he developed paresis. While performing in his last hit, *Mavourneen* in 1891, the dementia became so serious that at the 102d performance he was withdrawn. He died at Bloomingdale Asylum in White Planes seven years latter.

Scanlan's demise left a void that had to be filled, especially since Pitou had a considerable stake in maintaining his share in the Irish theatrical market. He sent off a wire to a singing actor, another tenor, whom he thought could step into Scanlan's roles. Chauncey Olcott had just completed an engagement in England, and he agreed to come to New York.

Neither his stage name nor his real name, John Chancellor, suggests the genuine Irish background of the man who would become the leading Irish-American performer of his day. Olcott's mother, Margaret Doyle, had been born in County Kilkenny and came to America as a babe in arms. The family lived for a time in a paddy camp along the Erie Canal while Olcott's grandfather worked on the locks. Margaret married a Yankee named Chancellor and Olcott was born in Buffalo on July 21, 1860. According to Rita Olcott, the singer's wife, young Chauncey heard tales of Ireland from his Irish grandparents while he was growing up.[5]

As a young man, Olcott was bitten by the theatrical bug and he ran away from home, several times, to join minstrel shows. Although he suffered the indignity of having one of his parents drag him by the ear out from his first minstrel parade, he eventually realized his ambition and sang with several popular minstrel troops. He graduated from the minstrel circuit and got his big break when he appeared with Lillian Russell in *Pepita, or The Girl with the Glass Eyes* in 1886. His career took him back and forth across the Atlantic several times. While in London, he landed the part of Chevalier Patrick Julius O'Flanagan in *Miss Decima*. In order to polish his Irish accent, Olcott made a quick trip across the Irish Sea. It was his first visit to Ireland and it lasted only a week. When the call came from Pitou, however, the accent was good enough to last for hundreds of performances as Olcott established himself as the reigning Irish tenor in the American theater.[6]

Olcott quickly moved into Scanlan's *Mavourneen*, which his wife later described as a "cloak and sword" drama, set in Grattan's Dublin. "When Chauncey sang [Scanlan's songs] he put into his voice all the bitter history, the broken homes, the fairy memories of the Emerald Isle. Irish hearts in his American audiences wept in their exile." Olcott was warmly received and he quickly established his credentials as the successor to Billy Scanlan.[7]

As Mari Kathleen Fielder has pointed out, Scanlan had been instrumental in pioneering for the American theater a new type of stage Irishman that Olcott later perfected. Eschewing the excesses of the hard-drinking Paddy, the Scanlan-Olcott figure was a handsome, witty, attractive, yet sentimental hero, who was not above shedding a manly tear for mother and motherland. He borrowed some of the humor and cleverness of Boucicault's peasant heroes and blended it with the virtues and good looks of the typical romantic lead of earlier Irish melodrama. As Fielder has suggested, the really new element in this hero, as epitomized by Olcott's characters, seemed to spring more from the Irish American than the Irish imagination. He was a good-humored hero who, while capable of daring-do, was more at home singing love songs and lullabies.[8]

Once Olcott had proved himself in Scanlan's *Mavourneen*, Pitou and other writers built a succession of vehicles around the new star: *The Irish Artist* (1894), *The Minstrel of Clare* (1896), *Sweet Inniscarra* (1897), *A Romance of Athlone* (1899), *Garret O'Magh* (1900), *Old Limerick Town* (1902), *Terence* (1903), *Ragged Robin* (1904), *Eileen Ashtore* (1906), *Barry of Ballymore* (1910), *Macushla* (1912), and *The Isle O' Dreams* (1913). Many of the plays were historical romances and a few revolved around figures out of Irish history, such as *Edmund Burke* (1905) and *O'Neill of Derry* (1907).

The musicals were enormously popular among middle-class Irish audiences. According to Fielder, the earlier plays were tried out in the Irish neighborhoods in the Bronx and Brooklyn before hitting Broadway. After Broadway moved beyond shamrocks and sentiment, Olcott simply toured the Irish areas of greater New York and other Hibernian strongholds across the country.[9]

Although the idea of an all-singing, all-dancing Edmund Burke may seem unlikely, Olcott's vehicles, built upon earlier Irish melodrama, gave Irish Americans a kind of "usable," if not very accurate, sense of the past. Unlike Thomas Moore, who offered a glorious past to be wept over in an inglorious present, Olcott and his associates gave Irish Americans a glorious, albeit fantastic, past upon which to build dignity and respectability. In the shift from melodrama to musical, there was an opportunity to clothe Ireland in more sentimental, sunnier aspects, without dwelling on such unpleasant details as eviction, famine, and revolution.

Olcott wrote or at least collaborated on a number of the songs used in his musicals. According to his wife, while Olcott did write some songs, he also came up with bits of melody and verse that were put into shape by the regular lyricists and composers whom Pitou had under contract.[10] He collaborated with some of the best Tin Pan Alley professionals of the day. The lyricists included George Graff Jr. and Rida Johnson Young, who also wrote the books for several of his musicals. Among the composers was Ernest Ball, one of the Alley's most successful tunesmiths. It was Ball who wrote the music for "When Irish Eyes Are Smiling" (1912), "A Little Bit of Heaven (Sure, They Call it Ireland)" (1914), and with Olcott, "Mother Machree" (1910). When we add Olcott's "My Wild Irish Rose" (1897) and J. R. Shannon's "Too-re-loo-ra-loo-ra (That's an Irish Lullaby)" from *Shameen Dhu* (1912), we have much of the sentimental core of twentieth-century Irish-American song.

Although Olcott was a handsome and apparently competent actor, a good bit of his success depended on his ability to combine his fine lyric tenor with what American audiences accepted as an appropriate Irish accent and singing style. For his turn-of-the-century, middle-class audiences, this meant the *bel canto* style that had come to represent artistic singing. As Fielder has pointed out, there was no hint of the Irish traditional singer in Olcott's delivery and he was, for a time, compared favorably with the young John McCormack.[11]

McCormack was one of the finest lyric tenors of the twentieth century. His recordings of the tenor arias from Mozart's *Don Giovanni* remain unrivaled for their purity of tone and the long flowing *bel canto* line. However, he was best known and is still best remembered for his renditions of popular Irish songs. The identification was so strong that William Jerome and Jean Schwartz wrote "When John McCormack Sings a Song" (1915), which claimed, "Sure you get a glimpse of heaven where all Irish hearts belong." Thus, while Scanlan and Olcott were recognized for their singing, it was John McCormack's recordings of the best of Olcott's material that gave those songs a high polish and made them popular well beyond the Irish-American community. It is significant that most of Olcott's recordings were on the "ethnic" labels made for the Irish market, while most of McCormack's were on the mainstream labels.[12]

To the extent that the Irish tenor produced an "ethnic" sound, it was based on an ethnicity defined by popular culture on both sides of the Atlantic, and, as suggested above, it had little to do with traditional singing in Ireland. In this context, Rita Olcott's account of the origins of "My Wild Irish Rose" is unintentionally revealing. When the Olcotts took his mother for a visit back to Ireland (a place she was very anxious to leave as soon as she saw it), they visited the Lakes of Killarney and found themselves being entertained by a local lad. To keep him from singing songs in Gaelic in the traditional (and, no doubt, to his auditors, nasal) manner, Olcott asked the boy the name of a local flower. When told that it was nothing but "a wild Irish Rose," Olcott supposedly had his inspiration for a song. The little story is revealing about the cultural distance that the American-born, middle-class Irish had already traveled. "Irish" songs were now to be written in America, by Americans, and sung by Americans in a style approaching that of classically trained singers.

MOTHERS MACHREE

The vogue of Irish mother songs in American popular culture owes much to "Mother Machree," written for *Barry from Ballymore* (1910).

> There's a spot in my heart which no colleen may own,
>> There's a depth in my soul never sounded or known,
> There's a place in my memory, my life that you fill,
>> No other can take it, no one ever will.

CHORUS:

> Sure, I love the dear silver that shines in her hair,
>> And the brow that's all furrowed, and wrinkled with care,
> I kiss the dear fingers so toil worn for me,
>> Oh, God bless you and keep you, Mother Machree.[13]

John McCormack's recording of the song eventually overshadowed Olcott's renditions. McCormack was so closely associated with the song that when he announced in 1919 that he would become an American citizen, fifteen hundred graduating naval trainees sang "Mother Machree" in his honor, followed by the national anthem and three cheers for the country's newest citizen.[14]

"Mother Machree" was a strong influence in a business where it was often safer to copy a trend than to innovate. In the decade after the song appeared in 1910, 16 percent of the Irish songs in the sample mention "mother," a considerable jump from previous decades. Ernie Ball himself cashed in on the dear one again in 1915 when he wrote "She's the Daughter of Mother Machree" with J. K. Brennan. The same year saw "When the Sun Sets in Galway (Mother Machree Waits for Me)," illustrated by a green-tinted reproduction of Whistler's mother on the cover. "Ireland Must Be Heaven for My Mother Came from There" (1916) was eventually featured in the film, *Oh You Beautiful Doll*. In "I'm Hearing from Erin and Mother O'Mine" (1917), the connection between an Irishman and his mother surpasses the miracles of modern technology. The messages the singer receives from over the sea are not via the "wireless" but from the heart. Brennan and Ball came back in the following year with "Goodbye Mother Machree" (1918), its cover depicting a soldier kissing his white-haired mother farewell. "That Old Irish Mother of Mine" was written by another pair of Alley veterans, Billy Jerome and Harry Von Tilzer (1920).

Of course, the Irish did not have a monopoly on mother songs. Sophie Tucker had a great hit with "My Yiddishe Mommy" (1926). Mothers had been one of the universal themes of Anglo-American popular music since the days of the parlor ballads. Nevertheless, the image of mother played an important role in Irish-American culture. Irish working-class fathers often died early, leaving the mother, as William V. Shannon reminds us, "as the children's only link to the happier days of the past and the symbol of the family's will to survive. . . . The widow woman thereby became a classic figure in the Irish community." Andrew Greeley states that the mother is a stronger figure within the Irish Catholic family structure than in most other ethnic communities. She is "more likely to play a solitary influential role, just as the cultural heritage, the folklore, and the literary tradition would have predicted." Charles Fanning points out that the Irish mother's traditional role as provider of religious instruction, strengthened by the "devotional revolution" in post-Famine Ireland, enhanced her position within her new home in America, reinforcing and encouraging a tendency toward matriarchal dominance. Moreover, before marriage, young Irish women could more easily get steady work in the textile mills or in domestics service than could unskilled Irishmen. Although they tended to stay at home with their children after marriage, many Irish women may have retained something from their experience of economic independence. "The result could easily have been a subtle transfer of power and family control from the struggling male provider to the grounded, less threatened woman of the house." While, as Fanning points out, the key position of the Irish mother was reinforced in Irish-American fiction, it also was reinforced in popular songs.[15] By Olcott's time, the Mothers Machree had become the common link in three sets of interlocking dyads that were at the core of twentieth-century Irish-American song: mother and son; mother and sweetheart, mother and Ireland.

Far from being a conceit of Broadway and Tin Pan Alley, the strong ties between mother and son seem to have been a genuine element in both Irish and Irish-American culture. Kirby Miller has suggested that the mother-son bond was in part the product of the changing social structure in post-Famine rural Ireland. The shift from partible to nonpartible inheritance gave the Irish father enormous power, since it was he who would decide which son would get the farm. At the same time, marriage in rural Ireland took on a more pronounced economic character as families sought to marry the daughter with the dowry to a "strong" farmer or local businessman. In Kirby's words, "Emotional bonds between mothers and sons were proverbially close, at times smotheringly so, as frustrated farmers' wives – often trapped in loveless marriages to men much older than themselves – lavished compensatory affection on male offspring who welcomed relief from their father's stern demeanor."[16]

The roots of Mother Machree also extended deep into the experience of Irish emigration itself. Miller emphasizes the burden of guilt laid upon young Irish men and women, who, in emigrating, had to deal simultaneously with the combined burdens of moving from adolescence to adulthood, while simultaneously leaving their parents to start life in a strange new country. Many of the emigrants of the last wave, from 1870 to 1921, were from the traditional, Gaelic-speaking communities of the western seaboard, where children were raised to be self-effacing, obedient, and responsible for the parents in old age. Thus, separation, especially from the mother, was hard. Miller quotes one emigrant as saying, "There is no friend that takes the place of mother. Who is so kind, so thoughtful . . . ? What [but the image of mother] attaches and keeps our thoughts continually centered on home?"[17]

The "American wake," a uniquely Irish institution modeled on the wake for the dead and held for every emigrant, seems to have been designed to instill grief and guilt upon the departing sons and daughters and to impress upon them the obligations they still had to the parents left behind. One emigrant, James Mitchell, wrote of the leave-taking, "It is impossible for anyone not experienced to have an adequate idea of the effect of a *last* look from a Father or Mother." The "wakes" sometimes featured lamentations, similar for those raised for the dead. Thus, one Kilkenny mother is supposed to have keened over her son who was about to emigrate: "O mavourneen, and why do ye break the heart of her who raired ye? Was there no turf in the bog, no praties in the pit, that ye leave the hairth of yer poor ould mother?" Another mother from Connemara cried out:

Is there anything so pitiful as a son and a mother
Straying continually from each other? I who reared him without
    pain or shame

And provided food and good clean sauce for him . . .
Isn't it little my painful disease affects him
And the many sorrows that go through my heart?

The songs sung at the emigrant's "wake" were a mixture of traditional, broadside, and popular pieces. To Miller they represent "a stylized dialogue between the emigrants and those who remained in Ireland," expressing the promise to return, the duties to parents, and the guilt of leaving.[18]

There are clearly sentiments in the Irish popular songs of the late nineteenth and early twentieth centuries that could have evoked guilt among some listeners. "That Old Irish Mother of Mine" tells us:

It's always, "Good luck and God bless you"
    Each time that she bids you good-bye;
For a poor broken heart that's love-hungry
    There's a sweet cheery smile in her eye.
When you gaze on that picture you see
    She's a *mother and sweetheart to me.*[19]

Few songs come closer to equating the mother with the beloved. However, in many of the popular Irish songs the two are closely associated. In "Let Me Glance at Dear Old Ireland Once Again" (1911), the singer envisions home and hearthside back in Ireland: "With my mother there, God bless her, and my sweetheart to caress her." To some extent, such sentiments represented a continuation of the sense of loss of home and family established in the parlor songs of the nineteenth century. The fact that these sentiments continued to be expressed into the twentieth century, however, suggests deeper cultural tides at work than simply the toilings of Tin Pan Alley. In "There's a Wee Bit of Blarney in Killarney" (1915), the singer vows to take his mother back to Ireland where he will then marry his girl who stayed behind. In "The Home of Killarney and You" (1916), we learn, "There's a mother whose waiting and watching, I know / And a colleen whose love still is true."[20]

In its enumeration of the qualities of a sweetheart suitable for an Irishman, "The Kind of Girl I Mean" (1918) concludes: "She may not be a goddess, or be fashion's raging queen, / But she must be like my mother, / That's the kind of girl I mean." When the boy tells the girl in "My Irish Song of Songs" (1917), "Sure, you have all the charms of my Mother Machree," what more could be said? Mark Slobin, in contrasting Irish and Yiddish songs written in America around the turn of the century, has pointed out that "'My Best Friend is My Mama' ('Mayn Libster fraynd iz mayn mamenyu') merely states that sentiment [of love for one's mother], without saying, as did the Irish song, 'Mother Machree,' that no 'other girl' can ever take her place. The attachment is seen as organic, not erotic."[21]

Fielder sees this idolization of mother and the close association between the mother and the beloved in these songs as emanating from the Irish Catholic exaltation of the ideal of "sexless love." Moreover, the insistence that the beloved measure up to the ideal of the mother may have helped justify the large numbers of unmarried men within the Irish-American community. If art was imitating nature in these songs, nature returned the favor on more than one occasion. An Irish American tells how he once met a woman who had known his father as a young man. Asked why they never married, she replied, "In 1925 we wanted to get married, but your father asked me to wait. He couldn't bring himself to marry while his mother was alive."[22]

The final dyad concerns the strong identification between the Irish mother and Ireland. In this context it is interesting to recall that Ireland often had been depicted as a woman in Gaelic songs and poetry, as well as in popular poetry in English. Moreover, the nationalist literature of the 1890s produced such influential works as William Butler Yeats's *The Countess Cathleen* and *Cathleen ni Houlihann,* in which women symbolize the spirit of Ireland. The revolutionary poet Patrick Pearse wrote poems and plays in which mothers speak of sacrificing their sons for the nationalist cause – in a sense, for "mother Ireland." The association of mother with Ireland in the popular songs was less dramatic but still very pervasive.

In "That Old Irish Mother of Mine" (1920) the singer acknowledges that he has never seen Ireland except in his dreams. Yet he knows that "Ireland must be heaven for my mother came from there." In the song, Ireland and mother become one:

> In her eyes there's the dew of Killarney
> On her cheek there's the rose of Kildare
> On her lips just a wee bit of Blarney
> And the snow of Athlone in her hair.[23]

And, of course, she was born on St. Patrick's Day.

In "That Tumble-Down Shack in Athlone" the focus continually shifts back and forth among mother, home, and Ireland. While the first verse announces the desire to return "To ould Erin far over the sea," the chorus hints at a return to the womb:

Oh! I want to go back to that tumbledown shack
Where the wild roses bloom round the door:
Just to pillow my head in that ould trundle bed,
Just to see my ould mother once more.[24]

In "I Had a Dream that Ireland Was Free among the Nations of the Earth" (1917), the singer's vision includes St. Patrick, Tara, and "My dear old mother came from far skies, The gold sunshine in her soft blue eyes." The cover carries a small photograph of the performer, the Irish tenor, Thomas Eagan, in chain mail and mantel, carrying a sword. This Celtic warrior who can dream simultaneously of motherland and mother may be an example of what Fielder calls the "feminization" of the Irish male, revealing "soft traits traditionally deemed feminine." Characters who could parade about in swashbuckler and, simultaneously, croon lullabies, weep for a lost childhood, and sing paeans to Ireland and to mother, were suitable heroes for an Irish-American middle class for whom the more traditional manly virtues of drinking and fighting had to be tamed.[25]

THE COLLEEN

The association of the colleen with mother and Ireland reveals the way in which the images of the Irish were moving away from the city in American popular music after the turn of the century. Based on the songs in the sample published after 1900, it seems clear that songwriters and their public were more comfortable in dealing with the Irish girl in a rural Irish, as opposed to an urban American, setting. Only 14 percent of the post-1900 songs in the sample are set clearly in the American city; most are set in Ireland. As a result, the rural colleen was a more typical subject for Tin Pan Alley than was the Irish-American girl.

After 1900, love songs regained their dominance in Irish-American popular songs. In the sample, love songs, having accounted for over 60 percent of the songs through the 1860s, had declined from 34 percent in the 1870s to a low of 23 percent in the 1880s, as comic songs became more prominent. The Gay Nineties saw the beginning of a revival. From 40 percent in the 1890s, the proportion of love songs grew to 62 percent in the 1900s and then declined slightly to 52 percent in the 1910s.[26]

The Irishness of the twentieth-century colleen is not easy to discern in the songs, once the trappings of setting, Gaelic endearments, and the generous sprinklings of key words such as "blarney" and "shamrock" are set aside. A direct descendant of the sweethearts of earlier, Victorian songs, about the only nod to modernity given the colleen is a tendency to balance her native shyness with a certain "roguish" quality, which often is suggested in song but never clearly defined. So while the modern Irish girls are perhaps a bit more lively and fun than their Victorian grandmothers, they are, like Mary of the Vale of Tralee, still pure, loyal, and faithful. However, Tin Pan Alley songwriters now identified these as particularly Irish traits. In one song published in 1915, we learn that, unlike the passions of the French and Spanish that flare up and die, "Irish Love (Like the Wine That Grows Sweet with Age)" steadily deepens and will last. The father in "Go Find a Sweetheart from the Emerald Isle" (1909) gives practical advice suitable to any upwardly mobile Irish-American man:

> Dutch girls are fickle, and the French girls wise,
> Italians lure you with their dreamy eyes;
> If you want a girl to help you win,
> And stick to you through thick and thin,
> Go get one from the Emerald Isle.[27]

This kind of practical approach to romance also turns up in "Plain Molly O" from *Mavourneen*, one of the first songs to bear Chauncey Olcott's name (although it is virtually the same as Billy Scanlan's song published earlier the same year, 1891): "She's plain Molly O, simple and sweet." "Plain" (as opposed to "fancy") or "simple" (instead of "sophisticated") were always virtues attributed to the beloved in the popular music of democratic America. However, their use in framing the Irish and Irish-American girl at a time when tastes were beginning to forsake Victorian verities might have helped to equate Irishness with certain old-fashioned qualities, as well as suggesting limited working-class or lower middle-class horizons.

> She's the daughter of Rosie O'Grady,
> A regular old fashioned girl,
> She isn't crazy for diamond rings
> Silks and satins and fancy things,
> She's just a sweet little lady . . . [28]

Whereas "Irish" had once signified people who were considered wild, rowdy, and undisciplined, by the turn of the century the word was beginning to suggest attitudes that were conservative and old-fashioned.

The physical attributes of the Irish beauty invariably center around her blue eyes, as in Olcott's "Each Day Til I Die" (1911): "By the spell of her smile, and the glint of her tresses, / The throat so milk-white and the blue of her eyes." In "The Girl I'll Call My Sweetheart Must Look Like You" (from *Macushla*, 1911), we learn that "The girl I'll call my sweetheart must have eyes of Irish blue, / And her cheeks must blush like roses fondly kiss'd by morning dew." "Blue eyes" and "roses" are closely associated with the Irish colleen in Olcott's "My Wild Irish Rose" (1897), although surprisingly "When Irish Eyes Are Smiling" (1912) favors no particular color. Whatever qualities of beauty and character that may be ascribed to the colleen, however, it is the very fact that she is Irish that makes the girls in these songs so desirable. After extolling her blue eyes and her "blarney," the singer in one song concludes simply, echoing the title: "I love you most of all *Because You're Irish*" (1917).[29]

THE EMERALD ISLE

Ireland was the apex of a triangle linking mother and the beloved. This trinity had come together in Alley songs by the end of the nineteenth century. In 1898 a hopeful songwriter summed them up in "Come Back to Old Ireland":

> Come back to old Ireland the place of your birth,
> Remember the Land of your sweetheart and mother,
> For well do you know, that no where on earth,
> Is a place that we love like Old Ireland.[30]

Appropriately enough, the song was dedicated to Chauncey Olcott. As we have seen, elements of one part of the triad could easily blend into the others. This is especially true regarding the connection between the beloved and Ireland. The lyrics of both "It's a Rocky Road to Dublin (But I'm Coming Back to You)" (1913) and "Where the River Shannon Flows" (1905) keep sliding between a longing for Ireland and a yearning for the sweetheart left behind. The titles of songs, such as "Take Me Back to Ireland to My Little Irish Rose" (1913), "When I Dream of Killarney and You" (1915), and "The Shannon, the Shamrock and You," carry the same essential message: Ireland and the beloved were two halves of the same yearning. Sometimes, however, Ireland herself becomes the beloved, as in "Ireland I Love You, Acushla Machree" (1910): "Home of my childhood, I'll think of you ever, / You're in my tho'ts, every night, every day." The cover depicts an Irish landscape set within the outline of a big shamrock.[31]

After 1900, more than ever before, the Ireland of song is the focal point for a great sense of nostalgia. In "Will My Soul Pass through Old Ireland?" (1900), a dying old woman asks the priest, a rare figure in the popular songs about the Irish: "Will my soul pass through old Ireland past my dear old Irish home? Will I see the winding river by whose banks I used to roam?" Such sentiments were not the exclusive product of Tin Pan Alley commercialism. They conveyed real meaning to homesick Irish emigrants. Kirby Miller quotes from a letter from an elderly immigrant who wrote back to Ireland to say that there were now too many friends and family members buried in America to allow him to return to Ireland. Then, thinking of his own death, he quotes the following lines: "the Breeze of Death shall waft that Dream among / The hills of Ireland lost when I was young."[32]

Tin Pan Alley song covers and lyrics emphasized the beauties of Ireland, and the association between the singer and the features of the landscape. The song "In Ould Ireland" (1911) places the beauties of Irish nature in the context of a yearning to return.

> How I long for each lov'd spot,
>> Winding road and straw thatch'd cot
> By Killarney's lakes and fells,
>> How sweet mem'ry weaves its spells,

The singer promises to return to "Beauty's home in ould Ireland."[33]

Inevitably, a place so grand could only be described as a veritable heaven on earth. J. K. Brennan and Ernie Ball pulled out all the stops for "A Little Bit of Heaven, Sure They Call It Ireland" (1914), from *The Heart of Paddy Whack*, an Olcott musical.

> Shure, a little bit of Heaven fell from out the sky one day,
>> And nestled in the ocean in a spot so far away;
> And when the Angels found it,
>> Shure it looked so sweet and fair,
> They said, "suppose we leave it for it looks so peaceful there,"
>> So they sprinkled it with star dust just to make the
>> shamrocks grow;
> 'Tis the only place you'll find them no matter where you go;
> Then they dotted it with silver, to make its lakes so grand,
> And when they had it finished, shure they called it Ireland.[34]

In the hands of the writers of "That's What Ireland Means to Me" (1917), the island becomes a mystical setting for everything pleasant and loving.

> What gladness means to a heart bowed down with sorrow,
>   What music means to those who cannot see,
> The love that first you knew, when your mother smiled at you,
>   That's what Ireland means to me.[35]

Such sentiments were all the more exquisite because they were accompanied with a certain quotient of sentimental pain. Thomas Moore had established the association of Ireland with "smiles" and "tears." Songs, such as "Erin, the Tear and the Smile in Thine Eye," suggested that the extremes of joy and sorrow explained the essence of the Irish character, as well as the Irish experience. This motif, which never quite left popular Irish song, enjoyed a revival, especially after 1910. Most writers of Tin Pan Alley knew little of Ireland's tragedies. Ever on the lookout for the formula of words and images that would click with an audience, they wove the facile sentiments of sorrow into the fabric of their Irish songs, relieved by flashes of "smiles" and "sunshine." Even "Danny Boy" (1913) promises, "I'll be there in sunshine or in shadow."[36]

A few of these songs were cast in the older mold of patriotic, nationalistic song, as in "Dear Ireland" (1905): "Many men have died, and women cried, upon that Isle so green, / It's a land that's suffered more than any land y'eve ever seen." Although "Erin Is Calling" (1916) is superficially nationalistic, the emphasis on the sorrows of Ireland has little to do with politics.

> Erin's tears have kept the shamrock flowering,
>   Erin's tears have kept the shamrock growing,
> You can hear a tear in every breeze that is blowing,
>   Erin is calling You.[37]

More typically, however, are the reflexive references to tears, as in "When John McCormack Sings a Song" (1915). Concerning the great tenor's singing, we are told, "Like the dew drops he can weave a veil of tears." In "Irish Eyes of Love" (1914) we hear that "The tear in your eye is the dew of the mornin'." Olcott worked the smiles and tears together in "Isle O' Dreams" (1911): "Dear land of love where laughter through ev'ry tear drop gleams." "What an Irishman Means by 'Machree'" (1915) includes "The gold of all smiles, and the salt of all tears." According to "Everyone Loves an Irish Song" (1916), "There's a tear drop in the laughter like a diamond in a crown, / There's a smile, a sigh in every note for a heart with care bow'd down."

Both "Mother Machree" and "When Irish Eyes Are Smiling" combine smiles with tears. The motif even appears in several song titles: "The Laugh with a Tear in It" (1908) by Olcott and Manual Klein and "Every Tear is a Smile in an Irishman's Heart" (1919).[38]

Smiling though the tears is a cliché in many popular love songs. However, in the Irish songs this motif is applied to, or at least associated with, a country and its people. It is difficult to decide which is more remarkable: that Tin Pan Alley managed to reduce the tragic elements in the Irish experience to a handful of clichés, or that some reflection of that experience, no matter how dim and shallow, managed to establish itself in these commercial popular songs.

The Ireland of American popular songs is more a place of dreams and memories than of mountains and lakes. It is a dreamland that, in the imagination of the singer, is always calling him home. Although the association between Ireland and dreams had been present in Moore's songs, it was not common in American popular Irish songs until after 1910. After that year, the words "dream" and "memory" occur in around 16 percent of the songs in the sample (as compared to between 7 and 9 percent in the preceding twenty years). In "A Song of Old Kilkenny" (1910), a man hears a street boy singing an Irish song and the memories and dreams of home come flooding back to him. More typically, as in "Sweet Eileen of Kilkenny" (1914), the singer starts off: "I'm dreaming tonight of my home o'er the sea, / And of my little sweetheart there waiting for me."[39]

As noted above, "Isle O' Dreams" (1911) is the title song from one of Olcott's musicals. About one-third of the song lyrics in the sample from Olcott's shows contain the words "dream," "dreams," or "dreaming." Other songwriters also used the words in their titles: "When I Dream of Old Erin (I'm Dreaming of You)" (1912), "When I Dream of Killarney and You" (1915), " 'Twas Only an Irishman's Dream" (1916), and "Don't You Love to Dream of Dear Old Ireland?" (1920).

The motif of the return to Ireland also becomes a more significant feature of the twentieth-century songs. This theme grows from 5 percent of the songs in the 1900s to around 15 percent after 1910. However, unlike many of the earlier songs in which the singer wants to return to Ireland to fetch his old mother and his sweetheart and bring them back to America, many of the twentieth-century songs actually suggest that the singer will go back to Ireland to stay. Thus, in "Where the River Shannon Flows" (1905), once the singer returns "to dear Erin's shore," he promises, "There I'll settle down for ever, / I'll leave the old sod never." The singer in "Back to Old Erin" (1914) looks forward to returning to his sweetheart in a cottage beside the Shannon. The man in "There's a Wee Bit of Blarney in Killarney" (1915) promises to take his mother back to Ireland where he will wed his girl and live there.[40]

Some Irish, having made money, did leave America and go back to Ireland to buy a farm or to retire. Others returned to Ireland defeated, unable to adjust to life in the industrial cities of the United States. Miller suggests that as many as 10 percent of post-Famine emigrés returned to Ireland. There were, of course, far fewer "birds of passage" among the Irish than there were among other immigrant groups of the period, as many as one-third of whom might have returned home. However, as Dennis Clark has pointed out, "A large proportion probably did aspire to repatriation, but many, many more yearned to return for family reasons, to share their American adventures and advancements." Certainly, enough Irish paid visits back home so that in American cities with large Irish populations there was usually at least one small company specializing in arranging such trips.[41]

For the most part, however, the songs of return were no more a part of Irish-American reality than were the fairies and leprechauns so often mentioned in the songs. However, the *idea* of returning to Ireland was apparently an integral part of the cultural baggage that some of the post-Famine generation brought with them to America. Miller suggests that the promises of return, so common in the songs sung at the wakes and so often made by the prospective emigrants during the emotional farewell scenes, were gratifying to both emigrants and to those left behind; they were a part of the "dialogue" about leave-taking and maintaining ties to home and family.[42]

SMILING EYES AND HAPPY HEARTS

Many songs, directly or indirectly, referred to the character of the Irish people. There were, of course, some continuities with the songs of the nineteenth century. Loyalty to Ireland was still a hallmark of the Irish character as depicted in American popular culture. It was his very tie to Ireland that supposedly defined the best qualities of the Irishman, as a father tells his son in "Take Off Your Hats to Old Ireland":

I-R-E, that's the ire and the fire, you admire in your sire,
    L-A-N-D, that's a land great and grand, on its merit it can stand,
I-RE-LAND is the place of a race that has never known disgrace.[43]

The depiction of the Irish as a merry people also was carried over from the old vaudeville songs, but without the Donnybrooks and heroic drinking bouts. True, some songs made playful references to the Irishman's alleged love of a good fight. In "The Irish Blues" (1915) we are informed that "The Irish are a fighten' race, A very hard to frighten race," who "if they cannot find a war, They start one of their own." The old pugnacious Paddy is absent from such songs, however. Instead, the Irish stereotype was tidied up for the new century to meet the demand for a new kind of ethnic pride. The cover of "In the Good Old Irish Way" (1907) shows respectably dressed dancers doing a four-hand reel before a piano. A small photograph of the song's performer, Maggie Cline, smiles on the scene. The lyrics present an up-to-date version of the old image of the singing, dancing, partying Irish.

> In the Good Old Irish Way,
>> We'll be merry while we may,
> Never mind how much innocent noise we make,
>> If you don't make enough, sure they'll think it 'twas a wake.
> In the Good Old Irish Way,
>> No one minds how long you stay,
> You can eat, drink or smoke, sing a song, crack a joke,
>> In the Good Old Irish Way.

"You Don't Have to Come from Ireland to Be Irish" (1917) also carries the suggestion of good times. The cover shows an accordion player and fiddlers with girls dancing amid shamrocks. In the 1880s and 1890s, such songs would have ended with a brawl, but no longer.[44]

The Irish character as portrayed in some songs had more transcendent qualities, however. "What an Irishman Means by 'Machree'" (1915), seems to suggest that the Irish feel more deeply than others and can convey their inner warmth in uniquely Irish ways.

> 'Tis the thrill of the hand, And the light of the eye,
>> The glow of the cheek, and the lips' parting cry;
> 'Tis father, 'tis mother, 'Tis brother or wife,
>> The music of woman's smile, the wine of man's life.

"Top of the Morning" (1920) explains the popular Irish greeting as follows:

> An Irishman's greeting comes straight from the heart,
>> It means more than "How do you do,"

Good luck and God bless you but never good-bye.
Is the "Top of the Morning to you."

The cover depicts mountains running down to the seas, set with the outline of a harp.[45]

"Heart" was a very important word in Tin Pan Alley's Irish lexicon. It
conveyed the essential quality of Irishness. In "You Don't Have to Come
from Ireland to Be Irish," we learn that "It's the heart of you that makes
you Irish." "It Takes a Great Big Heart to Sing an Irish Song" (1917) assures us: "For there's warmth in the heart of the Irish, There's a thrill in
the grip of the hand." In "Every Tear Is a Smile in an Irishman's Heart"
(1919), the reason for this phenomenon is: "For his heart is as big as can
be, And the smile on his face is a trait of his race, A happy-go-lucky is he."[46]

In song after song, Irish-American self-esteem is high: "I'm Awfully Glad
I'm Irish" (1910) simply asserts "Everyone loves the Irish." "When Irish Eyes
are Smiling" (1912) assures us that "When Irish hearts are happy, Sure 'tis
like a morn in spring." "Why Not Sing 'Wearing of the Green'?" (1915) offers
to extend the scope of Irishness to everyone: "Sure there must be Irish in
us all / From the way it's coming out."[47] The old negative elements that
had once accompanied the image of the gregarious, fun-loving Irish were
gone. The Irish now were presented as good-hearted, friendly people whom
anyone would enjoy knowing.

"ALL I WANT IS IN IRELAND"

The Shamrocks, the Shannon, the Lakes of Killarney,
> The green rolling hills and the valleys between;
I had to forsake them, Shure, I couldn't take them,
I left them along with my Irish colleen,
> The voice of my mother is calling me homeward,
And I sigh for a puff of my daddy's dudeen;
Shure'en all that I had and all that I have,
> *And all that I want is in Ireland.*[48]

In the early decades of this century, there were still many recent Irish immigrants for whom Ireland represented the home and family
abandoned for a new life in America. Many continued to entertain fond
memories of the youth they had spent in the Irish countryside. As Dennis
Clark remarks, "The sentimental lure of childhood scenes and memories,

the romanticism of selective recollection, and the elemental ties of family were potent psychological factors."[49] For some of these immigrants, the sentiments of "All I Want Is in Ireland" might have given expression to a genuine nostalgia for places and people they had once known. However, for those who had built successful lives in America, and especially for their American-born children and grandchildren, what could it have meant to sing "All I Want Is in Ireland?" What did this Ireland of song, a product of the "negotiation" between the Irish and American popular song culture, actually mean to Irish Americans in the twentieth century?

For many Irish Americans, Ireland had become a mythical place, the Emerald Isle, an ideal within which various vaguely defined but deeply felt needs could be met. The real Ireland had been depopulated by famine, poverty, and lack of opportunity. The Ireland of imagination was transformed by commercial popular culture into a rural paradise peopled by handsome young men, beautiful colleens, cherished parents, glowing hearthsides, and friends and neighbors, all of whom were white and blue-eyed. The pipes and fiddles were always sounding and the dances were always about to begin. Sex was a hard-won kiss and love was eternal. A very different place, this imagined Ireland, from the gritty, crowded, multi-ethnic urban cities where most of Irish America lived. The Eden-like quality of this mythical Ireland of popular song was reinforced by the fact that this was a "lost" land. Its beauties and joys, like the childhood of the singers, were gone, lost in time or inaccessible across the miles of the gray Atlantic. Thus, the Emerald Isle was drenched in nostalgic yearning for the unattainable.

All of this is in keeping with the theme of nostalgia introduced into popular Irish song by Moore and maintained throughout the nineteenth century. Some of those songs, however, kept at least a toe-hold on reality, unlike the songs written after 1900, which no longer stressed the reasons why the beloved homeland had been "lost." As we saw in chapter 9, the songs of Irish nationalism that came out of Tin Pan Alley rarely attacked Britain or even mentioned the horrors of famine and eviction. Within American popular culture, Irish nationalism had become a quality that defined Irish-American character rather than Irish-American politics. Moreover, Irish Americans were less anxious than their parents had been to be reminded that the Irish had been driven out of Ireland by English injustice, by famine, and by poverty – images that did not count for much within the success-driven culture of America. Thus, the importance of the "smiling-through-the-tears" motif; it vaguely acknowledged the past without having to define its unpleasantness.

As for really returning to Ireland, this was not something most American-born Irish intended to do. First, there was no work in Ireland. Second, being urbanites, they would have been bored and probably very uncomfortable in an Irish environment that might have been less beneficent when experienced directly on a rain-swept "bohoreen" than when sung about on Broadway. Finally, one could not "return" to a place one did not know. For those born here, America, not Ireland, was home. What was the point, then, of singing about returning to a land one had never seen?

The image of Ireland in American popular culture had become essential to the maintenance of a positive image of the Irish in America. Somehow, the qualities of Ireland had become embodied in her people. The myth of Ireland maintained the myth of the Irish: torn from a fair and perfect land, from homes and loved ones, the Irish came to America, where, in the face of many difficulties, they prospered. In other words, for many Irish Americans, the idea of "Ireland" was predicated upon success in America. Conversely, success and acceptance here was based on the popular image of Ireland. To get the Yankees to love Ireland was to get them to love the Irish. As the song said, "There's Something in the Name of Ireland That the Whole World Seems to Love."[50]

At one level these songs of nostalgic longing for Ireland reflect the Irish-American form of a feeling common to many Americans: the impossible desire to recapture some sense of security, comfort, and love embodied in a real or imagined past. To be American has always meant leaving home too soon and too frequently, enduring too many changes. As Alexis de Tocqueville noted long ago, Americans never have enough and always want more. Identities cobbled up out of the passing demands and fancies of the day crumble away and have to be continually repaired or replaced. There must be some wellspring, some source to which we can return, at least in imagination, for a replenishing of the spirit. Although we are supposed to turn to religion, philosophy, or nature for such support, one of the major functions of popular culture has been to "keep the home fires burning," so to speak, to provide readily accessible images of that one perfect state of being about which we can dream but never achieve. In the "Emerald Isle," Irish Americas had at least a consistent and ethnically logical source for their identity and the values for which it stood.

Yet, that a nostalgic fixation on their rural, emerald utopia should occupy such a central place in the image of the Irish in twentieth-century American popular culture still seems an anomaly, especially when we consider the extent to which Irish Catholics had become an urban people –

our first real urbanites. In spite of their peasant origins, they had none of the Jeffersonian suspicion of or disdain for the city. Having no place else to go to, the Irish burrowed into American cities and came to understand them, literally from the ground up. They understood them better than many Yankees, as they turned urban politics into a profession, instead of a nose-holding duty, a function of upper-class *noblesse oblige*.[51] Indeed, in the 1890s there had been a brief burst of urban nostalgia in Irish-American songs. "The Sidewalks of New York" (1890) and some of Ned Harrigan's later songs already had a kind of afterglow about them when sung by the successful "solid" men who bawled them out at gatherings of the Harrigan Club in New York City.

Since so much of the image of post–Civil War Irish America had come from the city, the shift in emphasis in the songs after 1900 suggests a kind of rejection of the city. It is as though the Irish had come to feel that an urban identity was not the key to Yankee acceptance after all. The WASPs made money in cities but they did not love them nor those who lived in them, especially those who looked and talked differently. WASPS sang of small-town homes in the South, the Midwest, or New England. They hymned the moon shining down on the Swanee, even the Hudson. In memory they smelled the new mown hay and heard the rustle of the sycamores. Very well; let them get a whiff of the turf smoke curling up from a thatched-roof cottage, listen to the Shannon's purling stream, and watch the moon rise over Killarney. Just like all true Americans, the Irish Americans, too, could be a people of rural roots, simple rural tastes, and wholesome rural character. According to the new image, the Irish were in the city but not of it. Their true character emanated not from the streets that Harrigan had once sentimentalized but from the glowing hearthside of a land that was geographically far off but in imagination so close it could be conjured up with a song.

Only in 1918 did America cross the statistical line that separated a rural from an urban society. Until then, the majority of Americans had been born and at least raised in rural or small-town environments. So much of urban America had been filled by people, strangers to each other, whose roots lay beyond the confines of the city in rural America or Europe. Even in the nineteenth century, the Irishman's longing for an idealized Irish cabin paralleled the American's yearning for a rural home. Twentieth-century Tin Pan Alley was equally adept at conjuring up visions of the banks of the Wabash, or the Swanee, or the Shannon. Moreover, the "Isle of Dreams" was the exact opposite of the industrial cities with their polyglot population of all creeds and colors. Like the WASPS, the Irish could at least dream of rural, ethnic homogeneity. Perhaps that is one reason why hardworking, disciplined, sober, competitive, Protestant America of the early twentieth century was willing to buy into the image of the light-hearted, home-loving, quick-tempered but genial, sentimental, loyal, extravagant, *occasionally* hard-drinking Irish, who dared to love an Ireland so compatible with the idealized image of rural America.

There were other reasons as well. In the early decades of the twentieth century, as the culture of factory and office began to reshape the American character, the popular image of Ireland and the Irish represented an alternative to the values of the white-collar, organizational man of the new urban, business culture. The Irish Americans were depicted as more relaxed, fun-loving, yet moral, sentimental and, for all of their Celtic exuberance, responsible, patriotic citizens. These supposedly Irish virtues extolled in song were really just the old-fashioned qualities that modern Americans feared were slipping away in the rat race of modern times.

THE PASSING OF THE IRISH POPULAR SONG: FROM MAINSTREAM TO SUBCULTURE

Chauncey Olcott died in the early hours of March 18, 1932, close enough to St. Patrick's Day to allow the symbolic date of his passing to supersede the actual date in many press accounts. His coffin, covered with violets, was attended by many of the leading lights of Irish America: George M. Cohan, John McCormack, film star Thomas Meighan, New York Mayor Jimmy Walker, and former New York governor Al Smith.[52] Although the funeral marked the passing of the great era of Irish-American entertainment, the general popularity of Irish songs had ended a decade earlier.

The year 1920 was perhaps the last good year for new popular songs about Ireland and the Irish. The sample contains thirteen songs published in that year. During the remainder of the decade, however, Ireland and the Irish were no longer hot topics in the popular music business. The number of new Irish songs coming out of Tin Pan Alley dropped off quickly.[53]

There are several reasons for this change. The domestic repercussions of America's involvement in World War I, culminating in the Red Scare and the revival of the Ku Klux Klan, helped to reduce the appeal within mainstream popular culture of ethnicity as a vehicle for entertainment. Even before the war, ethnic humor itself was in decline. By the early 1920s, when an out-of-work Irish step dancer named Gracie Ethel Cecile Rosalie Allen teamed up with a down-at-the-heel vaudeville comic named Nathan Birnbaum, the resulting team of Burns and Allen did not focus on either the Hibernian or the Jewish *shtick*. Vaudeville itself, which had once been so hospitable to Irish themes and Irish performers, had begun its slow decline under the impact of the cinema, the radio, and the automobile. In fact, after 1900 the Irish were no longer ubiquitous in American entertainment, as they had been in the 1880s and early 1890s.[54]

At the same time, Tin Pan Alley may have driven the Irish genre so far into the fantastic realms of novelty and nostalgia that even George M. Cohan's songs for *Little Nelly Kelly* and *The Merry Malones*, shows set in America, could not effect a rebirth of musical interest in urban Irish America. Also, things Irish, so long identified with nostalgia, mothers, and the Emerald Isle, may have seemed too old-fashioned for a popular music, which after 1920 was influenced by jazz rhythms and sophisticated lyrics. Irish themes had survived the impact of ragtime and the other dance crazes of the early twentieth century, but they no longer seemed compatible with the musical idioms of the Jazz Age.

Of course, Tin Pan Alley songs about Ireland did not suddenly disappear from the popular culture, as anyone even vaguely aware of St. Patrick's Day in America can attest. Irish Americans themselves continued to enjoy them on a daily basis. Richard Spottswood, in his discography of ethnic recordings, provides a glimpse into the musical tastes of Irish-American culture in the interwar years. Within the seventy pages of lists of records made for Irish Americans, there are about 660 song titles that I can identify to some degree as to period and place of origin. Of these, about one-third appear to belong to the nineteenth century. A little more than half of them are parlor songs composed before the Civil War – songs by Moore and his successors. Only about sixty songs suggest vaudeville and early Tin Pan Alley sources. Of these, only one half, including some Harrigan and Braham songs, are comic. Nothing could be a clearer reflection of the rejection of Paddy than this minuscule trickle of the once great tide of post–Civil War comic stage Irish songs.

Roughly another third of the recordings that I could identify in Spottswood appear to be late nineteenth and twentieth-century songs from across the Atlantic: music hall songs from London and Dublin, sentimental and comic pieces, such as songs by Percy French, and over seventy "rebel songs" dating from 1898 to the Anglo-Irish War. The presence of these songs (which generally did not appear in sheet music or song collections in America), along with the enormous number of recordings of jigs and reels listed by Spottswood, suggests the role of the last wave of immigrants among both performers and record buyers.

The final one-third of the songs appear to be products of twentieth-century Tin Pan Alley, most of them written before 1920. Their strong presence in the post–World War I recordings is evidence that Irish America took these products of the Alley to heart. No longer a vibrant part of commercial music, however, these songs gradually faded from the mainstream of popular song. After 1920 they belonged to an ethnic subculture.[55]

The evolution of the image of the Irish in America did not come to an end in the twenties, of course. It continued on the stage and in the new media of radio and, especially, the cinema. Even before the First World War, more modern and more complex characterizations of the Irish were beginning to appear in film. There was, as we have seen, some backsliding within the early Hollywood studios, but according to Joseph Curren, *The Last of the Callahans* was also the last of its type. By the 1930s and 1940s there were a variety of Irish types portrayed in films – tough cops and tough gangsters, romantic lovers and celibate (but crooning) priests, fiery redheads and good-hearted moms. On the whole, there were no more protests.[56]

Perhaps the most important thing these films accomplished was to bring the Catholic Church, an institution seldom even alluded to in the songs, into the mainstream of American popular culture. Moreover, while Hollywood's Catholic Church was, as Lawrence McCaffrey has suggested, more social service agency than agency of the divine, it was also free from the Protestant's sense of it as alien and mysterious.[57] This was due in part to Hollywood's decision to give the church an Irish face. Spencer Tracy, Pat O'Brien, and Bing Crosby achieved great popularity for their portrayal of Irish-American priests.

The films also helped to restore the balance between the rural and urban images of the Irish. The popular liberalism of the depression and war years temporarily made cities seem like a part of America, and many of the most vibrant Hollywood films with Irish-American characters were those set in America's cities. By the 1940s the ghost of Ned Harrigan might have been satisfied. While the occasional songs did not always sound very "Irish" and the humor was greatly subdued, the old Irish-American urban sentimentality was intact. When Hollywood turned to Ireland it reiterated in film the Tin Pan Alley romantic image of the Emerald Isle. In fact, much of Hollywood's image of Ireland and the Irish had already been established in the popular songs by the 1920s.

In over a century the images of the Irish in popular song had evolved from the romantically exotic exile and rollicking clown, through comic representations of a vast urban underclass, to equally comic strivers after the lace curtain, to patriotic immigrants who still loved their homeland, to sentimental dreamers of the Emerald Isle, to good-natured, solid citizens who represented middle-class core values. Throughout the years, the Irish themselves accepted, and sometimes rejected, these various images. Occasionally, individuals and Irish-American organizations tried to push the image in one direction or another. Toward the end of the nineteenth century, these self-conscious efforts at image building had an impact. However, it was largely through the give-and-take of commercial popular culture, the informal negotiations, especially in the marketplace, that these changes occurred.

The image of Ireland did not change as dramatically as did that of the Irish. Erin, a poetical invention of Anglo-Irish poets like Thomas Moore, remained steeped in beauty and sorrow, sunshine and shadow. By 1900, however, the sorrow had been reduced to reflexive references to tears and the beauties took on the gaudy colors of Chauncey Olcott stage sets. It was an invented Ireland that could act as a repository for the virtues Irish Americans were supposed to represent. It was a dreamland that in some songs could even be superimposed on America.

> Sure, the shamrocks were growing on Broadway,
> Every girl was an Irish colleen,
> And the town of New York was the county of Cork,
> All the buildings were painted green,
> Sure, the Hudson looked just like the Shannon,
> Oh, how good and real it did seem,
> I could hear mother singin',
> The sweet Shandan bells ringin',
> *'Twas only an Irishman's dream.*[58]

To the extent that such sentiments represented a desire on the part of the Irish to make their Irishness compatible with being Americans, the dream came true.

Conclusion

In this study I have presented the changing images of the Irish and Ireland in American popular song as the product of cultural negotiations between Irish Americans and the WASP-dominated mainstream. In trying to understand the nature of the cultural interactions between the Irish and the WASP communities, it is essential to remember that the stereotype of the Irish Catholics preceded the emergence of an Irish-American identity. The Irish arrived, therefore, facing a double burden: they were poverty-stricken immigrants who were also culturally suspect. Within the negotiations over Irish-American identity, class tensions were complicated by ethnic tensions. The immigrants had to define and assert their identity in the face of the WASP middle-class need to maintain economic as well as social and cultural control. Without doubt, Irish-American identities were shaped and limited to some degree by the dominant Protestant, Anglo-American, bourgeois culture the immigrants encountered.[1]

Although the Yankees were prepared to cast the Irish in the already established Paddy mold, this stereotype based on the Irish Catholic peasant was too ludicrously limited to serve as a predictor, much less guide, for the future. When Irish Catholics started arriving in large numbers after 1820 they had few models of immigrant adjustment to follow. True, those Protestant Irish who had chosen to assert an Irish identity had laid some of the political and cultural groundwork by linking the cause of Irish liberty to the American republican, revolutionary tradition. Nowhere, however, was there a large, non-WASP ethnic group already established in our cities to suggest to the Irish what they were to do, how they were to act. Indeed, it would be the Irish themselves who would eventually create and assume this role for other immigrant groups later in the nineteenth century.

The challenge of creating an ethnic identity was a very complex one for both the Irish immigrants and the receiving population. It has been two hundred years since J. Hector St. John de Crèvecoeur asked his famous question, "What is an American?" We are still working on the answer. The instability of the national identity in the nineteenth century meant that the Irish in America had considerably more room to maneuver, to create a place for themselves within the culture, than they had in England, where they encountered similar prejudices. It also meant that it was the Irish who would provide answers to a series of questions that had never occurred to many of Crèvecoeur's generation. The Irish arrived at a time when we had barely begun to ask, "What is an *urban* American – or an *industrial work-ing-class* American – or a *Catholic* American?" Answers to those questions came as much from Irish Catholics and other immigrants as from the WASP community.

The negotiations over the definition of Irish-American ethnicity took place, then, on many levels and within many spheres of American society. In this study we have looked at only a very limited, although significant aspect of those negotiations: those that involved the commercial popular culture centering on theater and song publishing. As we have seen, these negotiations were more concerned with the stereotype of the Irish than with the reality of their lives in America. As a result, the negotiations were nev-er truly open to all possibilities. The Irish could not abolish the stereotype of themselves that they encountered upon landing; they could only change it. The negotiations were, therefore, conducted around and through the stereotype – the discourse between the Irish and the broader spectrum of American culture being conducted *through* the stereotype, and the dialogue within the Irish-American community taking place *around* it.

It is interesting to note how long it took the Irish-American communi-ty to reject Paddy, who, even in his reincarnation as an Irish-American workingman, maintained his popularity until the end of the nineteenth century. There were always complaints about the stage Irishman from with-in the Irish community. However, it appears that many Irish found the comic Irish songs of the late nineteenth century entertaining, especially when sung by Irish performers. Perhaps nineteenth-century Irish Ameri-cans found an audacious vitality in Paddy, as he lurched his way through the American urban scene. Since the Irish stereotype had developed as the antithesis of Anglo-American culture, there must have been some satis-faction in cheering on a figure who made hash of snobbish, Protestant, Yankee values. Assaulting WASP sensibilities might have been seen as something of a virtue. Similarly, the satires on Paddy aspiring to the lace curtain were always double-edged. On one level they appeared to echo Yankee anti-Irish prejudice; on the other they voiced Irish suspicion about accepting Yankee values of material success and upward mobility that would threaten the cohesion of the parish (suspicions that were voiced in more serious ways by Catholic writers).

Irish-American performers and audiences were, therefore, slow to give up the edge of wildness that was so much a part of Paddy's historical nature. All those songs about Hibernian soirees, wakes, baptisms, and celebrations that ended in chaos, while hardly edifying from the Yankee point of view, may have been satisfying from that of the Irish working class. In his plays, even Edward Harrigan mixed the blunderings and melees of the traditional Paddiad with sentimental portraits of Irish working-class families.

Of course, Paddy also entertained the WASPs. That is why he had been invented in the first place. If the Irish immigrants could find something of value in him, then so could those middle-class Protestants who enjoyed him. Therefore, while all aspects of a stereotype may be taken as negative, since they project the same set of traits on all members of a group regardless of individual experiences and abilities, a stereotype may generate positive or negative reactions, depending on the observer. Paddy had a dual nature. Jigging about, brandishing a shillelagh, he could personify either the *joi de vivre* of the Celtic spirit or the threat of a looming Celtic underclass. To the extent that Yankees came to perceive Paddy in terms of the former rather than the latter, the stereotype became more positive. As I have tried to suggest in this study, Irish and Irish-American performers, playwrights, and songwriters helped to emphasize the genial side of Paddy's nature. As a figure of unrestrained joy, Paddy could appeal to both Irish and non-Irish. In terms of stereotypes, of course, "positive" and "negative" are relative terms. It was one thing to cease to be seen as a threat; it was another to be seen as a solid citizen. What Yankee male would have wanted his daughter to marry Paddy, regardless of his virtues?

By the end of the nineteenth century, the contexts surrounding the negotiations over the Irish-American identity were changing. New immigrants from the peasant societies of southern and eastern Europe made the Irish seem less alien to Yankees. Simultaneously, the growth in Irish status was accompanied by a powerful desire for matching respectability in image. As the element of chaos became less characteristic of Irish life in industrial America, there was less need for Paddy's entertaining teetering on the brink of anarchy. Judging by the songs and what was happening in vaudeville after 1900, the Irish seem to have decided once and for all that they could have an Irish identity *without* Paddy; or, at least, with a greatly subdued Paddy standing genially in the background. Occupying the center of the new identity was a thoroughly Americanized, yet sentimental citizen and patriot who drew his or her strengths from a mythical land known as the Emerald Isle.

Perhaps the most extraordinary thing about the whole process was the acceptance of the Tin Pan Alley version of Ireland by both Irish and Yankees alike. Even before Moore's *Irish Melodies*, Ireland had its own existence in Anglo-American popular culture, quite apart from her people. Once regarded as a wilderness, Ireland had emerged at the end of the eighteenth century as a land of singular beauty, even while most of her people sank deeper into poverty. Moore popularized in English the feminine persona that Gaelic poets had already bestowed upon Ireland. As "Erin," Ireland was depicted as a beautiful woman, betrayed and enslaved, smiling in hope of her liberation, weeping over her tragic fate. Her children, sad exiles and immigrants, carried her sorrows with them. Even Paddy took on a certain pathos, even dignity, in his unrelinquished love for her.

Yet, while the Irish people sometimes were regarded as tragic exiles, they were more often seen either as figures of fun or a tribe of unruly paupers. Thus the discrepancy between Anglo-American love for a song like "Come Back to Erin" and the general dislike of the flesh-and-blood Irish who crowded into the cities of England and America. Far from inspiring such songs, the Irish-Catholic immigrants had to coopt them. Within American popular culture they had to reclaim Erin, the creation of Anglo-Irish and English songwriters, as their own. In doing so, they provided themselves with the one image available to them that was already acceptable to the WASPs. The Irish, in their ceaseless proclamation of devotion and loyalty to their homeland, were gradually able to transfer her positive qualities to themselves, as we have seen in the Tin Pan Alley songs. It was as children, not of historical Ireland, but of Erin, or in her twentieth-century transformation, the Emerald Isle, that the Irish finally gained acceptance within American popular culture.

The myth of the Emerald Isle provided the meeting place for the two strains of the Irish stereotype: the sentimental, nostalgic myth, launched by Moore, of exiles from a lost land; and the genial, good-hearted, and dependable character of the Tin Pan Alley Irish American, the direct, albeit a greatly reformed descendant of the stereotypical Paddy. Compared to traditional mythologies, the myths of modern popular culture tend to be rather mundane. There were no Fianna, no Red Branch knights, and no battles of Moy Tura for the Irish Americans. Yeats might entertain himself with such stuff in his remote tower at Ballylee, but in the Irish neighborhoods of Philadelphia, New York, Boston, Chicago, and in scores of industrial towns in the East and Midwest, Irish Americans, intent on acceptance and on getting ahead, found more cultural utility in songs that told them that they were a grand people from a grand country and that they had successfully established themselves in America.

To a remarkable degree, Irish Americans managed to make their devotion to what they called Ireland absolutely compatible with their devotion to America. No other ethnic group managed so neatly to turn the "hyphen" into a bridge. Yet, it was a bridge that went nowhere, or, rather, it only went from one part of America to another. The Ireland of the songs was, in the end, an aspect of America, an isle of American-born dreams. The Emerald Isle provided an uncomplicated, usable "homeland" for those who had not been born in Ireland and who had little inclination to visit it, yet who needed something more than the vast, grimy industrial cities to call "home." The Ireland of song was a cleaned up, pretty place, where decent, rural simplicity replaced poverty. It was an Ireland one could invite the Yankees to admire and even occasion a sentimental tear over.

After the turn of the century, the popular culture images of Ireland and the Irish were addressed increasingly to the second and third generations instead of the immigrants. The problem for the immigrants had been to find an *American* identity. The problem for the American born was to maintain some sense of an *Irish* identity that could be accepted within American popular culture, their primary source of identity, the Roman Catholic Church, being held suspect by much of the Protestant majority. One of the paradoxes of American society is that as a group ceases to be the "Other," it may find itself becoming just another.[2] In becoming thoroughly American, the Irish wanted somehow to remain identifiably Irish. After the turn of the century, Irish Americans laid claim to a redefined ethnicity even as they relinquished many of the customs and habits of mind of the immigrant generation.

Herbert Gans suggests that the "functions" of ethnic culture – Irish, or Polish, or Jewish – diminish over the generations, until "identity becomes the primary way of being ethnic, ethnicity takes on an expressive rather than an instrumental function in people's lives, becoming more of a leisure-time activity and losing its relevance, say, to earning a living or regulating family life." The resulting "symbolic ethnicity" is "characterized by a nostalgic allegiance to the culture of the immigrant generation, or that of the old country; a love for and a pride in a tradition that can be felt without having to be incorporated into everyday behavior."[3] Symbolic ethnicity is a way of "feeling" ethnic without "being" ethnic; that is, living with all of the privations and restrictions that may have characterized the lives of one's parents and grandparents. Old homelands are, Gans notes, particularly useful as ethnic symbols, "because they are far away and cannot make arduous demands on American ethnics; even sending large amounts of money is ultimately an easy way to help, unless the donors are making major economic sacrifices."[4]

Ethnic symbolism may exist as much for the benefit of the outsider as for the reaffirmation of those inside the group. In fact much of the function of "ethnic symbolism" may lie in its public, semiotic role; it provides a way of signifying one's ethnicity to others, assigning and assuming places within the society. This is especially true of symbols created and perpetuated within the commercial popular culture. By 1900, songs of the Emerald Isle and of the happy, hearty Irish people became convenient vehicles for symbolic ethnicity for the Irish.[5]

The Irish succeeded to a remarkable degree in guiding their stereotype within American popular culture along generally favorable lines. In the process they accomplished two very important things. Working with the grain of American culture, the Irish helped to shape an image of themselves and their old homeland that enabled them to put forward a distinct but positive ethnic identity. At the same time, this identity did not wall them off from the mainstream of American society. On the contrary, Americans came to love the blarney and shamrocks, Killarney's rocks and fells, and Macnamara's Band. The old negative traits were blurred or were reinterpreted in a more positive light. Within American popular culture, the Irish were defined as a patriotic, hardworking, happy people, exemplars of the old verities of family and community. The image of Ireland became an appendage of the American myth of the rural Eden.

There was a price to be paid for this success, however. By 1920, the Irish, more than any other ethnic group, had participated in shaping an image of themselves within American popular entertainment, and, then, they embraced it. They themselves knew that there was much more to being Irish than shamrocks and shillelaghs. In their parishes and neighborhoods, in factories and saloons, at home and at dances they experienced a sense of Irishness that was rich and complex, with real pain and sadness interlocked with real triumphs and successes. Within the Irish community, Irishness – American Irishness – was real. However, the language, images, and symbols that might have expressed that reality to other Americans had been preempted by the clichés of popular culture.

It is characteristic of much of the scholarship about popular culture in America to accept its products, no matter how skewed by the marketplace, as the result of the democratic process. If the public likes green beer and

"Kiss Me, I'm Irish" buttons on St. Patrick's Day, it is not the scholar's business to make aesthetic caveats. Moreover, the effectiveness of popular culture may be judged by what "works" at any given time, depending on how "works" is defined. The images of the Irish that came out of popular entertainment did work for them for a while. However, within the popular culture, problems emerge over the long haul. While the real Ireland was painfully forging a new national culture, assisted by some of the foremost modern writers, Irish America had to make do with a series of ethnic symbols that often lacked substance. In Ireland the discourse about Irishness was often passionate and sometimes acrimonious, but it was rich in images and symbols. In America, the virtues and values that supposedly defined Irishness were admirable, but they were not, after all, uniquely Irish. The Emerald Isle, that mythical land that was somehow the source for those values, was a Tin Pan Alley artifact. "Irishness," then, as presented within our popular culture, emerged as a form of show business: just a wisp of a "Rosie O'Grady" waltz song, the sound of taps on a stage, a cheery white-haired old lady in a black shawl, some old Pat and Mike jokes, a pair of blue eyes, a big smile and hearty handshake . . . just shamrocks and shillelaghs. It was only an Irishman's dream.

Introduction

1. Blessing, "Irish Emigration to the United States," p. 11.
2. McCaffrey, *Textures of Irish America*, p. 125.
3. Potter, *To the Golden Door*, p. 168.
4. Geist, "From the Plantation to the Police Station," p. 159.
5. Hoppenstand, "Yellow Devil Doctors and Opium Dens," p. 171.
6. Nye, "Notes on a Rationale for Popular Culture," p. 27.
7. Pickering and Green, "Toward a Cartography of Vernacular Milieu," p. 1.
8. Prior to the Civil War, a twenty-five- or thirty-cent piece of sheet music would have cost $5.63 to $6.75 in 1977 dollars. See Tawa, *Sweet Songs for Gentle Americans*, p. 108.
9. Middleton, *Studying Popular Music*, p. 11.
10. See, for example, Frith, "Why Do Songs Have Words?" p. 97.
11. Quoted in ibid., p. 95.
12. Pickering and Green, "Toward a Cartography of Vernacular Milieu," p. 3.
13. Middleton, *Studying Popular Music*, p. 249.
14. Ibid., p. 229.
15. Ibid., p. 247.
16. See Williams, "Base and Superstructure in Marxist Critical Theory."
17. Eric Lott's approach to popular culture is particularly relevant. He sees the popular as "neither . . . entirely the 'social control' of the ruling classes nor the 'class expression' of the dominated. Because the popular is always *produced*, capitalized, it is hardly some unfettered time-out from political pressures, a space of mere 'leisure'. . . nor does it arise in some immediate way from collective popular desires." Far from being a passive mirror of political domination or something totally determined by class or ethnic hegemony, Lott suggests that popular culture is formed "at the intersection of received symbolic forms," including those of authority and subordination, as well as "new articulations" by local leaders and entertainers. In Lott's view, popular culture represents an area of "contestation, with moments of resistance to the dominant culture as well as moments of supersession" (*Love and Theft*, pp. 17–18).
18. From this point on, the term "Irish song," unless otherwise qualified, will refer only to the popular songs about Ireland and the Irish that appeared in sheet music. The term will not include folksongs, that is, songs from the oral and broadside ballad traditions, unless they were published in sheet music.
19. Among the types of things I was able to track with the database were references in songs to fighting and drinking, to "Paddy," the stereotypical stage Irishman, as well as references to more positive elements, such as a sense of community among Irish Americans and their sense of family. I was also able to track whether a song was set in Ireland or in America and whether or not it reflected an urban environment.

20. Some songs in both the Lilly and Cincinnati collections carry handwritten dates provided by the original collector or the librarians. In some cases, using Richard J. Wolfe's study of music publishers in early nineteenth-century America, I was able to match a publisher's address printed on the song cover with the period during which his office or shop was known to have been occupied, and I have, therefore, assigned a corresponding range of dates to the song. In a few cases I have had to rely on the style of cover art and typeface, or on biographical information about the composer, to try to determine if an undated song was published before or after the Civil War.

Some songs, such as the most popular of Thomas Moore's *Irish Melodies*, remained in print for decades. There has been no attempt to represent this phenomenon in the database where a song is listed only once under the year in which it first appeared or was copyrighted.

Prior to 1890, before music publishing was centralized in New York City, a song may have been carried by as many as a dozen publishers in as many cities. My citations provide only the publisher whose name appears on the particular copy cited in the study or, in cases of multiple listings, the publisher whose name appears first.

Introduction to Part 1

1. See Miller, *Emigrants and Exiles*, pp. 137, 193; Doyle, *Ireland, Irishmen and Revolutionary America*, pp. 137, 191, 209.

2. MacDonagh, "Irish Famine Emigration to the United States," p. 370.

3. Wittke, *Irish in America*, p. 5; MacDonagh, "Irish Famine Emigration to the United States," p. 366.

4. Quoted in MacDonagh, "Irish Famine Emigration to the United States," p. 366.

5. See O'Tuathaigh, *Ireland before the Famine*, p. 203. About 45 percent of the holdings over one acre were under five. Only 7 percent were more than thirty acres. See Edwards and Williams, *Great Famine*, p. 89.

6. Miller, *Emigrants and Exiles*, p. 291; O'Tuathaigh, *Ireland before the Famine*, p. 204; MacDonagh, "Irish Famine Emigration to the United States," pp. 430, 432.

7. See MacLochlainn, "Gael and Peasant," pp. 20, 24; O'Tuathaigh, *Ireland before the Famine*, p. 206.

8. MacLochlainn, "Gael and Peasant," p. 25.

9. MacDonagh, "Irish Famine Emigration to the United States," pp. 426–30.

10. Miller, *Emigrants and Exiles*, pp. 347–48.

Chapter 1: Dear Harp of My Country

1. See Finson, *Voices That Are Gone*, p. 273. James Hewitt, a British musician who emigrated to America, produced *The Music of Erin* (1807), a collection of songs

based on traditional Irish harp tunes, one year before the publication of the first series of Moore's *Melodies*. However, Hewitt's collection appears to have had minimal impact upon the genre of popular songs about Ireland.

2. Snyder, *Celtic Revival*, pp. 190–92. For the Irish side of the Celtic Revival see Leerssen, *Mere Irish and Fíor-Ghael*.

3. Carpenter, "Changing Views of Irish Musical and Literary Culture," p. 23.

4. Jordan, *Bolt Upright*, p. 142. For the harping conventions and Bunting, see O'Sullivan, *Irish Folk Music and Song*, pp. 10–12.

5. White, *Tom Moore*, p. 76. For "the only art," see Welch, *Irish Poetry from Moore to Yeats*, p. 23. For "better able to vouch," see DeFord, *Thomas Moore*, p. 35; see also Rafroidi, "Thomas Moore," p. 55. For Moore's London connections, see Davis, "Irish Bards and English Consumers," pp. 13–15. Davis points out that the Power brothers had originally intended to use several poets, but Moore's first collection of the *Melodies* was so successful, they contracted him to complete the series.

6. Finson, *Voices That Are Gone*, p. 41. As Derek B. Scott suggests, Irish music had been coming to terms with the Italian style during the eighteenth century. The itinerant harpers encountered the popular Italian music in the important Anglo-Irish establishments, especially in Dublin. The capital city was an important musical center that attracted many foreign composers, including Thomas and Michael Arne, Francesco Geminiani, and Tommaso Giordani. The *Messiah* had its premiere there during Handel's 1741–42 visit. It is possible that Turlough O'Carolan, the best known of the harpers, met Geminiani in one of the ascendancy houses where the Italians usually stayed. Certainly, it was in these venues where the harper encountered the music of Corelli and Vivaldi. See Scott, *Singing Bourgeois*, pp. 26–27; Dower, "Dublin and Musical Culture," pp. 44, 47. After the Power brothers fell out, James Power replaced Sir John Stevenson with Henry Rowley Bishop, composer for John Howard Payne's "Home, Sweet Home," to complete the series of Moore's *Irish Melodies*.

7. See O'Boyle, *Irish Song Tradition*, p. 13. For "musical snuff-box," see DeFord, *Thomas Moore*, p. 36.

8. See Tessier, *Bard of Erin*, p. 84; see also Strong, *Minstrel Boy*, p. 131. In his performances, Moore's approach to rhythm and measure were apparently very free. He used pauses and *ritardandi* to effect. He is sometimes described as having delivered his songs in a kind of recitative style, "spoken" as much as sung (Tessier, *Bard of Erin*, p. 83). More than the result of aesthetic considerations, this style may have reflected a sensible strategy for preserving a light voice over many evenings of performing.

9. White, *Tom Moore*, p. 74. In "Shall the Harp Then Be Silent?" one of the rare cases where his verses are not particularly singable, Moore warns his public that only the first two verses of the song were actually intended for performance.

10. Hamm, *Yesterdays*, p. 44. For "He seems to think in music," see Jordan, *Bolt Upright*, p. 142. See also Welch, *Irish Poetry from Moore to Yeats*, p. 41.

11. Quoted in Rafroidi, "Thomas Moore," p. 58.

12. See Tessier, *Bard of Erin*, pp. 42–43.

13. Quoted in Grobman, "Ballads of Thomas Moore's *Irish Melodies*," p. 106.

14. James N. Healy points out that "Erin," more properly *Éireann,* is the genitive form in Irish of *Éire* and, therefore, has no grammatical sense at all when used, for instance, in the title "Erin Mavorneen" (*Mercier Book of Old Irish Street Ballads,* p. 349).

15. For Emmet, see Jordan, *Bolt Upright,* p. 115. Harold Ferrar refers to the "Emmet tradition" in Irish popular literature – the romantic presentation of Emmet, Sarah Curran, and Emmet's circle of friends – all of which owed much to Moore. Ferrar notes that one of Emmet's biographers claims that the revolutionary might have been forgotten if it had not been for Moore. See Ferrar, "Robert Emmet in Irish Drama," p. 23. In later editions of the *Melodies,* Moore did use his footnotes to tie his songs to contemporary Ireland. However, the references in the sheet music and the earlier editions were only to ancient Ireland. See Davis, "Irish Bards and English Consumers," p. 17.

16. Welch, *Irish Poetry from Moore to Yeats,* pp. 11, 28.

17. Davis, "Irish Bards and English Consumers," p. 11.

18. Quoted in Tessier, *Bard of Erin,* p. 5. See also Strong, *Minstrel Boy,* pp. 138–39.

19. Hamm, *Yesterdays,* p. 61.

20. Ibid., p. 51; see also Tessier, *Bard of Erin,* p. 23.

21. Grobman, "Ballads of Thomas Moore's *Irish Melodies,*" p. 109.

22. Quoted in White, *Tom Moore,* pp. 72–73 (emphasis added).

23. Welch, *Irish Poetry from Moore to Yeats,* p. 21. For similar sentiments expressed by eighteenth-century Irishmen, see Leerssen, *Mere Irish and Fíor-Ghael,* pp. 73, 75.

24. Tessier, *Bard of Erin,* pp. 47, 106; Welch, *Irish Poetry from Moore to Yeats,* pp. 38–39. "Green" is used in seventeen songs. The shamrock appears in eleven songs and is celebrated in "Oh the Shamrock." The harp appears in seven titles and in the lyrics of thirteen songs.

25. Joseph Leerssen briefly traces the growing admiration for Irish landscape in travel books. He quotes Charles Topham Boden, who, in his *Tour through Ireland* (1791), called Ireland "'the most romantic island in the world'" (Leerssen, *Mere Irish and Fíor-Ghael,* p. 80).

26. Davis, "Irish Bards and English Consumers," pp. 20, 21 (including Moore quote).

27. Austin, *"Susanna," "Jeanie," and "The Old Folks at Home,"* p. 131.

28. See Hamm, *Yesterdays,* pp. 46, 57–58; Fanning, *Irish Voice in America,* p. 12. For Moore's popularity in the United States, see Tessier, *Bard of Erin,* pp. 111, 136.

29. Hamm, *Yesterdays,* p. 174. Lover took to the stage when his failing eyesight threatened his livelihood as a miniaturist. He debuted in London in 1844. For his performances, see Symington, *Samuel Lover,* p. 122.

30. Whether by accident or design, Lover's songs of legend and superstitions do reflect one characteristic of the "grand airs" of the Gaelic tradition. Unlike Anglo-Scottish ballads, Gaelic songs rarely narrate the story, which it is assumed the audience already knows. Instead, the lyrics present the thoughts and emotions of one of the principal characters in the story.

31. Yerbury, *Song in America,* p. 162.

Chapter 2: Romantic Irish Popular Songs in Antebellum America

1. Finson, *Voices That Are Gone*, pp. 8, 12.

2. For copyrights, see Tawa, *Sweet Songs for Gentle Americans*, p. 112. For pianos, see Loesser, *Men, Women and Pianos*, pp. 20, 236, 519.

3. See Finson, *Voices That Are Gone*, p. 8.

4. Tawa, *Sweet Songs for Gentle Americans*, p. 15.

5. Scott, *Singing Bourgeois*, p. x.

6. Middleton, *Studying Popular Music*, pp. 12–13.

7. Scott, *Singing Bourgeois*, p. vii. Scott points out that during the first half of the nineteenth-century, songs published in sheet-music form were generally referred to as "popular songs" to suggest widespread demand: "A guarantee of quality followed, because a song could be popular in a commercial sense only by attracting sufficient numbers of musically literate bourgeois consumers" (p. vii).

8. Tawa, *Sweet Songs for Gentle Americans*, pp. 8, 11.

9. Lee, *Music of the People*, p. 9.

10. For the Irish genre of popular music, see Yerbury, *Song in America*, p. 162. Information for the following sections is derived from the electronic database referred to in the Introduction. Throughout the remainder of this study, the database will be referred to as "the sample." The songs of Thomas Moore and the non-comic songs by Samuel Lover are not represented in the database. We have already seen that few of Moore's titles suggest an Irish theme and, taken on the surface, many of the song lyrics had few direct references to Ireland. Although Samuel Lover wrote several of the classic Paddy songs of the era, most of his serious songs were about Irish superstitions and legends. There is seldom an Irish signifier in the primary titles to these songs. Nor do the lyrics themselves suggest the Irish theme, which was often dealt with in brief notes at the head of the song. The works of both Moore and Lover were, therefore, unique. Although they did help to establish some of the themes dealt with in Irish songs, the particular manner in which they framed and wrote their lyrics was not generally followed by other songwriters working in the Irish genre. Their presence would, therefore, tend to distort the sample.

11. Scott, *Singing Bourgeois*, p. 54.

12. This iconography had been already well established by the eighteenth-century Irish antiquarians. See Leerssen, *Mere Irish and Fíor-Ghael*, p. 440.

13. "The New Hibernian Quadrille," arr. Thomas Baker (New York: Waters, 1859). Nicholas E. Tawa states that about one-third of the body of pre–Civil War sheet music consisted of either dances or variations on popular melodies. See *Sweet Songs for Gentle Americans*, p. 4.

14. "Ellen Asthore," John Inman and James Gaspard Maeder (New York: C. E. Horn, 1841); "The Irish Mother's Lament (Introducing the Irish Cry for the Dead)," John Barton (New York: Firth, Hall, [1831–43]) (the dates are based on the publisher's address, according to Wolfe, *Secular Music in America*). See also Finson, *Voices That Are Gone*, pp. 276–77.

15. See Hamm, *Yesterdays*, pp. 55–57.

16. Finson, *Voices That Are Gone*, p. 37. At least one of Foster's melodies is

claimed by the Irish. In the liner notes to *Eugene O'Donnell: Slow Airs and Set Dances* (Innisfree/Green Linnet SIF 1015), Mick Moloney claims that Foster borrowed the melody for "Gentle Annie" from an Irish air, *Ni Fheicim Nios Mó Thu a Mhúirnín.*

17. Scott, *Singing Bourgeois*, pp. 99, 101.

18. Since they contain no lyrics, instrumental pieces are excluded from the following calculations, reducing the sample to ninety-one songs for the antebellum period.

19. For various types of love songs, see Tawa, *Sweet Songs for Gentle Americans*, pp. 131–38.

20. Ibid., pp. 125–26.

21. For the qualities of the beloved in song, see Tawa, *Music for Millions*, pp. 79–80.

22. "The Rose of Tralee (An Irish Ballad)," Charles Glover, [words by William Pembroke Mulchinock] (New York: Daly, [1852–69]); emphasis added. Various stories are told about the love affair between Mulchinock and the real "Mary." By far the nicest one is found in James Healy, *Second Book of Irish Ballads*. Other stories, less flattering to Mulchinock, can be heard around Tralee. The tune to which "The Rose of Tralee" is sung is not by Mulchinock but by Charles Glover and was first published in 1846. The song was so popular in Ireland, especially in the writer's home district, that a monument was raised to him in Kerry Town. Mulchinock's house was still standing in the 1960s in Clahane, where it overlooked the vale his song made famous. See Healy, *Second Book of Irish Ballads*, p. 76.

23. Tawa, *Music for Millions*, p. 71.

24. "Yes! 'Tis True That Thy Kate Now Is Sleeping," Rosa Hughes and Charles Jarvis (Philadelphia: Gould, 1853).

25. "Answer to the Lament of the Irish Emigrant," J. S. Murphy and T. Bissell (Boston: Keith, 1844). See also "Lament of the Irish Emigrant," Mrs. Price Blackwood and William R. Dempster (Boston: Reed, 1843). The man on the cover stands by the turnstile mentioned in the first line of the song: "I'm sitting on the stile Mary, where we sat side by side." An early favorite of John McCormack, this song remained popular into the twentieth century, by which time the title was sometimes taken from the song's opening line.

26. Finson, *Voices That Are Gone*, p. 113.

27. Hamm, *Yesterdays*, p. 77.

28. "Kathleen Mavourneen," Mrs. Crawford and Frederick Nicholas Crouch (New York: Benteen, 1840). The lyrics, with a different melody by Edward Allan, were published by Benteen of Baltimore (n.d.) around the same time.

29. Turner and Maill, *Just a Song at Twilight*, p. 202; see also Fitz-Gerald, *Stories of Famous Songs*, vol. 1, pp. 173–74.

30. "Come Back to Erin," Claribel [Charlotte Alington Barnard] (New York: 1866). Barnard helped to popularize this verse-refrain type of song. She wrote at a time when the ballad market was opening to women, although, like many of her predecessors in the field, she chose to remain anonymous. She may have taken the name of "Claribel" from a poem of that name by Tennyson, who was also from

her native Lincolnshire. She usually wrote her own lyrics as well as melodies. See Scott, *Singing Bourgeois*, p. 74. See also entry for Barnard in Gammond, *Oxford Companion to Popular Music*.

31. "Give Me Three Grains of Corn, Mother," Mrs. A. M. Edmond and O. R. Gross (Boston: Ditson, 1848). See also Elson, *Guardians of Tradition*, pp. 125–26; Tawa, *Sweet Songs for Gentle Americans*, p. 145.

32. "Dying Emigrant's Prayer," Henry Plunkett Gratten and George P. H. Loder (New York: Firth, Helf, 1847); "The War Ship of Peace," Samuel Lover (New York: Firth and Hall, 1847); "The Emigrant's Farewell," R. H. Eaton of Syracuse, New York, and L. V. H. Crosby (Boston: Reed, 1852).

33. Lee, *Music of the People*, p. 69; Tawa, *Music for Millions*, pp. 89, 90–91. For the enthusiasm with which the British middle class greeted sentimental songs about slaves, see Bratton, *Victorian Popular Ballad*, p. 106. Jon W. Finson has a chapter on "The Romantic Savage," in *Voices That Are Gone*, pp. 240–69. There is a clear parallel with songs expressing longing for Ireland in Isaac Woodbury's "The Indian's Prayer" (1846): "Let me go to my home in the far distant west," a "wild forest land" where "the tall cedars wave" and "wild fawns leap" (Finson, *Voices That Are Gone*, p. 243).

34. Fitz-Gerald, *Stories of Famous Songs*, vol. 1, p. 188. "Exile of Erin or Erin Go Bragh," [Thomas] Campbell [and Edward Knight] (Boston: Bradlee, [1819–30]) (the dates are from Wolfe, *Secular Music in America*). The words appeared in American songsters as early as 1819. For its use in Pilgrim's plays, see Flynn, "Ethnicity after Sea-Change," p. 169.

35. "The Emigrant's Farewell," R. H. Eaton of Syracuse, New York and L. V. H. Crosby (Boston: Reed, 1852).

36. "Mavourneen Machree," Mdm. Anna Ablamowicvz and E. W. Mason (Louisville: Tripp and Cragg, 1852); "The Irish Emigrant," Lady Dufferin [Mrs. Frederick Temple Hamilton Blackwood] and George Barker, [ca. 1845]. Lady Dufferin was Helen Selina Sheridan, granddaughter of the great Anglo-Irish playwright, Richard Brinsley Sheridan. Her sister Caroline, the Hon. Mrs. Norton, wrote "The Arab's Farewell to His Steed," one of the great favorites of the Victorian era. Lady Dufferin's husband was Frederick Temple Hamilton Blackwood, Lord of Dufferin and Ava, and author of *Irish Emigration and the Tenure of Land in Ireland*.

37. "Mary Astore," Mrs. Crawford and Stephen Glover (Boston: Ditson, [1844–57]).

38. See Austin, *"Susanna," "Jeanie," and "The Old Folks at Home,"* pp. 132, 137. As we have seen, Moore frequently used the word "dream" in many of his *Irish Melodies*, and the word appears in the texts of 8 per cent of the antebellum songs in my sample.

39. Hamm, *Yesterdays*, p. 54. See also Austin, *"Susanna," "Jeanie," and "The Old Folks at Home,"* pp. 123–62.

40. Turner, *Parlour Song Book*, p. 18.

41. "The Irish Peasant," Charles Harding and George Barker (Philadelphia: Lee, Walker, [1856–67]); "Aileen Mavourneen," Mrs. S. C. Hall and A. D. Roche (Philadelphia: Burns, [ca. 1840]); "You'll Soon Forget Kathleen," W. Langton Williams

(Boston: Ditson, [1858–76]) (the dates are based on publishers addresses in Wolfe, *Secular Music in America*).

42. "The Irish Patriot's Farewell to His Country," Richard B. Taylor (Boston: Keith, 1842).

43. "Hail! Glorious Apostle (A Hymn for St. Patrick's Day)," Thomas Comer (Boston: Donahoe, 1833).

44. Tawa, *Music for Millions*, pp. 63, 67.

45. "Killarney," Edmund Falconer [Edmund O'Rourke] and Michael William Balfe (New York: Daly, 1867). The beauties of Killarney had already been described in the eighteenth-century travel books on Ireland. In 1767 Irish-born Samuel Derrick described Killarney as "one of the most beautiful and romantic spots in this kingdom." See Leerssen *Mere Irish and Fíor-Ghael*, p. 76.

46. Nelson, "From Rory and Paddy," p. 95.

47. Many of the best of the Victorian parlor songs are well represented in the "ethnic recordings" made for Irish Americans in the 1920s and 1930s. See Spottswood, *Ethnic Music on Records*.

Introduction to Part 2

1. Knobel, *Paddy and the Republic*, pp. 12, 13. Knobel also points out that while they accepted much of the English stereotype of the Irish, Americans added to it their own perceptions of the ills of the Old World. Not being born and raised in the environment of freedom was taken as a distinct liability. Thus, the Irish became heirs to criticisms previously directed at both the French and the British (pp. 51–52).

2. Ibid., pp. 31–32, 33, 15–16.

3. Miller, *Emigrants and Exiles*, p. 350. For the Strong quote see Knobel, *Paddy and the Republic*, p. 87. In 1800 half of the population of Ireland were Gaelic-speaking monoglots. By 1851, towards the end of the vast Famine exodus, the proportion had fallen to just 5 percent. Although by that date only a quarter of the population could speak Irish at all, there were still well over a million Gaelic speakers in the country. See O'Tuathaigh, *Ireland before the Famine*, p. 157.

4. MacLochlainn, "Gael and Peasant," p. 31.

5. O'Tuathaigh, *Ireland before the Famine*, p. 150.

6. Niehaus, *Irish in New Orleans*, pp. 60, 65. Niehaus adds: "The attitude of the city toward violence among the Irish, like that of the South toward the Negro later, was also a determining factor . . . the city authorities exercised little restraint" (p. 63). Irish-on-Irish violence was pretty much accepted, although clan feuds, carried over from the Old Country, were recognized as being particularly dangerous. For the quote from Carleton, see Harmon, "Cobwebs before the Wind," p. 137.

7. MacDonagh, "Irish Famine Emigration to the United States," p. 368.

8. For an excellent account of old Irish wake customs see O'Súilleabháin, *Irish Wake Amusements*.

9. Croker, *Researches in the South of Ireland*, pp. 278, 280–81.

10. Evans, *Irish Folk Ways*, pp. 256–57; Light, "Role of Irish-American Organizations," p. 13.

11. Croker, *Researches in the South of Ireland*, p. 225.

12. Wilgus, "Irish Traditional Narrative Songs in English," p. 124.

13. See Miller, *Emigrants and Exiles*, p. 107. Miller attributes much of this premodern mentality to some of the peculiar characteristics of Irish Catholicism as interpreted by many peasants in the pre-Famine years. They "viewed the universe as static and tradition bound, within which they were merely passive recipients of whatever bounties or ills God or fate saw fit to ordain. . . . [They] regarded themselves not as independent agents but as dependent patients, bound to their communal traditions and subject to the 'twists and turns' of fate or to what one Donegal man called '*rotha mór an tsaoghali*' (the great wheel of life)" (p. 110). The expression recalls the medieval image of Fortuna with her wheel.

Chapter 3: From Teague to Paddy

1. Kibred, "Fall of the Stage Irishman," p. 451. For earlier representations of the Irish on the English stage, see Bartley, *Teague, Shenkin and Sawney*; Duggan, *Stage Irishman*; and Truniger, *Paddy and the Paycock*. Truniger points out that while Shakespeare did not invent the stage Irishman, his MacMorris is the first in a long line of Irish soldiers in the English theater (p. 26).

2. See Snyder, "Wild Irish," p. 149.

3. Hayton, "From Barbarian to Burlesque," pp. 5, 7. For the Irish as "savages," see Jones, *O Strange New World*, pp. 167–73; for Quinn's quote, see Quinn, *Elizabethans and the Irish*, p. 26.

4. Bartley, *Teague, Shenkin and Sawney*, p. 37. To this day, "the bogs" is an English slang term for lavatory.

5. Gallagher, *Foreigner in Early American Drama*, p. 115; Bartley, *Teague, Shenkin and Sawney*, pp. 127, 164.

6. Hayton, "From Barbarian to Burlesque," p. 11.

7. Text from Chappell, *Ballad Literature and Popular Music*, vol. 2, p. 572. The song first appeared between late 1687 and 1688 as an attack on James II's appointment of Richard Talbot, Earl of Tirconnell, as Lord Deputy in Ireland.

8. See under "Irish" in Partridge, *Dictionary of Historical Slang*; for "weep Irish," etc., see Curtis, *Anglo Saxons and Celts*, p. 52; for American usage, see Dohan, *Our Own Words*, p. 234. See also Hayton, "From Barbarian to Burlesque," p. 15. In contemporary Ireland "Belfast confetti" refers to bricks and paving stones hurled at the constabulary and the military.

9. Hayton, "From Barbarian to Burlesque," pp. 16–18.

10. For the Dunton quote, see Leerssen, *Mere Irish and Fíor-Ghael*, p. 73.

11. Bartley, *Teague, Shenkin and Sawney*, pp. 164–65; Duggan, *Stage Irishman*, p. 290.

12. Bartley, *Teague, Shenkin and Sawney*, p. 193.

13. See Leerssen, *Mere Irish and Fíor-Ghael*, p. 131; Duggan, *Stage Irishman*, pp. 289–90.

14. According to Leerssen this change in attitude, which appears around the middle of the eighteenth century, is evidenced only in the theater, not in any other type of literature (*Mere Irish and Fíor-Ghael,* pp. 82, 88).

15. Duggan, *Stage Irishman,* p. 284. Duggan points out that the dialect change took place during the Williamite era. For the humor of the brogue, see Bratton, *Victorian Popular Ballad,* p. 213.

16. Krause, *Dolmen Boucicault,* pp. 39–40.

17. Ibid., p. 40. Annelise Truniger points out that guile and cunning originally developed as the traits of the Irish servant in English drama (*Paddy and the Paycock,* p. 25). Paddy the peasant inherits Teague's deviousness, but renders it harmless, as Paddy is, more often than not, a "dacent" fellow.

18. Truniger, *Paddy and the Paycock,* p. 41. For the Swift quote see Smith, "From Stereotype to Acculturation," p. 53. There has been some confusion about the word "brogue." In its customary English spelling it has a double meaning – "shoe" and "accent." In Gaelic, references to shoes and accent derive from two different, although similarly sounding, words. *Bróg* means "shoe." See de Bhaldralthe, *English-Irish Dictionary.* However, *barróg* means "to hug, embrace," or to have a hold upon. See O'Siochfhradha, *Learner's Irish-English Dictionary.* Thus, "brogue" did not, as some scholars have suggested, derive from the idea that the Irishman sounded as if he had his shoe in his mouth. Rather it meant that the Irishman of Gaelic background, in speaking English, spoke with an accent that figuratively had a "hold" upon his tongue. I am grateful to Alf MacLochlainn for calling my attention to this.

19. See Waters, *Comic Irishman,* p. 11. Here is Waters's example of a bull: "Well Mick . . . I've heard some queer stories about your doings lately. 'Och, don't believe thim, surr,' replied Mick. 'Sure half the lies tould about me by the naybours isn't thrue'" (p. 11).

20. Duggan, *Stage Irishman,* pp. 293, 295.

21. Fanning, *Irish Voice in America,* p. 12.

22. Dodge, "Irish Comic Stereotype," p. 120.

23. Gallagher, *Foreigner in Early American Drama,* pp. 121, 123, 125; quote on p. 126.

24. Ibid., pp. 118, 121, 131–33; Fanning, *Irish Voice in America,* p. 13.

25. For Pilgrim quote, see Grimsted, *Melodrama Unveiled,* p. 189. See also Gallagher, *Foreigner in Early American Drama,* p. 117; Niehaus, *Irish in New Orleans,* p. 121. A similar process was at work in the fiction of the early republic. Teague O'Regan in Hugh Henry Brackenridge's picaresque novel *Modern Chivalry* (1792–1815) represents the transfer of the stage Irishman to the American novel. Charles Fanning describes Teague as: "Drinking, whistling, blarneying, and brandishing a shillelagh, Teague heads a long parade of stereotypical Irish figures in mainstream American fiction" (*Irish Voice in America,* p. 13). Herbert Joseph Smith has suggested that Brackenridge's characterization of Teague was "the first major ethnic fool to appear in American fiction," a national prototype of the bumbling immigrant-on-the-make that would serve as a model throughout the nineteenth century ("From Stereotype to Acculturation," pp. 4–5, 25).

26. Toll, *Blacking Up*, p. 169; Lott, *Love and Theft*, p. 91. Lott suggests that minstrelsy was also "an Americanizing" ritual that gave "socially insecure Irishmen" a sense of superiority over the blacks they parodied (p. 96).

27. See Wittke, *Tambo and Bones*, pp. 210, 214, 223, 235, 245.

28. Ibid., p. 77.

29. Ibid., p. 200; see also Toll, *Blacking Up*, p. 176. Eric Lott suggests that the use of Irish dialect and songs by blackface performers is evidence of a connection between Irish low comedy and minstrelsy (*Love and Theft*, p. 95).

30. See Waters, "No Divarshin," p. 57.

31. Foster, "Irish Wrong," pp. 35–36, 44. See also Symington, *Samuel Lover*, p. 94. According to Symington, at least one of the author's characters, Handy Andy, was based on a man who served the Knight of Glin, at Glin Castle in County Kerry. Symington maintains that some of the incidents attributed to Andy were basically true (pp. 114, 119–23).

32. Power, *Impressions of America*, vol. 1, pp. 181–82.

33. See the Barney Williams interview in *The Spirit of the Times*, April 10, 1875, p. 208. Concerning Power's birth, Christopher Fitz-Simon suggests that Power's father may have been the Marquess of Waterford "or at least . . . a member of that family" (*Irish Theatre*, p. 95). Barney Williams, a Corkonian who took over many of Power's roles, reported to *The Spirit of the Times* that Power was rumored to have been a Welshman whose "true name was Thomas Powell" (April 10, 1875, p. 208). Williams is the only source I have found for this story. In alleging that Power was Welsh (and that he initially spurned Irish roles), he may have been slandering the man with whom he was so often compared, not always to his, Williams's, credit.

34. Potter, *To the Golden Door*, p. 609; Waters, *Comic Irishman*, p. 42.

35. See Nelson, "From Rory and Paddy," pp. 88, 89–90; Fitz-Simon, *Irish Theatre*, p. 96.

36. Ireland, *Records of the New York Stage*, pp. 29–70; see also Meserve, *Heralds of Promise*, p. 111.

37. See Ireland, *Records of the New York Stage*, p. 69. It was a case of the sea claiming what it had once lost. Young Power and his mother had survived a shipwreck off the Welsh coast on their original journey from Ireland. See Fitz-Simon, *Irish Theatre*, p. 95.

38. Winter, *Other Days*, pp. 108, 110; Young, *Famous Actors and Actresses*, vol. 1, p. 135.

39. Hornblow, *History of the Theatre in America*, vol. 2, p. 144.

40. Ryan, "Hibernian Experience," pp. 36–37.

41. Root, *American Popular Stage Music*, p. 77.

42. *Spirit of the Times*, April 17, 1875, p. 237. In William Winter's opinion, it was the Irish gentleman more than the Irish peasant roles that elicited Brougham's best efforts. See Winter, *Other Days*, pp. 102–3.

43. Hutton, *Curiosities of the American Stage*, pp. 104–5.

44. Ireland, *Records of the New York Stage*, p. 332. For "a portion" see McConachie, "Cultural Politics of 'Paddy,'" p. 4.

45. Williams interview in *The Spirit of the Times*, October 3, 1874, p. 195.

46. McConachie, "Cultural Politics of 'Paddy,'" p. 4.

47. Young, *Famous Actors and Actresses*, vol. 1, pp. 298–99.

48. Meserve, *Heralds of Promise*, p. 112.

49. Williams interview in *The Spirit of the Times*, April 10, 1875, p. 208. For Collins see also Niehaus, *Irish in New Orleans*, p. 123.

50. Quoted in Potter, *To the Golden Door*, p. 610.

51. See Meserve, *Heralds of Promise*, pp. 160, 165; Bogard et al., *Revels History of Drama in English*, pp. 176–77.

52. "Paddy Carey's Fortune or Irish Promotion," Cherry and Whitaker (Philadelphia: C. Tawes, [1813–19]). The dates "1800–33" are written on the cover. Based on the publishers' addresses given in Wolfe, *American Secular Songs*, this copy might have been printed between 1813 and 1819.

53. "Fine Ould Irish Gintleman," John Brougham (Boston: Reed, 1845). This was a much-parodied song. Dickens is supposed to have written one. In America there was "The Fine Old Southern Gentleman," and Daniel Decatur Emmett wrote "The Fine Old Colored Gentleman" around 1836. See Tawa, *Sweet Songs for Gentle Americans*, p. 92.

54. "The Irishman's Shanty," Matt Peel (New York: Firth, 1859).

55. "Teddy O'Neale," Eliza Cook and James G. Maeder (Boston: Oakes, 1843).

56. "Barney Brallaghan," P. K. Moran (New York: Bourne, 1830).

57. "There's Monny a Shlip (An Irish Song)," by Pro Basso [pseud.] (Cincinnati: Church, 1874).

58. "Larry O'Gaff (A Comic Irish Song)," as sung by Jack Welch (Boston: Ditson, [1844–57 penciled on cover]).

59. "The Poor Irish Boy," Eliza Cook and John Frazer (New York: Waters, 1854).

60. "Rory O'More," Samuel Lover (New York: Hewitt, Jaques, [1837–41]).

61. "Paddy Reilly's Pledge," Robert Clarke and Lady Clarke (Dublin: Pigott, n.d.). The Lilly Library copy of this song has the date 1872 penciled on the cover. However, it may have been written much earlier. Father Theobald Mathew's great temperance movement swept through Ireland in the late 1830s and the 1840s.

62. Earl F. Niehaus reports a New Orleans joke about an Irish toper who had turned up dead drunk and had been waked once too often. He suggested that the next time he was found comatose his companions should just bring him the glass "an' if I don't rise up an' dhrink, then bury me" (*Irish in New Orleans*, p. 128).

63. "The Birth of Green Erin," by James R. Thomas (New York: Pond, 1866). In spite of the date, the song has every appearance of something written at least a generation earlier.

64. "Lanigan's Ball," Tony Pastor, Neil Bryant, and Charles Glover, arr. (New York: Pond, 1863). Another copy published by Pond in 1865 credits Baumbach as the writer. However, there can be little doubt that the piece is Irish in origin. James M. Healy asserts that the song originated near Athy, mentioned in the song, around 1860. Local tradition had it that the song was based on an actual occurrence, which, in fine Irish tradition, was satirically commemorated by one of the guests. See Healy, *Ballads from the Pubs of Ireland*, pp. 26–28.

Colm O Lochlainn claims to have seen a sheet music version in Ireland dating from the 1870s in which the words were attributed to "Mr. Gavan, the Celebrated Galway poet." The song was also common in ballad sheets and, indeed, is composed very much in the Irish broadside tradition. See O Lochlainn, *Irish Street Ballads*, p. 223 n. 52. The tune, the traditional "Hurry the Jug," is still played by Irish musicians but is as likely to be known by the song's title.

65. "Father Molloy," as sung by Harry Drayton (Boston: Ditson, 1861).

66. Bratton, *Victorian Popular Ballad*, p. 190. For "The Guide's Song," see Symington, *Samuel Lover*, pp. 48–49. The Irish mile was in fact longer than the English mile.

67. "Fair Rose of Killarney," Eliza Cook and Stephen Glover (Baltimore: Willig, [1824–31]); "Beautiful Erin," Mrs. Wellington Boate and William Glover (New York: Hall, [1848–58]); dates for both songs derived from Wolfe, *Secular Music in America*. "Green Hills of Erin, A National Song," F. W. N. Boyley and T. B. Phipps (London: [1821–31 penciled on cover]).

68. Symington, *Samuel Lover*, p. 96 (emphasis added).

Chapter 4: Ethnicity and Parlor Songs

1. In the Starr Collection at the Lilly Library I found 165 titles, most of them published before 1860, filed under "Scotland." Of course, as with the term "Irish," "Scottish" or "Scotch" refers to a genre or style of a song rather than to a song's actual origins or composer. Jon W. Finson suggests that until 1840, Scottish songs outnumbered Irish songs in American popular music (see *Voices That Are Gone*, p. 278). On the basis of my sampling, it seems that while there appear to have been more songs associated with the Scots in the earlier decades of the nineteenth century, the number of Irish songs increased considerably by the middle of the century and continued to expand as interest in Scottish songs declined.

2. Van der Merwe, *Origins of the Popular Style*, p. 17.

3. See Scott, *Singing Bourgeois*, pp. 94–96.

4. Only 22 percent of the titles in my sample carry the word "Scottish" or "Scotland" in the secondary title, while it was common for pre–Civil War Irish songs to have some direct reference to Ireland or the Irish in the title. This suggests a greater familiarity with the Scottish genre on the part of the song-buying public. Publishers could rely on other clues to signify a Scottish song. Twenty-six percent of the Scots songs in the Lilly Collection are identified by the word "Highland" or some particular Scottish place name (only 6 percent of the Irish songs used place names in the titles published before the Civil War). Forty-seven percent were identified by some simple linguistic signifier, such as "wee," "bonny," and "auld," whereas only 16 percent of Irish songs used similar identifiers. On the other hand, only 17 percent of the titles used obviously Scottish personal names, compared to over 40 percent of the Irish songs. Given the predominance of the stage Irishman over his other Celtic counterparts, Irish names were probably more familiar to the Anglo-American public.

5. Finson, *Voices That Are Gone*, p. 49.

6. For the original version of "John Anderson, My Jo" see Barke and Smith, *Robert Burns*, pp. 142–43.

7. Scott, *Singing Bourgeois*, pp. 93–94. See also Van Der Merwe, *Origins of the Popular Style*, p. 16.

8. See Middleton, *Studying Popular Music*, pp. 10, 134–35.

9. Here is a sampling of the contents of songsters published around the middle of the century: *Beadle's Dime Song Book No. 4*, out of seventy songs, five Scottish and twelve Irish; in *Beadle's Dime Song Book No. 5*, out of seventy-three songs, seven Scottish, six Irish; *Gentle Annie Melodist No. 1*, out of sixty-three songs, eight Scottish and three Irish; *Gentle Annie Melodist No. 2*, out of forty-eight songs, three Scottish and four Irish; and *The Love and Sentimental Songster*, out of eighty-eight songs, three Scottish and twelve Irish. Significantly, in *Fred Shaw's Dime American Comic Songster*, nine of the thirty-eight songs were Irish, none were Scottish.

10. Hamm, *Yesterdays*, pp. 187, 189–90, 195–98.

11. I reviewed the pieces arranged alphabetically by title in the folders from "A" through "H."

12. That publishers assumed that the audience for these songs included Germans is suggested by the fact that all but eleven of the ninety-five songs I sampled have lyrics in German as well as in English. Nevertheless, the fact that in over three-quarters of the songs the English words are printed above the German, placing them closer to the melody line, and that in all cases the English words were in a more readable typeface, suggests that English speakers were an important, if not the primary, audience for these songs.

13. Quoted in Turner and Maill, *Just a Song at Twilight*, p. 10.

14. Toll, *Blacking Up*, p. 175. Jon W. Finson finds it "incredible" that there was so little American sheet music dealing with German ethnicity, given the number of German speakers in the country, even before the immigration of the 1850s. See Finson, *Voices That Are Gone*, pp. 283, 289–90, 309.

15. Lott, *Love and Theft*, p. 35. Lott's emphasis on men refers to cross-dressing in minstrel acts, which along with issues of ethnicity and working-class identities, make up the complexity that he addresses. See also Toll, *Blacking Up*, pp. 161–62, 176.

16. See Dennison, *Scandalize My Name*, p. xi; Geist, "From the Plantation to the Police Station," p. 161. Geist goes on to point out that blacks were generally considered to be docile, a trait rarely associated with the Irish.

17. Quoted in Knobel, *Paddy and the Republic*, p. 21. See also Boskin, *Sambo*, p. 13.

18. Boskin, *Sambo*, p. 42.

19. Niehaus, *Irish in New Orleans*, p. 131. For Dunton quote, see Leerssen, *Mere Irish and Fíor-Ghael*, p. 73.

20. Boskin, *Sambo*, p. 14.

21. Ibid., pp. 56, 58, 61.

22. See Dennison, *Scandalize My Name*, p. 102; for quote see p. 86.

23. Ibid., p. 192; Van den Merwe, *Origins of the Popular Style*, pp. 17, 18. Denni-

son is sometimes too eager to find race in songs. In his comments on "The Black-bird," which he found in a songster, he suggests that the song is a rare example of a white woman taking a black lover (*Scandalize My Name*, pp. 130–32). The song turns out to be a broadside version of an Irish patriotic "ashling" or vision song. The "Blackbird," whose loss the woman (Ireland) in the song laments, originally represented Bonnie Prince Charlie.

24. Kibred, "Fall of the Stage Irishman," p. 452.

25. The similarities between Paddy and Sambo break down, of course, in regard to the unique situation that engulfed African Americans. The difference between a poor, suspected minority group and the victims of a system of chattel slavery based on race is, in the end, too great to be bridged by a comparison of stereotypes. The fact that the Irish were free to respond to their stereotype made all the difference in the world. For a glimpse into the complexities of the relationships between the Irish and African Americans, see Ignatiev, *How the Irish Became White*.

26. Mercier, *Irish Comic Tradition*, p. ix.

27. Lebow, "British Images of Poverty," pp. 59, 80, 82.

28. Young, *Famous Actors and Actresses*, vol. 2, p. 931. For the Daniels quote see Nelson, "From Rory and Paddy," p. 88 (emphasis added).

29. Winter, *Other Days*, p. 101 (emphasis added).

30. For quotes from the *Cork Examiner*, see Young, *Famous Actors and Actress-es*, vol. 2, p. 1180 (emphasis added). For the quote from the *New Orleans Picayune*, see Rossman, "Irish in American Drama," p. 51 (emphasis added).

31. Symington, *Samuel Lover*, p. 51.

32. Nelson, "From Rory and Paddy," pp. 81, 83.

33. Knobel, "Vocabulary of Ethnic Perception," p. 53. In spite of the sophisti-cation of Knobel's content analysis, one has to question the validity of classifying words as simply either "positive" or "negative" when, within the broader context of the popular culture, the qualities a word might conjure up could cover a wide range of feelings. For example, under the category of "Negative Relational" Kno-bel counted the occurrence of words in plays that "'depict the target group and its members as strange or alien as opposed to familiar and native'. . . or 'empha-size those characteristics which make group members undesirable and unattrac-tive interpersonal problems'" (p. 55). Among the words placed in this category are "curious," "droll," "extraordinary," "amusing," "funny," and "saucy." Likewise, in the category "Emotional" we find words such as "enthusiastic," "frolicking," "imag-inative," and "romantic" (pp. 55, 57). While within certain dramatic contexts the intent of such words may have been to convey negative impressions, they also suggest an ambiguity toward Paddy. They may be negative in that the characters described may lack seriousness. However, they may also suggest some lurking sym-pathy and even admiration for the characters. More important, the aspects of the Irish stereotype represented by these words were those that I believe eventually helped to move the stage Irishman from a primarily negative to a increasingly positive position in American culture by the late nineteenth century.

34. Knobel, *Paddy and the Republic*, p. 60.

35. Niehaus, *Irish in New Orleans*, p. 125 (emphasis added).

Introduction to Part 3

1. Wittke, *Irish in America*, p. 35.

2. Rosenwaike, *Population History of New York City*, p. 43; Ernst, *Immigrant Life in New York City*, pp. 43, 68, 69, 105.

3. Quoted in Daniels, *Coming to America*, p. 137.

4. *Beadle's Dime Song Book No. 4*, pp. 37–38.

5. Curran, *Hibernian Green on the Silver Screen*, p. 6.

6. Rosenwaike, *Population History of New York City*, pp. 80, 108; Wittke, *Irish in America*, pp. 44–45.

7. For the Irish demographics see MacDonough, "Irish Famine Emigration to the United States," pp. 369, 435. On Irish workers, see Wittke, *Irish in America*, p. 23.

8. Edwards and Williams, *Great Famine*, p. 113. For clachans, see Evans, *Irish Folk Ways*, pp. 23–25; Miller, *Emigrants and Exiles*, pp. 27–28. "Clachan" is apparently the anglicization of *clohán*, which means variously "a jumble of stones" or "village." While the clachans were emptied by the Famine, the enclosures, and the evictions, some survived in the "Congested Districts" of the west of Ireland late into the nineteenth century. See Miller, *Emigrants and Exiles*, p. 470. One of the most famous clachans, a fishing village known as "The Cladagh" on the edge of Galway city, lasted into the 1920s. The Cladagh is immortalized in the song "Galway Bay" by Dr. Arthur Colahan (1947).

9. Wittke, *Irish in America*, p. 62. In order to appreciate the importance of the Ulsterman's complaint, see the discussion of the "ceili" or visiting in contemporary rural Ireland in Glassie, *Passing the Time in Ballymenone*.

10. Miller, *Emigrants and Exiles*, pp. 274, 516.

11. For densities around 1850 see Clark, *Hibernia America*, p. 52. For later densities, see Sante, *Low Life*, 32.

12. McCaffrey, *Irish Diaspora in America*, p. 66.

13. Clark *Hibernia America*, p. 56.

14. Daniels, *Coming to America*, p. 142; Miller, *Emigrants and Exiles*, p. 500.

15. Archdeacon, *Becoming American*, p. 99.

16. McCaffrey, *Irish Diaspora in America*, p. 66. For the American Protective Association, see Higham, *Strangers in the Land*, pp. 60–61, 80–85. Better known as the APA, the association had its origins in an earlier group, the American Protestant Association, a smaller and secretive organization formed in the 1850s.

17. Clark, *Irish Relations*, p. 131; Curtis, *Anglo-Saxons and Celts*, p. 109.

18. Doyle, *Ireland, Irishmen and Revolutionary America*, p. 224.

19. Many of these pieces were serialized in the Irish-American press before appearing in book form. See Walsh, "Lace Curtain Literature," p. 140.

Chapter 5: "To the Land We Left and to the Land We Live In"

1. Barney Williams interview, *Spirit of the Times*, April 10, 1875, p. 208.

2. Flynn, "Ethnicity after Sea-Change," p. 171.

3. Ryan, "Hibernian Experience," pp. 44–45. For the quote, see Blaney, "City Life in American Drama," p. 116.

4. Staples, *Male-Female Comedy Teams*, p. 20.

5. Wittke, "Immigrant Theme on the American Stage," pp. 218, 219.

6. McConachie, "Cultural Politics of 'Paddy,'" p. 11.

7. Krause, *Dolmen Boucicault*, p. 25.

8. Watt, *Joyce, O'Casey, and the Irish Popular Theater*, p. 52.

9. Krause, *Dolmen Boucicault*, p. 13.

10. Ibid., p. 32. See also Kosok, "Image of Ireland in Nineteenth-Century Drama," p. 59; Graves, "Stage Irishman among the Irish," p. 35.

11. Watt, *Joyce, O'Casey, and the Irish Popular Theater*, p. 75; Kosok, "Image of Ireland in Nineteenth-Century Drama," p. 65.

12. See Flynn, "Ethnicity after Sea-Change," p. 165; Rahill, *World of Melodrama*, p. 190.

13. Flynn, "Ethnicity after Sea-Change," pp. 166, 3, 146, 34.

14. Ibid., p. 174; quote in following paragraph from ibid., p. 23.

15. "I'll Take You Home Again, Kathleen," Thomas P. Westendorf (Cincinnati: John Church, 1876). Westendorf was not the only songwriter to suggest an Irish theme in the title while avoiding a clear Irish identification in the lyrics. William Shakespeare Hays, a prolific songwriter in the 1860s and 1870s, wrote a number of songs with Irish names in the title, some even suggesting Irish themes, such as his emigration song "Barney Don't Forget" (1878), while never mentioning Ireland. It was a way of using an Irish hook while appealing to the largest possible audience.

16. Staples, *Male-Female Comedy Teams*, p. 32.

17. "A Handful of Earth from the Place of My Birth," W. H. Clark (New York: Fisher, 1884).

18. "Pat Malloy," Dion Boucicault (New York: Pond, 1865). The song was so popular that it inspired a broadside ballad, "Return of Pat Malloy," as well as a parody (see Wright, *Irish Emigrant Ballads and Songs*, pp. 262–67). There was also "Mary of Fermoy (The Answer to Pat Malloy)," J. E. Fitzgerald and Frank Howard (Chicago: Merrill, 1866). See also Finson, *Voices That Are Gone*, p. 287.

19. "Maggie, Darling, Now Good Bye," C. A. White (Boston: White, Smith, 1872). The cover proclaims that the song was "written expressly for, and sung with great success by the Freeman Sisters," who may be depicted on the cover, one dressed as a boy in knee breeches with a bundle over the shoulder.

20. *Pat Rooney's "Day I Played Base Ball" Songster*, p. 9.

21. "Sad-Fated Erin," George Russell Jackson and J. L. Gilbert (New York: W. A. Evans, 1882).

22. "The Irish Emigrant's Return," George Russell Jackson and George Dana (Boston: Russell, 1881); "The Exile's Lament, or Lay Me on the Hillside," J. F. Mitchell (New York: Harding, 1886). The song was used in McCarthy, *True Irish Hearts*.

23. Quoted in Potter, *To the Golden Door*, p. 161. See also Miller, *Emigrants and Exiles*, pp. 102–30.

24. "Must We Leave Our Old Home (or Queenstown Harbor)," W. J. Alexander (San Francisco: Broder, 1890).

25. *Pat Rooney's "Day I Played Base Ball" Songster*, p. 7.

26. "There Never Was a Coward Where the Shamrock Grows," Frank Wilson (New York: Harms, 1880). The song must have been popular, for it featured in a joke in *Puck* in 1895 (see Donovan, "Good Old Pat," p. 10):

> Mrs. O'Houlihan: "Sure, an' Oi hear there was nigh a murther committed at Casey's party last night."
> Mr. Duffy: "Oho! Oho! An' what started the ruction?"
> Mrs. O: "Casey sung 'there never was a coward where the shamrock grew,' an' someone said they all came to Americay."

27. "Where the Grass Grows Green," Harry Clifton (Philadelphia: Lee, Walker, [1856–67]); dates suggested in Wolfe, *Secular Music in America*. This song also appeared in broadsides of the period. It is reprinted without attribution in Healy, *Mercier Book of Old Irish Street Ballads*, vol. 1, p. 11.

28. As a key word in the song texts, however, the shamrock appears most frequently in the 1870s, 20 percent of the sample for the decade, and rapidly declines to an average of 7 percent for the 1880s and 1890s. Mention of the shamrock in song lyrics picks up again after the turn of the century, appearing in 10 percent of the sample for the 1900s and 23 percent for the 1910s.

29. "Dear Little Colleen," George Cooper and C. M. Pyke (New York: Spear, Dehnhoff, 1877).

30. "Good Bye Mavourneen," T. P. Westendorf (New York: Gordon, 1877).

31. "Three Leaves of Shamrock," J. McGuire (New York: Harding, 1889). See also Wright, *Irish Emigrant Ballads and Songs*, p. 51.

32. "Dear Little Shamrock," W. Jackson (Boston: Ditson, 1870). The lyrics are attributed to Andrew Cherry; reprinted in Healy, *Mercier Book of Old Irish Street Ballads*, vol. 1, p. 20. "The Love of the Shamrock," J. K. Emmet (Cincinnati: John Church, 1879); from the musical *Fritz in Ireland*.

33. *Pat Rooney's "Day I Played Base Ball" Songster*, p. 6.

34. "Viva Hibernia," H. L. M., M. A. Gilsinn (St. Louis: L. J. Debuque, 1873).

35. "When Erin Shall Stand Mid the Isles of the Sea," Mrs. A. L. Ruter Dufour and Solon Nourse (New York: J. L. Peters, 1874); "Home Rule for Old Ireland," Charles Sweetland and Edward Kendall (Boston: White, Smith, 1878). Sweetland and Kendall also performed the song.

36. "Ireland's Freedom," Artane and Gerald O'Brien (n.p., 1880), was included as a supplement in the March 13, 1898, edition of the New York *Family Story Paper*; "Dear Ireland, When You're Free," P. J. Sweeney (New York: J. A. Nobel Simpson, 1898), printed as special insert in the *New York Sunday World*, March 13, 1898.

37. "Leaving Old Ireland and Thee," A. A. Walls and F. Fauciulli (Boston: Evans, 1884).

38. "The Wearing of the Green," [Dion Boucicault] (Boston: Ditson, 1864, 1865). For background on the song, see Zimmermann, *Songs of Irish Rebellion*, pp. 167–70. Boucicault's version went through a number of sheet music editions in 1864,

1865, and 1866. Most of them show the character of Shaun the Post as variously played by Boucicault, J. E. McDonough, or T. H. Glenney – all wearing knee breeches and large green cloaks. There were also instrumental versions. One edition was dedicated "To the Fenian Brotherhood." The song continued in sheet music well into the twentieth century.

39. *Delaney's Irish Song Book No. 2*, p. 23.

40. *Twentieth Century Songster* (ca. 1899).

41. "Bridget Donahue," Johnny Patterson ("The Irish Clown"), arr. A. S. Josselyn (Boston: Blair, Lydon, 1882). The "eagle" in question was probably on a piece of U.S. currency. Some sheets give the name of A. S. Josselyn as the composer. However, according to Watters and Murtag, Patterson never bothered to copyright his songs. In addition to "Bridget Donahue" they claim that Patterson wrote such sentimental favorites as "The Stone Outside Dan Murphy's Door" and "The Garden Where the Praties Grow." Patterson, who was born in Clare, actually did a clown act in circuses on both sides of the Atlantic, performing for Ringling Brothers when in America. He met a strange end. While performing in a circus at Castleisland in County Kerry on May 19, 1890, he tried to sing a song calling for unity among Irishmen split by the Parnell-O'Shea divorce case. He was injured in the resulting riot and died, a rare Irish martyr to the cause of moderation. See Watters and Murtag, *Infinite Variety*, pp. 81–82.

42. See Potter, *To the Golden Door*, p. 116. See also Meagher, *From Paddy to Studs*, p. 36.

43. "Goodby Johnnie Dear," H. Martin and W. Dean (Cincinnati: Groene, 1890). For remittances see Miller, *Emigrants and Exiles*, p. 510; McCaffrey, *Irish Diaspora in America*, p. 62; Fortune, "Culture of Hope," pp. 45–46.

44. "The Day We Celebrate," Edward Harrigan and David Braham (New York: Harding, 1875).

45. Brown, *Irish-American Nationalism*, p. 21.

46. Ibid., pp. 24, 64.

47. See Greene, *American Immigrant Leaders*, p. 28. Greene points out that O'Connor's argument is evidence that his *Shamrock and Hibernian Chronicle* was shifting from being an organ for transplanted Europeans to becoming a voice for immigrant Americans. See also Brown, *Irish-American Nationalism*, p. 28.

48. Greene, *American Immigrant Leaders*, pp. 20–21.

49. Ibid., p. 21.

50. For the connection between Fenianism and Irish participation in the American Civil War, see McCaffrey, *Irish Diaspora in America*, pp. 120–21.

51. "Pat Murphy of the Iron Brigade," in Silber, *Songs of the Civil War*, p. 177.

52. *Delaney's Irish Song Book No. 4*, p. 22.

53. "The Irish Volunteer," S. Fillmore Bennett and J. P. Webster (Chicago: Higgins, 1862).

54. *Delaney's Irish Song Book No. 4*, p. 22.

55. Ibid., p. 20.

56. *Stephens' Fenian Songster*, pp. 51–54; reprinted in Wright, *Irish Emigrant Ballads and Songs*, pp. 429, 439–40.

57. Quoted in LaGumina and Cavaioli, *Ethnic Dimension in American Society*, pp. 51–52.

58. "The Flag of Ireland Free," Harry Pierce (Chicago: National Music, 1884). The cover states that the song was sung by Alex Rourke's Cook County Quartet and dedicated to the Irish-American Club.

59. "That Sweet Bunch of Shamrocks," C. C. Tidball and Harry Earl Brandt (Chicago: National Music, 1890). For the Collins quote, see Greene, *American Immigrant Leaders*, p. 38.

60. Quoted in Potter, *To the Golden Door*, p. 511.

61. See Jolliffe, *Third Book of Irish Ballads*, p. 105. Tim Sullivan was born in 1827 and died in 1914. A native of West Cork, he was, with his brother A. M. Sullivan, an editor of the *Nation* in Dublin. He is best remembered in Ireland for his poems and songs, such as "Deep in Canadian Woods" (or "Ireland, Boys, Horray"), which was sung by Irish soldiers on both sides during the Civil War, and "Michael Dwyer." He also wrote Ireland's unofficial national anthem, "God Save Ireland," the hymn to the Manchester Martyrs. He visited America in 1890. See ibid., pp. 104–5; see also Boylan, *Dictionary of Irish Biography*, p. 373.

Chapter 6: The Irish and Vaudeville

1. See Moody, *America Takes the Stage*, pp. 40–42; Wittke, *Tambo and Bones*, p. 148.

2. Snyder, *Voice of the City*, pp. 9, 46.

3. Ibid., pp. 14, 172.

4. Gilbert, *American Vaudeville*, p. 62.

5. Laurie, *Vaudeville*, pp. 319–20.

6. For vaudeville teams, see ibid., pp. 319–21; Gilbert, *American Vaudeville*, pp. 71–72. For the Cohans, see the early chapters in McCabe, *George M. Cohan*.

7. Staples, *Male-Female Comedy Teams*, pp. 23–27.

8. See Snyder, *Voice of the City*, p. 48; Loesser, *Humor in American Song*, p. 142. For the Boucicault quote see Beer, *Mauve Decades*, p. 150. In their Irish act, Weber and Fields dressed in green satin breeches, black frock coats, green bow ties, and green derbies. They would sing songs like "Success to the Shamrock" and end with "Achushla Gall Machree" without any notion as to what they were singing about. See Adams, "Minority Characters on the American Stage," p. 21.

9. Pre-dating vaudeville, the influence of Irish step dancing in minstrelsy is suggested in several lithographs of minstrel dancers. One of the greatest solo dancers of the antebellum era was William Henry Lane, a black performer who danced under the name of Juba. A lithograph depicts him with his hands at his sides, his right foot on three-quarters point and his left leg cocked, ready to tap out the rhythm. Another period picture shows two men in blackface and African wigs in the classic pose of the Irish step dancer ("Irish Mornings and African Days," cover and p. 49). Lane, who died in 1852, was the greatest minstrel dancer of the era. He inaugurated the "challenge" or competition jig and beat all the professional

white dancers. Although he undoubtedly drew upon the Irish dance tradition, his white competitors picked up some of the African-American elements he added. For Lane and for the Irish contribution to minstrel dance, see Stearns and Stearns, *Jazz Dance*, pp. 36, 46–49.

10. Cohan discovered his style when, during a rehearsal, the orchestra leader, instead of launching into a rapid 6/8 time tune as expected, introduced Cohan's dance solo with a tune in a very slow 2/4 time. In trying to fit his steps into this unfamiliar tempo, Cohan invented his new dance style. See Cohan, *Twenty Years on Broadway*, pp. 141–44. For Keeler see Frank, *TAP*, pp. 32–33. See also Burns, *Gracie*, pp. 28–30.

11. See Gilbert, *American Vaudeville*, pp. 62–65, 128.

12. Staples, *Male-Female Comedy Teams*, p. 28.

13. *Pat Rooney's "Day I Played Base Ball" Songster*, p. 24.

14. Arthur Flynn in *Irish Dance* makes reference to the fishermen of the Aran Islands using their wooden-soled clogs to tap out rhythms for dances (see p. 77). John P. Cullinane states that some Irishmen wore boot protectors on the heels and toes of their shoes and that these enhanced the sound of the dancer. Later male dancers used large-headed nails with coins inserted between the nail heads and the sole. Cullinane gives no dates for these practices but the context suggests early twentieth century, in which case it is possible that Irish traditional dancers may have been inserting theatrical practices into their traditional dances. See Cullinane, "Aspects of the History of Irish Dance," pp. 68–69. For the relationship between Irish step dancing and American theatrical clogging, see Stearns and Stearns, *Jazz Dancing*, pp. 49–51; Culliname, "Irish Dancing World-Wide," pp. 201–2.

15. Gilbert, *American Vaudeville*, pp. 66–70. For Delaney, see Stearns and Stearns, *Jazz Dance*, pp. 50–51.

16. Slide, *Vaudevillians*, pp. 127–28.

17. Jennings, *Theatrical and Circus Life*, pp. 417, 420.

18. Ibid., p. 421. For the stage Irishman's whiskers, see Gilbert, *American Vaudeville*, pp. 62, 66. Jennings, however, calls the side whiskers "Galway sluggers" or "Carolines" (p. 424).

19. *Pat Rooney's "Day I Walked against O'Leary" Songster*, p. 21.

20. Watters and Murtag, *Infinite Variety*, p. 85.

21. *Pat Rooney's "Day I Walked against O'Leary" Songster*, p. 13. The song around which the patter was developed has survived and, under the title of "Dick Darby the Cobbler," has been recorded by Ulster Singer Tommy Makem, among others.

22. Barth, *City People*, p. 217.

23. Jennings, *Theatrical and Circus Life*, p. 426.

24. Page, *Writing for Vaudeville*, pp. 66–67.

25. Higham, *Send These to Me*, pp. 25–26.

26. For information on Touhey and the Taylors, see O'Neill, *Irish Minstrels and Musicians*, pp. 313–15; Williams, "Irish Traditional Music in the United States," pp. 290–91; Mitchell and Small, *Piping of Patsy Touhey*, pp. 1–11.

27. See the double cassette *James Morrison: The Professor* (Viva Voca 001, n.d.).

The cover combines a photograph of Morrison between pictures of the Statue of Liberty and the Dartry Mountains in County Sligo. Morrison, along with Michael Coleman and Paddy Kilorlan, was one of the great exponents of the "Sligo" long-bow style of fiddle playing, which, through the power of their recordings, became the dominant style of Irish-American fiddling in this century and greatly influenced playing techniques and style back in Ireland.

28. Staples, *Male-Female Comedy Teams*, p. 30.

29. Small, "Performance as Ritual," pp. 7, 8–9. Small's own analysis is based on looking at the symphony concert as a ritual.

30. See Barth, *City People*, pp. 205–6.

31. McLean, *American Vaudeville as Ritual*, p. 106.

32. Ibid., pp. 2–3.

33. Steinberg, *Ethnic Myth*, p. 52.

34. Barth, *City People*, p. 215.

35. Steinberg, *Ethnic Myth*, p. 53.

36. Snyder, *Voice of the City*, p. 117.

37. Ibid., p. 110.

38. Grimsted, *Melodrama Unveiled*, pp. 194–95.

39. Snyder, *Voice of the City*, p. 114.

40. Bratton, *Victorian Popular Ballad*, pp. 188–89.

41. Krause, *Profane Book of Irish Comedy*, pp. 27, 31, 173.

42. Doyle, *Ireland, Irishmen and Revolutionary America*, p. 224.

Chapter 7: The Irish American in Post–Civil War Song

1. A study of *Delaney's Irish Song Book*, nos. 2 and 4, both published in the 1890s, reveals the same pattern. Taken together both volumes contain 344 songs, 41 percent of which are comic. Forty-four percent of the songs have names in the titles and 63 percent of these songs are comic. Again masculine names predominate. Sixty-seven percent of all of the names in the titles are male, as are 77 percent of the names in comic song titles, most of which are Gaelic surnames. There can be little doubt that these songsters and others like them were intended for an Irish market. In addition to a few traditional Irish songs (in English), they contain patriotic airs and recitations that would appeal only to the Irish community. More than half of the material in Delaney's songsters came from sheet music, which could be ordered at three for a dollar (in stamps).

2. Curran, "From 'Paddy' to the Presidency," p. 107. See also "No Irish Need Apply," John F. Poole (ca. 1860). The song apparently originated in Britain and was brought over by performer Kathleen O'Neil. According to Finson, the cover of the original British sheet quotes a London advertisement for a cook cautioning "No Irish need apply" (*Voices That Are Gone*, pp. 290–91). For various versions and "answers," see Wright, *Irish Emigrant Ballads and Songs*, pp. 650–52, 525, 527. Greenway has a version in *American Folk Songs of Protest*, pp. 41–42.

3. "Poor O'Hoolahan," Hugh Morton and Gustave Kerker (New York: Harms,

1898). For "Drill Ye Tarriers, Drill," see Cohen, *Long Steel Rail*, pp. 553–59; Gilbert, *American Vaudeville*, pp. 71–72. Thomas Casey, who had once worked with drill and blasting powder, was an entertainer associated with Tammany Hall. His song became popular when it was interpolated into one of Charles H. Hoyt's farce comedies, *The Brass Monkey*. See Marcuse, *Tin Pan Alley in Gaslight*, p. 84.

4. Potter, *To the Golden Door*, p. 165.

5. "It's the Irish, You Know," J. W. Wheeler (Boston: Blake, 1885); "The Men Who Come Over from Ireland," J. J. O'Grady (New York: Spaulding, Gray, 1896).

6. For "Dan Maloney," see *Delaney's Irish Song Book No. 2*, p. 23; for "The Gintleman from Kildare," see *Delaney's Irish Song Book No. 4*, p. 10.

7. "Is That Mr. Reilly?" Pat Rooney (New York: Harding, 1883). The unpleasant reference to the Chinese is a reflection of the competition that many Irish laborers felt they were facing from imported Chinese workers.

8. "Are You There Moriarty?" Edward Harrigan and David Braham (New York: Pond, 1876).

9. Kahn, *Merry Partners*, p. 41; see also Sante, *Low Life*, p. 238.

10. "McGinty, the Ladies' Pride," Charles Graham and W. D. Hall (Boston: White, Smith, 1889).

11. "Tammany," Vincent Bryan and Gus Edwards (New York: Witmark, 1907). For Irish in the police, see Sante, *Low Life*, p. 244; Potter, *To the Golden Door*, p. 530.

12. "He's on the Police Force Now," *Delaney's Irish Song Book No. 4*, p. 8; "Oh, Gilhooley," *Pat Rooney's "Day I Walked against O'Leary" Songster*, p. 6.

13. Riordon, *Plunkitt of Tammany Hall*, pp. 31, 6. For Mann quote, see ibid., p. xvii.

14. *Williams Irish Songster* (Chicago: Frank Williams, n.d.).

15. *Pat Rooney's "Day I Walked against O'Leary" Songster*, p. 53.

16. Quoted in Kahn, *Merry Partners*, p. 98. "Oh, He Promises," Edward Harrigan and David Braham (New York: Pond, 1880).

17. "McGonigle's Led Astray," C. F Horn (Boston: Evans, 1883); "Reagan's Evening Out," C. F. Horn (Boston: Evans, 1883).

18. *Delaney's Irish Song Book Number 4*, p. 10. The song was written by a bricklayer's assistant, Dennis Morgan from County Monaghan. See also Miller, *Emigrants and Exiles*, pp. 330–31.

19. "Old Boss Barry," Edward Harrigan and David Braham (New York: Pond, 1888). Cherry Hill marked one of the boundaries of the historic Irish slums in New York City. Corlear's Hook, where Harrigan was born, marked another.

20. See Levy, *Give Me Yesterday*, pp. 139, 140.

21. "Dear Ireland," A. Baldwin Sloane (New York: J. W. Stern, 1905).

22. Greeley, *Irish Americans*, p. 115. See also Light, "Role of Irish-American Organizations," p. 135; McCaffrey, *Irish Diaspora in America*, p. 78.

23. "Miss Mulligan's Home Made Pie," C. F. Horn (Milwaukee: Rohlfling, 1885). There are several versions of this song, such as "Miss Hooligan's Christmas Cake" and "The Trinity Cake," all of them funnier than Horn's. Whether or not Horn's is the original, there must have been some sort of folk process at work on the vaudeville/music hall circuits as the song passed back and forth across the Atlantic.

24. *Delaney's Irish Song Book No. 4*, p. 10.

25. "There Goes McManus," B. H. Janssen (New York: Harms, 1889); "Learning McFadden to Waltz," M. F. Carey (Albany: Cluett, 1890); "Casey's Social Club," Edward Harrigan and David Braham (New York: Harding, 1878).

26. "John James O'Reilly," Flora Moore (Cincinnati: J. L. Groene, 1890).

27. "The Irish Jubilee," J. Thornton and Charles Lawlor (New York: Witmark, 1890).

28. Slobin, *Tenement Songs*, p. 106.

29. "The Irish Spree," Tom Browne and Edmund Forman (New York: Harding, [ca. 1880]).

30. "If I Catch the Man," William J. Scanlan (New York: Harms, 1882).

31. "Down Went McGinty (Dressed in His Best Suit of Clothes)," Joseph Flynn (New York: Spalding, Kornder, 1889); "McGinty's Wake (Answer to Down Went McGinty)," J. Flynn (Brooklyn: Spaulding, Kornden, 1889); "I'll Paralyze the Man That Says McGinty," Ed E. Pidgeon and Monroe H. Rosenfeld (Brooklyn: Spaulding, Kornder, 1890). See also Wittke, *Tambo and Bones*, p. 108.

In spite of its use by post–Civil War political cartoonists such as Thomas Nast, the simian caricature of the Irishman (which arrived from England in the late 1860s) appears to have been rare on sheet music covers. I found only six examples in my sample. For a discussion of the caricature, see Curtis, *Apes and Angels*.

32. "Throw Him Down, M'Closkey," J. W. Kelly (New York: Harris, 1890). For performances of this song, see Jasen, *Tin Pan Alley*, p. 26; Marcuse, *Tin Pan Alley in Gaslight*, p. 101. The song was suggested to Kelly by an actual barroom brawl in which he was almost involved. See Marcuse, *Tin Pan Alley in Gaslight*, pp. 101–2. For other songs written by Kelly, see ibid., pp. 93, 103; Marks, *They All Sang*, p. 131.

33. McCaffrey, *Irish Diaspora in America*, p. 69.

34. Clark, *Hibernia America*, p. 52. See also Asbury, *Gangs of New York*, p. 9. For Dicken's quote see ibid., pp. 11–12.

35. Sante, *Low Life*, pp. 199, 201.

36. For gangs, see Asbury, *Gangs of New York*, pp. 226–30. For Dr. O'Connell, see Mitchell, "View of the Irish in America," p. 10.

37. For the *Times* quote, see Meagher, *From Paddy to Studs*, p. 9. Andrew Greeley notes that early alcohol studies began at Yale with the comparison of the Jews, Italians, and Irish in New Haven. Since, within this context, the Irish seemed to have the highest incidence of alcoholism, the researchers concluded that they were "culturally deviant," a term which, if applied to blacks, Greeley maintains, would be considered racist. Greeley believes that myth and stereotype directed the research. See Greeley, *Irish Americans*, pp. 171–72.

38. *Beadle's Dime Song Book No. 5*, p. 59.

39. *Nellie Seymour's "I'm Going to Tell on You, Kate" Songster*. See also "McCarthy's Widow" (1887), *Barnum and Bailey Songster*; "Larry Mulligan," Dave Reed Jr. (1894), *Gems of Songs*.

40. Bratton, *Victorian Popular Ballad*, p. 156.

41. "The Mountain Dew," Edward Harrigan and David Braham (New York: Pond, 1882); "Taking in the Town," Edward Harrigan and David Braham (New York: Pond, 1890); "John Riley's Always Dry," Edward Harrigan and David Braham (New York: Pond, 1881).

42. "The Pitcher of Beer," Edward Harrigan and David Braham (New York: Pond, 1880).

43. "Irish Potheen," William Scanlan (New York: Harms, 1882). For "Drinking with Daniel Maloney," see *Delaney's Irish Song Book No. 2*, p. 26.

44. Clark, *Irish Relations*, p. 63.

45. For Philadelphia, see ibid., pp. 65–73. For Worcester, see Rosenzweig, *Eight Hours for What We Will*, pp. 46–47.

46. Fanning, *Finley Peter Dunne and Mr. Dooley*, p. 34; Sante, *Low Life*, pp. 111–20.

47. For *Mulhooly*, see Clark, *Irish Relations*, p. 67. For *Lampoon*, see Ryan, *Beyond the Ballot Box*, p. 75. For Stivers's quote, see Stivers, *Hair of the Dog*, p. 13.

48. Stivers, *Hair of the Dog*, p. 14; Greeley, *Irish Americans*, pp. 175–76.

49. Stivers, *Hair of the Dog*, p. 129.

50. Malcolm makes the point that "the drunken 'Paddy' is only one side of the coin; the other side is the teetotal 'Paddy.'" She suggests that the question is not so much "Why did Paddy drink?" but "Which Paddy drank?" See Malcolm, *"Ireland Sober, Ireland Free,"* pp. 324, 331, 332–33.

51. Stivers, *Hair of the Dog*, p. 128.

52. Burns, "Plays of Edward Green Harrigan," p. 184 (emphasis added). The phrase "drop of the cratur" (or "craythur") appears in various vaudeville/music hall songs, such as "Tim Finnigan's Wake" and "Ode to Whiskey." Most Irish Americans and some Irish interpret "cratur" to mean "creature." Eric Partridge claims that "cratur" was a slang term for liquor from the sixteenth to the eighteenth centuries and was used for whiskey (especially Irish whiskey) in the nineteenth and twentieth centuries. He claims it is derived from "creature comforts." See Partridge, *Dictionary of Historical Slang*, p. 202. The Gaelic word for "creature" is *créatúr*. It was the late Robin Dudley Edwards, Professor of Modern Irish History at the National University of Ireland, Dublin, who once suggested to me in conversation that "craythur" as in "a drop of the . . ." meant "jar" and was related to the old Greek word *krater*.

53. *Delaney's Irish Song Book No. 2*, p. 16. See also "The Irish Wedding," D. Maguinnis (Boston: White, Smith, Perry, 1872).

54. "The Flaming O'Flannigans," in *Fred Shaw's Dime American Comic Songster*, pp. 61–62.

55. Levy, *Give Me Yesterday*, p. 287 (emphasis added).

56. Mitchell, "View of the Irish in America," pp. 9–10; O'Connell quote on p. 7.

57. From the recording *Kilkelly* by Mick Moloney, Robbie O'Connell, and Jimmy Keane (Green Linnet SIF 1072). Moloney collected it from Mike Flanagan of the Flanagan brothers.

58. Douglas, "Jokes," p. 297.

Chapter 8: The Theater and Songs of Edward Harrigan

1. Most of those who have written about Harrigan agree that his father's background was Irish. Warren Burns, however, claims that the background was Welsh ("Plays of Edward Green Harrigan," p. 15). Richard Moody, who wrote *Ned Harrigan* with the cooperation of the Harrigan family, stresses the Irish connection (pp. 7–8).

2. For San Francisco Irish see Sarbaugh, "Exiles of Confidence," p. 165.

3. See Burns, "Plays of Edward Green Harrigan," p. 23; Kahn, *Merry Partners*, p. 14.

4. See Clark and Morris, "*Scherzo, Forte*, and *Bravura*," p. 465; see also Taubman, *Making of the American Theater*, p. 110.

5. Quoted in Koger, "Critical Analysis of Edward Harrigan's Comedy," p. 137; Wittke, "Immigrant Theme on the American Stage," p. 212; Taubman, *Making of the American Theater*, pp. 108–9.

6. For the Harrigan quote, see Kahn, *Merry Partners*, p. 265. See also Bordman, *American Musical Comedy*, p. 46. Isaac Goldberg once suggested that Harrigan's approach to play writing was influenced by the fact that he worked in what Goldberg called "the actor tradition" rather than the "play tradition." Harrigan devised characters from his experience onstage and from the interplay between actor and audience. See Goldberg, "Harrigan and Hart," p. 202.

7. Kahn, *Merry Partners*, p. 37; Moody, *Ned Harrigan*, pp. 79, 60.

8. Kahn, *Merry Partners*, pp. 38, 267.

9. Quoted in Hewitt, *Theater U.S.A.*, p. 249. See also Moody, *Ned Harrigan*, p. 78. By the mid-1880s Harrigan was attracting the attention of some of the major critics of his day, such as Brander Matthews, William Winter, and William Dean Howells. Howells compared Harrigan's work to the Venetian comedies of Goldonia. See Koger, "Critical Analysis of Edward Harrigan's Comedy," p. 132.

10. Quoted in Koger, "Critical Analysis of Edward Harrigan's Comedy," p. 127.

11. Rinear, "F. S. Chanfrau's Mose," p. 212. For background on Mose, see Dorson, "Mose." For Chanfrau's stage persona see Hutton, *Curiosities of the American Stage*, p. 51; Young, *Famous Actors and Actresses*, vol. 1, p. 176.

12. For "I'm Bilein'," see Dorson, "Mose," p. 293. See also Hutton, *Curiosities of the American Stage*, p. 51; Moody, *Ned Harrigan*, p. 13. Maureen Murphy sees Mose as "based on an Irish immigrant type" ("Irish-American Theatre," pp. 223–24). Carl Wittke believes that the Mose character "strongly suggests an Irish ancestry, and was the forerunner of the full-grown stage Irishman of the next decade." He also notes that Chanfrau and his wife did Irish sketches in New York before the Civil War. See Wittke, "Immigrant Theme on the American Stage," p. 214. For origins of "b'hoy," see Dohan, *Our Own Words*, p. 233; Partridge, *Dictionary of Historical Slang*.

13. For the Boucicault quote see Kahn, *Merry Partners*, p. 67. Maureen Murphy points to Harrigan's early satire, *Arrah-na-Brogue* (a take off on Boucicault's *Arrah na Pogue*), as well as his own Irish melodramas, as evidence of Boucicault's influence ("Irish-American Theatre," p. 226).

14. Moody, *Ned Harrigan*, p. 190.

15. Kahn, *Merry Partners*, p. 189.

16. Moody, *Ned Harrigan*, pp. 175–76.

17. Braham was one of the foremost theater composers in the 1870s and 1880s. For his influence, see Root, *American Popular Stage Music*, pp. 59–62. According to Maxwell Marcuse, Braham played an important role in the evolution of Tin Pan Alley tunes. In addition to writing for Harrigan, he composed music for other lyricists with whom he had hits. He wrote the music for George L. Catlin's "Over the Hill to the Poor House" and G. L. Stout's "Eily Machree." See Marcuse, *Tin Pan Alley in Gaslight*, p. 26. For the role of songs in Harrigan's plays, see Koger, "Critical Analysis of Edward Harrigan's Comedy," pp. 126, 264; Burns, "Plays of Edward Green Harrigan," pp. 35–36.

18. Koger, "Critical Analysis of Edward Harrigan's Comedy," p. 175. See also Hamm, *Yesterdays*, p. 281; Scheurer, "'Thou Witty,'" p. 105. Some of the most popular Harrigan and Braham songs were among the "Songs of the Past" recorded by Victor in 1916. See Root, *American Popular Stage Music*, p. 60.

19. Unless otherwise noted, all songs referred to in this chapter are by Harrigan and Braham and were published in New York City by Pond.

20. See Moody, *Ned Harrigan*, p. 2. Around the turn of the century Smith was the "Commodore" of the Harrigan Club, a banqueting, drinking, and singing society that included a number of prominent New Yorkers, especially politicians.

21. Connaught is a province, not a county in Ireland. Harrigan did not visit Ireland until late in his career, therefore, his sense of Irish geography was casual at best.

22. McCaffrey, *Textures of Irish America*, pp. 65–66.

23. These plays suggest the influence of Brougham, who also may have written the first satire on the lace curtain in his 1855 play *The Game of Love*. For Brougham's influence on Harrigan, see Koger, "Critical Analysis of Edward Harrigan's Comedy," p. 61; Hawes "John Brougham as Playwright," p. 188.

24. Quoted in Moody, *Ned Harrigan*, p. 138.

25. Quoted in Koger, "Critical Analysis of Edward Harrigan's Comedy," p. 163.

26. Quoted in Bordman, *American Musical Comedy*, p. 44.

27. Koger, "Critical Analysis of Edward Harrigan's Comedy," p. 168.

28. Doyle, *Ireland, Irishmen and Revolutionary America*, p. 224; Meagher, *From Paddy to Studs*, p. 80.

29. Koger, "Critical Analysis of Edward Harrigan's Comedy," pp. 169, 227; Murphy, "Irish-American Theatre," p. 227.

30. Although best known for his characterization of Dan Mulligan, as an actor, Harrigan, along with his partner Tony Hart, successfully portrayed a variety of ethnic types onstage. They played Italian immigrants in *The Italian Padrone, or Slaves of the Harp*, by John F. Poole (1873). In Harrigan's *Waddy Googan* (originally entitled "The Metropolis"), which dealt with the increasing number of Italians in New York, Harrigan played a variety of ethnic characters. He even played Tom in *Uncle Tom's Cabin* to Hart's Topsy. Harrigan's African American character in his own *Old Pete* was one of his favorite parts. He also wrote and starred in *Mordecai Lyons*, a

play ahead of its time in providing a sympathetic treatment of the Jew onstage. See Koger, "Critical Analysis of Edward Harrigan's Comedy," p. 214; see also Finson, *Voices That Are Gone*, p. 305.

31. Quoted in Kahn, *Merry Partners*, pp. 263–64. For "Below Fourteenth Street," see ibid., p. 58. For "sort of thick an' mixed," see Moody, *Ned Harrigan*, p. 109.

32. Quoted in Kahn, *Merry Partners*, p. 64.

33. Koger, "Critical Analysis of Edward Harrigan's Comedy," pp. 36–37.

34. The songs Harrigan and Braham gave to the African-American characters were usually group pieces, marches and pseudo-spirituals, typical of the "plantation" or "camp meeting" choruses that whites accepted as genuine African-American music.

35. Koger, "Critical Analysis of Edward Harrigan's Comedy," p. 167.

36. Kahn, *Merry Partners*, p. 67. See also Koger, "Critical Analysis of Edward Harrigan's Comedy," pp. 145, 152, 165.

37. See Moody, *Ned Harrigan*, pp. 102, 123.

38. Quinn, *History of the American Drama*, p. 86.

39. Strang, *Celebrated Comedians*, pp. 119–20.

40. McLean, *American Vaudeville as Ritual*, p. 106.

41. Burns, "Plays of Edward Green Harrigan," p. 23.

Introduction to Part 4

1. See Knobel, *Paddy and the Republic*, pp. 176–77. See also Donovan, "Good Old Pat," pp. 8, 9.

2. See Skerrett, "Development of Catholic Identity," p. 133. For the quote see Mitchell, "'They Do Not Differ Greatly,'" p. 62.

3. Miller, *Emigrants and Exiles*, p. 493.

4. McCaffrey, *Textures of Irish America*, p. 29; Meagher, *From Paddy to Studs*, pp. 8–9.

5. Meagher, *From Paddy to Studs*, p. 7. See also Greeley, *Irish Americans*, pp. 111, 112.

6. Meagher, *From Paddy to Studs*, p. 183.

7. Fallows, *Irish Americans*, p. 48.

8. Mitchell, "'They Do Not Differ Greatly,'" p. 57.

9. Light, "Role of Irish-American Organizations," p. 113.

10. Miller, *Emigrants and Exiles*, pp. 489, 492.

11. Ibid., p. 352.

12. Ibid., pp. 349–50.

13. See ibid., pp. 502, 522. For "culture of exile," see ibid., pp. 102–30.

Chapter 9: Paddy on the Alley

1. For "Of the sixteen songs," see Hamm, *Yesterdays*, p. 291. For Middleton quotes, see Middleton, *Studying Popular Music*, p. 13. For the generally accepted

story regarding the origins of the name "Tin Pan Alley," see Ewen, *Life and Death of Tin Pan Alley*, pp. xii–xiii. For the shifting locations of the Alley, see Jasen, *Tin Pan Alley*, p. xxii; Ewen, *Life and Death of Tin Pan Alley*, p. 22.

2. See Hamm, *Yesterdays*, pp. 286–87; Jasen, *Tin Pan Alley*, pp. xvi–xvii.

3. Jasen, *Tin Pan Alley*, pp. 6–7.

4. Kanter, *Jews on Tin Pan Alley*, p. 15.

5. For Van Tilzer quote, see Tawa, *Way to Tin Pan Alley*, p. 32. See also Jasen, *Tin Pan Alley*, p. xvi.

6. Finson, *Voices That Are Gone*, p. 63.

7. Ewen, *Life and Death of Tin Pan Alley*, p. 5.

8. Ibid., pp. xii, 12; Hamm, *Yesterdays*, p. 289.

9. Ewen, *Life and Death of Tin Pan Alley*, pp. 73–75.

10. Marcuse, *Tin Pan Alley in Gaslight*, p. 13; Hamm, *Yesterdays*, p. 287. The price of songs varied. On the average, sheet music sold for fifty cents a piece. However one could get a copy for a dime in the five-and-ten-cent stores. Around the turn of the century, the average take-home wage for a family of four was $12.75 a week. But, since entertainment in the home was still a central feature of American life, the buyer might get a good deal of use out of a song. See Jasen, *Tin Pan Alley*, p. xx.

11. Tawa, *Way to Tin Pan Alley*, pp. 75–76; Kanter, *Jews on Tin Pan Alley*, p. 26.

12. Tawa, *Way to Tin Pan Alley*, pp. 90, 107, 163–64. See also Hamm, *Yesterdays*, pp. 292–93.

13. McGlennon was a Manchester-based Scot who claimed to have "written" over four thousand songs for British parlors and music halls, the melodies plucked out on a child's instrument. Apparently one of the costs of producing "rubbish" was getting tangled up in what Dave Russell calls "perplexing ideological inconsistencies." McGlennon, for example, did his share of Irish pieces, including settings for some poems by Thomas Davis, poet of the Young Irelanders. As Russell points out, he could crank out "Who Fears to Speak of '98" and eviction ballads, such as "Spare the Old Mud Cabin" (1903), along with songs praising imperial triumphs. See Russell, *Popular Music in England*, pp. 92–93, 103, 116; see also Bratton, *Music Hall*, pp. 9–10.

14. "Remember the Boys of '98," Brandon Tynan (New York: Tynan, 1902).

15. "It's the Song That Reaches Irish Hearts (The Wearing of the Green)," Bartley Costello and Albert Von Tilzer (New York: Yorke, 1909).

16. "Ireland's Flag of Green," Mack Keller and Frank Orth (New York, 1907).

17. "Independence Day in Dublin Town (A Novelty Song)," Bob Harty and Ernest Breuer (New York: Witmark, 1914); "What's the Matter with the Irish? (They're Getting Better Every Day)," Howard Johnson and Jack Glogau (New York: Feist, 1916).

18. "Keep a Place Down in Your Heart for Ireland," Stanley Murphy and Albert Von Tilzer (New York: Broadway, 1916).

19. "All Aboard for Ireland," C. Bang and H. C. Jordan (New York: Bang and Jordan, 1919). The publisher apparently sought to cover all bases by running "Here's Hoping We Get Home Rule" above the title.

20. "Soldiers of Erin: The Rallying Song of the Irish Volunteers," Peter Kearney and Victor Herbert, edited and published for the benefit of the Gaelic League of Ireland by Rev. Robert F. O'Reilly (New York: Irish Industries Depot, 1917). Herbert took his Irish heritage seriously, especially during the years between 1912 and 1920. Whenever his busy schedule and the occasion permitted, he lent his musical skills and public stature to promoting Irish causes. As president of the Friendly Sons in 1915, he greeted the members on "The Day" with his version of the ritual of dual allegiance: "Unbounded as is our loyalty to the country of our adoption – and we have done our best to reward America for opening her maternal arms to us – we are still fond lovers of that Green Isle beyond the Sea." Herbert wrote several operetta's on Irish themes, most notably *Hearts of Erin*, which opened in 1917. Built around the Rising of 1798, the work was eventually renamed *Eileen*. The operetta closes with "When Ireland Stands among the Nations of the World" (a paraphrase of a line from Robert Emmet's speech from the dock). See Waters, *Victor Herbert*, pp. 470, 481, 501.

21. "God Made Ireland a Nation," Rose Villiar (New York: Villiar, 1919); "I'm Coming Back to Old Ireland (When It's a Nation of Its Own)," Frankie Williams and Otis Spencer (New York: Williams, 1919); "Strike the Blow for Independence," Gus Troxler and A. I. McKenzie (Newark: Big Four, 1919).

22. "When Ireland Comes into Her Own," Jeff Brennan and Jack Stanley (New York: Broadway, 1919).

23. As the best example of Irish-American patriotism, Meagher cites the founding of the Knights of Columbus, a militant Catholic, super-patriotic organization that was primarily Irish. It grew from its founding in 1882 to one-half million members by 1920. Members were mostly American born and upwardly mobile, "suggesting the deeply rooted commitment of the new generation of prosperous Celts to the land of their birth" (Meagher, *From Paddy to Studs*, pp. 12–13).

24. "Let's Help the Irish Now," Bernie Grossman and Billy Frisch (New York: Joe W. Stern, 1919); "Irish Liberty," Charles B. Lawlor and Alice Lawlor (New York: Ireland a Nation Music, 1920).

25. "King Gilhooly," Edgar Smith and John Stromberg (New York: Witmark, 1899); "The Mick Who Threw the Brick," William Cahill Davis and Charles B. Lawlor (New York: Schlam, 1899).

26. Middleton, *Studying Popular Music*, p. 44.

27. "Nora Malone, Call Me by Phone," Junie M. McCree and Albert Von Tilzer (New York: A. Von Tilzer, 1909); "In My Irish Aeroplane," by Stanley Murphy and Harry Tierney (New York: Remick, 1917).

28. "Mister Dooley," William Jerome and Jean Schwartz (New York: Shapiro, Bernstein, 1902).

29. "Bedelia (The Irish Coon Serenade)," William Jerome and Jean Schwartz (New York: Shapiro, Bernstein, 1903). Nicholas Tawa notes, "From the late nineties on, coon and rag were considered different aspects of the same song style. Several writers seem to have associated the label 'coon' with the text and 'rag' with the music" (Tawa, *Way to Tin Pan Alley*, p. 186).

30. "My Irish Molly O," William Jerome and Jean Schwartz (New York: Remick,

1905). See Cohen-Stratyner, *Popular Music*, p. 256. The Flanagan Brothers, Joe and Michael, were among the most prolific of the Irish artists who recorded on the "ethnic" labels put out by major companies in the 1920s and 1930s. Although they started out as instrumentalists playing jigs, reels, and hornpipes, they introduced vocals, as well as vaudeville-type comedy routines. See Spottswood, *Ethnic Music on Records*, vol. 5, pp. 2762–68.

31. "Kerryanna," Jack Drislane and George W. Meyer (New York: Haviland, 1910).

32. "The Irish Tango," J. Brandon Walsh and Ernest Breuer (New York: Witmark, 1914); "Dublin Rag," Harold R. Atterridge and Phil Schwartz (New York: Feist, 1910).

33. "Everything at Reilly's Must Be Done in Irish Style," John and William West (New York: Rob Reucker, 1899).

34. "My Irish Song of Songs," Al Dubin and Dan J. Sullivan (New York: Witmark, 1917), from the Chauncey Olcott musical *Once Upon a Time* by Rachel Crothers.

35. "Ha-Le Ha-Lo or That's What the Germans Sang," Will A. Heelan and Fred J. Helf (New York: Stern, 1901); "It's the Irish," Austin Benson (Alcony, Ohio: Benson, 1915); "McElwee," George Whiting and T. N. Snyder (New York: Ted Snyder, 1909); "A Little Bit of Irish," Gus Kahn and Grace Le Boy (New York: Shapiro, 1911). Maggie Cline introduced this last song and it was eventually recorded.

36. "Arrah Wanna (An Irish Indian Matrimonial Venture)," Jack Drislane and Theodore Morse (New York: Haviland, 1906). Improbable as the song was, it was a great hit. Both the vocal and the instrumental two-step version were recorded. See Cohen-Stratyner, *Popular Music*, p. 18.

37. "Since Arrah Wanna Married Barney Carney," Jack Drislane and Theodore Morse (New York: Haviland, 1907).

38. "O'Brien Is Tryin' to Learn to Talk Hawaiian," Al Dubin and Rennie Cormack (New York: Witmark, 1916); "Since Maggie Dooley Learned the Hooley Hooly," Ed Leslie, Bert Kalmer, and George W. Meyer (New York: Waterson, Berlin, Snyder, 1916); "Sing a Good Old Irish Song for Me," Joe Hiller, Joe Weston, and George B. McConnell (New York: Welch, 1917).

39. "Mister Pat O'Hare," B. Hapgood Burt (Detroit: Remick, 1910); "Arrah-Arabia," Ed Madden and Dorothy Jardon (New York: Stern, 1908); "I've Got Rings on My Fingers (or Mumbo-Jumbo-Jijjiboo J. O'Shay)," Weston and Barnes and Maurice Scott (New York: Harms and Francis, 1909). The song was a great hit, thanks to the catchy melody and the singing of Blanch Ring, who introduced it in *The Midnight Sons* (1909).

40. "Kelly's Gone to Kingdom Come," Sax Rohmer and Thurban W. Thurban (Chicago: Rossiter, 1910); "I'm the Man They're Looking for, Kelly, That's My Name," Ed Rogers (New York: Ted Snyder, 1910).

41. "Yiddisha Luck and Irisha Love (Kelly and Rosenbaum, That's Mazeltoff)," Alfred Bryan and Fred Fisher (New York: Shapiro, 1911); "Moysha Machree (They're Proud of This Irisher, Yiddisher Boy)," James Kendis (New York: Kendis, 1916).

42. "There's a Little Bit of Irish in Sadie Cohen," Alfred Bryan and Jack Stern (New York: Remick, 1916); "My Yiddisha Colleen," Ed Madden and Leo Edwards (New York: George Edwards, 1911).

43. Riordon, *Plunkitt of Tammany Hall*, p. 48.

44. "If It Wasn't for the Irish and the Jews," William Jerome and Jean Schwartz (New York: Jerome, Schwartz, 1912).

45. Some films on this theme were *Becky Gets a Husband, Two Blocks Away, Abie's Irish Rose, Kosher Kitty Kelly, Frisco Sally Levy, Rosa Machree, Izzie and Lizzie, Private Izzy Murphy, Sailor Izzy Murphy, The Princess of Hoboken, The Life of Riley, Clancy's Kosher Wedding, A Harp in Hock,* and *Sally in Our Alley.* According to Thomas Cripps, "By the end of the silent era, the symbolic marriage of Jew and Irishman outstripped all other ethnic themes" ("Movie Jew," p. 201). See also Fielder, "Fatal Attraction." Two successful plays with the Irish-Jewish theme are Edward Everett Rose's *Rosa Machree* (1921) and Anne Nichols's *Abie's Irish Rose* (1925). Lily Carthew (Lillian Heydemann) had earlier parodied the genre in *The American Idea*, where the apparently Irish interloper into a Jewish family turns out to be Yan Kele [Kelly] Operchinsky. See Flynn, "Melting Plots," pp. 428–29.

46. See Mark Slobin's study of Jewish popular songs in America. Slobin makes the point that the popular songs in Yiddish tended to be more complex, more ironic, and even bitter about the American experience than songs written in English (*Tenement Songs*, pp. 119–63).

47. "My Mariuccia (Taka a Steamboat)," George Ronklyn and Al Piantadosi (New York: Barron, Thompson, 1907); "Tony Spagoni's Cabaret," Al Dubin and Clarence Gaskill (New York: Witmark, 1917).

48. "The Dago Banana Peddler," Frank Dumont (New York: Willis Woodward, 1888); "Go On, Good-a-bye," M. J. Murphy and Al W. Brown (Chicago: Kremer, 1910).

49. "Mosha from Nova Scotia," L. Wolfe Gilbert and Melvin Franklin (New York: Stern, 1915); "Marry a Yiddisher Boy," J. S. Brown and George Botsford (New York: Remick, 1911).

50. "My Rose of the Ghetto," Donaghey, Burkhardt, and Jerome (New York: Charles K. Harris, 1911); "My Yiddisher Blonde," M. Alexander and Anatol Friedland (New York: Remick, 1912).

51. I have found no songs in this period pairing Irish with blacks. This would have been considered beyond the boundaries of humor. However, songs mentioning the "coon" or ragtime style played at the edges of Irish prejudice against African Americans.

52. Curran, "From 'Paddy' to the Presidency," pp. 104, 109.

53. Friedman, *Hollywood's Image of the Jew*, p. 33.

54. Curran, *Hibernian Green on the Silver Screen*, p. 36. See also Clark and Lynch, "Hollywood and Hibernia," p. 100.

Chapter 10: Irish America in Search of an Image

1. Quoted in Flynn, "Ethnicity after Sea-Change," p. 36.

2. See Clark, *Erin's Heirs*, p. 41. Mick Moloney interviewed an old accordion player, Gene Kelly, originally from County Kilkenny, who related how he used to

take part in these vigilante-style disruptions of stage acts that he and his contemporaries considered un-Irish. See Moloney, "Irish Ethnic Recordings," p. 90.

3. Snyder, *Voice of the City*, p. 110; Staples, *Male-Female Comedy Teams*, p. 86. For the *Gaelic American* quote, see Murphy, "Irish-American Theatre," p. 229.

4. Flynn, "Ethnicity after Sea-Change," pp. 2–3; Waters, *Comic Irishman*, p. 79.

5. Cripps, "Movie Jew," p. 198.

6. Appel, "From Shanties to Lace Curtains," p. 371. See also Distler, "Ethnic Comedy," p. 36; Donovan, "Good Old Pat," pp. 8–9.

7. Appel, "From Shanties to Lace Curtains," pp. 369, 372, 373. See also Donovan, "Good Old Pat," pp. 12–14.

8. See Staples, *Male-Female Comedy Teams*, pp. 86, 87. See also Clark, *Erin's Heirs*, pp. 40–41; Fielder, "Wooing a Local Audience," about the Mae Desmond Players who specialized in Irish-American material in Philadelphia.

9. Walsh, "Lace Curtain Literature," p. 143. See also Meagher, *From Paddy to Studs*, p. 9.

10. "Who Threw the Overalls in Mistress Murphy's Chowder?" George L. Giefer (New York: Mullen, 1898).

11. Quoted in Fanning, *Finley Peter Dunne and Mr. Dooley*, pp. 77–78.

12. Ibid., pp. 81–82.

13. Staples, *Male-Female Comedy Teams*, p. 88.

14. Ibid., pp. 84–85. For the Ryan quote, see ibid., p. 88.

15. Ibid., p. 89.

16. Galewitze, *Bringing Up Father*, p. v; Staples, *Male-Female Comedy Teams*, p. 272n.

17. See Donovan, "Good Old Pat," p. 11.

18. "Bridget McGuire" [also known as "Since My Daughter Plays on the Typewriter"], Thomas P. Getz and George W. Hetzel (New York: Thomas P. Getz, 1889).

19. "O'Brien Has No Place to Go," S. Murphy and George Evans (New York: Remick, 1908). The color red first appears in an obvious way in the 1890s, when it was used on 34 percent of the song covers. The use declined after the turn of the century to 14 percent for the 1900s and 10 percent for the 1910s.

20. "The Belle of Avenoo A," Safford Waters (New York: Howley, Haviland, 1895).

21. "The Idol of Donovan's Row," Lou Sully (New York: Howley, Haviland, 1898); "The Sunshine of Paradise Alley," Walter H. Ford and John W. Bratton (London: Witmark, 1895).

22. Quoted in Ewen, "City Lights," p. S55.

23. See Levy, *Give Me Yesterday*, p. 284. One character in Hogan's Alley became so popular that within a month Outcault had to give him his own cartoon: "The Yellow Kid," one of the first well-known newspaper comic characters, was born. He was featured on the cover of Myer's "Dance of the Hogan Alley Hoboes." It should be noted, however, that Outcault's strips, with their crowds and sense of confusion, not to mention violence, gave a more realistic hint of the chaos of urban poverty than conveyed by even Harrigan's best plays. See Berger, *Comic-Stripped American*, pp. 25–27.

24. McCabe, *George M. Cohan*, p. 2.

25. "Harrigan," George M. Cohan (New York: Mills, 1907). For the quote, see McCabe, *George M. Cohan*, p. 51.

26. Finson, *Voices That Are Gone*, p. 309.

Chapter 11: All That I Want Is in Ireland

1. Marcuse, *Tin Pan Alley in Gaslight*, p. 48.

2. Spaeth, *History of Popular Music*, p. 217.

3. "Remember Boy, You're Irish," William J. Scanlan (New York: Harms, 1886).

4. Pitou, *Masters of the Show*, pp. 173–74.

5. Olcott, *Song in My Heart*, pp. 16–19.

6. Ibid., pp. 124–28.

7. See ibid., pp. 143, 146. This brief quotation reveals how dedicated Olcott's wife was, even after the singer's death, to maintaining the image of this new type of stage Irishman that her husband had represented.

8. Fielder, "Chauncey Olcott," pp. 7–8

9. See ibid.

10. See Olcott, *Song in My Heart*, p. 179. Until around 1912, Olcott is listed as the songwriter for most of the songs for his shows. Most of his acknowledged collaborations, primarily on the lyrics, took place from 1907 to 1913. After 1913, most of his songs were written for him.

11. Fielder, "Chauncey Olcott," p. 12.

12. "When John McCormack Sings a Song," William Jerome and Ray Goetz, Jean Schwartz (New York: Waterson, Berlin, Snyder, 1915). For Olcott's recordings see Spottswood, *Ethnic Music on Records*, vol. 5, pp. 2838–39.

13. "Mother Machree," J. R. Young, Chauncey Olcott, and Ernie Ball (New York: Witmark, 1910). Fielder suggests that these Irish mother songs represent "the passive female value of self-denial, self-sacrifice, and patient endurance" at just the time that the "New Woman" (the Bridget Typewriter McGuires) was emerging (see "Chauncey Olcott," p. 15).

14. Foxall, *John McCormack*, p. 79.

15. Fanning, *Irish Voice in America*, p. 158. See also Greeley, *Irish Americans*, p. 125; Shannon, *American Irish*, p. 38.

16. Miller, *Emigrants and Exiles*, p. 482.

17. Ibid., p. 515.

18. Ibid., pp. 489, 559, 562.

19. "That Old Irish Mother of Mine," Billy Jerome and Harry Von Tilzer (New York: Harry Von Tilzer, 1920; emphasis added).

20. "Let Me Glance at Dear Old Ireland Once Again," Robert Vaughan and Tom Sherman (New York: Morris, 1911); "There's a Wee Bit of Blarney in Killarney," A. J. Jackson and L. W. Gilbert, M. Ager (New York: J. W. Stern, 1915); "The Home of Killarney and You," John C. Sycamore (New York: Marvel, Sycamore, 1916).

21. Slobin, *Tenement Songs*, p. 125. Writing of the Irish-American community, Ellen Horgan Biddle notes that "men in tender moments often call their wives

'mother'" ("American Catholic Irish Family," p. 108). For songs see also "The Kind of Girl I Mean," Anna Nichols, Fiske O'Hara, and George Gartlan (New York: Leo Feist, 1918), from *Marry in Haste;* "My Irish Song of Songs," Al Dubin and Dan J. Sullivan (New York: Witmark, 1917).

22. O'Connell, "Irish I," p. 677. See also Fielder, "Chauncey Olcott," p. 35.

23. "That Old Irish Mother of Mine," Billy Jerome and Harry Von Tilzer (New York: Harry Von Tilzer, 1920).

24. "That Tumble-Down Shack in Athlone," R. W. Pascoe, Monte Carlo, and Alma M. Sanders (New York: Waterson, Berlin, Snyder, 1918), used in the Olcott vehicle *The Voice of McConnell,* produced by George M. Cohan.

25. "I Had a Dream That Ireland Was Free among the Nations of the Earth," Gordon Johnston and Samuel S. Krams (New York: Waterson, Berlin, Snyder, 1917). See also Fielder, "Chauncey Olcott," pp. 9–13.

26. These changes were accompanied by a shift back to the use of women's names in the song titles. Women's names had predominated in song titles until the 1870s, when male names, signifying comedy, took over. The pendulum began to shift back to women in the 1890s and by the 1910s 60 percent of the names appearing in song titles were feminine. Moreover, after 1910, for the first time more women than men began appearing on the song covers.

27. "Irish Love (Like the Wine That Grows Sweeter with Age)," Al Bryan and Leo Edwards (New York: Edwards, 1915); "Go Find a Sweetheart from the Emerald Isle," Herbert Ingraham (New York: Shapiro, 1909).

28. "The Daughter of Rosie O'Grady," Monty C. Brice and Walter Donaldson (New York: Witmark, 1918); "Plain Molly O," William Scanlan (New York: Harms, 1891); "Plain Molly O," Chauncey Olcott (New York: Harms, 1891). By copyrighting virtually the same song with minimal changes, Olcott presumably shifted the royalties over to himself.

29. "Each Day Til I Die, an Irish Love Song," Chauncey Olcott (New York: Witmark, 1911); "The Girl I'll Call My Sweetheart Must Look Like You," Chauncey Olcott and Dan J. Sullivan (New York: Witmark, 1911); "Because You're Irish," Gus Kahn and Egbert Van Alstyne (New York: Remick, 1917). The association of the colleen with roses and blue eyes began to appear in the 1880s, when over 20 percent of the Irish love songs presented blue-eyed sweethearts surrounded by roses. The proportion increased somewhat in the 1890s and then decreased to around 15 percent after the turn of the century. After 1910, however, over 30 percent of the love songs made the connection between blue eyes, roses, and the beloved. It seems possible that Olcott's "Wild Irish Rose" and various songs about "Irish Eyes" increased the popularity of these symbols of the Irish colleen.

30. "Come Back to Old Ireland," Annie B. O'Shea (Chicago: Root, 1898).

31. "Ireland I Love You, Acushla Machree," Raymond Browne (New York: Witmark, 1910).

32. Miller, *Emigrants and Exiles,* p. 512; "Will My Soul Pass through Old Ireland?" Vincent P. Brayn and H. W. Armstrong (New York: F. A. Mills, 1900).

33. "In Ould Ireland," Arthur Gutman (New York: Seymour, Furth, 1911). The phrase "Beauty's home" is taken from the earlier parlor ballad "Killarney."

34. "A Little Bit of Heaven, Sure They Call It Ireland," J. K. Brennan and Ernest Ball (New York: Witmark, 1915).

35. "That's What Ireland Means to Me," Joe Goodwin and James F. Hanley (New York: Shapiro, Bernstein, 1917).

36. "Danny Boy (Adapted from an Old Irish Air)," Fred. E. Weatherly (New York: Bossey, Hawks, 1913).

37. "Dear Ireland," A. Baldwin Sloane (New York: J. W. Stern, 1905); "Erin Is Calling," William Jerome and Milton Ager (New York: W. Jerome, 1916).

38. "Irish Eyes of Love," J. Edward Killalea and Ernest R. Ball (New York: Witmark, 1914); "Isle O' Dreams," George Graff Jr. and Chauncey Olcott, Ernest Ball (New York: Witmark, 1911); "What an Irishman Means by 'Machree,'" Francis Donnelly, S. J., and George H. Gartlan (New York: Feist, 1915); "Everyone Loves an Irish Song," William J. McKenna (New York: Haviland, 1916).

39. "A Song of Old Kilkenny," Charles E. Baer and Johann G. Schmid (New York: Remick, 1910); "Sweet Eileen of Kilkenny," J. A. Pedersen and Abe Olman (Chicago: La Salle, 1914).

40. "Where the River Shannon Flows," James I. Russell (New York: Witmark, 1905); "Back in Old Erin," Joe Hill (Kansas City: Hill, 1914); "There's a Wee Bit of Blarney in Killarney," A. J. Jackson and L. W. Gilbert, M. Ager (New York: J. W. Stern, 1915).

41. Clark, *Irish Relations*, p. 78. For returning Irish immigrants, see Miller, *Emigrants and Exiles*, pp. 426, 519. According to Clark, by the 1880s families would pool funds to send immigrant parents back for visits. In fact, tours of Ireland became an organized feature of the trans-Atlantic travel business (see *Irish Relations*, pp. 78, 80–81).

42. Miller, *Emigrants and Exiles*, pp. 560–61.

43. "Take Off Your Hats to Old Ireland," Stanley Murphy and Percy Wenrich (New York: Remick, 1910).

44. "The Irish Blues," J. B. Walsh and Ernie Edrman (New York: Rossiter, 1915); "In the Good Old Irish Way (A Celtic Waltz Song)," W. A. Heelan and H. B. Blanke (New York: Remick, 1907); "You Don't Have to Come from Ireland to Be Irish," George Graff, Bert Grant (New York: Waterson, Berlin, Snyder, 1917).

45. "Top of the Morning," Anne Nichols and George H. Gartlan (New York: 1920), from *Spring Time in Mayo*.

46. "You Don't Have to Come from Ireland to Be Irish," George Graff, Bert Grant (New York: Waterson, Berlin, Snyder, 1917); "It Takes a Great Big Heart to Sing an Irish Song," Barry Costello and Theo Morse (New York: Feist, 1917); "Every Tear Is a Smile in an Irishman's Heart," Dan Sullivan, Monte Carlo, and Alan M. Sanders (New York: Harry Von Tilzer, 1919).

47. "I'm Awfully Glad I'm Irish," Edgar Leslie and Al Piantadosi (New York: Feist, 1910); "When Irish Eyes Are Smiling," Chauncey Olcott, George Graff Jr., and Ernest Ball (New York: Witmark, 1912); "Why Not Sing 'Wearing of the Green'?" Howard Johnson and Jack Glogau (New York: Feist, 1915).

48. "All I Want Is in Ireland (All That I Had and All That I Have)," Jeff Branden and Evans Lloyd (New York: Branden, 1917); emphasis added.

49. Clark, *Irish Relations*, p. 77.

50. "There's Something in the Name of Ireland That the Whole World Seems to Love," H. Johnson and M. Ager (New York: Feist, 1917).

51. See McCaffrey, *Textures of Irish America*, p. 166.

52. Fielder, "Chauncey Olcott," p. 24.

53. In the Lilly Library collection I could find only fifteen songs published after 1920. The situation was similar in the collection of the Cincinnati Public Library. This considerable decline in the number of new songs dealing with Ireland and the Irish after 1920 does not appear to be an artifact of the collections. Barbara Naomi Cohen-Stratyner's compilation of song titles for the period 1900–1919 reveals thirty-seven songs dealing with Ireland and the Irish for the first decade and twenty-eight for the next. By contrast, Nat Shapiro's listing for 1920–29 produces only five titles for the period. Of course, neither index lists all the songs published those years; only those songs the editors consider "significant" because they had been recorded or used in films or shows. See Cohen-Stratyner, *Popular Music;* Shapiro, *Popular Music.*

54. Staples has noted that of 450 known male-female teams appearing in New York City between the 1894–95 and 1903–4 seasons, only twenty can be positively identified as Irish, a marked decrease from 1880s. And, although the number of mixed teams jumped to 650 during the next decade, the number of Irish teams remained the same. See Staples, *Male-Female Comedy Teams*, pp. 89, 206.

55. Since these recordings were made primarily for the Irish market, it is interesting that only about a quarter of the nineteenth-century songs, less than 10 percent of the entire sample, could be considered "folksongs." I was able to identify only fifteen songs with Gaelic titles.

The results of my survey of Spottswood are suggestive at best. First of all, I did not factor in duplicate song titles. Second, some of my identifications are "informed guesses," based on the fact that it is generally possible to identify songs belonging to the Victorian parlor tradition, vaudeville, Tin Pan Alley, and the British music hall by the nature of their titles. Finally, out of 900 records titles that are clearly vocals, there are around 240 I cannot identify either as to time or place. There is no reason to expect that this group would necessarily reflect the breakdown I found in the 660 songs I believe I can identify. If the majority of them were of British/Irish origin, for example, then the role of immigrants in interwar Irish-American song culture would turn out to be even greater than I have suggested. For the discography of Irish ethnic recordings, see Spottswood, *Ethnic Music on Records*, vol. 5, pp. 2737–869.

56. See Curran, *Hibernian Green on the Silver Screen*, pp. 17–18, 35. For the variety of Irish screen types and the role of Irish Americans in Hollywood, see Woll and Miller, *Ethnic and Racial Images*, pp. 261–62, 264–65, 268. Clark and Lynch suggest that the new Irish characters seen in films were merely more modern versions of the older stage-Irish types ("Hollywood and Hibernia," p. 112). However, being "modern" also meant that they were acceptable to mainstream America, something that was not always true of the old stage-Irish images.

57. McCaffrey, *Textures of Irish America*, p. 40.

58. "'Twas Only an Irishman's Dream," John J. O'Brien and Al Dubin, Ronnie Cormack (New York: Witmark, 1916).

Conclusion

1. We must understand this process within a larger perspective. In Ireland itself, Irish-Catholic bourgeois culture had a profound effect in reshaping the society.

2. Williams, "Immigration as a Pattern."

3. Gans, "Symbolic Ethnicity," p. 204.

4. Ibid., p. 206.

5. It is important to remember that by 1920, the point when this study ends, Irish communities in America were a mixture of first, second, and third generation, each, as groups and as individuals, at varying points on the spectrum from "functional" to "symbolic" ethnicity.

Adams, Harold E. "Minority Characters on the American Stage." In *Studies in the Science of Society*. Ed. George Peter Murdock. 1937. Freeport, N.Y.: Books for Libraries, 1969. 1–28.

Appel, John J. "From Shanties to Lace Curtains: The Irish Image in *Puck*, 1876–1910." *Comparative Studies in Society and History* 13 (1971): 365–75.

Archdeacon, Thomas J. *Becoming American: An Ethnic History*. New York: Free Press/Macmillan, 1983.

Asbury, Herbert. *The Gangs of New York: An Informal History of the Underworld*. New York: Knopf, 1928.

Austin, William W. *"Susanna," "Jeanie," and "The Old Folks at Home": The Songs of Stephen C. Foster from His Time to Ours*. 2d ed. Urbana: University of Illinois Press, 1989.

Barke, James, and Sydney Goodsir Smith. *Robert Burns: The Merry Muses of Caldonia*. London: W. H. Allen, 1965.

Barnum and Bailey Concert Songster. New York: New York Publishing Co., [ca. 1888].

Barth, Gunther. *City People: The Rise of Modern City Culture in Nineteenth-Century America*. New York: Oxford University Press, 1890.

Bartley, J. O. *Teague, Shenkin and Sawney; Being an Historical Study of the Earliest Irish, Welsh and Scottish Characters in English Plays*. Cork: Cork University Press, 1954.

Beadle's Dime Song Book No. 4. New York: Beadle, 1859.

Beadle's Dime Song Book No. 5. New York: Beadle, 1860.

Beer, Thomas. *The Mauve Decade: American Life at the End of the Nineteenth Century*. New York: Knopf, 1926.

Berger, Arthur Asa. *The Comic-Stripped American*. Baltimore: Penguin, 1974.

Biddle, Ellen Horgan. "The American Catholic Irish Family." In *Ethnic Families in America: Patterns and Variations*. Ed. Charles H. Mindel and Robert W. Habenstein. New York: Elsevier, 1976. 89–123.

Blaney, Glenn H. "City Life in American Drama, 1825–1860." In *Studies in Honor of John Wilcox*. Ed. A. Dayle Wallace and Woodburn O. Ross. Detroit: Wayne State University Press, 1958. 99–128.

Blessing, Patrick J. "Irish Emigration to the United States, 1800 to 1920: An Overview." In *The Irish in America: Emigration, Assimilation and Impact*. Ed. P. J. Drudy. New York: Cambridge University Press, 1985. 11–38.

Bogard, Travis, Richard Moody, and Walter J. Meserve. *The Revels History of Drama in English*. Vol. 7. New York: Barnes and Noble, 1977.

Bordman, Gerald. *American Musical Comedy: From Adonis to Dream Girls*. New York: Oxford University Press, 1982.

Boskin, Joseph. *Sambo: The Rise and Demise of an American Jester*. New York: Oxford University Press, 1986.

Boylan, Henry, ed. *A Dictionary of Irish Biography.* 2d ed. New York: St. Martin's, 1988.

Bratton, J. S. *The Victorian Popular Ballad.* Totowa, N.J.: Rowman, Littlefield, 1975.

——, ed. *Music Hall: Performance and Style.* Philadelphia: Open University Press, 1986.

Brown, Thomas N. *Irish-American Nationalism, 1870–1890.* New York: J. B. Lippincott, 1966.

Burns, George. *Gracie: A Love Story.* New York: Putnam, 1988.

Burns, Warren Thomas. "The Plays of Edward Green Harrigan: The Theatre of Intercultural Communication." Ph.D. dissertation. Pennsylvania State University, 1969.

Carpenter, Andrew. "Changing Views of Irish Musical and Literary Culture in Eighteenth-Century Anglo-Irish Literature." In *Irish Literature and Culture.* Ed. Michael Kenneally. Savage, Md.: Barnes and Noble, 1991. 5–24.

Chappell, W. *The Ballad Literature and Popular Music of the Olden Time.* 2 vols. 1855–59. New York: Dover, 1965.

Clark, Dennis. *Erin's Heirs: Irish Bonds of Community.* Lexington: University Press of Kentucky, 1991.

——. *Hibernia America: The Irish and Regional Cultures.* Westport, Conn.: Greenwood Press, 1986.

——. *The Irish Relations: Trials of an Immigrant Tradition.* Rutherford, N.J.: Fairleigh Dickinson University Press, 1982.

Clark, Dennis, and William J. Lynch. "Hollywood and Hibernia: The Irish in the Movies." In *The Kaleidoscopic Lens: How Hollywood Views Ethnic Groups.* Ed. Randall M. Miller. Englewood, N.J.: Jerome S. Ozer, 1980. 98–113.

Clark, John R., and William E. Morris. "*Scherzo, Forte,* and *Bravura:* Satire in America's Musical Theater." *Journal of Popular Culture* 12.3 (1978): 459–81.

Cohan, George M. *Twenty Years on Broadway and the Years It Took to Get There.* Westport, Conn.: Greenwood Press, 1971.

Cohen, Norm. *Long Steel Rail: The Railroad in American Folksong.* Urbana: University of Illinois Press, 1981.

Cohen-Stratyner, Barbara Naomi, ed. *Popular Music, 1900–1919: An Annotated Guide to American Popular Songs.* Detroit: Gale Research, 1988.

Cripps, Thomas. "The Movie Jew as Image of Assimilation, 1903–1927." *Journal of Popular Film* 4.3 (1975): 190–207.

Croker, Thomas Crofton. *Researches in the South of Ireland.* 1824. New York: Barnes and Noble, 1968.

Cullinane, John P. "Aspects of the History of Irish Dance in Ireland, England, New Zealand, and Australia." Souvenir program for the World Irish Dancing Championship, Galway City, Ireland, 1987.

——. "Irish Dancing World-Wide: Irish Migrants and the Shaping of Traditional Irish Dance." In *The Creative Migrant.* Ed. Patrick O'Sullivan. New York: Leicester University Press, 1994. 192–220.

Curran, Joseph M. *Hibernian Green on the Silver Screen: The Irish and American Movies.* New York: Greenwood Press, 1989.

Curran, Thomas J. "From 'Paddy' to the Presidency: The Irish in America." In *The Immigrant Experience in America*. Ed. Frank J. Coppa and Thomas J. Curran. Boston: Twayne, 1976. 95–114.

Curtis, L. P., Jr. *Anglo-Saxons and Celts: A Study of Anti-Irish Prejudice in Victorian England*. Bridgeport, Conn.: University of Bridgeport Press, 1968.

——. *Apes and Angels: The Irishman in Victorian Caricature*. Washington, D.C.: Smithsonian Institution Press, 1971.

Daniels, Roger. *Coming to America: A History of Immigration and Ethnicity in American Life*. New York: Harper-Collins, 1990.

Davis, Leith. "Irish Bards and English Consumers: Thomas Moore's 'Irish Melodies' and the Colonized Nation." *Ariel: A Review of International English Literature* 24.2 (1993): 7–25.

de Bhaldraithe, Thomás, ed. *English-Irish Dictionary*. Baile Átha Claith [Dublin]: Oifig an tSoláthair, 1959.

DeFord, Miriam Allen. *Thomas Moore*. New York: Twayne, 1967.

Delaney's Irish Song Book No. 2. New York: Delaney, [ca. 1887].

Delaney's Irish Song Book No. 4. New York: Delaney, [ca. 1887].

Dennison, Sam. *Scandalize My Name: Black Imagery in American Popular Music*. New York: Garland, 1982.

Distler, Paul Antonie. "Ethnic Comedy in Vaudeville and Burlesque." In *American Popular Entertainment: Papers and Proceedings of the Conference on the History of American Popular Entertainment*. Ed. Myron Matlaw. Westport, Conn.: Greenwood, 1979. 33–42.

Dodge, Robert K. "The Irish Comic Stereotype in the Almanacs of the Early Republic." *Éire-Ireland* 19.3 (1984): 111–20.

Dohan, Mary Helen. *Our Own Words*. New York: Knopf, 1976.

Donovan, Kathleen. "Good Old Pat: An Irish-American Stereotype in Decline." *Éire-Ireland* 15.3 (1980): 6–14.

Dorson, Richard. "Mose, the Far-Famed and World Renowned." *American Literature* 15 (1943): 288–300.

Douglas, Mary. "Jokes." In *Rethinking Popular Culture: Contemporary Perspectives in Cultural Studies*. Ed. Chandra Mukerji and Michael Schudson. Los Angeles: University of California Press, 1991. 291–310.

Dower, Catherine. "Dublin and Musical Culture in the Eighteenth Century." *Éire-Ireland* 22.1 (1987): 44–58.

Doyle, David Noel. *Ireland, Irishmen and Revolutionary America, 1760–1820*. Dublin: Mercier Press, 1981.

Duggan, G. C. *The Stage Irishman: A History of the Irish Play and Stage Characters from the Earliest Times*. London: Longman's Green, 1937.

Edwards, R. Dudley, and T. Desmond Williams. *The Great Famine: Studies in Irish History, 1845–52*. 1956. Dublin: Browne, Nolan, 1962.

Elson, Ruth Miller. *Guardians of Tradition: American School Books of the Nineteenth Century*. Lincoln: University of Nebraska Press, 1964.

Ernst, Robert. *Immigrant Life in New York City, 1825–1863*. New York: King's Crown Press/Columbia University, 1949.

Evans, E. Estyn. *Irish Folk Ways*. London: Routledge and Kegan Paul, 1957.

Ewen, David. *The Life and Death of Tin Pan Alley: The Golden Age of American Popular Music*. New York: Funk and Wagnalls, 1964.

Ewen, Elizabeth. "City Lights: Immigrant Women and the Rise of the Movies." *Signs: A Journal of Women in Culture and Society* 5.3 suppl. (1980): S45–S66.

Fallows, Majorie. *Irish Americans: Identity and Assimilation*. Englewood Cliffs, N.J.: Prentice-Hall, 1979.

Fanning, Charles. *Finley Peter Dunne and Mr. Dooley: The Chicago Years*. Lexington: University Press of Kentucky, 1978.

——. *The Irish Voice in America: Irish-American Fiction from the 1760s to the 1980s*. Lexington: University Press of Kentucky, 1990.

Ferrar, Harold. "Robert Emmet in Irish Drama." *Éire-Ireland* 1.2 (1966): 19–28.

Fielder, Mari Kathleen. "Chauncey Olcott: Irish-American Mother-Love, Romance, and Nationalism." *Éire-Ireland* 22.2 (1987): 4–26.

——. "Fatal Attraction: Irish-Jewish Romance in Early Film and Drama." *Éire-Ireland* 20.3 (1985): 6–18 .

——. "Wooing a Local Audience: The Irish-American Appeal of Philadelphia's Mae Desmond Players." *Theatre History Studies* 1 (1981): 50–63.

Finson, Jon W. *The Voices That Are Gone: Themes in Nineteenth-Century American Popular Song*. New York: Oxford University Press, 1994.

Fitz-Gerald, S. J. Adair. *Stories of Famous Songs in Two Volumes*. Philadelphia: J. B. Lippincott, 1910.

Fitz-Simon, Christopher. *The Irish Theatre*. London: Thames and Hudson, 1983.

Flynn, Arthur. *Irish Dance*. [Republic of Ireland]: Folens, n.d.

Flynn, Joyce Ann. "Ethnicity after Sea-Change: The Irish Dramatic Tradition in Nineteenth-Century American Drama." Ph.D. disseration. Ann Arbor, Mich.: University Microfilms International, 1992.

——. "Melting Plots: The Racial Ethnic Amalgamation in American Drama before O'Neill." *American Quarterly* 38.3 (1986): 417–38.

Fortune, Robert S. "The Culture of Hope and the Culture of Despair: The Print Media and 19th-Century Irish Emigration." *Éire-Ireland* 13.3 (1978): 32–48.

Foster, Sally E. "Irish Wrong: Samuel Lover and the Stage-Irishman." *Éire-Ireland* 13.4 (1978): 34–44.

Foxall, Raymond. *John McCormack*. Staten Island, N.Y.: Alba House, 1963.

Frank, Rusty E. *TAP: The Greatest Tap Dance Stars and Their Stories, 1900–1955*. New York: William Morrow, 1990.

Fred Shaw's Dime American Comic Songster. New Orleans: R. Coburn, [ca. 1858].

Friedman, Lester D. *Hollywood's Image of the Jew*. New York: Frederick Ungar, 1982.

Frith, Simon. "Why Do Songs Have Words?" In *Lost in Music: Culture, Style and the Musical Event*. Ed. Avron Levine White. London: Routledge and Kegan Paul, 1987. 97–106.

Galewitze, Herb, ed. *Bringing Up Father by George McManus.* New York: Scribners, 1973.

Gallagher, Kent G. *The Foreigner in Early American Drama: A Study in Attitudes.* The Hague: Mouton, 1966.

Gammond, Peter. *The Oxford Companion to Popular Music.* New York: Oxford University Press, 1991.

Gans, Herbert J. "Symbolic Ethnicity: The Future of Ethnic Groups and Cultures in America." In *On the Making of Americans: Essays in Honor of David Riesman.* Ed. Herbert J. Gans, Nathan Glazer, Joseph R. Gusfield, and Christopher Jencks. Philadelphia: University of Pennsylvania Press, 1979. 193–220.

Geist, Christopher D. "From the Plantation to the Police Station: A Brief History of Black Stereotypes." In *The Popular Culture Reader.* Ed. C. D. Geist and Jack Nachbar. 3d ed. Bowling Green, Ohio: Bowling Green University Popular Press, 1983. 157–70.

The Gems of Songs Introduced in "Colonell and I." New York: Witmark, [ca. 1894].

Gentle Annie Melodist No. 1. New York: Firth, Pond, [ca. 1858]).

Gentle Annie Melodist No. 2. New York: Firth, Pond, 1859.

Gilbert, Douglas. *American Vaudeville: Its Life and Times.* 1940. New York: Dover, 1968.

Glassie, Henry, *Passing the Time in Ballymenone: Culture and History in an Ulster Community.* Philadelphia: University of Pennsylvania Press, 1982.

Goldberg, Isaac. "Harrigan and Hart – and Braham." *American Mercury* 16 (Feb. 1929): 201–10.

Graves, Robert. "The Stage Irishman among the Irish." *Theatre History Studies* 1 (1981): 29–38.

Greeley, Andrew M. *The Irish Americans: The Rise to Money and Power.* New York: Harper and Row, 1981.

Greene, Victor R. *American Immigrant Leaders, 1800–1910: Marginality and Identity.* Baltimore: Johns Hopkins University Press, 1987.

Greenway, John. *American Folksongs of Protest.* 1953. New York: Barnes, 1960.

Grimsted, David. *Melodrama Unveiled: American Theater and Culture, 1800–1845.* Chicago: University of Chicago Press, 1968.

Grobman, Neil R. "The Ballads of Thomas Moore's *Irish Melodies.*" *Southern Folklore Quarterly* 36.2 (1972): 103–20.

Hamm, Charles. *Yesterdays: Popular Song in America.* New York: Norton, 1983.

Harmon, Maurice. "Cobwebs before the Wind: Aspects of the Peasantry in Irish Literature from 1800 to 1916." In *Views of the Irish Peasantry, 1800–1916.* Ed. Daniel J. Casey and Robert E. Rhodes. Hamden, Conn.: Archon Books, 1977. 129–60.

Hawes David S. "John Brougham as Playwright." *Educational Theatre Journal* 9.3 (1957): 184–93.

Hayton, David. "From Barbarian to Burlesque: English Images of the Irish c. 1660–1750." *Irish Economic and Social History* 15 (1988): 5–31.

Healy, James N., ed. *Ballads from the Pubs of Ireland*. Cork: Mercier, 1965.

———. *The Mercier Book of Old Irish Street Ballads*. Vol. 1. Cork: Mercier, 1967.

———. *The Second Book of Irish Ballads*. 2d ed. Cork: Mercier, 1964.

Hewitt, Bernard. *Theater U.S.A., 1668 to 1957*. New York: McGraw-Hill, 1959.

Higham, John. *Send These to Me: Immigrants in Urban America*. Rev. ed. Baltimore: Johns Hopkins University Press, 1984.

———. *Strangers in the Land: Patterns of Nativism, 1860–1925*. New York: Atheneum, 1965.

Hoppenstand, Gary. "Yellow Devil Doctors and Opium Dens: A Survey of the Yellow Peril Stereotypes in Mass Media Entertainment." In *The Popular Culture Reader*. Ed. C. D. Geist and Jack Nachbar. 3d ed. Bowling Green, Ohio: Bowling Green University Popular Press, 1983. 171–85.

Hornblow, Arthur. *A History of the Theatre in America: From Its Beginnings to the Present Time*. 2 vols. Philadelphia: J. B. Lippincott, 1919.

Hutton, Laurence. *Curiosities of the American Stage*. New York: Harper Brothers, 1891.

Ignatiev, Noel. *How the Irish Became White*. New York: Routledge. 1995.

Ireland, Joseph N. *Records of the New York Stage, 1750–1860*. Vol 2. 1866. New York: Benjamin Bloom, 1966.

"Irish Mornings and African Days on the Old Minstrel Stage: An Interview with Leni Sloan." *Callahan's Irish Quarterly* 3.2 (1982): 49–53.

Jasen, David A. *Tin Pan Alley: The Composers, the Songs, the Performers and Their Times – The Golden Age of American Popular Music from 1886 to 1956*. New York: Donald I. Fine, 1988.

Jennings, John J. *Theatrical and Circus Life; or, Secrets of the Stage, Green-Room and Sawdust Arena*. St. Louis: M. S. Barnett, 1882.

Jolliffe, Maureen. *The Third Book of Irish Ballads*. Cork: Mercier, 1970.

Jones, Howard Mumford. *O Strange New World: American Culture – The Formative Years*. 1952. New York: Viking, 1964.

Jordan, Hoover H. *Bolt Upright: The Life of Thomas Moore*. Ed. James Hogg. Vol. 1. Salzburg: Institut für Englische Sprache und Literatur, Universität Salzburg, 1975.

Kahn, E. H., Jr. *The Merry Partners: The Age and Stage of Harrigan and Hart*. New York: Random House, 1955.

Kanter, Kenneth Aaron. *The Jews on Tin Pan Alley: The Jewish Contribution to American Popular Music, 1830–1940*. New York: Ktav Publishing House, 1982.

Kibred, Declan. "The Fall of the Stage Irishman." In *The Genres of the Irish Literary Revival*. Ed. Ronald Schliefer. Special issue of *Genre: A Quarterly Devoted to Generic Criticism* 12.4 (1979): 451–72.

Knobel, Dale T. *Paddy and the Republic: Ethnicity and Nationality in Antebellum America*. Middletown, Conn.: Wesleyan University Press, 1986.

———. "A Vocabulary of Ethnic Perception: Content Analysis of the American Stage Irishman, 1820–1860." *Journal of American Studies* 15.1 (1981): 45–71.

Koger, Alicia Kea. "A Critical Analysis of Edward Harrigan's Comedy." Ph.D. dissertation. Ann Arbor, Mich.: University Microfilms International, 1984.

Kosok, Heinz. "The Image of Ireland in Nineteenth-Century Drama." In
Perspectives of Irish Drama and Theatre. Ed. Jacqueline Genet and Richard
Allen Cave. Savage, Md.: Barnes and Noble, 1991. 50–67.

Krause, David, ed. *The Dolmen Boucicault.* Chester Springs, Pa.: Dufour Press,
1965.

——. *The Profane Book of Irish Comedy.* Ithaca, N.Y.: Cornell University Press,
1982.

LaGumina, Salvatore J., and Frank J. Cavaioli, eds. *The Ethnic Dimension in
American Society.* Boston: Holbrook Press, 1974.

Laurie, Joe, Jr. *Vaudeville: From the Honky-Tonks to the Palace.* New York:
Henry Holt, 1953.

Lebow, Ned. "British Images of Poverty in Pre-Famine Ireland." In *Views of the
Irish Peasantry, 1800–1916.* Ed. Daniel Casey and Richard Rhodes. Hamden,
Conn.: Archon Books, 1977. 57–85.

Lee, Edward. *Music of the People: A Study of Popular Music in Great Britain.*
London: Barrie and Jenkins, 1970.

Leerssen, Joseph Th. *Mere Irish and Fíor-Ghael: Studies in the Idea of Irish
Nationality, Its Development and Literary Expression prior to the Nineteenth
Century.* Amsterdam: John Benjamins, 1986.

Levy, Lester S. *Give Me Yesterday: American History in Song, 1890–1920.*
Norman: University of Oklahoma Press, 1975.

Light, Dale B., Jr. "The Role of Irish-American Organizations in Assimilation
and Community Formation." In *The Irish in America: Emigration,
Assimilation and Impact.* Vol 4. Ed. P. J. Drudy. New York: Cambridge
University Press, 1985. 113–41.

Loesser, Arthur. *Humor in American Song.* 1942. New York: Howell, Soskin, 1974.

——. *Men, Women and Pianos: A Social History.* New York: Simon and Schuster,
1954.

Lott, Eric. *Love and Theft: Blackface Minstrelsy and the American Working
Class.* New York: Oxford University Press, 1993.

*The Love and Sentimental Songster: A Choice Collection of Popular Love and
Sentimental Songs by Stephen Foster and Others.* New York: Dick, Fitzgerald,
1862.

MacDonagh, Oliver. "The Irish Famine Emigration to the United States." In
Perspectives in American History. Ed. Donald Fleming and Bernard Bailyn.
Vol 10. Cambridge: Harvard University Press, 1976. 357–446.

MacLochlainn, Alf. "Gael and Peasant: A Case of Mistaken Identity?" In *Views
of the Irish Peasantry, 1800–1916.* Ed. Daniel J. Casey and Robert E. Rhodes.
Hamden, Conn.: Archon Books, 1977. 17–36.

Malcolm, Elizabeth. *"Ireland Sober, Ireland Free": Drink and Temperance in
Nineteenth-Century Ireland.* Dublin: Gill and Macmillan, 1986.

Marcuse, Maxwell F. *Tin Pan Alley in Gaslight: A Saga of the Songs That Made
the Gray Nineties "Gay."* Watkins Glen, N.Y.: Century House, 1959.

Marks, Edward B., as told to Abbott J. Liebling. *They All Sang: From Tony
Pastor to Rudy Valle.* New York: Viking Press, 1935.

McCabe, John. *George M. Cohan: The Man Who Owned Broadway*. Garden City, N.Y.: Doubleday, 1973.

McCaffrey, Lawrence J. *The Irish Diaspora in America*. Bloomington: Indiana University Press, 1976.

———. *Textures of Irish America*. Syracuse, N.Y.: Syracuse University Press, 1992.

McConachie, Bruce A. "The Cultural Politics of 'Paddy' on the Midcentury American Stage." *Studies in Popular Culture* 10.1 (1987): 1–13.

McLean, Albert F., Jr. *American Vaudeville as Ritual*. Lexington: University Press of Kentucky, 1965.

Meagher, Timothy J. *From Paddy to Studs: Irish-American Communities in the Turn of the Century Era, 1880–1920*. Westport, Conn.: Greenwood Press, 1986.

Mercier, Vivian. *The Irish Comic Tradition*. Oxford: Clarendon Press, 1962.

Meserve, Walter J. *Heralds of Promise: The Drama of the American People during the Age of Jackson, 1829–1849*. New York: Greenwood Press, 1986.

Middleton, Richard. *Studying Popular Music*. Philadelphia: Open University Press, 1990.

Miller, Kirby A. *Emigrants and Exiles: Ireland and the Irish Exodus to North America*. New York: Oxford University Press, 1985.

Mitchell, Arthur. "A View of the Irish in America, 1887." *Éire-Ireland* 4.1 (1969): 7–12.

Mitchell, Brian C. "'They Do Not Differ Greatly': The Pattern of Community Development among the Irish in Late Nineteenth-Century Lowell, Massachusetts." In *From Paddy to Studs: Irish-American Communities in the Turn of the Century Era, 1880–1920*. Ed. Timothy J. Meagher. Westport, Conn.: Greenwood Press, 1986.

Mitchell, Pat, and Jackie Small. *The Piping of Patsy Touhey*. Dublin: Na Píobarí Uillean, 1986.

Moloney, Mick. "Irish Ethnic Recordings and the Irish-American Imagination." *Ethnic Recordings in America: A Neglected Heritage*. Washington, D.C.: Library of Congress/American Folklife Center, 1982.

Moody, Richard. *America Takes the Stage: Romanticism in American Drama and Theatre, 1750–1900*. Bloomington: Indiana University Press, 1955.

———. *Ned Harrigan: From Corlear's Hook to Herald Square*. Chicago: Nelson Hall, 1980.

Murphy, Maureen. "Irish-American Theatre." In *Ethnic Theatre in the United States*. Ed. Maxine Schwartz Seller. Westport, Conn.: Greenwood Press, 1983. 221–35.

Nellie Seymour's "I'm Going to Tell on You, Kate" Songster. New York: Henry J. Wehman, [ca. 1895].

Nelson, James Malcolm. "From Rory and Paddy to Boucicault's Myles, Shaun and Conn: The Irishman on the London Stage, 1830–1860." *Éire-Ireland* 13.3 (1978): 79–105.

Nickerson's The "I'll Not Go Out with Riley Any More" Songster. New York: Henry J. Wehman, [ca. 1895].

Niehaus, Earl F. *The Irish in New Orleans, 1800–1860*. Baton Rouge: Louisiana State University Press, 1965.

Nye, Russell B. "Notes on a Rationale for Popular Culture." In *The Popular Culture Reader*. Ed. C. D. Geist and Jack Nachbar. 3d ed. Bowling Green, Ohio: Bowling Green University Popular Press, 1983. 21–27.

O'Boyle, Seán. *The Irish Song Tradition*. Dublin: Gilbert Dalton, 1976.

O'Connell, "Irish I." In *The American Irish Revival: A Decade of the "Recorder," 1974–1983*. Ed. Kevin M. Cahill. Port Washington, N.Y.: Associated Faculty Press, 1984. 677.

Olcott, Rita. *Song in My Heart*. New York: Fields, 1939.

O Lochlainn, Colm. *Irish Street Ballads*. New York: Corinth Books, 1960.

O'Neill, Francis. *Irish Minstrels and Musicians*. 1913. Cork: Mercier Press, 1987.

O'Siochfhradha, M., comp. *Learner's Irish-English Dictionary*. New ed. Dublin: Talbot, n.d.

O'Súilleabháin, Seán. *Irish Wake Amusements*. Cork: Mercier, 1967.

O'Sullivan, Donal. *Irish Folk Music and Song*. Rev. ed. 1952. Dublin: Three Candles, 1961.

O'Tuathaigh, Gearóid. *Ireland before the Famine, 1798–1848*. Dublin: Gill and Macmillan, 1972.

Page, Brett. *Writing for Vaudeville*. Springfield, Mass.: Home Correspondence School, 1915.

Partridge, Eric. *A Dictionary of Historical Slang*. Abridged. Ed. Jacqueline Simpson. Harmondsworth, U.K.: Penguin, 1972.

Pat Rooney's "Day I Played Base Ball" Songster. New York: A. J. Fisher, 1878.

Pat Rooney's "Day I Walked against O'Leary" Songster. New York: A. J. Fisher, 1878.

Pickering, Michael, and Tony Green. "Toward a Cartography of Vernacular Milieu." In *Everyday Culture: Popular Song and the Vernacular Milieu*. Ed. Michael Pickering and Tony Green. Philadelphia: Open University Press, 1987. 1–38.

Pitou, Augustus. *Masters of the Show*. New York: Neale, 1914.

Power, Tyrone. *Impressions of America during the Years of 1833, 1834, and 1835 in Two Volumes*. London: Richard Bently, 1836.

Potter, George. *To the Golden Door: The Story of the Irish in Ireland and America*. Boston: Little, Brown, 1960.

Quinn, Arthur Hobson. *A History of the American Drama from the Civil War to the Present Day*. 1927. New York: F. S. Crofts, 1936.

Quinn, David Beers. *The Elizabethans and the Irish*. Ithaca, N.Y.: Cornell University for the Folger Library, 1966.

Rafroidi, Patrick, "Thomas Moore: Towards a Reassessment?" In *Irish Literature and Culture*. Ed. Michael Kenneally. Savage, Md.: Barnes and Noble, 1991. 55–62.

Rahill, Frank. *The World of Melodrama*. University Park: Pennsylvania State University Press, 1967.

Rinear, David L. "F. S. Chanfrau's Mose: The Rise and Fall of an Urban Folk Hero." *Theatre Journal* 33.2 (1981): 199–212.

Riordon, William L. *Plunkitt of Tammany Hall.* Ed. Arthur Mann. New York: Dutton, 1963.

Root, Deane L. *American Popular Stage Music, 1860–1880.* Ann Arbor, Mich.: UMI Research Press, 1977, 1981.

Rosenwaike, Ira. *Population History of New York City.* Syracuse, N.Y.: Syracuse University Press, 1972.

Rosenzweig, Roy. *Eight Hours for What We Will: Workers and Leisure in an Industrial City, 1870–1920.* New York: Cambridge University Press, 1983.

Rossman, Kenneth R. "The Irish in American Drama in the Mid-Nineteenth Century." *New York History* 21.1 (1940): 39–53.

Russell, Dave. *Popular Music in England, 1840–1914: A Social History.* Kingston: McGill-Queen's University Press, 1987.

Ryan, Dennis P. *Beyond the Ballot Box: A Social History of the Boston Irish, 1845–1917.* Amherst: University of Massachusetts Press, 1983.

Ryan, Pat M. "The Hibernian Experience: John Brougham's Irish-American Plays." *Melus* 10.2 (1983): 33–47.

Sante, Luc. *Low Life: Lures and Snares of Old New York.* New York: Farrar, Straus and Giroux, 1991.

Sarbaugh, Timothy. "Exiles of Confidence: The Irish-American Community of San Francisco, 1880–1920." In *From Paddy to Studs: Irish-American Communities in the Turn of the Century Era, 1880–1920.* Ed. Timothy J. Meagher. Westport, Conn.: Greenwood Press, 1986. 161–79.

Scheurer, Timothy E. "'Thou Witty': The Evolution and Triumph of Style in Lyric Writing, 1890–1950." In *American Popular Music: Readings from the Popular Press.* Vol. 1: *The Nineteenth Century and Tin Pan Alley.* Ed. Timothy E. Scheurer. Bowling Green, Ohio: Bowling Green University Popular Press, 1989. 104–19.

Scott, Derek B. *The Singing Bourgeois: Songs of the Victorian Drawing Room and Parlour.* Philadelphia: Open University Press, 1989.

Shannon, William V. *The American Irish.* Rev. ed. New York: Macmillan, 1966.

Shapiro, Nat, ed. *Popular Music, 1920–1929: An Annotated Index of American Popular Songs.* Vol. 5. New York: Adrian Press, 1964.

Silber, Irwin, comp. and ed. *Songs of the Civil War.* New York: Columbia University Press, 1960.

Skerrett, Ellen. "The Development of Catholic Identity among Irish Americans in Chicago, 1880–1920." In *From Paddy to Studs: Irish-American Communities in the Turn of the Century Era, 1880–1920.* Ed. Timothy J. Meagher. Westport, Conn.: Greenwood Press, 1986. 117–38.

Slide, Anthony. *The Vaudevillians: A Dictionary of Vaudeville Performers.* Westport, Conn.: Arlington House, 1981.

Slobin, Mark. *Tenement Songs: The Popular Music of the Jewish Immigrants.* Urbana: University of Illinois Press, 1982.

Small, Christopher. "Performance as Ritual: Sketch for an Enquiry into the True Nature of a Symphony Concert." In *Lost in Music: Culture, Style and the Musical Event.* Ed. Avron Levine White. New York: Routledge and Kegan Paul, 1987. 6–32.

Smith, Herbert Joseph. "From Stereotype to Acculturation: The Irish-American's Fictional Heritage from Brackenridge to Farrell." Ph.D. dissertation. Kent State University, 1980.

Snyder, Edward D. *The Celtic Revival in English Literature, 1760–1800.* 1923. Gloucester, Mass.: Peter Smith, 1965.

——. "The Wild Irish: A Study of Some English Satires against the Irish, Scots, and Welsh." *Modern Philology* 17.12 (1920): 147–85.

Snyder, Robert W. *The Voice of the City: Vaudeville and Popular Culture in New York.* New York: Oxford University Press, 1989.

Spaeth, Sigmund. *A History of Popular Music in America.* New York: Random House, 1948.

Spottswood, Richard K. *Ethnic Music on Records: A Discography of Ethnic Recordings in the United States, 1893–1942.* 5 vols. Urbana: University of Illinois Press, 1990.

Staples, Shirley. *Male-Female Comedy Teams in American Vaudeville, 1865–1932.* Ann Arbor, Mich.: UMI Research Press, 1984.

Stearns, Marshall, and Jean Stearns. *Jazz Dance: The Story of American Vernacular Dance.* New York: Schirmer, 1968.

Steinberg, Stephen. *The Ethnic Myth: Race, Ethnicity, and Class in America.* 1981. Updated and expanded ed. Boston: Beacon, 1989.

Stephens' Fenian Songster. New York: Murphy, 1866.

Stivers, Richard. *A Hair of the Dog: Irish Drinking and American Stereotype.* University Park: Pennsylvania State University Press, 1976.

Strang, Lewis C. *Celebrated Comedians of Light Opera and Musical Comedy in America.* Boston: L. C. Page, 1901.

Strong, L. A. G. *The Minstrel Boy: A Portrait of Tom Moore.* New York: Knopf, 1937.

Symington, Andrew James. *Samuel Lover: A Biographical Sketch with Selections from His Writings and Correspondence.* New York: Harper Brothers, 1880.

Taubman, Howard T. *The Making of the American Theater.* Rev. ed. New York: Coward, McCann, 1967.

Tawa, Nicholas E. *A Music for Millions: Antebellum Democratic Attitudes and the Birth of American Popular Music.* New York: Pendragon Press, 1984.

——. *Sweet Songs for Gentle Americans: The Parlor Song in America, 1790–1860.* Bowling Green, Ohio: Bowling Green University Popular Press, 1980.

——. *The Way to Tin Pan Alley: American Popular Song, 1866–1910.* New York: Scheirner Books, 1990.

Tessier, Thérèse. *The Bard of Erin: A Study of Thomas Moore's Irish Melodies, 1808–1834.* Trans. George P. Mutch. Salzburg: Institut für Anglistik und Amerikanistik, Universität Salzburg, 1981.

Toll, Robert C. *Blacking Up: The Minstrel Show in Nineteenth-Century America.* New York: Oxford University Press, 1974.

Truniger, Annelise. *Paddy and the Paycock: A Study of the Stage Irishman from Shakespeare to O'Casey.* Bern: Francke, 1976.

Turner, Michael R., ed. *The Parlour Song Book: A Casquet of Vocal Gems.* London: Michael Joseph. 1972.

Turner, Michael R., and Anthony Maill, eds. *Just a Song at Twilight: The Second Parlour Song Book.* London: Michael Joseph, 1975.

Twentieth Century Song Collection. Chicago: Phoenix House, [ca. 1900].

Van der Merwe, Peter. *Origins of the Popular Style: The Antecedents of Twentieth-Century Popular Music.* Oxford: Clarendon, 1989.

Walsh, Francis. "Lace Curtain Literature: Changing Perceptions of Irish American Success." *Journal of American Culture* 2.1 (1979): 139–46.

Waters, Edward N. *Victor Herbert: A Life in Music.* New York: Macmillan, 1955.

Waters, Maureen. *The Comic Irishman.* Albany: State University of New York Press, 1984.

——. "No Divarshin: Samuel Lover's Handy Andy." *Éire-Ireland* 14.4 (1979): 53–64.

Watt, Stephen. *Joyce, O'Casey, and the Irish Popular Theater.* Syracuse: Syracuse University Press, 1991.

Watters, Eugene, and Matthew Murtag. *Infinite Variety: Dan Lowrey's Hall, 1879–97.* Dublin: Gill and MacMillan, 1975.

Welch, Robert. *Irish Poetry from Moore to Yeats.* Totowa, N.J.: Barnes and Noble, 1980.

White, Terence de Vere. *Tom Moore: The Irish Poet.* London: Hamish Hamilton, 1977.

Wilgus, D. K. "Irish Traditional Songs in English, 1800–1916." In *Views of the Irish Peasantry, 1800–1916.* Ed. Daniel J. Casey and Robert E. Rhodes. Hamden, Conn.: Archon Books, 1977. 107–28.

Williams Irish Songster. Chicago: Frank Williams, n.d.

Williams, Raymond. "Base and Superstructure in Marxist Critical Thought." In *Rethinking Popular Culture: Contemporary Perspectives in Cultural Studies.* Ed. Chandra Mukerji and Michael Schudson. Berkeley: University of California Press, 1991. 407–23.

Williams, William H. A. "Immigration as a Pattern in American Culture." *Proteus* 11.2 (1994): 5–9.

——. "Irish Traditional Music in the United States." In *America and Ireland, 1776–1976: The American Identity and the Irish Connection.* Ed. David Noel David and Owen Dudley Edwards. Westport, Conn.: Greenwood Press, 1980. 279–95.

Winter, William. *Other Days Being Chronicles and Memories of the Stage.* New York: Moffat, Yard, 1908.

Wittke, Carl. "The Immigrant Theme on the American Stage." *Mississippi Valley Historical Review* 39.2 (1952): 211–32.

——. *The Irish in America.* 1956. New York: Russell, Russell, 1970.

——. *Tambo and Bones: A History of the American Minstrel Stage.* 1930. Westport, Conn.: Greenwood Press, 1968.

Wolfe, Richard J. *Secular Music in America.* 3 vols. New York: 1964.

Woll, Allen L., and Randall M. Miller. *Ethnic and Racial Images in American*

Film and Television: Historical Essays and Bibliography. New York; Garland, 1987.

Wright, Robert L., ed. *Irish Emigrant Ballads and Songs.* Bowling Green, Ohio: Bowling Green University Popular Press, 1975.

Yerbury, Grace D. *Song in America: From Early Times to about 1850.* Metuchen, N.J.: Scarecrow Press, 1971.

Young, William C., ed. *Famous Actors and Actresses on the American Stage: Documents of American Theater History.* 2 vols. New York: R. R. Bowker, 1975.

Zimmermann, Georges-Denis. *Songs of Irish Rebellion: Political Street Ballads and Rebel Songs, 1780–1900.* Dublin: Allen Figgis, 1967.

"Give Me Three Grains of Corn, Mother," 42
Glover, Charles, 250n22
Glover, Stephen, 76
"God Made Ireland a Nation," 187
"Go Find a Sweetheart from the Emerald Isle," 222
"Go On, Good-a-bye," 196–97
"Going Home with Nelly after Five," 163
Goldberg, Isaac, 270n6
Golden, Harry, 198
"Good Bye Mavourneen," 107
"Goodby Johnnie Dear," 111
"Goodby Mother Machree," 217
Grace, William R., 94
Graff, George, Jr., 215
Gratten, Henry Plunkett, 42
Greeley, Andrew, 142–43, 152, 176, 217, 268n37
Green, Tony, 4, 7
Green (color): in songs, 27, 248n24
"Green Hills of Erin," 76
Greene, Victor, R., 112–13
Grimstead, David, 131
Gross, O. R., 42
"The Groves of Blarney," 30, 38
"The Guide's Song," 76
Gwynn, Stephen, 63

"Hail! Glorious Apostle (A Hymn for St. Patrick's Day)," 46
Hale, Edward Everett, 105
"Ha-Le Ha-Lo or That's What the Germans Sang," 193
"The Haleys from Mullingar," 103–4
Hamm, Charles, 21, 25, 37, 45, 163, 184
"A Handful of Earth from the Place of My Birth," 102
"Hang the Mulligan Banner Up," 169
"Happy Hooligan," 154–55
Harp: as symbol, 27, 29, 35; woman as, 27, 36; in songs, 248n24
Harpers: Irish, 20, 21, 38
"The Harp That Once through Tara's Halls," 43

Harrigan, Edward, 10, 111–12, 128, 138, 144, 158–72 passim, 175, 239; on police, 139; on politicians, 141, 142; satire on rising Irish, 143; on drinking, 150–51; early life, 158, 270n1; Mulligan Guard series, 159, 169–70; as playwright, 159–62, 270nn6,9,12–13, 271n23; realism of plays, 159–60; his audience, 162; as songwriter, 162–69, 271n18; and Irish-American community, 164–68; class elements in plays, 167–68; multiethnic plays, 168–71, 271n30, 272n34; mentioned, 65, 119, 120, 153, 157, 176, 181, 191, 200, 205–9 passim, 232, 235, 277n23
–Plays: The Mulligan Nominee, 141; Waddy Googan, 142; The Blackbird, 150; The Mulligan Guard's Christmas, 150; Mulligan's Silver Wedding, 150; Reilly and the Four Hundred, 150, 162, 165, 167, 171; Squatter Sovereignty, 154, 167; The Last of the Hogans, 163; The Mulligan Guard's Picnic, 163, 169; The Mulligan Guards, 164, 169; The O'Reagans, 165; Cordelia's Aspirations, 166, 167, 168; Dan's Tribulations, 166, 168, 169; McSorley's Inflation, 167, 168; The Mulligan Guards' Surprise, 167; The Major, 169
"Harrigan," 209
Harris, Charles K., 182
Hart, Tony (Anthony J. Cronin), 119, 120, 158, 159, 160, 181, 200, 213
"Has Any One Here Seen Kelly?," 195
Haweis, Rev. H. R., 82
Hays, William Shakespeare, 261n15
Hayton, David, 58, 59
Healy, James M., 256n64
Herbert, Victor, 182, 187, 274n20
Herne, James A., 100
"He's on the Police Force Now," 139
Hewitt, James, 246n1

"McElwee," 193

McFadden's Row of Flats, 200–201

McFlinn, Dennis (A. G. Weeks), 142

"McGinty in Town," 146

"McGinty's Wake," 147, 151

"McGinty, the Ladies' Pride," 139

McGlennon, Felix, 185, 273*n13*

"McGonigle's Led Astray," 135, 141

McGuire, J., 107

McHenry, James, 97

McLean, Albert F., Jr., 129

McManus, George, 206

"McNally's Row of Flats," 168–69

McNish, Frank, 65

Meagher, Timothy J., 176, 203

"The Meeting of the Waters," 27–28

"The Men Who Come Over from
    Ireland," 137–38

Mercier, Vivian, 85

Meserve, Walter, 68, 71

"Mick McCarthy's Wake," 150, 189

"The Mick Who Threw the Brick,"
    189

Middleton, Richard, 6, 7, 33, 80, 181,
    189

"Mike McCarthy's Wake," 135

Miller, Kirby, 17, 52, 55, 93, 105, 110,
    217–18, 227, 253*n13*

Minshull, John, 64

"The Minstrel Boy," 25

Minstrelsy, 65–66, 82, 83, 118, 146,
    264*n9*

"Miss Mulligan's Home Made Pie,"
    143, 267*n23*

"Mister Dooley," 190

"Mister Pat O'Hare," 194

Mitchell, J. F., 104–5, 107

Moloney, Mick, 276*n2*

Moody, Richard, 160

Moore, Emmett, 188

Moore, Ernest C., 151

Moore, Flora, 144

Moore, Thomas, 19–31 passim; sense
    of music, 20–22; as performer, 21,
    247*n8*; as songwriter, 21–22; sense
    of nationalism, 22–24, 28; and

Robert Emmet, 23, 248*n15*;
    Corruption and Intolerance, 24;
    politics of, 24; view of Irish
    character, 25–27; mentioned, 46,
    72, 78, 82, 214, 225, 230, 234, 236

—*Irish Melodies*, 19–31 passim, 240;
    musical character of, 21, 247*n6*;
    Irish character of, 22; Irish legends
    in, 23; melancholy character of, 23;
    patriotic themes in, 23; sense of
    Irish past in, 23–24, 25; and
    freedom, 24–26; in Anglo-
    American culture, 25, 27; nostalgia
    of, 25–26, 44–46; sunshine-
    shadow/smiles-tears motif, 26–27,
    212, 225; Irish nature of, 27–28;
    influence on Anglo-American
    songs, 28–29, 37–38, 44; Irish
    nationalism in, 28; influence on
    American song publishing, 29; in
    database, 249*n10*; dream motif of,
    251*n38*; mentioned, 47, 226

Moran, Peter K., 30

Morrison, James, 127, 265*n27*

Morse, Theodore, 193

Morton, Will H., 107–8

Mossap, George, 71

"Mother Machree," 215, 216, 226

"The Mountain Dew," 150

"Moysha Machree," 195

"Mrs. McCarthy's Party," 144

"Mulberry Springs," 165

Mulchinock, William Pembroke, 39,
    250*n22*

"Muldoon, the Solid Man," 138

"Mullaly's Groc'ry Bill," 145

Munster (province of Ireland), 17

Murphy, John, 65

Murphy, Joseph, 65

Murphy, Maureen, 168, 270*nn12–13*

"Must We Leave Our Ould Home (or
    Queenstown Harbor)," 105

"My Dad's Dinner Pail," 166

Myers, Gene, 208

"My Irish Molly O," 190–91

"My Irish Prairie Queen," 193

"My Irish Song of Songs," 192, 219
"My Little Side Door," 166
"My Mariuccia (Take a Steamboat)," 196
"My Nellie's Blue Eyes," 211
"My Rose of the Ghetto," 197
"My Wild Irish Rose," 127, 215–16, 223, 279n29
"My Yiddisha Colleen," 195
"My Yiddisher Blonde," 197

Nast, Thomas, 94, 147, 152, 202, 268n31
Nelson, James Malcolm, 48, 68, 87
New Orleans, La., 53, 64, 71, 88, 91, 252n6
New York, N.Y., 139, 140, 141, 148, 152; Irish plays in, 71, 158–72 passim; Irish in, 91–93; center for music and theater, 181–85
Niehaus, Earl F., 53, 64, 87, 252n6
"The Night That Paddy Murphy Died," 156
"No Irish Need Apply," 136, 266n2
"Nora Malone, Call Me by Phone," 189
Norman, Mabel, 191
Nugent, Maude, 191
Nye, Russell, 4

O Boyle, Seán, 21
O'Brien, Artane, 108–9
O'Brien, Gerald, 108–9
O'Brien, Hugh, 94
"O'Brien Has No Place to Go," 207, 277n19
"O'Brien Is Tryin' to Learn to Talk Hawaiian," 193–94
O'Bryan, Daniel Webster. See Bryant, Dan
O'Carolan, Turlough, 247n6
"Och! Paddy, Is It Yerself?," 149
O'Connell, Daniel, 2, 15–16, 108, 112
O'Connell, Dr. P., 149, 155–56
O'Connor, Batt, 112
O'Connor, Thomas, 112

O'Flaherty, Barnard. See Williams, Barney
O'Grady, J. J., 137
O'Halloran, Sylvester, 19, 22
"Oh! Breath Not His Name," 23
"Oh, Gilhooley You're a Lad!," 139–40
"Oh, He Promises," 141
"Oh! The Days Are Gone, When Beauty Bright," 21
"Oh! Think Not My Spirits Are Always as Light," 26
O'Keefe, John, 60, 64
Olcott, Chauncey (John Chancellor), 65, 182, 183, 190, 223, 226, 233, 236; background, 213–14; as songwriter, 214–15, 222, 279nn28–29; as singer, 215–16, 278n12
Olcott, Rita, 213, 215, 278n10
"Old Boss Barry," 142
"The Old Featherbed," 167
"Old Folks at Home," 38
O Lochlainn, Colm, 257n64
O'Neal, Kitty, 119, 121, 266n2
"One Bumper at Parting," 26
Opper, Frederick Burr, 154, 202
Organs, parlor, 5, 32
"The Origin of the Harp," 27
O'Rourke, Edmund. See Falconer, Edmund
Osborne, Harry, 105
Ossian, epic of. See Macpherson, James
O'Tuathaigh, Gearóid, 52–53, 252n3
Outcault, Richard, 208, 277n23

Paddy. See Ethnic stereotypes: Irish; Sheet music: Irish; Stage Irishman
Paddy camps, 91
"Paddy Carey's Fortune or Irish Promotion," 72
"Paddy Duffy's Cart," 167
Paddy making, 2
"Paddy on the Canal," 91–92
"Paddy Reilly's Pledge," 74
Page, Brett, 125

Russell, Henry, 29
Russell, Lillian, 213
Russell, Mark, 149
Russell Brothers, 201
Ryan, Desmond, 41
Ryan, Pat M., 98
Ryan, Redman, 71
Ryan, Thomas, 205–6

"Sad-Fated Erin," 104
Saloons, 151–52
"Savourneen Deelish," 43, 185
Scanlan, William J., 100, 151, 211–15, 222
Scheurer, Timothy E., 163
Schwartz, Jean, 189–91, 215
Scott, Derek, 33, 38, 80, 247n6
Scott, Sir Walter, 22, 79
Seabrooke, Thomas Q., 171
Shakespeare, William, 57, 58, 61, 253n1
Shamrock: as symbol, 5, 29, 35; in songs, 27, 42, 106–8, 248n24
Shamrock and Hibernian Chronicle, 112
Shannon, William V., 217
"The Shannon, the Shamrock and You," 223
Shaw, George Bernard, 99
Sheet music: cultural negations in, 4–5; characteristics of, 5–7; commercial nature of, 5, 32–33; illustrated covers, 5; limitations for analysis, 5–6; and the middle class, 5, 32–34, 249n7; dating of, 6, 11, 246n20; lyrics, 7–8, dream motif in, 25, 251n38; smiles-tears motif in, 27, 212; music publishing, 32; price, 32, 245n8, 273n10; home motif in, 45–46; ragtime, 190, 274n29; and ethnic stereotyping, 192–99; as popular cultural artifact, 249n7. *See also* Parlor Songs; Popular song; Tin Pan Alley
—African-Americans: in songs, 85
—Germans: compared to Irish songs, 82

—Irish: illustrated covers, 4, 35–36, 40, 45–46, 72, 74, 103, 106, 183–91 passim, 207, 216, 223, 224, 228, 249n12, 261n19, 268n31, 277nn19,23, 279n26; defining Irishness, 6; database, 9–12, 245n19, 246n20, 249n10, 250n18; "Irish song" defined, 9–10, 245n18; sunshine-shadow/smiles-tears motif in, 26–27, 212, 225–26, 230; Gaelicisms, 34–35, 41–42; Irish names in, 34, 77, 135, 144–45, 185, 257n4, 266n1; men in, 34, 36, 135–36, 266n1; titles of, 34–35, 257n4; women in, 34–35, 36, 39–40, 135, 279n26; Ireland and nature, 35, 42, 47–48, 224; Irish place names in, 35; instrumental dance pieces, 36–37, 249n13; music, 36–38; about love, 38–42, 221; about death, 39–40, 44, 46; about parted lovers, 40; about emigration and leave taking, 42–46, 46–48, 101–8; about sense of loss, 42–43, 48, 219, 230; about childhood, 44, 45–46, 212; about eviction, 44, 45, 104–5, 109; about home, 44–46; comic songs, 71–77, 103, 134–36, 143, 145, 185, 189–97, 203, 221, 234, 266n1; about drinking, 73–75, 149–51, 154, 166, 203; about violence, 75–76, 144, 145–49, 154, 203, 228; compared to songs about Scots, 79–81, 257n4; compared to songs about Germans, 81–83, 102; about immigrants, 101–5, 106–8, 110–13; theme of return, 101, 224, 226–27, 231, 280n41; about remittances, 110–11; urban settings in, 134, 163–66, 168–69, 171, 210, 221; working men, 136–37; "solid man," 137–38; satire on mobility, 142–44, 204–7; sense of community, 164–68; immigrant experience of, 165–67; satire on Irish mobility, 167–68; multiethnic themes, 169–71, 192–

WILLIAM H. A. WILLIAMS, a professor in the College of Undergraduate Studies at The Union Institute (Cincinnati) and former project director for the Organization of American Historians, has published articles on a variety of topics in Irish and American studies. He is currently revising his book *H. L. Mencken* (Twayne, 1977) and studying how English travelers to Ireland perceived the Irish landscape.